The Poetics of the
Common Knowledge

SUNY Series, The Margins of Literature
Mihai I. Spariosu, Editor

THE POETICS
OF THE COMMON
KNOWLEDGE

Don Byrd

State University
of New York
Press

Published by
State University of New York Press, Albany

© 1994 State University of New York

All rights reserved

Production by Susan Geraghty
Marketing by Dana Yanulavich

Printed in the United States of America

For information, address State University of New York
Press, State University Plaza, Albany, N.Y., 12246

Library of Congress Cataloging in Publication Data

10 9 8 7 6 5 4 3 2 1

Byrd, Don, 1944–
    The poetics of the common knowledge / Don Byrd.
        p.   cm. — (SUNY series, the margins of literature)
    Includes Bibliographical references and index.
    ISBN 0-7914-1685-2 (hc : alk. paper). — ISBN 0-7914-1686-0 (pbk).
    : alk. paper)
    1. Language and languages—Philosophy. 2. Poetry. 3. Knowledge,
theory of. I. Title. II. Series.
    P106.B96   1994
    401—dc20   92-42637
                                                           CIP

That is: life is absolutely simple. In any civilized society everyone should know EVERYTHING there is to know about life at once and always. There should never be permitted, confusion—
—William Carlos Williams

I have ever found your plain things the knottiest of all.
—Herman Melville, as Ishmael

CONTENTS

ACKNOWLEDGMENTS

The present book—volume two of *The Nomad's Encyclopedia*, announced in my *The Great Dimestore Centennial* (1986)—arose from conversations with Charles Stein, almost weekly over a period of ten years, and an ongoing correspondence with Jed Rasula. I think also of sitting on Cressy Beach above Gloucester Harbor with Gerrit Lansing, who prompted me to the title of this book; of a dinner with Beth Schultz in Lawrence, Kansas, when she, Marge, and I realized that in middle-age one may begin to live with the rhythms one's body has always relentlessly declared; of a spectacular autumn afternoon in the Catskills with David Matlin and Gail Schneider, when David diagnosed the amnesia that releases Americans from their violence and Gail was doing the rabbit paintings; of George Butterick, who, when I told him that I was afraid my book was getting too long, said, "Don't worry, and write your butt off" (I will miss George's clarity of mind and advice; I wish he could have seen the end results: *in memoriam*, 1942–1988); of visits with Paul and Nancy Metcalf and with Neil and Wendy Rolnick; of Ed Sanders, who insisted, "Don't let yourself be burned-out"; of talks with Kenneth Irby, Robert Duncan (*in memoriam*: 1919–1988), Jackson Mac Low, Clark Coolidge, Madeline Gins, George Quasha, Jack Clarke (*in memoriam*: 1933–1991), Nathaniel Mackey, Bob Grenier, Christer Hennix, Robert Bowen, David Levi Strauss, Pierre Joris, Judith Johnson, Gene Garber, Michael Blitz, Jondi Keane, Derek Owens, Joe Amato, and John Winner; and of the time when Jerome and Diane Rothenberg showed up in Albany for a semester with the combination of talk and testimony that carried me through a critical juncture in the writing. Also, there was a lunch with Judith Malina, who said the task in the 1950s and 1960s had been to wake people up, but now, people are wide awake and scared to death–the problem is to give them courage. Her theater is a monument to these tasks. This insight allowed me to find my proper focus when I got lost in the details. These friends and many others are implicated in my thought; love and the common knowledge circulate in the community. Marge and Anne Byrd, above all, are my tutors in the common and the necessary.

Although the deaths pile up and fill the previous paragraph with ugly parentheses, the private discussions continue. Of their necessity and depth, I have no question. The passage from private to public however is fraught with doubt and uncertainty. No one knows enough to write confidently of the matters for which we are responsible as agents of the community. Unfortunately, our responsibility is not relieved by our ignorance.

CHAPTER 1

The Parable of Beginning

In full imagination poetry issues
like blood on Lady Macbeth's hand,
nails of the dead making the ship
move which carries her epiphany
into the continuum at the risk of
heart's awakening to the old ways
wanting, this final mystery
once set upon yields the all from
which you were cut away, for I have
seen the star, rise and embodied,
no ghost, but the real thing ritual
murder could not produce, the war
of oneself given over as instrument
immersed now in a cowl of sound.
—John Clarke, "Beginning the Other Side"

MAKING THE WORKING SPACE

In the process of their becoming, the literal thinking, writing, and rewriting, these essays revealed a fact of composition that may have been first noticed by Pascal: "The last thing one discovers when writing a work is what one should put first." The process is endless: each rewriting yields a new first thing. In the working, each site—chapter, paragraph, even sentence—reaches toward completion only to reveal, if one attends with care, its incompletion, so it discovers a new first thing, turns back on itself, and seeks to be more inclusive, until every constituent tries to become the monad in which the whole is reflected. Language is recursive: it implicates more and more language until it rediscovers itself or some suggestion of what it had been, for, as it reaches near the critical point of recapitulation, it suffers a phase shift, enters a new dimension, and becomes itself an object of study, an open and indeterminate site rather than a tool. It opens again and again in the pursuit of its own closure, always beginning.

The perspectives through the course of the text consequently shift, sometimes rapidly. Juxtaposed sites engage with and fail

1

their own self-containment. The use of such a text is not to cut through the cone of the matter in order to show this or that parabolic section—there is no one parable—but to manifest the interior complexity of the cone and the numerous parables it concretely contains.

The *content* might have been entirely different. In the following essays, I pay special attention to Descartes, Hegel, and Freud. I am critical of their simplistic representationalism, their implicit doctrines of force, their submissions of the individual to generalized, abstract formalisms. I might have taken up Spinoza, Darwin, and William James, or Locke, Hume, and Whitehead, arriving at much the same place by different and, for me, more sympathetic routes. The point is not a particular historical narrative. For that matter, the content might have been completely non-narrative. The *thing* I want to reveal is neither form nor content but the conditions of manifestation as such. I am interested in beings who cause themselves, define themselves, and enclose themselves in their radical uniqueness. I am interested in how they may be understood as acting not from their theories—that is, generalities about their possible formal condition—but from their singularities. I do not mean to depreciate theory. It has it uses in describing possibilities. The acts of living however are insistently and beautifully singular. They are not general or generalizable: "One chance each time."* It is this insistence that I propose to understand, and this beauty I hope to affirm.

We have languages and bodies—macrocosm and microcosm, themselves only parables. We are too often missing the mesocosm—the dense locale of the common, that is absorbed by the exaggeration of symbolism, on the one hand, and by mere biology, on the other. I am interested not in the phenome*logy* of spirit which is disciplined by the dialectic of master and slave, subject and object, teacher and student, but in the *phenomena* of spirit which are common. To make a logic of phenomena, to objectify them and attend to their ratios, introduces at the outset a displacement that can never be overcome.

We have suffered from an inadequate logic—perhaps from logic as such—which reduces everything to a structure of likes and

---

*Charles Stein in conversation (about 1987).

differences without measure and a sentimental poetics, which treats measure as convention. Logic is a collection of techniques for a theater, a representational space. It accounts adequately, therefore, for closure, for endings and deaths. Logics, however, typically do not account for beginnings. "We can assume nothing and assert nothing dogmatically," Hegel writes on the first page of his *Logic;* "nor can we accept the assertions and assumptions of others. It seems as if it were impossible to make a beginning at all" (Hegel, 1975, 3). As logics are necessarily founded upon that which is unconditioned and underived, any beginning is too late. To begin logically, thus, is to make a violent symbolic gesture, to throw certain elements together, as the etymology of "symbol" suggests. Dr. Johnson's famous comment on the violent yoking of ideas in metaphysical poetry is also relevant. The world that modern discourse addresses is fashioned of symbols bound by abstract force. Western culture has compensated for its belatedness by violence, and everyone who declares a logic—psycho-logics, socio-logics, or any science that proposes to reveal the unitary logical structure of a body of knowledge—is implicated. The modern western tradition is inherently technological; it uses the machine or social machinations to compensate for its failure to get in on the first creation.

Once a logic is established, its continuation is assured by its inherent mechanism. The dialectic needs argument as the souls of the Homeric underworld need blood. One is tempted by the Nietzschean hope that it might be overwhelmed or at least contained by the aphorism, the argument that dramatizes all of its dialectic ramifications in the *adequacy* of its language. The dialectic, however, resolves only in the apocalypse. To contradict it is to continue it: such are the desperate terms of modern history.

Wilson Harris writes, "Our grasp of time tends—everyone knows—to incorporate tragic proportions of determined futures and to overlook unspectacular resources of futurity and imagination that may alter perception through and away from fixed habit, greed and monoliths of terror" (Harris, 1983, xvi). And in this connection, he speaks of "blocked muses," the muses hemmed in by the massive compulsion in rationalism to repeat and, as Freud notes, submitting to its own mechanistic designs, to have the aim to live by having the aim to die.

Freud might have said more precisely that the aim of all *abstract* life is death. Inanimate matter was never more than a medium of life: protein happened to be available for the use of the living. Life requires *some* medium, and protein is complex enough to embody its dense, complex forms. In manifesting itself in protein, however, life is subject to the laws of protein, which are deathly, mechanical, repetitive. In manifesting itself in consciousness, in language, in desire, in family, in society, in technology, it is subject to the laws of these media and their mechanisms as well. All of the *resources* of life are machines, the resources of life are death, the resources of freedom are laws. The ancient fantasy is that we can annihilate the medium—the body and its laws—and have life, *pure* life, spirit, angelic matter. We have many rituals for the annihilation of the medium—not only religion but also art and work. All of life, according to Freud, is just such a ritual.

We cannot now afford to be sentimental about our vocabulary. We hear of the end of Man or the Subject, the end of Nature, the end of Culture, the end of History, Sex, Family, Desire, Power. The announcements seem dramatic and important. Writers compete for public space by trying to discover some still more fundamental Reality that has ended. (The end of Reality too has been announced.) The theoretical excitement arises from the vague hope that living will step free at last. All of the logics of liberations, however, are machines that are efficacious because they inexorably repeat themselves; thus they recur to the ritual of liberation and "die trying."

As a matter of fact, none of these concepts are important in themselves; they are *only* concepts. Certain conceptual institutions have collapsed. Conceptuality as such, however, has not ended. The end of the usefulness of these great, organizing terms signals a staggering *increase* in available abstraction. Abstraction has freed itself from theology, which is to say, it has freed itself from this or that abstraction; now we have pure abstraction, the abstraction of abstraction. Life is manifested in various media from which it is never free. The freedom of living appears only in the density that arises in the interference patterns where living realizes itself profusely and declares its *mastery* of media. Life is no longer required to seek death to manifest itself.

Unlike logic, which must be prior to its own practice, poetics is properly *after* the fact of the poem. Charles Stein writes:

IT ISN'T A MATTER OF REPETITION:
        THE THING THAT EXCITES NARRATION
    HASN'T
        happened yet

                          (Stein, 1985, 6)

The problem for the writer of poetics is the opposite of the logician's: it is always too soon. The common intuition of the whole cannot be represented by symbols; it cannot be mediated. The purest moments of beginning are silent: the world is mute. Everything is what it is; everything is clear. The continuous space in which humans act, where they not only gesture and walk but also think, talk, and write, cannot be symbolized. In it, there are no infinitesimals, no discrete breaks, no logical atoms such as the units that Wittgenstein calls "facts" or the phonologists call "phonemes"; it can be made manifest only by action. Symbols are inherently symbols of division.

The emergence of the common knowledge from the silence is always disruptive and uncertain. Now we must know, in Philip Guston's words, "Where to locate everything and where everything can exist" (Guston, 1965, 38). Things can be located *or* they can exist; located existence is difficult. Guston discovered the problem in his careful attention to the paintings of Piero della Francesca; it may be discovered in any common space. Existent things do not have simple locations. This is the problem of the common knowledge. Everything is located in and exists in space—a completely real space that is familiar as a quotidien condition of living. It cannot, however, be symbolized; we can make no direct reference to it. It must be constructed: it can be lived, but *as knowledge* it must be constructed. For this reason, a poetics, not an epistemology, is required. We can no longer abide the scaleless world in which theory and its prose disciplines dislocate us.

I could say, simply, that the following essays attempt to explain what Ezra Pound meant in the imagist manifesto by "Go in fear of abstraction" and William Carlos Williams meant by the thematic line in *Paterson,* "No ideas but in things." Probably no two statements in twentieth-century poetics, however, have been more influential and less understood. It was not understood that a statement composed exclusively of concrete nouns and action verbs may be utterly abstract. Abstraction is a matter not of diction but of organization, of movement, of rhythm. Therefore I should say that the

purpose of the following essays can be specified in the words of
Charles Olson, from *The Maximus Poems,* Volume 3:

> an actual earth of value to
> construct one, from rhythm to
> image, and image is knowing, and
> knowing, Confucius says, brings one
> to the goal: nothing is possible without
>   doing it.
>   (Olson, 1983, 584)

Or the words of Louis Zukofsky in "*A*"–12:

> So goes: first, *shape*
> The creation—
> A mist from the earth,
> The whole face of the ground;
> Then rhythm—
> and breathed breath of life;
> Then *style*—
> That from the eye its function takes—
> "Taste" we say—a living soul.
> First, glyph; then syllabary,
> Then letters. Ratio after
> Eyes, tale in sound. First Dance. Then
> Voice. First, body—to be seen and to pulse
> Happening together.
>   (Zukofsky, 1978, 126)

These passages are not equivalent: Olson favors the ear,
Zukofsky the eye; both however propose an unfamiliar and diffi-
cult orientation in relation to the common world. The task is not
to interpret these passages but to create the working space in which
their proposals renovate the possibility of action.

Western epistemology has distinguished rigorously between
emotion and thought—between thought that agitates the body,
rhythm, and thought that does not. Distinguishing these domains
and enforcing their separation have been primary tasks of educa-
tion and art. The poetics of the common knowledge proposes to
fill the void in the breakdown of that epistemology, that education,
and that art. Now all thought agitates the body. Now all knowl-
edge is emotional. There are no inert facts, no cold ideologies, no
contemplative reliefs from acting and being acted upon; all knowl-
edge is potentially dangerous.

In this culture, we deal with the epistemological stress, for the most part, with narcotica, literal drugs, the distractions of the media, or the mechanisms of work. These are the functions of Thanatos. The promise of amelioration is not the promise of ideological critique and reform but the promise of a better drug, a bigger shopping mall, a more entertaining satellite network, a more spectacular amusement park, a more absorbing baseball game.

The poetics of the common knowledge looks not to drug the agitated body into the passivity that imitates the inanimate but to redeem emotion. Now everyone is responsible for their feelings as they were once responsible for their beliefs.

The break of modern methodology with classical metaphysics was profound. Modernism's claim of a continuous Western tradition of logocentrism beginning with the Greeks was a desperate ploy, the acceptance of which represents an almost universal failure of scholarly nerve. Metaphysics has been for more than three centuries a sentimentality—necessary to the prevailing cultural strategy but in an important sense, which has been at least half-understood and half-accepted, phony. It has been maintained and enforced by an aesthetic tradition, often masquerading as religion. Modern humanistic culture has been an exercise in bad faith ever since its inception.

The philosophic enterprise of Jacques Derrida—and his work is a notable instance of a *kind* of undertaking that has been central to the refashioning of the humanities and social sciences during the last two decades—is poised on an implicit history of the Western intellectual adventure that underwrites this sentimentality by way of negation. At best it is an eccentric history, a Nietzschean willing of a particular Platonism which is to be identified and rooted out. Derrida's readings are breathtakingly profound and gloriously subtle. Under his scrutiny, the most unlikely texts yield extraordinary passages of philosophic thought. His essays are engaging reading. The kind of personal authority that he assumes, however, removes him from the company of the common world. His texts can be read but not shared. As readers, if we engage his texts in the terms they themselves require, we too follow an idiosyncratic trajectory of textual production. For the true poet, as Blake notes, there is no other, and Derrida is a poet of this authoritarian kind. He enters the pleasure dome where his word is final. His texts are to be tested, as Blake's visionary poems are tested, for their depth, their beauty, and their use. Derrida's writings present vision, not knowledge. This is not to deny the importance of Derrida's thought. His nihilism is rigorous and its methods demanding. It is not, as it is sometimes suggested, a justification of an any-thing-goes-know-nothingism. When vision is mistaken for knowledge, however, the culture is in the direst danger.

To be sure, if ones test of objectivity is sufficiently rigorous, all claims of truth fail, and we inherit a tradition that has required *absolute* rigor. Knowledge of the common world has been tested by the impossibly rigorous requirements that prevail in mathematics, logic, and the physical sciences.

The question of truth, however, is prior to epistemology. Epistemology is an administrative, not a foundational, science. Truth cannot be *founded* on another truth; such a thought obviously implies an infinite regress. A truth claim can be founded only upon an agreement concerning what constitutes a legitimate or adequate proof—that is, upon an ethical consideration.

Skepticism is irrefutable and empty. *The Poetics of the Common Knowledge* maps a space in which the ethical grounds of knowledge can be considered.

THE FIX

To be certain, we are in a *fix*.

The term *fix* cannot be easily resolved: we are placed, fastened securely, stabilized and unalterable, nonvolatile, killed and kept as a specimen under glass, directed, adjusted, ascribed, allotted, set aright, made ready, prepared, focused, repaired, de-sexed, hardened, bribed, provided for, doped up. We undertake a fix in the face of a breakdown. It is a word of people who confuse their lives and their knowledge of their lives with the structures of their machines. We have taken up an abode; we are in a predicament. It is the classic premise of comedy. A fix is possibly deadly, and it is, therefore, also a premise of tragedy.

When one is in the profoundest fix, every attempt to extricate oneself from it makes it worse. It is the hair of the dog, the spike in the vein. The crooked gambler, the crooked politician, and the hit man, *fix* things. We fix our attentions, purposes, affections, or eyes—the fix locks mind to body in a self-overcoming mechanism.

We are determined, dedicated to a teleology, which we are expected to discover and maintain: almost already something else, so being the very thing we destroy ourselves—victims of our own references to genetics, evolution, history, who must constantly tamper with our own mechanisms in order to stay on course. Our enterprise is not viable.

The *OED* quotes John Donne in an example of the alchemical jargon "fixion": "There must be a fixion, a settling thereof, so that it shall not evaporate into nothing." But if it is volatility itself that we want to fix? The alchemical drama is tragicomedy. It tells of a marriage of opposites, a merging of life into death: this is the boldest formulation of the fix. It is at least one way out of the dialectical mess. Near the end of *Phenomenology,* Hegel writes: "death becomes transfigured from its immediate meaning, viz. the non-being of the *particular* individual, into the *universality* of the Spirit who dwells in His community, dies in it every day, and is daily resurrected." (Hegel, 1977, 475)

To say nothing of belief, is it even possible to *think* this thought? We can, of course, say it. The grammar is correct: *death is life.* Structurally, it is correct—that is, this is the unstructuring required by structure. In the face of actual death, it means nothing. Grammatical rectitude or even grammatical necessity is not enough. Is it a thought, or is it a grammatical condition, a logical requirement, just beyond thought?

Everything now is in question. Everything, *including this statement,* is in question. The liar's sentence ("I always lie"): if it is true, it is false; if it is false, it is true. The classic fix. Its value flickers back and forth with the speed of the mind, which hurries in an attempt to catch itself in the act of changing or slows down in an attempt to see how it works. It is not just this strange self-embracing sentence, this narcissistic grammatical aberration—and a presumably insignificant group of similar self-referential statements—however, which enters this peculiar oscillation. The language as a whole ultimately refers back to itself. Of course, it is possible to formalize important fragments of a language. Saussure, Chomsky, Montague, and many others have developed useful techniques, and, within their domains, the formalisms give statistically reliable results, but Wittgenstein writes: "All propositions are of equal value" (Wittgenstein, 1961, 145). And he realizes that "All propositions, *including this one,* are of equal value." Describing

itself as a proposition, it is no "higher"; it cannot master itself any
more than it can master language as a whole. Thus, Wittgenstein
ends the *Tractatus* with the declaration that all of his own proposi-
tions are nonsensical—all of his propositions, including that they
are all nonsensical, are nonsensical—the *reductio ad absurdum* of
the philosophic tradition.

A *fixion* is a fiction, an untruth that is true or posited as truth,
a narrativization of the fix, so the liar of the paradox is given time
to elaborate both the false as true and the true as false—that is, the
dialectic. The production of language goes into infinite regression
and self-proliferation, so the conditions that are proposed for
thought turn out themselves to be unthinkable.

Since the seventeenth century, if not since the sixth century
B.C., the formal structure of language has been confused with the
structure of mind and world. So variable, vast, and fascinating is
this medium that we have pursued it, or consumed it, as if it might
be meaning in itself. The interplay of the abstract concept, on the
one hand, and the concrete event, on the other, generated an over-
whelming historical dynamism. For every advance in abstract
thought, a renewed aesthetic commitment generated new energies
and realized new possibilities. Conversely, every aesthetic break-
through called forth and required an ever more athletic abstract
mind. Now, however, the *formal* possibilities, both in art and sci-
ence, have been realized. The new, nondialectical logic that ap-
peared in the aftermath of World War II can isolate and formalize
this or that aspect of the world without regard to totality. Unlike
the old logics, the new requires nothing of the world it describes.
Therefore, nothing can be learned about the world by studying
logic or grammar. The content of the new logic is purpose and
desire, not the necessary forms of mind or substance. In cyberne-
tics and information theory, one draws distinctions in spaces that
are called into existence by the distinctions themselves. The tech-
niques of abstraction are no longer underwritten by an originating
unity. We are, thus, of a time that does not find its origin in the
logos; we are *beyond* the closure of metaphysics. "In the beginning
there was information," Fred Dretske writes. "The word came
later" (Dretske, 1981, vii). Granted, as the critics of the tradition of
the *logos* will note, Dretske's formulation defers the problem that
they take as primary, but, from the new perspective, the deferment
is not critical; the new logic does not require the pursuit of the

infinite regress. The slack or difference that was fatal to metaphysics is a built-in feature of the new procedures, indeed a requirement of their practicality. Difference is precisely the quantity that cybernetics measures.

We consign our lives to a mysterious semiotic domain, which is so vast and various that it cannot be theorized or it can be theorized only piecemeal in relation to this or that particular project. The institutions in the culture, in order to preserve their systemic nature, define a universe of possibility in relation to the particular function that they serve rather than to a universal theory. The power of this new thought derives *not* from the methodological reduction of multiplicity to universal rules but from the discovery of techniques by which complex and rigorously effective structures can be generated *without* universal reference. Knowledge is now statistically reliable.

We do not know how to characterize our own time, except by the fact that it is *after* something else that was definitive: modernism or industrialism or structuralism, for example. The one positive designation that has gained some currency is "the age of information." To say the least, the mere *quantity* of information affords the term considerable usefulness: according to one prediction, "as much information will be generated and distributed between 1987 and 1990 as in all of previous human history" (Bunnell, 1987, 14). The indexing systems that proved barely adequate to organize and access printed materials begin to break down in the face of this amount of information. It might be more accurate to speak of an age clogged with information.

In one of the most important essays in literary theory of the past decade, "Local Transcendence: Cultural Criticism, Postmodernism, and the Romanticism of Detail," Alan Liu provides a devastating critique of what he calls "cultural criticism . . . in high postmodernist forms: cultural anthropology, new cultural history, New Historicism, New Pragmatism, new and/or post-Marxism, and finally that side of French theory—overlapping with post-Marxism—that may be labeled French pragmatism . . ." (Liu, 1990, 76). In a short essay, he demonstrates that the foremost strategies for generating cultural analysis produce only "a culture-*spiel* as determinedly depthless in its play with representational surfaces, facades, screens, and media of all sorts as a vinyl LP hand spun by a rap artist, that master of culture-*spiel* able to fragment long-play metanarrative into *petits récits*" (Liu, 1990, 48). These spiels, he tells us, recycle a familiar, and tired, romanticism that *appeals* to practice but provides no practice other than the appeal to practice. He writes: "If I had to put my criticism of high postmodern cultural criticism in brief, it would come to this: 'context' is not the same as 'culture.' Context throws over the surface of culture an articulated grid, a way of speaking and thinking culture, that allows us to model the scenes of human experience with more felt significance—more reality, more practicality, more aesthetic impact—than appears anywhere but on the postmodern version of romantic 'nature': a screen" (Liu, 1990, 99).

"Culture" is now available only by way of the virtuoso performances of the expert. We are dazzled by the generation of meaning out of details so arcane that they are not even shared by a cult of initiates. The culture critic addresses the question of meaning in relation to a local pastiche that is determined by the contingency of a particular reader's reading. The hope is that, if the texture of a particular cultural swatch can be examined in enough detail, the larger pattern will be implied.

We now enter a time of utter fragmentation. In contrast to the high postmodernist cultural critics, we must see that we are radically local. We entertain the fragments of no whole. Languages are invented again and again before our eyes, and in the perpetually perishing present. They manifest themselves and remain or disappear by virtue of whatever contingencies of attention they engage. *Beyond* the birth trauma and the Oedipal dilemma, we attend daily the regeneration of a common world. The 'things' we compose—it is hard give them a more specific name—are local and carry no force beyond the locality in which their actual *uses* are their only principles.

We have thought that there is one logic and many possible worlds that satisfy it. Rather there are many logics and only one, *postlogical* world. Logics are the content, not the structures, of the world. The conception of the artist has been that he or she observes the universal logic and fills in the colors of its particular occasions. All freedom has been conceived in terms of variant images of the controlling logic. Literary theory now, rather than descrying the logical preconditions of literary activity, must give attention to the richness of concrete action that proliferating logical spaces afford. Thus, it does not attend to absence and longing for lost logical origins, to the self-resistance of theory, or to the density of local texture that bespeaks the residue of the great nineteenth-century intellectual systems such as Marxism and Freudianism; it attends to the *amplitude* of time and space, which is nonlogical in its proliferation of niches for living and casual in its destruction of them.

There is no way out of the fix. We are recursive beings. If the species is caught in an infinite loop, the condition is hopeless. The resources of a finite earth will be destroyed before our philosophic needs are satisfied. If, however, the recursive loop can be conceived as finite, humans as psychological, sociological, and cosmological beings can achieve stability *without* coercion.

RADICAL MODERNISM

The abiding problem that Descartes left us is uncertainty over proper human scale. Descartes's tricky little argument proves something about the grammar of "ego" but not about the grammar of proper names: I can know that I am I without knowing who my "I" is. Descartes's *cogito* was of a different scale than René Descartes himself. As Nietzsche discovered, on solid Cartesian grounds, he was all of the names in history. Nietzsche's argument and its repetition in this century is solid evidence of our lack of a concrete realm of history that comes into existence as concretely measured time, actual ratios between actual events, not between events and presupposed, theoretical backgrounds. Nietzsche might have argued as justifiably that his ego had no name, that all names belong only to history. We measure ourselves, though they are useless as measures, by scaleless archetypes—Jesus or Oedipus, or by the Nietzschean self-sublating hero. Likewise, the lack of meaningful scale is apparent in the architecture of cityscapes, sprawling suburbs, and art. The music of Wagner, Mahler, and Bruckner suffer from a lack of scale as does the music of Webern—the nineteenth-century composers as arbitrary in their gargantuanism as the twentieth-century composer in his miniaturism. More recently, Stockhausen and Glass, for all of their differences from the earlier composers and from one another, are similarly scaleless. Tolstoy's great work fails not from its lack of center, as Henry James and Percy Lubbock complain, but from its lack of scale, as do Browning's *The Ring and the Book* and Joyce's *Finnegans*

Wake. The problem is not the mere size of these texts but our inability to know how big they actually are.

Since the seventeenth century, the official philosophy of the West has been unable to account for the profoundest subjectivity or the profoundest objectivity. We have known, rather, an objective subject and a subjective object. In our relative subjectivity, we discover an arena in which we become giddy with talk, and in contemplation of our relative objectivity, we discover certain predictable patterns that afford significant control over nature. As William Carlos Williams notes, however, "Without measure we are lost. But we have lost even the ability to count. . . . I repeat, a new measure by which may be ordered our poems as well as our lives" (Williams, 1969, 340). Lacking scale and measure, we can define the world only by halves, and our definition requires a reconciliation of radically different modes of discourse, a reconciliation that is possible only in a generous theoretical sense. We have been required to subvert the structures on which we stake our conceptions of the world. The intellectual tradition seems bent upon its own self-cancellation. It bespeaks the possibilities of a renewal that at the same time it denies. This is the agony of modernism, clearly apparent in Descartes, and most poignant perhaps in the *angst* of a Heidegger, Schönberg, or Eliot, but now, sadly and widely suffered by the masses, who turn their backs on the modern and seek comfort in the teachings of Khomeini, Moon, Swaggart, Robertson, and Falwell, or who, in the same spirit of fundamentalism, take up learned jargons of aesthetics or the social sciences. We are caught between idolatry and nihilism. The dialectic produced the irresistible force and the unmovable object and then stalled. In the infinite domain that opens, the most spectacular kinesis produces no measurable motion: having travelled an immense distance, there is still an infinite distance to go.

Modernism and postmodernism are not philosophies, nor do they belong to particular historical epochs; they are modes of historical action. Modernism expresses the will to begin again by identifying language with being. The new beginning inevitably upsets the conventional practice of life catastrophically. It is concerned not with the purity of beginning but with the stability that arises from beginning again—the reality that is never reduced to familiarity and predictability. Modernists quickly despair of language and are happy to return to inarticulation, opening logical space after logical space, sometimes in dizzying proliferation. The

Plato of the dialogues is a modernist in this sense. Postmodernism is administrative and pedagogical. Sometimes the divergence between being and language becomes so intense that it can be enforced only by totalitarian organization and violence, an all too familiar fact of this century.

From the fifth century B.C. until the nineteenth century, the equation of being and language continued to produce at least occasionally new and unexpected relationships. Hegel, however, spoke for a crisis in modernism—a crisis for the possibility of intellectual renovation. A profound modernist himself, he expressed the enthusiasm of a culture that was committed not only to beginning again but to including both beginning and end in its beginning. Nineteenth-century European culture was imperialistic even on the transcendental scale: the time-honored modernist strategy entered a postmodern infinite regress. Thereafter modernism was not a philosophic strategy but a historical fact. The century between the revolutions of 1848 and the end of World War II was a time of unparalleled intellectual, military, political, and industrial upheaval. For the lack of a better name, we have referred to it as a time of "modernism," which means only, "we have never seen anything like this before," and truly we had not. This modernism is not a collection of styles that had its day and faded. It was thrust upon us as an effect of our prodigious—and perhaps cancerous—productivity.

Postmodernism, the response to the time *after* the apocalypse, is a philosophy of administration, the business of business schools. It is necessary to manage the inevitable divergence of being and knowing which follows the modernist catastrophe. As a social concern, it is a counterpart of the solid waste problem. If we have too much garbage, we also have too much "good" stuff, too much poetry, too many paintings, too much music. The immense proliferation has turned even the modernist masterpieces into embarrassments of riches, so we must work as hard to distribute the spiritual booty as we do to bury the waste. If we are now postmodern, it means only that the newness has worn off, that dadaist goofiness has become commonplace.* It remains to realize the dadaist sanity.

The Poetics of Common Knowledge is an unapologetic mod-

---

*See, for example, Greil Marcus's *Lipstick Traces: A Secret History of the Twentieth Century* (Marcus, 1989).

ernist essay, concerned not with *carrying-on* but with beginning and beginning again, with the rhythm of beginning, and the measure of "true necessity" by that rhythm. I assume not only that beginning again is possible but that about 1910, a vast energy gathered toward a new beginning, manifesting itself in the continuous world war and utter technological renovation that dominated the first half of this century. By this propulsion we escaped the gravity of Western humanism. The human creature has internalized its machinery in its evolution. We have entered the cyborgian world of science fiction where we confront creatures—indeed all of us—to which the distinction between living things and mechanism does not apply. Donna Haraway notes: "By the late twentieth century, our time, a mythic time, we are all chimeras, theorized and fabricated hybrids of machine and organism; in short, we are cyborgs. The cyborg is our ontology; it gives us our politics" (Haraway, 1985, 66). Our fascination to ourselves as cyborgian creatures is that we combine in our beings the predictability of machines with the reckless, independence of singular creatures. It is an attractive but dangerous combination. Machines do not began again, do not renovate themselves, do not produce the freshness and new variety which is required to maintain the order of the system. The cyborgian world is an adventure in order, a construction of the world from unique components that are always in danger of being overwhelmed by their own inherent tendency to repeat, simulate, and generalize.

The failure to attend to the strange centaur world—half industrial waste land and half computer simulation—that we inhabit is extraordinary. Thus, Roland Barthes, in 1971: "The break, as is frequently stressed, is seen to have taken place in the last century with the appearance of Marxism and Freudianism; since then there has been no further break, so that in a way it can be said that for the last hundred years we have been living in repetition" (Barthes, 1977, 155–56). Fredric Jameson, in 1981: Marx "alongside Freud and Nietzsche [is] one of the great negative diagnosticians of *contemporary* culture" (Jameson, 1981, 281, my emphasis).

Is it not remarkable that these giants of nineteenth-century materialism are accounted contemporary? The thought of Marx, Freud, and Nietzsche not only belongs to the twilight time of classical physics, it is profoundly predicated upon the Newtonian worldview. To be sure, there has been no "break," no new coherent world picture; it has been rather a rupture and a flowing, which is the condition of radical modernity. No century in human history has seen such radical change in the material conditions of life as the one just past. The results of systematic research and technological development as the basis of an ever-expanding world economy are obvious and profound. The refusal to recognize the accompanying intellectual upheaval borders on psychosis.

Barthes writes: "Just as Einsteinian science demands that the relativity of the frames of reference be included in the object studied, so the combined action of Marxism, Freudianism and structuralism demands, in literature, the relativization of the relations of writer, reader and observer (critic)" (Barthes, 1977, 156). It is an ill-informed metaphor. This "relativistic" object that Barthes discovers is not the "object" of modern physics: Einsteinian physics does not turn physical space-time into textual hash. On the contrary, Einstein declares that *every* locus of observation is absolute. Barthes's prevalence represents a serious setback, a loss of fifty years at least. Charles Beard (Beard, 1934) and Carl Becker (Becker, 1932) were further along this line of thought in the 1930s; Ezra Pound in "Cavalcanti: Medievalism" (Pound, 1965, 129–200), William Carlos Williams in "The Poem as a Field of Action" (Williams, 1969, 280–90), and Gertrude Stein in *Lectures in America* (Stein, 1985) were further along. The great materialistic systems of the nineteenth century, bereft of the science that underwrote them, have been recycled as aesthetic and reactionary political strategies. The technological procedures that dominate contemporary culture have been assimilated by the cultural studies industry to antiquated notions of critique.

"The Newtonian-Euclidean subconscious," to use Milič Čapek's term, has powerfully reasserted itself. Čapek writes, "the mental habits which constitute what may be called our 'Newtonian-Euclidean subconscious,' and whose roots lie deep in the phylogenetic heritage of man are too obstinate to be modified by a bare mastery of mathematical formalism, which merely suppresses without eliminating them" (Čapek, 1961, xv). Čapek, of course, speaks of thinkers who have mastered the mathematics and *still* have trouble consistently thinking the new intellectual world (it is so strange), not the students of culture who, in the face of mathematical ignorance have retreated to the safety of a bedraggled romanticism that forestalls criticism by criticizing itself. Much of the literary theoretical activity of the past two decades has been a willful attempt to regenerate the illusion of Newtonian-Euclidean space as a cultural arena. It has been profoundly reactionary, profoundly unwilling or unable to deal with a world that is as alien as the world our science describes. We are radically uprooted from the neat theoretical worlds that relieve our confusions with talk of material objects and physical forces. The Marxist notion of conflict, the Nietzschean notion of will, and the Freudian notion of desire now have the status that angels had for the classical physicists.

The distinction that Barthes obscures—and it is almost universally obscured in contemporary literary theory—is between the continuous manifold of physical space and the discreet manifold of logical space. In a continuous manifold, there are no objects—no Cartesian space-points, no atoms, no phonemes (i.e., discrete semantic atoms). Everything is dispersed throughout the spatial field. From any particular frame of reference everything is precisely located, but from a universal perspective the entire spatial field is densely saturated with every object in it. Like many other theorists who work in the aftermath of structuralism, Barthes comprehends only the discrete manifold of logical or grammatical space. His textualized object is the Newtonian object that must absorb the vagueness of location that absolute time and space require. Barthes speaks not for a meaningful relativism but for a Euclidean-Newtonianism with the jitters: "Each poetic word is thus an unexpected object, a Pandora's box from which fly out all the potentialities of language; it is therefore produced and consumed with a peculiar curiosity, a kind of sacred relish. This Hunger of the Word, common to the whole of modern poetry, makes poetic speech terrible and inhuman." (Barthes, 1967, 48) Barthes suggests that modernity moves toward a new Eden, where it will overcome the crippling double bind that it suffers and produce a "literature" that is not literature, a "history" that is not history. He speaks for a desperate romanticism.

This does not mean that we must now adjust our paradigms to relativity theory, quantum mechanics, chaos theory, or the theory of self-organizing systems. These are in fact, for the most part, probably irrelevant to human life; they do not deal with the common scale. We cannot expect a new epochal paradigm. It is paradigmatic thought itself that has come to an end. Of course, we have local paradigms that provide administrative procedures for particular purposes, but language does not contain a picture of itself. We have reached the profoundest level of abstraction. The *intellectual* adventure is over. The *logic* of the situation is revealed: certain rules produce certain results. The linguistic media define zones of logical possibility, and they are all inhabited. We cannot cover every point in the space, of course, but as in the infinitesimal calculus, we can approach the limit and forget the remainders that are not significant anyway. Life is not now renovated in relation to the *logos* or in relation to the absence of the *logos*. It is like updated software: the intellectually new is not *fundamentally* different from the old, but there is a lot of new documentation to read. Radical modernism equates not being and language but being and consciousness. Mind does not carry out beyond knowledge into the unconscious structures of language. Knowledge is, Gertrude Stein reminds us again and again, what we know.

POETIC KNOWLEDGE

We are the daily victims of an addictive aestheticism: a huge distraction industry produces consumable images of meaning and efficacious action, creating a universal environment for egos that are at once highly prized and literally superfluous. The Self is, at this point, a luxurious reference to a bygone era—as it were, a collectable antique. For example, we support symphony orchestras the size of the army of Renaissance city-states to play music that was written a century or more ago while excluding most contemporary music from the concert halls. Beethoven's evocation of the historical individual's relationship to eternity becomes for the posthistorical listeners an Image that relates them to a reality requiring their participation and, at the same time, systematically excluding them. The German tradition in music, as it is now purveyed, is a perfect cultural product because it cancels itself out, allowing its audience the feeling of meaning without the world in which that kind of meaning can be realized.

The education industry is deeply implicated in the recycling of history. Harold Bloom writes: "The teacher of literature now in America, far more than the teacher of history or philosophy and religion is condemned to teach the presentness of the past, because history, philosophy, and religion have withdrawn as agents from

the Scene of Instruction, leaving the bewildered teacher of litera-
ture at the altar, terrifiedly wondering whether he is to be sacrifice
or priest" (Bloom, 1975, 39). Professor Bloom's terror and wonder
are explicable. History, philosophy, and religion are disciplines of
knowledge; literature is a discipline of taste. In a culture that has a
taste for history but no historical foundation, the aesthetic domain
is inflated. Moral, political, and religious meanings are pig-
gybacked on abstract languages that relate only to their own sys-
tematic requirements. They are statistical manifestations, shared
hallucinations, that appear when light hits abstract forms at cer-
tain angles. It is a powerful strategy. The only limits are practical
and pedagogical: initiating everyone into a second world—a world
quite alien to the one the student discovers on the street—is a
massive job. In monolithic cultures, which limit themselves to a
few controlling images, education can provide the necessary her-
meneutical tools. The abstract code, however, is able to assimilate
endless particulars and, moreover, requires a continually broaden-
ing base of particulars to feed its ravenous generalizing powers;
soon more images and interpretations than can be reasonably
managed accrue. Students can be exposed to great diversity, but
they cannot be given the confidence of a culture. Without the
convenience of a relatively small canon, the field is simply too vast.

The literature teacher's anxiety for which Professor Bloom elo-
quently speaks, however, should be mitigated by the fact that the
privileged scene of instruction and its priestcraft have been effec-
tively replaced by a universal media environment that instructs the
masses directly. The institutions of high art are the product of an
ideology that has itself eroded away. Art activity has not changed,
but the culture has changed around it, giving it a different status.
Although the forms of artistic production are still vital, and the
jargon of the art business—classifications of genres, categories of
judgement, and so forth—is still in common use, art has ceased to
be a producer of value and has become merely a producer of de-
scriptions and commodities in a statistical field. Ideology is re-
placed with the Nielsen ratings and the opinion polls.

The replacement of the elite tradition with the popular media is
now more or less complete. The change appears democratic be-
cause of the size of the population involved, but in practical terms
it is not a significant change. A people can be better tyrannized by
itself than by an elite. Aura is not necessary in an aesthetically

dense world. The principles of the high-cultural canon are now enforced not by awe but by the omnipresence of the popular media. The symphony, for example, must be impressive in both its quality and its scale so its themes will be remembered after the audience has left the hall. Popular music need not be memorable, because it is unavoidable. Similarly, television drama is always there. Although video recorders are now widely available, there is little reason to record anything. One sitcom can be substituted for another without loss. We do not need memorable music, poems, plays, paintings: the values that the memorable "objects" manifested are now literally repeated in the electronic furnishing of homes and cities. The information covers us, flows over our surfaces; we are in a great Jacuzzi of information. The field of radical contradictions has given way to a completely forgiving medium, which can be transmitted electromagnetically to create a universal productive environment.

Post-Hegelian intellectual history confirms that universal entailment is true. Its logical circuits, unfortunately, are infinite. Our paths of thought never fail to confirm our assumptions, but the thought never reaches its goal: the Truth or the Revolution or Self-Knowledge are endlessly deferred; the analyses of nature, history, and person are interminable. "The revolution of poetic language," in Julia Kristeva's ringing phrase, the language of the post-Hegelian bacchanal, revealed the heterogeneity and indeterminacy of the semiotic field. Ultimately, the rationalization of the symbolic domain was drawn into the dark side of the associative logic that it had exploited. Kristeva: "Magic, shamanism, esoterism, the carnival, and 'incomprehensible' poetry all underscore the limits of socially useful discourse and attest to what it represses: the *process* that exceeds the subject and his communicative structures." Poetry, which had striven to express perfected consciousness, the *unity* of the idea and the thing, became the source of, again in Kristeva's words, "the essential element of a practice involving the sum of unconscious, subjective, and social relations in gestures of confrontation and appropriation, destruction and construction— productive violence . . ." (Kristeva, 1984, 16).

Against the proliferation of meaningless production, I will argue that it is poetry, *workings in poetic language and action,* not mere submission to its violence, that can redeem us from the post-Hegelian pathology, driving us further into spiritual and ecological disequilibrium. In Alfred North Whitehead's words, "there can be an intuition of probability respecting the origination of some novelty" (Whitehead, 1978, 207), and this probability is *nonstatistical*. The unique occasions of this intuition are not the production of a mechanism nor are they predictable by induction. If history represents our intuition of more or less permanent patterns in life against which loss is realized and measured, nonstatistical intuition represents—again in Whitehead's terms—"a creative advance into novelty" (Whitehead, 1978, 349). The statistical knowledge by which we describe our accommodation to the world has an inside as well as an outside, and it is on this axis, not on the axes of mind and matter, subject and object, or general and particular— these are all terms of absolutist metaphysics—that our knowledge must be turned.

We are primitives of poetic knowledge. Poetry's conventions have been sadly vitiated by over two millennia of obedience to theory, from Aristotle to current theorists, such as Kristeva, who value poetry only because it concretizes and negates theoretical totality. Much of what passes for poetry is mere decoration and sentiment—poetry produced, consciously or unconsciously, as the illustration of this or that abstraction or, more recently, as the illustration of an-*arché*-ism—that is, to show that there is nothing to show. The poetics of the common knowledge proposes to understand the making of a knowledge that is not theoretical. If it is anti-intellectual, it is not hopefully a know-nothing anti-intellectualism. Indeed, mind itself is a gross simplification, the substitution of a schematic image for a rich participation in the articulation of living space.

We have much to learn from the cultures that articulate cosmologies without writing, but we cannot put on the shaman's cloak and appropriate their cultural traditions as we appropriate the natural resources of their lands. In spiritual practices, they have a sophistication that we will forever lack. It is our advantage—and the terms of the danger in which we find ourselves—that we have worked our way *through* theory. While we now return to that perpetually unfamiliar place of endless chance and *changing* that can be safely called "the real," we engage it not as spirit but as information. The common can be specified as that which remains more or less constant in any medium of information storage and transmission. Myth was the quintessential content of oral culture, metaphysics was the quintessential content of literate culture. The poetics of common knowledge now begins to prepare the legacy of literacy for the electronic media.

My claim for the redemptive powers of poetry may seem hopelessly optimistic and probably even foolish. Indeed the level of literacy required to read even the least demanding poetry is now fairly rare. *Poetic knowledge,* however, is not exclusively or even most significantly what appears in those peculiar and despised writings known as "poems." It is the knowledge of finitude, of words and things that happen once and once only, measurable but not repeatable, the intuitions of *nonstatistical* probabilities that are *creative,* not merely re-creative (or recreational). It is not clear what conventions might best embody this knowledge. The most pervasive forms, to which many people *pay attention* are perhaps musical. Television, of course, is omnipresent, but its viewers are only partially conscious at best. Indeed it appears to be impossible to pay close attention to television. I suspect the new poetics will have more to do with pedagogy and engineering than traditional aesthetic objects. The literary form as such, poetry itself, is of small consequence; it has been perhaps already absorbed into life. The same could be said to a greater or lesser degree of all of the traditional art forms. If Marx once believed the philosophic task was not to interpret the world but to change it, the task now is not to replicate the world but to make it. Marx hoped to put the worker in control of the productive or more precisely *r*eproductive institutions; the poetics of the common knowledge proposes to put the individual in control of creation and *the* Creation.

The common is given, but the common knowledge is not. It should not be confused with "common sense"—which is to say, the lore of compromise a culture builds up with its own ignorance. *The common knowledge might be properly contrasted to disciplined knowledge.* The domain of the common knowledge has no preexistence. It comes into being only when contingent beings come into contingent relationship. The common knowledge leads not to certainty of mind but to confidence of action. It consists not of propositions to be communicated from A to B but of orientations in fields of meaning, measures by the scales in which humans share not a perspective or a belief but a world that opens to this or that particular vantage and practice. In order to constitute an effective community rather than a symbolic machine for social production, organized beings must orient themselves in their mediascapes. For those of a common orientation, knowledge is not transmitted through a channel (sender to receiver by way of code, in Jakobson's well-known paradigm); it is, rather, the condition of action that permeates the space of the community. That it cannot be spoken is not "mysterious." There is no occasion to speak it; it is what makes speaking possible. It is however perpetually made manifest in the acts of creation. Whitman's barbaric yawp *says* nothing, it manifests the creation of the world that can be shared. Louis Zukofsky reminds us, "Measure/tacit is" (Zukofsky, 1978, 131). We hear the sounds, but the *measures* are made manifest.

The disciplined knowledge that might guide us from this crisis and the perpetual violence of our times is flawed: to understand has come to mean to be able to give an explanation of a phenomena as a symbolic machine. When information that *was* shared is interpreted and thus found meaningful, it is removed from the common; it becomes epistemic property. One situation is interpreted in terms of another, so the one becomes a mere logical function of the other. The modern psyche, the modern, human psyche itself, represents the triumph of our first attempt to create an artificial intelligence machine—a discipline of knowledge. That the project now continues, constructing models in silicon rather than in a fictional Self, should not be surprising. In the mode of this self-willed robot, language as such is a device for binding a relatively low-order of abstraction to a higher order. The binding of energy by symbols involves establishing relationships between two levels of abstraction, between, for example, the simple idea of a thing and the idea of a thing that includes itself by way of its self-aware creatures. Knowledge in this sense involves a double bind and is compromised with unreality from the outset. Symbolic binding is the underlying device of Western epistemology in all of its common forms—its various totalitarianisms, both right and left, as well as the totalitarianism of what Herbert Marcuse called "repressive tolerance," its artistic conventions, its theologies and atheologies.

Wallace Stevens's jar has become an essential of undergraduate education because it reveals in anecdotal form the fundamental cultural strategy. It tells of symbolically bound energy:

> I placed a jar in Tennessee,
> And round it was upon a hill.
> It made the slovenly wilderness
> Surround that hill.
>   (Stevens, 1982, 76)

In terms of theory, this is all one needs to know about technology. The artifice of the jar and its strategic placement *bind* not the wilderness, which is irrelevant to its symbolic use, but the *energy* of wilderness. The difference of potential between the juxtaposed images creates, as it were, a voltaic power cell that energizes the hermeneutic process that in turn binds its own informational flow in some form. This generation of energy *ex nihilo* suffices to drive the symbolic machine ultimately into the profoundest fix: the process exploits the very conditions that make it possible.

The contrast between Stevens's "Anecdote of a Jar" and Gertrude Stein's "A Carafe, That Is a Blind Glass," from *Tender Buttons,* is clear: "A kind in glass and a cousin, a spectacle and nothing strange a single hurt color and an arrangement in a system to pointing. All this and not ordinary, not unordered in not resembling. The difference is spreading" (Stein, 1962, 461).

Information here, rather than tending toward the creation of stasis, is unbounded. The carafe, rather than defining discrete objects in a discrete manifold, is a flowing in a continuous manifold. It communicates nothing but itself. Stein pursues objects past their discrete eidetic solidity, generating linguistic surfaces, continuous spaces in which every distinction is returned through its reference to itself. Language is no more internal to the psyche than any other object of attention. Both its content *and* its grammatical structures are contingent. In a totally different context, that of theoretical physics, David Finkelstein proposes a logic "which is itself a dynamic ingredient in the physical theory, an actor rather than part of the stage" (Finklestein, 1969, 213). This is a fundamental disruption.

"No one has been able to pose the problem of language," Gilles Deleuze and Félix Guattari write, "except to the extent that linguists and logicians have first eliminated meaning; and the greatest force of language was only discovered once a work was viewed as a machine, producing certain effects, amenable to a certain use" (Deleuze and Guattari, 1977, 109). Although we are free to assert a preference for this or that disposition toward language, its mechanism—as it were, its time and space—is still largely unquestioned. By the same token, *the problem of meaning* is posed only to the extent that poets first eliminate Language. This is not to say, of course, that they have eliminated the sounds or marks of words, the medium of measured speech, but they have eliminated *Language,* that peculiar abstraction which since Parmenides has confused its own systematic requirements with the world's and which in modern linguistic science has become the prime philosophic datum.

"We are led back," Foucault writes "to that place Nietzsche and Mallarmé signposted when the first asked: who speaks? and the second saw his glittering answer in the Word itself." And he adds, "The question as to what language is in its being is once more of the greatest urgency" (Foucault, 1970, 382). The precise nearness *and* distance of this Word to the Word of the New Testament should not be missed. It is not a particular Word, a word made flesh, but the infinite structure of wordiness in worldliness, which we can know piecemeal but not in totality. Although it never allows the comfort of certainty, it does offer an infinitely commodious setting for writing. It is not however Mallarmé who now gives the profoundest evidence concerning the being of language but the cyborgian engineers who write the code for fifth-generation computers, and the rhetoric of television, rock music, and shopping malls. For those who address the being of language these are the proper objects of study.

Foucault announces the imminent end of Man, that is, the end of abstraction, and of Man as the trope of that abstraction. For Foucault, the inevitable outcome of the dialectic that he traces is the dissolution of Man into language. He does not, however, follow this thought to its conclusion. Just because the language cannot be systematized as a totality does not mean that it cannot be systematized in parts. To say that every sign is haunted by its opposite, every yes is haunted by a no, every conscious meaning haunted by an unconscious meaning, may represent a great insight (it does) or it may be a symptom of neurosis (it is). Although the truth of any proposition is undecidable against the background of the whole of language, language only *plays* in that vast context, it *works* in locally specified environments. A jail sentence has a decidable value as does a Dear John or the sentence that is signified by a pink slip tucked in with a pay check. These are are among some of the drearier domains of the common knowledge.

The end of Foucault's Man may be the beginning of the machine as "human," not the great machine of the paranoid vision that Foucault so dramatically invokes but the humble machine— not the great Mainframe in the Sky but myriad personal computers in open networks, each following its mechanistic program in its random, meaningless, linguistic environment.

Foucault's work might be seen as a poetics of *disciplined*

knowledge, and it is to his horrific vision in which all knowing is hedged in sadomasochism, that I hope to propose an alternative. *The Poetics of the Common Knowledge* does not argue with *Civilization and Madness, The Order of Things,* or Foucault's later, brilliant histories of power, but it takes another route through the history from the seventeenth century to present. The poetics of common knowledge answers Nietzsche's question not with Mallarmé but Melville. In a letter to Hawthorne, he writes: "We incline to think that God cannot explain his own secrets, and that he would like a little information upon certain points Himself. We mortals astonish him as much as He us. But it is this *Being* of the matter; there lies the knot with which we choke ourselves. As soon as you say *Me,* a *God,* a *Nature,* so soon you jump off from your stool and hang from the beam. Yes, that word is the hangman. Take God out of the dictionary, and you will have Him in the street" (Melville, 1960, 125).

As stable objects, Melville's three terms—"Me," "Nature," and "God"—are the apexes of the stable triangle of Western metaphysics, the termini of the Cartesian geometry, the beginning, middle, and end of Hegelian logic, the ego, id, and superego of Freudian psychology. They are the terms of a simple combinatorial logic that, for more than three hundred years, has created a history by adjusting and readjusting the ratios. It is as if we have have able to count to three and no further.

These noun-objects arrange themselves around the hero, the king, the movie star—the father—the one allowable perspective, the one true subjectivity, to which all others have reference. The peculiar quality of the hero or king is to be the one of all people who is self-sufficient. His is the only individuality. He writes the poetry he wants to read because his subjects' writings, like their dreams, as Freud tells us, are inscribed on his royal body. The king is the image of the Will to Power, and we should not underestimate the nostalgia that invests this figure, though now his authority is dispersed through the whole medium of social intercourse. We now come to the crisis of democracy, when we might give every individual his or her authority in relation to the medium. Otherwise, our knowledge will continue to be deathly and administered in relation to power structures that must always increase the total sum of power that they organize until finally the structure fails and the power disperses.

Melville recognizes that to identify any object is to submit it to a logic that is largely independent of the identification itself. Davis and Gilman, the editors of Melville's letters, misunderstand the grammatical awkwardness of the passage, conjecturing that Julian Hawthorne (who transcribed from the now-lost original) miscopied the phrase "the Being of the matter." They want to substitute terms that present precisely the problem that Melville tries somewhat awkwardly to avoid. Their suggested emendations— "Being that matters" and "Being that maddens"—both make Being into a noun-agent, thus putting God back into the dictionary. To Melville, the truth is neither transcendental nor imagined to be in some uncanny, hidden place, such as the unconscious. All of that which in this century would be studied as language or would be objectified and become the subject of scientific disciplines is the content of the visible truth. For the first time since perhaps the pre-Socratics, the representations of language are the *content* of the world, not its structure. Language is completely plastic; it is no longer possible to hold part of it back to create a shape for the remainder. The medium flows and is therefore subject to measure.

I do not know how to say this more emphatically: *the structure of the world is not the logic of language but the meaning of language*. Logical entailment involves one kind of necessity, and facts involve another. The requirements of the world are not logical but factual, and we have no reason to believe that factual necessity presupposes logical necessity. This writing desk *has to* be here because it is in fact here. If I want a book from the shelves on the south wall of my study I *have to* walk over there; I *have to* walk on the blue and red carpet. There is nothing logical in these requirements. They are requirements of measure in the physical world and the nature of my ongoing physical relationship with it. Jean Piaget writes: "If man, as Michel Foucault puts it, is only a 'a kind of rupture in the order of things,' to which has corresponded (but for less than two centuries) 'a mere wrinkle in our knowledge,' it is nevertheless worth remembering that this rupture and this wrinkle are the product of a great upheaval—but a well-organized one— which is constituted by life as a whole" (Piaget, 1970, 50). The organization of this upheaval can be known, not in absolute terms, to be sure, but in terms that are at least as certain as anything to which one might turn for a guarantee. No greater certainty is required for effective control of an enterprise. The poetics of the common knowledges proposes a practice that dwells, to recall

Whitehead's words, in the domain of nonstatistical probability, where creative advances into novelty are possible. The language is fluid, public, a communal store of signs; it is useful precisely because its signs have no particular referent. If one says language is destroyed by the poet, it is not a large or heroic act. If Language—that vast interlocking grammatical system that science posits but that has never been observed—exists at all, it is a low grade of existence. Its ontological status is like the government or the moral order; it is so compromised with things that are not-Language that it is really impossible to investigate the matter to anyones satisfaction. Language takes value when its generality is measured by specific acts of living.

AN ORIENTATION

The "proofs" of my many assertions, unfortunately, are lengthy and cumbersome. The very notion of proof involves the kind of abstract binding that I hope to expose. The task is to make concrete realities manifest.

In the domain of the common and only in the domain of the common, true poiesis occurs; the rest is technology and decoration. We get no additional leverage by trying to characterize the *medium* of knowledge—language, labor, sex, power—as if we might know what we do not know. The common knowledge is the knowledge of time and body, the end points of the continuum that is mediated, the waves and particles of open systems. Any act creates a space and a discrimination, an orientation and a nature, information and meaning, like the elusive conjugate pairs of quantum physics. In totalitarian systems, we lose one or the other; in mediation, we lose both and substitute a third. The possibility of these losses attend any writing. They plague the following essays. The ultimate goal, of course, is, as Walt Whitman realized, for *everyone* to be a poet—that is say, for everyone to language a world that provides orientation for the community.

In a pervasive change of the cultural mind in the seventeenth century, a complex descriptive model was substituted for nature, so *something* in the model corresponded to *everything* in nature. The model was a formal system or linguistic machine—in contemporary jargon, a computer program. It was assumed that the world consists of a few types of simple objects—atoms of some kind, some limited and enumerable set of simple things, that can be represented by linguistic tokens—and a finite set of specifiable rules by which these tokens can be combined. Thus, the rules can be applied to the tokens; and linguistic models of the world, corresponding point by point to the physical world, can be created. "To *understand* a phenomenon," thus, means "to be able to construct a corresponding linguistic machine." Of course, if the model corresponds precisely to the original, it is not clear what has been gained. The locus of the object is changed. Humans seem to feel that the model, being a "human thing," as it were, is more understandable than the world itself.

The testimony of the poststructuralists in this connection has been important: we now know that language is not a unified thing, even as an object of study. It is, rather, a collection of "programs," virtual machines, that define their operations in terms only of themselves. They all prove to be ultimately circular. Some of the loops—in fact, most of them—generate simple patterns that repeat dully as they continue on their endless paths; a few create interesting, nonrepeating textures. The Romantic poets discovered, or at least capitalized upon, linguistic loops of the latter kind, and poststructuralist theoreticians are still fascinated by them. The nonrepeating loop produces a "text," not resolution but the ongoing difference that is always the same. The resonances are rich and attractive, echoing out through their infinite logical spaces, but after a while they become so rich that finite information processing mechanisms such as human minds become overloaded, and the density can be heard only as white noise. It is then a matter of theology whether the roar is the sound of the absolute, of Being, or of terrifying emptiness. The great modern synthesis that poses these vastly inclusive uncertainties has proven to be resilient. Although it has closed, it has not ended; the terms of its virulent inertia are still to be understood.

The eighteenth-century philosophers could not explain organic forms. Newtonian machines, which they could model accurately and the behavior of which they could predict, did not grow. It was obvious, however, that somehow the warring elements of traditional chemistry—earth, air, fire, and water—combined to change the acorn into the oak tree. These simple natures that were defined by their conflict or, as we would now say, "difference," were brought into harmony to produce the phenomena of life. The *source* of the harmony, however, was necessarily transcendental: manifest nature did not, as Hume had so strikingly shown, require any *particular* order. The model of the organism that emerged in the latter half of the eighteenth century was not so much a new Idea as a kind of ragbag for ideas into which almost anything could be thrown. It was not exactly a paradigm—because blatantly incoherent elements were included—but a strategy to stand in the place of a paradigm. The phenomena of mind in Hegel's masterful account, for example—the mind responsible to both nature and transcendental order—is endlessly conflicted. In the Hegelian view, mind receives input in the form of difference, processes the differences according to transcendental principles, which arise and erase themselves, and issues output, again in the form of self-conflicted products. The Romantic organism simultaneously constructs and deconstructs its infinite being. In its constructive phase, it is totalitarian; in its deconstructive phase, it is cynical. J. Drummond Bone puts the matter succinctly: "The idea of the 'organic' contained for the Romantic period in Britain both notions of completeness and the impossibility of completeness, of a state of true being (the 'organic whole') and a state of truth which was eternal becoming (the 'infinity' of the organic). In the first lies a tendency towards the elaborately formal, indeed even the mechanical. In the second lies the temptation of the abandonment of form" (Bone, 1987, 195).

Romantic organism produced a reconciliation of Newtonian mechanism and organic teleology by fiat. In the interstices of organic creativity, a place was found for free interaction between natural perception and transcendental intuition. The various organic theories were distinguished from the mechanism of classical physics on the grounds that organic processes are irreversible. Embodying purposes and thus the possibility of progress, their development is not symmetrical with respect to time: organisms receive inputs from several sources, transform their constituent materials by reconciling contradictory forces, and *creatively* adapt themselves to novel environments. There was however no way to explain the workings of bodies except in Newtonian terms—that is, in terms of *forces* working on matter. The problem of interaction between mind and body, which plagued Cartesian thought, was given an *ad hoc* but metaphorically cogent solution. Language itself was figured as a kind of psychic head of steam that, like the heated gasses in the great industrial engines, transmitted its force (spiritual in its intangibility) from nature to mind and, in literary form, from mind to mind. Wordsworth imagines in *The Prelude* that nature impresses upon "all forms the characters of danger or desire," thus forcefully inscribing a sermon upon the heart of the boy who can, as an adult, profitably recollect these marks so thoughtlessly received. In the organicist understanding of perception and memory, nature's force literally rends a path through the neural material, abrading and consuming psychic space, in order to inscribe itself on the subjective tablet, and this mechanism is understood in a fundamentally consistent sense from Locke to Freud to Lacan and Derrida. Since the nineteenth century, the mechanism of inscription and the vitalism of purposive organisms have been maintained in uneasy synthesis.

This incoherent vitalism was not the failure of certain theorists. It was a requirement of the state of knowledge that made itself manifest in the years of the American and French Revolutions. Its power derives from the fact that it was able to find a place for so many blatant contradictions in a working cultural strategy. A *consistent* account of the static forms of Newtonian physics, on the one hand, and the progressive unfolding of industrial economies and new political institutions, on the other, was not possible. To a large degree, moreover, both dualism and various attempts to reconcile dualism were inherent in Western philosophy. The standard accounts of organicist theory, such as M. H. Abrams's, correctly invoke both Plato and Aristotle as contributors to the synthesis (Abrams, 1958, 184–85). This is, perhaps, to say only that Western epistemology has been consistently representationalist and universalist. Ever since Plato posed the problem of knowledge in terms of conjecture about essences that pervade shadowy phenomena, it has been necessary for systematic philosophy to account for an Image, an Idea or a source, *and,* as the achieved Idea was itself a source of something else, a purpose or teleology. The organism was the middle term, a trace between an origin and a result, an input and an output. The finite unity was required to include all that it was not—consciousness must include the other; the finite, the infinite; the static object, the becoming object; and so forth. This, of course, leaves us in a fix of the first order.

The nature of the fix now becomes apparent because the culture has successfully *implemented* organicist teleology. The vegetable mind of the Romantic theorists was reiterated in social, economic, and cultural domains to produce the technological progressivism that took *growth* as the fundamental measure of value, even, in a sense, as the necessary mark of existence itself. In practice, the imagination of transcendental perfection generated growth that was out of homeostatic control, or to put the matter more bluntly, the Romantic arrogance was underwritten by an organism that confused the scale of its ecological niche and the scale of its infinitely generative dialectical language and represented cancerous proliferation. Thus, we face impending ecological disaster on several fronts.

Since World War II, however, the conception of the 'organism' has undergone a profound change, so profound indeed that it is only the same concept by virtue of answering the same question—what is the nature of the living. With the appearance of the cybernetic view of organism, the distinction between mechanism and vitalism no longer carries its classical force. Norbert Wiener writes: "the modern automaton exists in the same sort of Bergsonian time as the living organism; and hence there is no reason in Bergson's considerations why the essential mode of functioning of the living organism should not be the same as that of the automaton of this time" (Wiener, 1965, 44). It had appeared that organism, with its teleological impetus, was exempt from mechanistic determinism, and it afforded a space for human dignity and values, perhaps even for divinity. Cybernetics, however, moves the question of mechanism and determinism to a higher level of abstraction. As it turns out, the Newtonian cosmos represents only a special case of automation. The circuit of the great machine, what I will call the "cynical" machine, is vitalistic—a construction of personal and social mechanisms which no longer observe the traditional distinction. Against it, the Heideggerian hope is not invalid but utterly misplaced.

The change cannot be simply schematized. Cybernetic thought is not a new paradigm. It is rather a science of paradigms and, as such, represents utterly unfamiliar levels of abstraction. In light of it, no paradigm or archetype carries more than local significance. Clearly, from the old paradigmatic perspective, we now enter a time of utter fragmentation. Representations of the world are pragmatic, related to particular purposes, ideological. There is no common *picture* of the world. The organism is now understood neither as a machine, which receives an input and produces an output, nor as a teleological entity, which derives from a source and tends toward some final end, but as a self-creating and self-organizing system. Such a description raises the specter of rampant subjectivism, and, without doubt, the nature of the object that is shared has radically changed. In fact, what is shared is not objects or representations but processes and rhythms.

If the old objective world picture limited what one could *see*, the limit on the common domain is a limit on what one can *do*. The limit is not epistemological but environmental. Organic dignity is now founded neither on a transcendental source nor on the immediate intuition of being itself. Organisms are to be valued for their autonomy, for their existence through themselves, not for their origination in something Other. This is to say, *organisms are the other*. They are so intimately involved with their environments, they are their environments. The rational hope of avoiding the paradoxes of self-reference turns out to be a hope to avoid life itself, which precisely and necessarily defines vitality in terms of the crisis of self-reference. This does not mean that knowledge is merely subjective: the shared knowledge, however, is not guaranteed by a common source but by the interaction of organisms with one another and a common environment.

It is a large view, which I hope to comprehend. Perhaps to look forward at the argument, focusing on the history of Force (motive, will), will clarify the position.

During the epoch that included both Descartes and Freud, the world as a History produced by the interaction of Nature and Person was constituted as a hybrid machine, half-matter and half-symbol. The symbols, however, like the things to which they were bound, were material. The pervasive metaphor extended Newtonian physics to the domain of the human soul, which was the necessary force binding the components of the symbolic machine into the required configurations. The materialism of the soul was obscured by a sentimental spirituality, but its force was no more— or less—mysterious than the forces that, according to Newton, bind objects, such as solar systems, across great distance. The poststructuralist theories of writing as a material trace—to say nothing of the current recycled versions of nineteenth-century materialisms such as Marxism and Freudianism—cling to metaphysical notions of force in the form of will or desire, while rejecting the metaphysical substances. That is, they retain a concept of vitalism or dynamism from the old concept of organism without retaining the concept of organism itself.

As modes of representation, the inadequacy not merely of the particular models but of this strategy of model making has been demonstrated. The symbolism itself, quite apart from it content, however, also has extraordinary requirements that are expressed as *force:* the "force" of History or, on another scale, the "force" of the individual's will to power. Poststructuralist methodology has freed us from the Cartesian-Newtonian *image* of the world without freeing us from its relentless and destructive dynamism. As David Lachterman writes in *The Ethics of Geometry: A Genealogy of Modernity,* "The Postmodernists, having become persuaded of the essential finitude of human knowing and speaking, to say nothing of writing, somehow leave intact the infinitude of a will embedded or embodied in a finite *and* inescapably deluded intellect" (Lachterman, 1989). *The Poetics of the Common Knowledge* proposes to deglamorize the mechanisms of will.

The following essays undertake to discover a dynamism proper to humankind to replace the wonderfully fascinating, beautiful, and ultimately self-destructive dynamism that has driven the culture now for over three centuries. William James states the alternative:

> I am as confident as I am of anything that, in myself, the stream of thinking (which I recognize emphatically as a phenomenon) is only a careless name for what, when scrutinized, reveals itself to consist chiefly of the stream of my breathing. The "I think" which Kant said must be able to accompany all my objects, is the "I breathe" which actually does accompany them. There are other internal facts beside breathing . . . and these increase the assets of "consciousness," so far as the latter is subject to immediate perception; but breath, which was ever the original of "spirit," breath moving outwards between the glottis and the nostrils, is, I am persuaded the essence of which philosophers have constructed the entity known to them as consciousness. That entity is fictitious, while thoughts in the concrete are fully real. But thoughts in the concrete are made of the same stuff as things are. (James, 1976, 19)

The theme is environmental in the most urgent and practical sense—a matter not of organic *thought* but of the literal organism itself, as a practical, active entity. The dynamism of the person is the dynamism not of will or desire or temporality but of breath. It is, thus, *spiritual* knowledge that I address.

The design of the study is simple. It traces progressive symbolization through four essays: "Symbolic Nature," "Symbolic History," "Symbolic Person," and "Symbolic Symbols." The "I think" thinks nature by way of a formal symbolic system; it thinks its temporal relationship with nature or history; and it thinks itself or person. In each of these critical moves, explored in certain epoch-forming texts of the modern West, the "I think" is driven by the search for content for its symbols. Ultimately, it finds only the symbols themselves, so symbols are symbolic not of Nature, History, or Person but of more symbols. Thus, I follow the search for content from Nature to History to Person (and the unconscious of person) to the moment of recursion, the moment at which language begins to eat its own tail (tale). This is a moment of paradox and consternation, to say nothing of a certain dizziness, that can be overcome only by taking the entire matter to a higher level of abstraction, a task that has fallen to the cyberneticists and information theorists. The chapter "Symbolic Symbols" begins with a consideration of them.

In each chapter, the movement is from the "I think" of theory to the "I breathe" of poetry, from an abstract structural*ism* to actual constructions, from logical objects to physical objects. Logic lets us think about all of the members of a particular class of objects, poetry lets us think about one thing at a time. Logic can account for all of the possibilities of a given world or set of axioms, but it cannot account for the way the world happens to be. Nothing can be simpler than this fact, but it is hard to say (this is the problem which troubled Wittgenstein through his entire career). Theoretical language—and in this sense, all Language is theoretical—is biased toward the general case. Poetry is made from sounds and marks, but, paradoxically, *not* language. Thus, in each chapter, the discussion moves from theory to poetry, in an attempt to expose the theoretical bias of language (not to argue with it, which of course is impossible, as the only instrument of argument is the biased one).

The persistent danger is that humans confuse themselves with their own mechanisms, with their technologies as well as their bodies and souls—both of which, isolated from one another, are also merely machines. They confuse life with the systematic background that they conceive for it. I think of Ornette Coleman's comments on the *Free Jazz* recording sessions: he speaks of the desire to express "our minds and emotions rather than being the background for emotions" (Coleman, 1961). Machines, including both those special kinds of machines that were called "organisms" by romantic theorists and those other necessary machines called "world systems" are the *backgrounds* of emotion. The baroque and romantic artists, whose heroic archetypes have prevailed now for more than three centuries, are allowed only to prepare the theater (theater and theory share a common etymological root). Theirs is profoundly theoretical art, an art of backgrounds. It is a contemplative art, demanding passivity and *re*presentation— "powerful emotion recollected in tranquility"—rather than a meditative art, an art of measure, of stepping off of boundaries, an activity that *is* life rather than a reflection upon it. Again, Ornette Coleman says of the ensemble playing on *Free Jazz*, "You can hear the others continue to build together so beautifully that the freedom even becomes impersonal."

The Poetics of the Common Knowledge attempts to define the dynamism that is neither abstract will to power nor desire or, more accurately, greed—the motives of cancerous acquisition figured in our theory as Newtonian force—but the impersonal freedom of sustainable communities. Unlike the ecologists who argue that we must, in order to survive as a species, return to some earlier form of technology, I argue that we must find a technology that expresses a sustainable dynamic, not merely a primitive version of what we have. There seems to be no "theory" of such a motive: theory inevitably commits us to expanding fields that ultimately "run us to death." It is a *practice* that is required, and we must learn to pay attention to the rhythms of the practice, not the abstract historical dynamism that theory necessarily involves. This practice can be characterized initially by the following claims (to be justified only by the study as a whole):

1. The sickness from which life on earth now suffers is diagnosed in these terms: the modern West mistook the tools of representation—the various languages—for the forms of human thought and experience. It failed to recognize tools as *expressions* of the world's attempts to know itself. In the short term, this

confusion generates immense force. Unfortunately, it is a force that requires humans as a resource as it requires fossil fuel, endless space in which to dump its waste, and so forth. In the long term, it destroys the viability of complex life in its environment.

This mistake has now been transported from the West to the remainder of the world.

2. The conscious ego is not the *subject* of knowledge, and information is not the *object* of knowledge. They are both, rather, the products of specific acts of knowing

3. Language in the simple, nontheoretical sense is a second-order operation of information on itself—that is, information describing itself. It represents subjectivity.

4. Theory or *logos* is a third-order operation of information on itself—information describing itself describing itself. It represents objectivity.

5. Object and subject wax and wane with purpose. The sustained intensities of objectivity and subjectivity are both ultimately destructive to the world that is their host.

There is also a purposeless intensity that generates information concerning values or the ends which purposes accomplish. This intensity is neither objective or subjective.

6. The common knowledge appears in the light of a theory of theories or a fourth-order operation on information—that is, *abstract expression* (the movement in American painting is incidentally relevant). It is not a knowledge of representation and, thus, the reconciliation of representational loci—subject and object—is unnecessary.

7. There are higher-level operations that it is our opportunity (and perhaps responsibility) to explore. Chaos itself is theorized. The oldest struggle is over. Chaos is understood as complexity. Again, every fragment is whole; again, every whole is fragmentary. We can now think these thoughts. The task, the completion of which may belong to another generation, is to think them until we can inhabit them.

8. Traditionally, a poetics would have been understood as the theory of the inevitable (and inevitably melancholic) return to a lower level of abstraction, the self-conscious practice of world construction in light of high-order self-reflection. The ability to confirm abstract concepts in terms of action was the redeeming quality of poetry for Aristotle, and, although the theory was given a dis-

tinct twist in the seventeenth century, a related notion still underwrites the academic study of literature. Poets are those sad creatures who, having surveyed the powerful theoretical engines that modern culture has promised, turn back, as Wallace Stevens noted, to take one last look at the ducks. Poetry, thus, has been for modern culture the reservoir of responsible nostalgia. It has been a concession to the archaic.

As it is now generally studied and practiced, especially in most creative-writing schools, poetry deserves the contempt that the current inattention to the genre bespeaks. It preaches, even in its most ironic posture, an obedience to abstraction or a rebellious refusal of abstraction—abstraction understood always in some seventeenth-century sense. Most often, it is so deluded about its own nature, it preaches obedience to abstraction in the name of rebellion against abstraction. The old, antitheoretical, workshop poets, frightened by the rigors of logical speculation, are mired in abstraction that they fail to recognize.

Poetics properly understood takes theory—theory well founded or unfounded, centered or decentered—as its content, not its form. It is now clear that hills and stones and trees are, as much as the great philosophic systems, abstract objects. The very notion of concretion is an abstraction. The modern poetry that creates the permanently modern is not a theoretical activities. It is a register not of thought but of feeling so rich as to comprehend all that might be thought of. It is the mastery of theory, the production of life value. Its concerns are quantitative and measurable. How much awareness? How much complexity of feeling? It measures richness not in terms of possessions but in terms of the intensity of living in a complex world. It is concerned with the uniqueness of its own event, not the normative requirements of thought (logic) or of society (propaganda enforced by tradition).

Theory is ruled by the law of noncontradiction; poetics is ruled by the law of non-self-exploitation. In theory, self-reference runs in a *vicious* circle; it is destructive and self-destructive, death seeking. In poetics, self-reference is the mechanism of a sustainable cycle of life.

The Constitution of Life as a Symbolic Machine: Some Sub/Versions

the zig zag mothers of the gods
of science   the lunatic fixed stars
& pharmacies
fathers who left the tents of anarchism
unguarded
the arctic bones
strung out on saint germain
like tom toms
living light bulbs
aphrodisia
"art is junk" the urinal
says "dig a hole
"& swim in it"
A message from the grim computer
"ye are hamburgers"
—Jerome Rothenberg, "That Dada Strain"

CHAPTER 2

Symbolic Nature

> Modern European philosophy, even before the *ego cogito* but certainly from then on, situated all men and all cultures—-and with them their women and children—within its own boundaries as manipulable tools, instruments. Ontology understood them as interpretable beings, as known ideas, as mediations or internal possibilities within the horizon of the comprehension of Being.
> —Enrique Dussel

THE TWO CULTURES

The Pursuit of the Infinite

The complaint of the seventeenth-century modernists against the scholastic tradition was justified: scholasticism neither progressed nor was interested in progression. Rather, it circled a persistent core of problems, inquiring about the nature of God, society, and man, mediating between the universal categories of logic and unique actualities. The static images that were produced in this contemplation bore witness to a fundamental incommensurability and, thus, to a perpetual ontological crisis. In the Aristotelian scheme each object is unique and each event requires a unique explanation. When a stone falls, according to traditional physics, it suffers an inward transformation that carries it to its "natural place." Until something happens there is nothing to explain; until the stone falls it *is* in its natural place. This knowledge is available only on a case-by-case basis; the disposition of each entity must be individually determined. The maintenance of a just relationship between *eidos* and *nous* was a massive contemplative chore, but it opened direct human participation in the cosmic dynamism.

The seventeenth-century search for a "method" of knowledge was motivated by the hope of discovering entire classes of phenomena that corresponded to the mathematical species of algebra. Unlike classical arithmetic, the new mathematics developed by Vieta and Descartes did not require an actual counting of actual things. Vieta speaks of "the zetetic art [which] does not employ its logic on

43

numbers—which was the tediousness of the ancient analysts—but uses its logic through a logistic which in a new way has to do with species" (Klein, 1968, 321). Mathematical analysis deals not with particular quantities but with classes of quantities, mathematical potentialities or functions—$y = f(x)$—which describe forms of relationships between *possible* individuals. We know, for example, the *form* of the acceleration of a ball on an incline plane; it can be expressed as a mathematical function. The equation itself tells us nothing, however, about particular balls and particular inclined planes; the relevant quantities must be measured and substituted for the generalized expressions of the formula. The functions in terms of which classical physics is expressed are independent of any *particular* world, and their advantage is precisely their avoidance of particular and sensuous means of expression. Unlike classical *mimesis*, seventeenth-century methodology models a world of which there is no unique image; it defines not images but *infinite classes* of images. Our world, the "real" world, is a contingent instance of the *possibilities* described by the formulae.

If Euclidean geometry is timeless, Cartesian geometry is also paradoxically spaceless. It removes mathematical expression from the realm of concrete intuition altogether. From the time Vieta's "*ars magna* found a place in the system of knowledge in general," Jacob Klein writes, "the fundamental *ontological* science of the ancients is replaced by a *symbolic* discipline whose ontological presuppositions are left unclarified" (Klein, 1968, 184). Thenceforth, the being of all things was not number in the classical sense but an unmeasured, formal property. It could be variously identified with ego, nature, or God, and it could be quickly and conveniently moved from one of these sites to another like the pea in the shell game. The modern view, thus, has a built-in fudge factor. The countable and accountable world was replaced with a formal structure, the content of which is arbitrary and, from a theoretical point of view, even superfluous.

Herman Weyl speaks of the seventeenth-century "leap into the beyond." Thereafter, the efficacious cultural forms became unavailable to intuitive scrutiny. The world to which the senses are responsible leaks out into the infinitely large and small. In an attempt to clarify the attitude of the algebraists, Weyl alludes to certain Indian and Buddhist texts that revel "in the possibilities of producing and designating prodigious numbers by means of the positional system, that is, by combination of addition, multiplication, and exponentiation." He adds: "In spite of their fantastic aspect there is something truly great about these efforts; the human mind for the first time senses its full power to fly, through the use of symbol, beyond the boundaries of what is attainable by intuition" (Weyl, 1949, 36). One feels this excitement in the writings of the seventeenth-century mathematicians. Vieta's *Introduction to the Analytic Art* (1591) ends by appropriating "to itself by right the proud problem of problems which is: TO LEAVE NO PROBLEM UNSOLVED" (Klein, 1968, 353). And even as he lays out the rules of his methodology, which insist upon the need for caution, Descartes notes simply, "there is no need for minds to be confined at all within limits" (Descartes, 1967, 1). The question of the ontological status of the universal is swept away by this enthusiasm. Herman Weyl:

> The leap into the beyond occurs when the sequence of numbers that is never complete but remains open toward the infinite is made into a closed aggregate of objects existing in themselves. Giving the numbers the status of ideal objects becomes dangerous only when this is done. The belief in the absolute is deeply implanted in our breast; no wonder, then, that mathematics was bold and naive enough to perform the leap. Whoever accepts as meaningful the definition 'n is an even or odd number according as a number x does or does not *exist* such that $n = 2x$,' which refers to the infinite totality of all of numbers . . . , already stands on the other shore; for him the system of numbers has become a realm of absolute existences which is "not of this world" and from which only gleams here and there are caught and reflected in our consciousness. (Weyl, 1949, 38)

This position is often called "Platonic," and there are Platonic arguments that indicate a clear longing for the other shore. In fact, however, Plato knew only a worldly mathematics in which the sequence of numbers, open toward the infinite and the infinitesimal, is never "made into a closed aggregate existing in themselves." Without entering the fray over the Platonic conception of number, which is fought by scholars of formidable learning and dialectical skill, it can be safely said that the modern number, unlike the ancient, does not depend upon actual counting and actual countable entities. The modern view is not simply more abstract but of a different order of abstraction. This is the first appearance of what Hegel will call "the right infinity," infinity as a real quantity, not just an endless succession.* The knowledge of the *mechanism* of this infinity is the profound gulf that separates modern from ancient culture, and it is only now that we have passed to a still higher level of abstraction that the seventeenth-century leap into the beyond can be fully comprehended.

The complexities of this situation created new a psychology: like an algebraic expression, the Cartesian ego was an ideal object that could be articulated only in formal language, especially the formal language of poetry and art. The rise of mathematical analysis and the poetic traditions of Milton, Donne, and Racine were cognate developments. The new poetry represented an ideal self as mathematics represented an ideal world, both of which are infinite and thus in some sense incomprehensible. The rhythm of the accentual-syllabic line, unlike classical verse, was not based on a real counting of intuitable quantities; it was, rather, a relationship, like an algebraic function, that defined rhythmic species and might be realized by a range of possible performances.

In the new regime each individual soul became the site of a "paradise within," as the archangel Michael tells Adam at the end of *Paradise Lost* and, at the same time, the cultivator of the garden, which reveals God's will by allegory. There were awful paradoxes hidden in this formula, but they were obscured by the substitution of the new methodology for the slower and less-powerful techniques of *mimesis*. The dissociation of sensibility that T. S. Eliot notes in Milton was not a failure of art but a necessary feature of the new program. In a revealing book, *Milton and the Postmodern*, Herman Rapaport argues that "Milton is not a poet of the logocentric, the theocentric book, but a poet who banishes the signified" (Rapaport, 1983, 13). That is, Milton was already a poststructuralist poet. As we shall see, every poet who absorbed and continued the methodological tradition from the beginning both does and does not banish the signified. In one sense, the poets obviously banish it: they create fictions. At the same time, how-

---

*Perhaps it will make the general direction of the argument clearer to note here that Hegel's right infinity is, from the point of view of the poetics of common knowledge, the *wrong* infinity. Finitism or the wrong infinity comes back into play seriously in this century in the mathematics of Henri Poincaré, L. E. J. Brouwer, Herman Weyl, and Alexis Yessinin-Volpin. A good introduction to this theory can be found in Charles Stein's introduction to *Being = Space × Action* (Stein, 1988, 1–45), in which an earlier version of this essay originally appeared.

ever, they create special fictions that are truer than the truth of the signified. The *mere* signified exists in an inferior world, a world itself banished and substituted for. For the solipsist who Milton was, the place of the signified is taken by more signifiers. The poststructuralists hardly provide a critique of the tradition: they expose some of the tricks which has it made effective.

Post-Cartesian solipsism was rigorous. Never before had individuals felt so keenly the responsibility for their own beliefs. For the few the intellectual challenge was unsurpassed; for the many only the enthusiasm of hymn singing and Bible thumping made the interior garden seem real at all. In time the intensities and insecurities of the situation became unbearable, and, after the great wave of religious psychosis and strife past, the rational spirit of the theology was attached to science, and the enthusiasm was attached to art. These two modes of the aesthetics of self came to pass for the objective and subjective realms, the one expressed by science, the other by *sentimental* reference to "the tradition." Humans, thus, became sadly subject to their own self-creations, metaphors in which they were weak and unreliable but oddly empowered as agents of change because the Other was created in the image of their reason. They were simultaneously master and slave, godlike creators of replicas on which they modeled themselves, disciplining themselves to their own mechanisms. Although idealism and materialism were their bleak *philosophic* alternatives, philosophy itself was largely irrelevant, except as symptom or official policy. A new psychology had taken hold, and inside it there were no true contraries, as Blake would note. Maintaining a subjectivity so large and commodious that physical mechanism and rational freedom could be simultaneously maintained involved a massive cultural project. The glorification of reason by the scientific community and the glorification of art by the aesthetic community involved claims that could not be responsibility demonstrated, but both were necessary to the emerging culture that valued only a progress that sacrificed all of its vitality to a vicious and infinitely circular regression.

Ideal Language

"Descartes" is our convenient name for the site of cognitive excitement that marks the essential assumption for the community of modern thinkers. The historical personage and his writings are by no means irrelevant, but the site as such is dependent upon neither. We honor him, rather than Vieta or Galileo and Bacon, who were prior to him in important respects, not only because he independently developed powerful techniques of mathematical analysis but also because he identified mathematical potentialities with pure space, thus creating the context of modern physics and, most significantly, for our purposes, defining the relationships between the common language and formal languages in terms that have persisted as fundamental structures of the culture. Or, if we emphasize the subject rather than the object, we can say that Descartes gave us the first complete image of the modern self, the solipsistic demiurge of modern technological psychology, an entity whose judgements call an unlocated and problematic world into being.

The Cartesian strategy creates a language of language, a writing of writing. It is evidence and understanding of this doubling that we seek in Descartes's work, which is the culmination of a profound culture change, closely associated with the development of printing and the development of linguistic forms appropriate to it. The question and answer format of classical dialectics gives way to a series of manic monologues. Descartes's *Rules for the Regulation of the Mind* consists not of questions and answers but of propositions and commentaries. The modern era is initiated not by catechism or dialogue but by *self*-interpretation. In addition to Descartes, one might think in this regard of the essays of Montaigne, Bacon, and Burton, or the solipsistic implications of the novel in the instigating hands of Cervantes and Defoe. The linearity of print-bred intelligence depends upon writing as an image of abstract temporality, a temporal sense that distinguishes it clearly from the linear duration of oral poetic performance, the temporal play of classical dialectics, and the oratorical time of classical rhetoric. The change from qualitative science to quantitative science parallels a shift in emphasis from ontology to epistemology, from grammar to rhetoric, and from poetry to prose.

The seventeenth-century implementation of a mechanical information-handling technology and its product—the printed book—required the revision of fundamental beliefs and institutions. The proposals for reform were diverse—some more or less useful; some, from our perspective, more or less absurd. Murray Cohen, in *Sensible Words: Linguistic Practice in England, 1640–1785,* gives a useful account of the linguistic projectors (Cohen,

1977). A remarkable number of these diverse projects—developing shorthand scripts or hieroglyphic writing, teaching the deaf and dumb, creating universal grammars, and so forth—shared a common theme of breaking the relationship between language and speech. The animadversions of the linguistic projectors on the centrality of the rhetorical voice anticipated and, in a sense, outdid the twentieth-century critique of voice led by Jacques Derrida. Respect for the voice as the guarantor of self-presence and for the associated metaphysics of the originating Word was undermined as far as the primary intellectual modes were concerned. In the seventeenth century, as in our own times, the fact that European writing was a mere transcription of vocal sounds that in turn referred to objects was a cause of special consternation. Phonetic language seemed to double the distance between a description and its object. As early as 1615, Matthew Ricci gave an influential account of Chinese ideographs, and proposals for visual languages were common. Even Francis Bacon commented on the advantages of glyphic over phonetic writing. Not only teaching the deaf but teaching as if *everyone* were deaf became a primary undertaking of a culture gearing up for book literacy and mathematical technology.

By the end of the century, the outline of a scheme that could compensate for the shortcomings of phonetic writing was articulated. The cultural solution to the problem that arose in the context of Cartesian thought was to create two languages: one formal, descriptive, and geometric; the other expressive, decorative, and historical. Although complex and often inefficient cultural institutions were required to oversee the practical relationship between these primary linguistic zones, the strategy afforded unprecedented intellectual leverage.

Descartes understands at least implicitly the necessary relationship between language reform and technology. In a letter to his friend, Mersenne, dating to about the time he was writing the *Regulae*, he suggests that an ideal language, which, like mathematics, would reveal the truth by virtue of its structure, is possible: "Order is what is needed: all the thoughts which can come into the human mind must be arranged in an order *like the natural order of numbers*." (Descartes, 1970, 4) The suggestion here is related to the *mathesis universalis* of the *Regulae* as well as Leibniz's plan for a universal calculus, Frege's symbolic logic, Russell's logical atomism, or any language that depends upon the identification and manipulation of "the simple ideas in the human imagination out of which all human thoughts are compounded." Descartes goes on to say: "The greatest advantage of such a language would be the assistance it would give to men's judgement, representing matters so clearly that it would be almost impossible to go wrong." The conception of a language that grammatically or structurally disallows falsity was a central philosophic fantasy from Descartes to the early Wittgenstein, and it persists, at least as a motivating fantasy, among certain researchers in cognitive science.

Descartes warns Mersenne, however, that he should "not hope ever to see such a language in use. For that, the order of nature would have to change so that the world turned into a terrestrial paradise; and that is too much to suggest outside of fairyland." (Descartes, 1970, 5–6) The recognition that such a language is possible but that it cannot be implemented without *a change in the order of nature* brings us to the moment of the technological crisis, the disjunction between what the order of nature produces of its own accord and what is possible. Most people, perhaps all people most of the time, are hopelessly mired in unreason. If the structure of reality is determined logically, and, therefore, unreasonable people are requirements of that structure, how does one establish the grounds for truth *outside* the habitual and determining language of the peasant or, for that matter, the intellectual salons? What conditions make reason possible? Although Descartes does not pose the question in quite these terms, which belong to Kant and the following century, he confronts the problem directly. If language is determined by habit and thought by language, how might it be possible to establish an arena of free intellectual renovation?

As an "instrument of knowledge," Descartes feels, the natural languages derive from or are secondary to a mathematical science that contains "the primary rudiments of human reason" (Descartes, 1967, 11). At the same time, his inability to develop mathematics *without* the "derivative" language is clear; he must have it in order to state the rules. This is a logical problem of the first order, and Descartes makes the only possible arguments: (1) truth can be established only in an ideal language and (2) the natural language *in the ironic and sentimental mode* can meet its metalinguistic requirements. He draws the analogy to the person who would practice the craft of a smith but who lacks the necessary tools and equipment. It would be necessary, he tells us, for the person first to fashion the required items in stone and wood and, then, in turn, to use these to make tools of more suitable but more intractable materials. "This method of ours," he writes, "resembles indeed those devices employed by the mechanical crafts, which do not need the aid of anything outside of them, but themselves supply the directions for making their own instruments" (Descartes, 1967, 25). The ideal language is a subset of the natural language, and, if a few clearly defined terms can be established, the remainder of the language can be constructed from these nodes of clarity, or at least that is the hope.

It is not clear, however, that one linguistic mode is the iron to another linguistic mode's stone. Descartes' argument is blatantly circular.* If a language as inclusive and fluent as the natural language is developed, how can it avoid all of the complexity and imprecision of the natural language? Descartes was athwart the problem of ideal languages, which the later Wittgenstein so cogently exposes: "When I talk about language (words, sentences, etc.) I must speak the language of every day. Is this language somehow too coarse and material for what we want to say? *Then how is another one to be constructed?*—And how strange that we should be able to do anything at all with the one we have!" (Wittgenstein, 1953, 49). As a logical problem, it is insoluable. It is possible, however, to create cultural institutions with enough tolerance that the problem can be absorbed, at least in sufficient measure to make ideal languages useful to technology, however uncertain their metaphysical foundations.

The Second House of Culture

The modern strategy for creating ideal languages has been to accept a traditional language as a kind of metaphysical halfway house, while articulating ideal structures that are alien to it. Before undertaking the process of doubt in *Discourse on Method*, Descartes notes that we do not rebuild the house in which we live without furnishing ourselves with "some other house in which we may live commodiously during the operations," so he adopts certain maxims to live by, as he carries out the reconstruction of

---

*This fact has generated a series of important essays by some of Descartes's most perceptive readers; these have been collected in a useful volume, *Eternal Truths and the Cartesian Circle*, edited by Willis Doney (Doney, 1983).

philosophy—for example, "to obey the laws and customs of my country, adhering firmly to the faith in which by the grace of God, I had been educated" (Descartes, 1967, 95). That is, he provisionally accepts the tradition that he is questioning and undermining.

The epistemic border that appeared in the seventeenth century was not between the known and the unknown but between two normative languages, the algebraic formalism and the aestheticized natural language. Although the supposed gap between the two cultures has occasioned much impassioned graduation-speech rhetoric, the two languages and the two cultures that serviced them were both essential. Thus, Descartes argues that "To study the writings of the ancients is right, because it is a great boon for us to be able to make use of the labours of so many men . . . But yet there is a great danger lest in a too absorbed study of these works we should become infected with their errors, guard against them as we may" (Descartes, 1967, 5–6). "The ancients" is a code term for what would be known as "culture" in the nineteenth century and "the humanities" in the twentieth. Descartes is thinking not only of the ancient texts but also the entire exegetical tradition, the lock, stock, and barrel of his own formal education, and, more generally, the tradition of letters itself. In counseling casual regard for the ancients, Descartes hits the keynote of subsequent rationalistic, technological, liberal thought. Since the seventeenth century, the *literary* tradition, in the broadest sense, the tradition of literature, of philosophy (to the extent that it has not been a pursuit of formal symbolic systems), of history, of colloquial thought in general, has been implicated in the sentimentality of a prephilosophic Golden Age. The modern West, the culture that has taken modernity as its definitive quality, has obsessively fantasized about its relationship to the ancients. Never has a culture so poised itself upon the dream of another so distant in time and space. Like Chronos with a time machine, we have devoured our ancestors. In audacious and inspired acts of scholarly piracy, we have appropriated classical images that are sensuous, timeless, and wholly inappropriate to the modern impulse. The fantasy has not been hampered by excessive knowledge; we do not know much about the Greeks. It is, at any rate, indirectly the Greece of the scholars that has figured in the modern imagination, but from the Italian neo-Platonists, Marlowe, and Shakespeare, to Joyce and Pound, the reservoir of classical imagery has been the target for a nervous meditation, a recalling and a casting away of a genealogy that we have created to justify and temper our rapaciousness.

The nostalgia for a time in which the particular is perfectly accommodated by the universal and vice versa is the instigating sentimentality of modern rhetoric. Georg Lukács writes: "For the question which engenders the formal answers of the epic is: how can life become essence?" (Lukács, 1971, 30). This is a clear and important formulation. In a preliterate poetry a great deal is forgotten, but the parts that are retained all have equal status. No part of the Homeric text exercises control over the remainder. It is the most parsimonious use of memory, and that which is remembered is worn down to the narrative nubs of myth. There are no irrelevancies: each image and piece of information retains its integrity; the value of information is not absorbed into a structural hierarchy. In Homer, the essences are made manifest, not named. The problem of the individual is solved by the fact that the epic discourse is structured by proper nouns; it never occurs as a problem, because the problem of the universal never arises.

The origin to which the modern West recurs is as much historical as metaphysical or, to say the least, the gap between the requirements of the theory and the practical workings of the culture is immense, and it is only the hopelessly intellectual who assume that the theory is more than an elegant afterthought. We conceive of a philosophic apocalypse in which thought will be sublated and the possibility of Odyssean action will reappear. Both of these conceptions, both the Golden Age and the dialectic that leads *forward* to it, are products of the philosophic tradition, and together they conspire to constitute a project, the program of which is nowhere clearly articulated.

As a rule of thumb in reading modern philosophy, one can assume that the gist of the position is never contained in an isolatable passage. For this reason the kind of textual attention that has been taught by Derrida and his disciples often produces deeply ramified incomprehension. To uncover the movement of the philosophic currents at a given time, it is necessary to examine the given details against the vastest background. The meanings of texts appear only in relation to a tacit knowledge of the complete tradition.

The center of interest is the propulsion toward the coherent truth. This fact discourages scholarship. Although the academy creates the appearance of isolated subject matters for microscopic scrutiny of expert researchers, it is not possible to test the generalizing sweep of even so cautious a philosopher as Descartes—to say nothing of Hegel or Freud—against all of the relevant material.

The histories that are implicit in modern thought, however, are not factual but mythological. Our dream-time happens also to have been an historical epoch from which we can recover texts, artifacts, ruins, and so forth. Our arguments over the nature of Greek social organization, the translation of pre-Socratic philosophic fragments, or the development of vase painting, therefore, are in effect theological.

Unlike the humanist scholars, the scientists and mathematicians were restoring not ancient texts but the pure thought of the Golden Age of science, which we know, if at all, in late and decadent form. Of this blest time, Simon Stevin, the mathematician, writes, "We call the wise age that in which men had a wonderful knowledge of science which we recognize without fail by certain signs, although without knowing who they were, or in what place or when" (Klein, 1968, quoted 187). Descartes goes so far as to accuse the ancients of harboring the secret of their discoveries for mercenary reasons—a practice that was not uncommon among Descartes's contemporaries. The scientists and mathematicians were "rearticulating" a world that never existed. Indeed, as Descartes and others well knew and proclaimed when their rhetoric moved into its other mood, they were drawing a world out of their own baseless creativity. They projected their own epistemological obsessions on a tradition that was largely interested in ontology, and the contradictions that were inherent in their project were deep and generative. The modern dialectic has been responsible to logic, to empirical evidence, and to personal freedom. The primary philosophic enterprise has been to discover a synthesis in which these contradictory claims can be satisfied. Such syntheses are, of course, necessarily unstable: personal freedom finds itself contending with the demands of *both* of the other terms, which are at odds with one another. It was in the creation of a theoretical world that a reasonable compromise seemed possible. The modern impulse has been to create a second world, a universal techno-environment, including perhaps replications of living organisms and, at least in computers, human intelligence—a replica that adds only its own predictability.

The Unacknowledged House

The two cultures, however, required a third culture, itself unspoken and even unrecognized. The languages of mathematics and poetry required the mediation of prose—a medium in which the ideal languages could be laundered. Jeffrey Kittay and Wlad Godzich write, "prose is considered omnipresent. . . Prose is meant to have no place; prose does not happen. Prose is what assigns place." The universal prose, which appeared in the seventeenth century, was not so much a literary genre as a new world, almost nature itself, which appeared to stand between the objective idealism of science and subjective idealism of poetry. Kittay and Godzich go on to say: "In relation to verse or indeed any other form, prose assumes the position of matter. . . It is there from the beginning, as the *hyle* of the world, and it is what will remain after the destruction of whatever may have been imposed on it. Unlike ancient *hyle*, however, prose is not inert; it does not wait for the inspirational breath to set it in motion, it animates and motivates, disposes, arranges, assembles, and orders by itself" (Kittay and Godzich, 1987, 197). As a self-energizing and motivating medium, prose is both a cultural motor and a persistent source of potential anarchy at the very heart of the culture. It is the resource of printed language: an undefined medium that implicitly encloses as a system all of the combinatorial possibilities of the alphabet. It paradoxically encloses the infinite with finite marks, thus creating an insoluable puzzle for the subject that identifies with its logical possibilities rather than its factual condition.

The terms of the debate over modern prose style were defined more than fifty years ago in classic essays by Morris W. Croll and R. F. Jones and have not been seriously disturbed by subsequent considerations. Croll emphasizes the reaction against the rhetorical style of Cicero by the Senecans—notably, Lipsius, Montaigne, and Bacon—thus seeing the matter as a continuing adjustment of modern practice to classical models. Jones, on the other hand, emphasizes the relationship of prose to science. He shows that many of the important concerns were immediate and utilitarian rather than literary. Therefore, he argues that the thoroughly modern prose style did not develop before the last half of the seventeenth century. To say the least, there were two strains of prose in the seventeenth century, and the problem has revolved around how to characterize them. Stanley Fish adds a new set of descriptive terms to the opposition without upsetting the distinction: "To the paired terms of my predecessors—Anglican-Puritan, Painted-Plain, Ciceronian-Senecan, Scientific-Rhetorical, Utilitarian-Frivolous—I add a new pair, Self-Satisfying and Self-Consuming" (Fish, 1972, 379). Fish rightly shows that the universal acceptance of the plain style after the Restoration was a result not of the triumph of this or that party but of an epistemological shift that all of the parties more or less shared. Prose style, thereafter, became the intellectual currency, the basis for a dialectic that was not possible as long as different formalisms represented radically divergence logical spaces. Allied with the newly available abstraction, prose was an awesome tool, and it proliferated as the utility of public information and entertainment. Formal beauty and expressiveness were incidental values. It was the raw material of thought or experience. The source of the formalism had been relocated.

Despite the divergence of the sources from which they trace the development, Croll and Jones agree that prose is *natural* language. Of Thomas Browne, Croll says: "He writes like a philosophical scientist making notes of his observation as it occurs. We see his pen move and stop as he thinks. To write thus, and at the same time to create beauty of cadence in the phrases and rhythm in the design—and so Browne constantly does—is to achieve a triumph in what Montaigne called 'the art of being natural'" (Croll, 1971, 70). This line of thought, given another half turn, justifies the automatic writing of the surrealists. Jones, on the other hand, emphasizes the naturalness of the self-effacing style that was favored by Puritan preachers and the scientists of the Royal Society, which are by no means mutually exclusive groups. John Wilkins, for example, who was one of the founders of the Royal Society, authored important statements on the style of both sermons and scientific reports. Jones finds the origins of modern prose style most clearly characterized in the often-quoted prescriptions from Thomas Sprat's *History of the Royal Society* (1667). In keeping with the necessary strategy of linguistic renovation, Sprat appeals to the precedent of a Golden Age, praising "primitive purity" that delivers "so many *things,* almost in an equal number of *words*" and "Mathematical plainness" (Sprat, 1958, 113). Croll conceives of the writer as a creature of nature and thus "natural," where Jones conceives of a writing as natural and thus as colorless as other objects of the Newtonian cosmos. Nature has to be conceived on a scale that could include a natural subject and a natural object. For one, style is the man, and, for the other, a completely styleless language is the equivalent of the objective world. Both speak of essential qualities of this new linguistic form; its allowance of equivocation is a necessary counterpart to the rigors of the idealized formal language of mathematics, on the one hand, and poetry, on the other.

The prose that developed in the seventeenth century and continued as the primary medium of knowledge cannot be simply defined. In a sense, its usefulness depends upon its lack of definition. It is the material from which both the formal language of mathematics and the formal language of poetry is refined. Of a passage from Pascal's essay on "Imagination," Croll says, "Nothing could better illustrate the 'order of nature,'" which is an order of definite objects but uncertain relationships, relationships that are—to use terms that have been common in poststructuralist cant—subject to "sliding or overturning of former categories," "slippage," and "decentering." Prose elegantly allows these imprecisions, which are excluded from both formal mathematical languages and poetry. Croll goes on to note that the sentence "begins by naming the subject, the *plus grand philosophe,* without foreseeing the syntax by which it is to continue. Then it throws in the elements of the situation, using any syntax that suggests itself at the moment, proceeding with perfect dramatic sequence, but wholly without logical sequence, until at last the sentence has lost touch with its stated subject. It is a violent, or rather nonchalant, anacoluthon" (Croll, 1971, 47–48). This is a fair characterization of one boundary of the "world of prose," which, according to Hegel's analysis, appears in the nineteenth century. The other boundary is formed by normative disciplines—rigorous grammars or empirical investigations. In effect, the resources of abstraction that mathematical analysis supplies requires an entire culture as its medium. It is the function of prose to communicate with the incommensurable elements that are necessarily involved in the synthesis—to translate, to absorb the slippage, to allow the play, and so forth. As Robert Adolph writes, "From the Restoration on, normal literary prose is, to use McLuhan's terms, a 'linear' product of the 'print culture.' The chief aim of such prose is useful public communication" (Adolph, 1967, 245). It becomes an instructional medium, devoted, as Stanley Fish notes, to the universal belief of the Restoration in "the ability of the mind to be instructed in the truth" (Fish, 1972, 380). There are some specialized vocabularies, of course, which distinguish certain professional groups, but prose itself becomes transparent and is only now called into question.

THE TWO LANGUAGES: SPACE

> For the modern scientist energy has no borders, it is a shapeless "mass" of force; even his capacity to differentiate it to a degree never dreamed by the ancients has not led him to think of its shape or even its loci. . . Perhaps algebra has queered our geometry.
>
> —Ezra Pound

Compendious Abbreviations

But Descartes sets a process into operation that moves us inexorably toward contemporary technoculture. The profoundest incoherence—incoherence invoked on behalf of an all-embracing totality—was required to break the sway of the old mentality, and open the cosmic possibilities of the printed book. From his earliest work, the suppressed essay, *The World; or Essay on Light*, Descartes assumes a thoroughly literate cosmos in which voice, like sight per se, has no significant relation to the abstract objects that constitute the field of knowledge. The voice bespeaks itself in language that is not heard, nature writes itself in signs that have no relation to the object, and the soul writes its emotions on the human countenance in signs that must be interpreted. Descartes's dualism divides meaning from voice as decisively as it does body from soul (Descartes, 1979, 4–5).

The central concern of Descartes's *Rules for the Regulation of the Mind* is the relationship between the common language and the conventions of mathematical formalism. His project relates directly to those of his contemporary linguistic projectors. He hopes to translate from the phonetic language to an algebraic language of geometric glyphs. In this connection, he recognizes the need for "certain compendious abbreviations," which supplement memory and aid "the continuous and uninterrupted action of a mind that has a clear vision of each step in the process" (Descartes, 1967, 8). The Cartesian method is fundamentally typographical: it is concerned with graphic arrangements that clearly reveal the structure of the argument, so mathematical proofs are easily read and the relationships between ideas made manifest. To think in terms of contemporary mnemonic technology, the rules for the regulation of the mind address the problem of programming, the creation of software for the printing press. It would not be over-dramatizing to say that Descartes's proposal borders on a mysticism of inscription: "since [memory] is liable to fail us and in order to obviate the need of expending any part of our attention in refreshing it, while we are engaged with other thoughts, art has invented the device of writing." And, he advises: "nothing that does not require to be continuously borne in mind ought to be committed to memory, if we can set it down on paper" (Descartes, 1967, 60).

What does the method require to be continuously borne in mind? Or, conversely, what cannot be committed to the formalism? These are practical questions, the kind of questions that must arise for a practicing mathematician, and questions of this kind, more significantly than questions of ontology, have motivated the history of the past three centuries and more. If the intuition and the expression of mathematical entities required the same kinds of objects, the questions would be simply answered, but they do not. The content of "naked understanding," in Descartes's terms, is "simple natures," entities as colorless and as empty as the natural integers that can be arranged in sequence by a simple enumerative process and then combined by rules to produce all possible valid combinations. For Descartes, these entities may be spiritual, corporeal, or *both at once.* He appeals to them first as ideal objects that must "be taken altogether outside the bounds of the imagination, if they are to be true." And again as merely pragmatic considerations: "It matters little, however, though they [the simple natures] are not believed to be more real than those imaginary circles by means of which Astronomers describe their phenomena, provided that you employ them to aid you in discerning in each particular case what sort of knowledge is true and what false" (Descartes, 1967, 40). There is an inherent contradiction in the idea of an imaginary ideal—that is, an imaginary object of which no image is possible. It is, however, precisely this imageless—which is also to say measureless—image that Descartes takes as the building block of his system (of the world) and that becomes the mark of modern thought. It is variously the infinitesimal point of mathematical analysis and the dimensionless, significant difference of phonology.

The Cartesian symbols, even more distinctly than the phonetic alphabet, are not merely indices of simple natures; they are images that visually replicate an object. Metaphysical purity, therefore, as Jacques Derrida is correct to note, necessitates that the entire argument be comprehended in a single view, as "present to itself." Descartes, however, explicitly makes no such claim: "what I have to do is to run over them [i.e., the properly concatenated propositions in the proof] all repeatedly in my mind, until I pass so quickly from the first to the last that practically no step is left to the memory, and *I seem to view the whole all at the same time*" (Descartes, 1967, 34, my emphasis). He is careful to stay within the *practical* limits of the method: the instantaneous apprehension of the whole that absolute knowledge requires is temporalized. He writes: "even though the understanding in the strict sense attends merely to what is signified by the name, the imagination nevertheless ought to fashion a correct image of the object, in order that the very understanding itself may be able to fix upon other features belonging to it that are not expressed by the name in question" (Descartes, 1967, 59). The ability to relate ideal simple natures to images—literally, marks on the page—is the essential equivocation of modern knowledge. The imagination integrates the names, which for "naked understanding" is in the realm of abstract potentiality, in its world-constituting function. In the century after Descartes, this practical function was sentimentalized and given responsibility for articulating an aesthetic world—the domain of artists and engineers alike.

The evidence for, in Derrida's words, the "unfailing complicity . . . between idealization and speech" (Derrida, 1978a), simply does not appear in Descartes or the work of the other essential thinkers—that is, the thinkers who contribute directly to the development of contemporary technoculture. Of the classical tradition, Derrida's assessment is no doubt accurate. In modern philosophy, however, presence was always and only a sentimentality, albeit a necessary sentimentality until it was, over a period of centuries, eroded away and replaced with its replica—a statistically fulgent zone in the media flux that can now be controlled by the machinations of popular culture, rather than by metaphysics and theology in collusion with art. Why Derrida's proposal of a grammatology has aroused such exaggerated interest at this late date is not clear. A deep reactionary spirit must need to believe that the question of rational ontology is still open, that the sentimentality that has invested terms such as *self, imagination,* and *environment* with their powerful resonances can be sustained, if only by negation.

If one emphasizes those features of methodology that underwrite its efficacy rather than those that attempt vainly to maintain its consistency, the complicity between idealization and *writing* is clear, and, when voice *is* idealized, typically its structure is bent to the demands of phonetic writing and not the reverse. Certain primitivists, Rousseau and Levi-Strauss, whom Derrida takes as typical, have invoked the classical tradition on behalf nonliterate people, and in a twentieth-century attempt to salvage the Cartesian project, Edmund Husserl idealizes voice, as Derrida elegantly demonstrates in *Speech and Phenomena,* but these are anomalous examples. To the extent that Husserl idealizes voice, he follows neither Descartes's lead, as we have seen, nor the lead of the other dominant strain of modern philosophy—that is, Locke's, with its insistence upon the primacy of writing. Locke's metaphor for the mind as a *tabula rasa* underscores the dominance of writing in the modern *episteme.* We have had a science of writing and *only* a science of writing for the past three and a half centuries.

The ideal self and the ideal object were not required by the Cartesian project; they were concessions to the human need for certainty, not to the practical requirements of the methodology. The power of the formalism, confirmed by the successes of technology, is now secure, and the fact that neither self nor object were functional is exposed. We are all Cartesian modernists, who, by staging an idealism as the pretext for a language without etymologies or sensuous content, have undergone a new beginning. The proliferating formalism often seems overwhelming. It has no outside and no concrete content. Increasingly we are its creatures. If we can expose its implementation, to see how we gradually replaced our intuition of the world and its measured language with a logic and an aesthetic, perhaps we can begin to reclaim a concrete common world as the content of a community.

Intuition

The seventeenth-century epistemologists reordered the relationship between the arts and the sciences as they were understood in classical and medieval times. In the classical view, art emphasized the practicality of judgement, and science emphasized theory for its own sake. Although the tradition of philosophic utopianism proposed to apply theory to politics, which was the highest art, the thought of applying theory to nature in a practical sense never occurred to the classical thinkers. The Cartesian position represents a change in desire, a reassessment of the relation between thought and the physical world. In the *Tractatus,* the last great document of the Cartesian tradition, Wittgenstein says, "anyone who understands me eventually recognizes . . . [my propositions] as nonsensical, when he has used them—as steps—to climb up beyond them. (He must, so to speak, throw away the ladder after he has climbed up it.)" (Wittgenstein, 1961, 151). In the first four rules of the *Regulae,* we witness Descartes's somewhat inelegant scramble up his own ladder of nonsense. Commentators have tried to explain his incoherence, but we must recognize that modernism involves not incoherence as a mere intellectual error but as a consuming and powerful intellectual foundation. Only thus is the logical impossibility of beginning again overcome.

The passages on intuition in the *Regulae* are some of the last tentative looks of Faustian man, self-creating man, whatever we should call the modern human, back to the firmly rooted ontology of the classical world. Descartes substitutes "clear and distinct ideas" for "intuition" in his later work, and when the term intuition returns to philosophic currency in the work of Kant, it has a different valence; it no longer relates to objects as such but to the conditions that make the apprehension of objects possible—that is, the forms of sensibility, time, and space. Descartes's definition of "intuition"—in its particular unclarity—is revealing: "*intuition* is the undoubting conception of an unclouded and attentive mind, and springs from the light of reason alone; it is more certain than deduction itself, in that it is simpler" (Descartes, 1967, 7). We learn a good deal more about what intuition is not than what it is:

it is not sense perception, it is not imagination, and it is not deduction. Although it is not reason as such, it is "born of the light of reason"—that is, apparently, to the mind which *shines with* reason, purely and attentively. His examples are of two sorts, intuitions of the self and intuitions of geometric properties: "Thus each individual can mentally have intuitions of the fact that he exists, and that he thinks; that the triangle is bounded by three lines only, the sphere by a single superficies, and so on" (Descartes, 1967, 7). We have knowledge of at least one singular object, the knowing self, and of certain classes of objects that are tautologies—the necessary constituents of judgements which are synthetic and a priori. The problem for epistemology is to join them. The argument that Kant finally articulates is implicit in Descartes's development of the idea.

Rule 1 states: "The end of study should be to direct the mind towards the enunciation of sound and correct judgements on all matters that come before it" (Descartes, 1967, 1). "Judgement," a common term of traditional logic, has to do with building up true propositions from simple elements, as opposed to syllogistics—the study of the relationships between propositions. The notion, however, that the *focus* of intellectual effort should be judgement rather than syllogistics was radically new. According to the methodologists, medieval logic had been lax in judgement, that is, in determining the truth of the premises. The importance of this distinction goes to the very root of Descartes's differentiation of his work from the Scholastics'. The problem for the thinker who is intent upon a thoroughgoing revision of the philosophic tradition is to adjust not merely the philosophic terminology but the relationships among the terms that inform the entire structure of thought. The meanings of the terms and the meanings of the terms in which the terms are defined must all be changed at once. Change of this order marks the difference between the profound modernist, such as Descartes, and, for example, the so-called modernists who fought the war between the ancients and the moderns in the eighteenth century. Those who complacently understand their position as "modern" are, in effect, already postmodern. The *Regulae* is a remarkable work precisely because of the insight into the perpetual modernist crisis that it affords. Modernism is that state of mind in which the system and the objects of one's thought wax and wane together.

In the commentary to the first rule, Descartes does not address the relationship between judgement and syllogistics directly. Rather, paraphrasing a passage from Aristotle, he renovates a series of related terms. Implicitly, the argument proposes that judgement is to syllogistics as the sciences are to the arts and as the mind is to the body. In this context, all of these central terms—and many others that depend upon them—come loose from their traditional moorings in scholastic thought and provide Descartes with a plastic medium in which to express himself. The precise meanings of the terms in the commentary are never specified; moreover, "judgement," which is the central term of rule 1, is given only indirect amplification.

The commentary focuses on the Aristotelian distinction between the sciences and the arts: "sciences . . . entirely consist in the cognitive exercise of the mind, [and] . . . the arts . . . depend upon an exercise and disposition of the body." The arts, with their physical involvements in the world, deal with *particular* subject matters and *particular* judgements or conclusions, rather than the theory of judgements as such. To his first examples of the arts, agricultural operations and harp playing, Descartes adds investigations into "human customs . . . the virtues of plants, the motions of stars, the transmutations of metals," and so forth. The sciences, on the other hand, "taken all together are identical with human wisdom, which always remains one and the same, however applied to different subjects, and suffers no more differentiation proceeding from them than the light of sun experiences from the variety of the things which it illumines." The science for which Descartes speaks represents Renaissance megalomania at its most dramatic: it has no specific content; it is rather the rules by which any possible content can be constructed; and, above all, it prepares the reasonable person "not for the purpose of resolving this or that difficulty of scholastic type, but in order that his understanding may light his will to its proper chance in all the contingencies of life" (Descartes, 1967, 1–2). The moderns propose to deal with the contingencies of life from the perspective of that which is *not* contingent and to renovate the physical world on behalf of the mind. Knowledge of particular things and events derives from judgements of universals, so the actual world is secondary to the Cartesian ego. "Judgement" is no longer a matter of building up isolated propositions from simple apprehensions; it is rather a world-constituting act. *The first proposition of modern philosophy is technology.*

Western science is neither simply a method nor a body of knowledge but a complex institution that coordinates method and knowledge with psychological forms. I know of no scholarly account of the crucial role that art, and especially the timed arts, poetry and music, played in the development of the scientific project of the seventeenth and eighteenth centuries. They too became in a sense technological, as implementations of the soul. Descartes sets the stage for a powerful movement in art that creates the requisite psychology of selfhood. In Milton and Donne, in El Greco, in Bach, and in the facades of Baroque churches, we can see signs of a new human creature that understands itself as infinite potentiality, as the generator of language that contains all knowledge and expresses not the outcome of science but its resources. It was the artist who supplies the profound *imagination* that methodology requires as a substitute for intuition. The new mode is clear, for example, in Bruno's attacks on Petrarch and in the widespread appearance of metaphysical poetries—"Concettismo," "Marinismo," "Gongorismo." The new images are not based on similitude. The vehicles of the metaphors are directly intuitable—a beloved and a compass in the famous example from the poem by Donne—but the relationships between them are not; how the terms relate must be explained. This strategy opens vast new metaphoric spaces: at *some* level of abstraction, everything is like everything else. The modern mind is more at home with paradoxes than with ontological mystery; it prefers recursive languages that require tireless but potentially entertaining interpretation to an hierarchical language that requires absorbed contemplation. Baroque art is the aesthetic leap into the beyond that corresponds directly to mathematical analysis.

The Equivocations

The difficulties that are presented by the self-reflective requirements of methodology appear in the commentary on rule 4: "There is need of a method for finding out the truth." In itself, this rule does not seem powerful, but it goes directly to the heart of the modernist objection to scholastic learning that made heavy concessions to contingency. Descartes writes: "So blind is the curiosity by which mortals are possessed, that they often conduct their minds along unexplored routes, having no reason to hope for success, but merely being willing to risk the experiment of finding whether the truth they seek lies there" (Descartes, 1967, 9). The failure to appreciate precisely this *risk* indicates a complete lack of interest in the primary form of intuition, which is mimetic rather than methodological. The mimetic sense of the world presupposes an object of imitation the nature of which is radically different from, perhaps even incommensurate with, the medium of imitation. That is, the classical tradition was profoundly, not just grammatically, dualistic. The *logos* of the tradition did not confuse Being with language. Discourse might be *about* the meditative object, but methodology institutes an inherently linguistic world as its field of operation. Only with Cartesian rhetoric do "discourse" and "meditation" begin to be synonyms.

Certain textual peculiarities in the *Regulae* and especially in the commentary to rule 4, which have been widely noted by readers of the work, are revealing. It is possible to see Descartes struggling with the complexities of his incoherent strategy. The first paragraph of the commentary more or less recasts the first three rules, and the second asserts the rediscovery of an ancient mathematical method. Although we do not know exactly when the *Regulae* was written, it was probably after Descartes had discovered algebraic geometry, a development that seems to be on his mind, because he tells us that he is thinking not of an "ordinary mathematics" but rather of an "instrument of knowledge . . . [that is] the source of all others." The confusion over the nature of this science has been far greater than is justified by the textual difficulties. The problems are logical, not textual, and they remain a constant of the philosophic tradition from Descartes himself, who found a way in the *Discourse* to sweep them under the rug, to Noam Chomsky and the foremost current French proponent of geometric mechanism, René Thom.

Although most of the "repetitions" in the *Regulae* can be accounted for in terms of perfectly normal thematic development that could have been worked out in revision (Descartes never prepared the manuscript for publication), there are a few passages in which Descartes is clearly struggling with serious philosophic problems. Consider, for example, this pair of passages:

1. For the human mind has in it something that we may call divine, wherein are scattered the first germs of useful modes of thought. Consequently it often happens that however much neglected and choked by interfering studies they bear fruit of their own accord. (Descartes, 1967, 10)

2. But I am convinced that certain primary germs of truth implanted by nature in human minds—though in our case the daily reading and hearing of innumerable diverse errors stifle them—had a very great vitality in that rude and unsophisticated age of the ancient world. (Descartes, 1967, 12)

These are not sentences of an inept or immature writer, as some commentators have suggested; they are written with a sensitivity to tone, nuance, and rhetorical impact. Whether the germs of truth are divine or natural might seem a matter of significant indecision, but it makes no difference to the actual *structure* of the argument. In either case they are *innate* and, equally important, they were known to the ancients; that is, a trace of them exists in the traditional learning. The *problem* is accounting for error. The tradition is obviously responsible for the "diverse errors" of the schoolmen, but it must, at the same time, somehow give evidence of these originary germs of learning. A logic never begins; it must have been so always. The old house of the new culture is not merely a convenience; it supplies a necessary component.

The same problem emerges dramatically in Descartes' account of the relationship between ancient and modern mathematics. Again, in these passages, Descartes is trying out alternative assessments of the modern renovation:

1. At the present day also there flourishes a certain kind of arithmetic, called Algebra, which designs to effect, when dealing with numbers, what the ancients achieved in the matter of figures (Descartes, 1967, 10).

2. For it seems to be precisely that science known by the barbarous name Algebra, if only we could extricate it from that vast array of numbers and inexplicable figures by which it is overwhelmed, so that it might display the clearness and simplicity which, we imagine, ought to exist in genuine mathematics (Descartes, 1967, 12).

As in the previous passages, Descartes's stance is already in the schematic world picture which depends upon a new formal language for its expression. If there is only the mechanism of unreasoning habit, on the one hand, and the invariant rules of the *mathesis universalis,* on the other, how does one make the transition from the false mind to the true? If knowledge is innate, it is impossible to account for the pervasiveness of error. If, however, it represents genuine innovation, it is impossible, having only the false tradition, to account for the ability to recognize the new truth.

These inconsistencies represent the efforts of a major philosopher, entering the mature phase of his thought, struggling with an insoluble problem at the center of his system. The fact that the system has had pervasive influence on the subsequent intellectual history of the West should perhaps be enough to make us doubt that logical consistency is as fundamental as we have believed. In terms of the increase of intellectual efficacy, in fact, the evidence might more fully support the usefulness of allowing thought to play back and forth between a willful dualism and a theoretical commitment to coherence. Any ideal language necessarily waffles in relationship to the common language it is intended to replace. The relationship between methodological thought and colloquial thought, between the new mathematics and the scholastic tradition, is necessary and necessarily obscure. Had Descartes prepared the manuscript for publication, he would have no doubt produced a text in which the problems are not so blatant, but the equivocation is essential to the program itself.

Rules 5 and 6 propose a method for analyzing complex arguments into their constituent parts and ordering simple natures in useable form, while rules 7 through 11 outline synthetic techniques for reconstituting the world in an ideal mathematical language. Rule 6, in particular, Descartes tells us, contains "the chief secret of method . . . For it tells us that all facts can be arranged in certain series, not indeed in the sense of being referred to some ontological genus such as the categories employed by philosophers in their classification, but in so far as certain truths can be known from others." (Descartes, 1967, 16) By carefully keeping track of absolute and relative terms—the structure of the hierarchy—it is possible to enumerate statements in order from the simplest and clearest to "whatever is said to be dependent, or an effect, composite, particular, many, unequal, unlike, oblique, etc." By exploiting the mnemonic technology of writing and particularly writing in the convenient and easily manipulated form of print, data can be managed in sure and powerful ways.

If the analytic function is the great secret of the Cartesian method, Descartes gives a much fuller and less-confusing account of the synthetic process. It is not necessary, for our purposes, to go into the procedures; more sophisticated versions of them are known to undergraduate mathematicians. The kind of *attention* that is being proposed beginning in rule 7, however, requires a radically new psychology. If thought can be regulated in its own operations and, thereby, released from the contingency of world, it can explore all possibilities. *Classical thought attended to the relation of form to thing; the modern, to the relation of form to form.* Descartes writes: "I am now able by attentive reflection to understand what is the form involved by all questions that can be propounded about the proportions or relations of things, and the order in which they should be investigated; and this discovery embraces the sum of the entire science of Pure Mathematics" (Descartes, 1967, 20). The confidence that the mind can extend its knowledge of actual structure to the structure of actuality is essential to the modern will to power.

In rule 12, which summarizes and concludes the first section of the *Regulae,* Descartes reintroduces the use of imagination, sense, and memory, but now their subordination to intuition and deduction—or the "understanding," in his term—is assured. The *mechanical* quality of imagination, sense, and memory is emphasized. The image of the human that Descartes presents is a being consisting of two texts or as existing at the intersection of two texts: one belongs wholly to the physical, mechanical world; the other is divinely or naturally inscribed in the mind in the form of combinatory techniques that encompass descriptions of all of the world's possibilities. In a metaphor that he carries through an extended passage, Descartes compares the body with its secondary intellectual faculties to a writing pen. In early modern grammatology, this passage must stand with Locke's discussion of the *tabula rasa.* Judgement is always judgement of a specific writing. He initially introduces the figure to explain how sense impressions are transmitted from the external world to some part of the body without the passage of "any real entity from one to the other":

It is in exactly the same manner that now when I write I recognize that at the very moment when the separate characters are being written down on the paper, not only is the lower end of the pen moved, but every motion in that part is simultaneously shared by the whole pen. All these diverse motions are traced by the upper end of the pen likewise in the air, although I do not conceive of anything real passing from the one extremity to the other. Now who imagines that the connection between the different parts of the human body is slighter than that between the ends of a pen, and what simpler way of expressing this could be found.

Conversely, the fancy manifests itself by the opposite motion of the pen. This example also shows how the fancy can be the cause of many motions in the nerves, motions of which, however, it does not have the images stamped upon it, possessing only certain other images from which these latter follow. Just so the whole pen does not move exactly in the way in which its lower end does; nay the greater part seems to have a motion that is quite different from and contrary to that of the other. (Descartes, 1967, 38)

It is unfortunate that the discussion of Descartes's mechanism has focused so heavily on the question of animals. Although his readers have been scandalized by the thought that horses and dogs may be automata, Descartes thinks of the larger part of *human* behavior as mechanistic and, as it turns out, *grammatological*. He argues that language is necessary to rational behavior and that the lack of language in animals is sufficient to prove that their actions are mechanical, but he does not say that language *assures* rational behavior. Self-directed activities of mind are rare and occur only when the germs of knowledge are awakened and utilized. Otherwise the stimulus-response circuit is merely robotic. These germs may, and presumably did, lay dormant for eons, and even in times when the method is known, true understanding is uncommon. The casual capacity for language—that one has a store of words, grammatical patterns, certain habitual uses, and so on—may be merely habitual and automatic. The other requirement of rational behavior is *method*.

Descartes's rhetorical strategy in the *Discourse* is to stage the epistemological question in terms of autobiography; thus shifting the question from matters of theoretical consistency to matters of education or development: "I shall endeavor in this discourse to describe the paths I have followed, and to delineate my life, in order that each one may be able to judge of them for himself," (Descartes 1967, 83) and so forth. Consequently, he is never required to make a whole-cloth translation from the common language to the ideal. The process, rather, is the initiation into error which is gradually recognized and corrected. The circularity of the argument is less obvious because we allow that people learn from their mistakes, while logical systems do not. It is the prototype of other self-improvement schemes. Since Descartes, we have increasingly placed our trust in our ability to construct the world (and self) we require, first as mathematical replicas in the seventeenth and eighteenth centuries, then as technological replicas in the nineteenth and twentieth centuries.

THE TWO LANGUAGES: TIME

> In English the poetics became meubles—furniture—
> thereafter (after 1630
> & Descartes was the value
>   —Charles Olson, "A Later Note of Letter #15"

The Cyborg

Let us quickly focus the issues: Descartes substituted the models of mathematical analysis for the external world. Newton, recognizing the mistake, tried to reverse the field, and he turned Descartes inside out—as later Marx would turn Hegel upside down—but it was too late. Substituting his own empiricism for Descartes's rationalism, Newton changed the perspective but not the metaphoric structure: he transferred the divinely underwritten logical structure of ego to a prior and absolute space, which he identified with divinity. That is, the founders of modern physics, despite their apparent oppositions, both conceived of the difference between the human and the divine as a matter of perspective. The chief intellectual project thereafter was the creation of human replicas to inhabit these perspectives that were oddly more rational than humans themselves. Descartes even conceived of constructing automata that might appear fully human.

His model of human beings, which treats the nervous system in terms of coding and information transfer, is a direct forerunner of contemporary models in cognitive science and artificial intelligence. Descartes could not, however, account mechanistically for functions that are considered "mental," that is, especially *purposive functions*. His automata might have behaved as if they were doubting, thinking, and knowing, but they could not doubt, think, and know.

Until this century, and the discovery of cybernetic self-organization, it was not clear how to reconcile purposive and mechanistic behaviors. They appeared to have different temporal structures. Cartesian science related the adequacy of causal explanation to the atemporality of geometry, thereby displacing scholastic teleology from the ontological to the cultural domain and rendering questions of purpose merely social and pragmatic. The cultural institutions at large became responsible for managing change or "progress" in a concrete realm that was implicitly technological; that is, teleology became a cultural and historical project, distinct from those other "timeless" processes of nature. The human agent as a purposive motor became the supreme cultural product.

Poetry and the Cartesian Circle

The prepublication manuscript of Descartes's *Meditations* was circulated among many of the important philosophers and theologians of the day, and Descartes responded to the objections in an appendix to the first edition. The objections of the logician of Port Royale, Antoine Arnauld, are the most telling. One might trace the beginnings of deconstruction to Arnauld's discovery that Descartes's arguments are circular or, perhaps more accurately, to the cultural decision to carry on Descartes's project despite its circularity. The foundation of modern epistemology involves putting off the proof of the premises until they can be supported by the conclusion. This is the basis for the progressive production of knowledge, and, if we can doubt its logical basis, we cannot deny its spectacular, material success.

Thus, deconstruction has not died, as it has been announced in various forums; it was, in the motto of the Hell's Angels, "born dead." It was the active principle of negation that fueled the dialectic, the sneer on the lips of the Cartesian demon, the car on what Hegel called "the way of despair." Though this movement of deathliness achieved a peculiar vitality during the Reagan era, it was not a fad: the other moment of deconstruction was the abstract, generalized systematicity of thought itself. If the construction of atemporal formalisms was the positive practice of post-Cartesian scientific culture—the persistence that tied it to the classical stasis—deconstruction was its historical motive. Time was not the intuition of change but a disciplined taking apart of taking apart, an analyzing of analysis. Together the stasis of the formal systems and the dynamism of their historical failures and reconstructions underwrote an ironic absolutism and a fundamental, ultimately corrosive cynicism.

We have space for only a cartoon history of deconstruction, but it will make the necessary points. Descartes discovered that it was possible to define a formal subset of the natural language that so exposed the logical structure that precise calculations were possible. That is, the rules for the regulation of the mind could be stated in the natural language and then the natural language could be criticized for its logical inadequacies from the special perspective that the new formal rules allowed. The construction of formal systems, pulling themselves up by their bootstraps, involved an implicit deconstruction of the natural language, and this somewhat inelegant mechanism of thought has been fundamental to the success of progressive knowledge during the past three centuries. As it turned out, the formal systems were never, as Descartes had hoped, complete or completable, but the natural language was forever in the process of being devalued from a succession of emergent formal perspectives. Of course, the first great formal systems—analytical geometry and infinitesimal calculus—were quantitative, but Descartes recognized from the beginning the possibility of a *mathesis universalis* which would embrace all discourse. As Chomsky has rightly noted, the science of linguistics was explicit in the Cartesian program. The interpretation of the natural language increasingly depended upon formal models, until finally it was understood in terms of the formal models of Chomsky and Montague.

The weakness of the new formal language was semantic. The structures themselves were elegant and powerful; the formal, generalized signs, however, did not have easy intercourse with the singularities of the world. Either the sign gained meaning by somehow pointing at things that were not themselves elements of the formal system—an idea that had strong commonsense appeal but proved to be theoretically awkward—or the signs were understood as having more signs as their meaning, so the coherent formal system was assumed to relate to the coherent world as a whole. In either case, it was necessary, at least implicitly, to bind symbols to their referents by force, and the history of philosophy from Descartes and Locke to Freud, the Vienna Circle, the early Wittgenstein, and many current cognitive scientists can be read as a series of strategies for the generation and management of that force.

The sign, the thoroughly modern sign, gained its shape from participation in a logical system based on distinctions that cut the universe of discourse into discrete entities. To name—and of course all naming in literate cultures is implicitly the naming of the phonemes—was to make a cut in universal logical space, differentiating a particular class from all possible classes. Although awful paradoxes lurked in the notion of a class of all possible classes, these *structures* were rich and useful. They underwrote Newtonian physics and thus subsequent European science and philosophy. Kant was Newtonian; Marx, Nietzsche, and Freud were Newtonians; Hegel, despite himself, was a Newtonian (he had no other cosmology available). The dialectic engaged language, and the entire content of its particular historical moment, thus energizing concrete change in the relationship between humankind and nature, between social classes, and so forth. Deconstruction involved at once the failure of philosophic theories and the fall of empires. Whatever the specific connections between Locke and Jefferson, Rousseau and Robespierre, Marx and the revolutions of 1848, Nietzsche and Bismarck, the dialectic of thought and the dialectic of action managed a complex intercourse. After World War II, however, if not after World War I, that profound synchronicity was erased. Thereafter, history was motivated not by abstract thought but by technology.

The deconstruction*ism* of the past quarter-century is the *generalization* of this dialectical unravelling. It understands that any *historical* construction is a shambles even from the moment of its conception. The dialectic is now almost exclusively academic: thought passes so graciously from thesis to antithesis, it does not, as it were, rough up the ground enough to generate significant historical movement. The logical field is so plastic that any claim can be adequately sublated in a few familiar gestures. The semantic resources of the natural language, which had provided a useful metalanguage from which new formal programs could be launched, has decayed, and now we suffer from something like intellectual heat death, that ultimate moment prophesied, in different ways, by the laws of thermodynamics and by Tristan Tzara, when all energy is equally dispersed throughout the cosmos. From his apocalytpic vantage, Hegel saw knowledge in the self-destructive play of self-reference. Given knowledge of the Absolute, the contradictions that propelled the dialectic were both resolved and not resolved: everything was itself *and* nothing was different than anything else; everything was the same *and* different; *everything* that was true was false and *everything* that was false was true. We live in the aftermath of this destruction. The mind was turned into a computer, and consciousness itself was turned into a television long before technology caught up. The earth is overrun with our representations of earth. We have entered a universal, grey medium—the postmodern blob. The representation cannot be represented.

The deconstructionists have cogently demonstrated that it is impossible, in absolute terms, for a writing to carry in itself the information that is necessary for its interpretation. They have not concluded however that the demand for such information is therefore nonsensical or that the rationalist project with its self-defeating mechanisms is bankrupt. In fact, many of them, under the melancholic influence of Freud and Lacan, figure that it is precisely the information, the lack of which is the cause of our misery. The private language has not been dismissed, but driven underground, and named the "Unconscious," so problems that resisted the fully confident and authoritative Cartesian self must now be puzzled out in the half-light (or less) of a fractured ego. We discover at this point—and the logical turns begin to appear with a dizzying rapidity—that the terms that define our condition are themselves unreliable. Jacques Derrida writes: "the Freudian concept of trace must be radicalized and extracted from the metaphysics of presence which still retains it (particularly in the concepts of consciousness, the unconscious, perception, memory, reality, and several others)" (Derrida, 1978b, 229). We are thus on the flip side of the liar's paradox. Radicalized and extracted, these concepts that map the essential Freudian structures are all subject to the paradox of self-reference: at least part of the time (and there is no way to know when), therefore, consciousness is unconscious, perception is hallucination, memory is forgetfulness, reality is illusion, and so forth. "Logically," one might replace any of the central terms with their opposites. Such, literally, is the sad condition of post-Hegelian logic.

Derrida's own address is an instance of a particular kind of decorum. The concepts in which we have sought the meaning of our lives turn out to be norms, statistically reliable zones of thought. We have no idea what their status might be, but it happens that the individual instances that they subsume are numerous or at least numerous enough, lacking an absolute accounting, to be persuasive. In this context, it is possible to entertain remarkable, fascinating and thought-defying questions, as when, Derrida asks, in the concluding paragraph of "Freud and the Scene of Writing," "How . . . , on the stage of history, can writing as excrement separated from the living flesh and the sacred body of the hieroglyph (Artaud), be put into communication with what is said in *Numbers* about the parched woman drinking the inky dust of the law; or what is said in *Ezekiel* about the son of man who fills his entrails with with the scroll of the law which has become sweet as honey in his mouth" (Derrida, 1978b, 231). It is of course a trick question. All of the variously possible answers are wrong and right. Points are given for style, and, by an unspoken agreement, style is judged by the canons of traditional French prose with all of its Cartesian assumptions, which is to say, of course, that there is no room for sloppiness; every detail must be clear and distinct. As it turns out, only the grand abstractions are equivocal. Stylistic requirements carry the weight of authority. Derridean "logic" has the rigor not of a Frege or Russell but of a Flaubert or Mallarmé.

"Can writing *as excrement* . . . ?" Derrida asks. We might also answer the question observing a different decorum. Tristan Tzara: "Dada remains in the European framework of weaknesses, still it is a bunch of excrement, but we want to shit in different colors to ornament the zoo of art of all the consulate flags." Although for Tzara language is utterly public, without interior dimensions, he shares with Derrida a logical form, the final reduction of the central concepts of the European dialectic to the logical rubble of self-reference. He also writes: "Anti-dadaism is a sickness: selfcleptomania, the normal human condition is DADA. But the true dadas are against DADA" (Tzara, 1973, 147). Those who favor Dadaism are mere avant-garde tourists, who haven't a clue as to the depths of outrage which Dadaism bespeaks. If you are for Dada, you are against it; if you are against Dada, you are for it.

The Derrida phenomenon in literary studies—quite apart from any assessment of Derrida's actual accomplishment—was symptomatic of an academic discipline in trouble. For twenty-five hundred years philosophy had concerned itself with the relationship between particular things and abstract categories, and poetry was the site on which these terms endlessly failed to fulfill the others' requirements—a site of primary cultural transactions, where the most abstract and reliable knowledge intersected with images of actual objects and events, where eternity and time played out their most spectacular dramas. Although individuals are common—indeed the very building blocks from which basic concepts are generalized—the adequate manifestation of the individual required all of the artifice the culture could muster. Western art was a wondrous *ad hoc* solution to the most enduring problem of Western philosophy. From the time of Hegel to the time of Norbert Wiener, philosophic attention shifted to the relationship between abstract categories and the nature of abstraction as such. The issues of the greatest philosophic consequences have not to do with the the relationship of the One and the Many but with the relationship of first- and second-order abstractions. The individual can now be assumed merely as a statistically reliable zone. The *One*, the concept, relates to the many, not by way of contradiction (and thus dialectical process), but by way of the bell-shaped curve. Thus, for Derrida, the central philosophic problem is not the relationship between Being and the individual chair or person, as it was for Parmenides and every philosopher until, at least, Hegel, but the relationship between Being and the abstract systematicity of phonetic writing as against the abstract systematicy of speech, on the one hand, and nonphonetic writing, on the other. Derrida's ploy is desperate but courageous: to seize not the constructive moment but the inevitable, deconstructive moment, when the dialectic produces not the heroic leader on the white horse but the markings on the pages of an infinite book as the occasion of ecstatic attention. To assert boldly and without reservation a commitment to writing as the image of death itself represents an ultimate self-sacrifice to the Idea of history as writing. This drives the silver stake through the heart of the vampiric ego, thus rendering a world, like the Flaubertian book, held together by almost nothing but style. Although Derrida takes up literary texts and reads them with much subtlety and grace, he does not take up the literary problem. Derridean philosophy declares, in effect, that the literary problem—the peculiar incommensurability of the individual thing and the concept to which it belongs—is solved. Indeed that clarity of image vis-à-vis concept, which was the motive of post-Aristotelian aesthetics, was a trick, a philosophically irresponsible and even dangerous trick that glossed over the failure of metaphysics.

Certain artists, however, posed individual entities that do not depend upon the *concept* for their definition or meaning. That is, when abstraction managed to name its concepts without deriving them from individuals, individuals likewise were freed their dependency upon conceptuality. It is the commonality of the individual, its freedom from disciplinary concepts, its *action* (rather than its image) that literary theory must now grasp.

What kind of motion is *e*-motion? Consider gestural space—the sum possibilities for human acts, internal and external, the movements of thought as well as the movements of arms, legs, and head, the acts of lungs, throat, teeth, and lips in the production of sounds. These acts of living are not representative of something else but meaningful in themselves. The arm moves through an infinite number of points, passing from one to the other, solving Zeno's paradox without difficulty. The gestural universe does not have to move toward deferred equilibrium; it *is* in equilibrium at every point. A gesture may stop or it may continue. If it stops, there is no dynamic residue.

By contrast, logic begins by taking a gesture as a *symbol* of a distinction: a formalism is introduced. The thing indicated is distinguished from everything else. The continuity of the gestural space is broken by reference. Logical space is not continuous but composed of a series of discrete objects or atoms. So long as the reference remains relatively local, the formalism is manageable and useful, but when it begins to refer to its own processes, it enters upon a self-destructive oscillation. What is required is the study not of logics but of poetics, the domain to which the gesture rather than the reference is fundamental. It is necessary not to deny reference—gestures sometimes point at things—but to confuse the value of the gesture with the value of the reference is deathly. Gesture is free and improvisatory, reference constitutes machines that it has been the Western habit—and confusion—to call "souls."

We know a good deal about the logical requirements of poetry (which turn out to be impossible to achieve) but too little about the *poetic* requirements of poetry. "I permit to speak at every hazard," Walt Whitman writes at the outset of "Song of Myself." Though it is too rare, we know such speech, the speech of free improvisation, without "talk of the beginning and the end," as we know such improvisation in painting and music in the work of Kandinsky, Schwitters, Guston, and Pollock, Cage, Coleman, Coltrane, Taylor, and others. If there are rules, they must belong to each hazard, each contingent occasion, not to a universal logos. We must see that such speech is required of a singularity, not of a generalized logical entity. Our ignorance is desperate. If meaning is representation, if X *means* because it can be exchanged for Y, "this process has no return," In poetics, however, things mean not because they can be exchanged for something else but precisely because they *cannot* be exchanged. Each gesture is unique; its value derives from its unrepeatable moment, not what it can be exchanged for. The dynamism, which has been attributed to historical dialectic, derives rather from the emotion of gesture. Intelligence does not significantly represent the world, it measures it by its acts.

Confidence beyond Thought

> For this is the company of the living
> and the poet's voice speaks from no
> crevice in the ground between
> mid-earth and underworld
> breathing fumes of what is deadly to know,
> news larvae in tombs
> and twists of time do feed upon,
>
> but from the hearth stone, the lamp light,
> the heart of the matter where the
> house is held
> —Robert Duncan, "Tribal Memories"

Pythagoras—or perhaps I should say, the thought that is mythologically bound to the name "Pythagoras"—casts a very long shadow over the intellectual history of the West. The authority that was associated with number before the rise of algebra is difficult for us to comprehend. The meditation on numbers which is a

consistent current of intellectual engagement before the sixteenth
century seems fanciful and superstitious. For St. Augustine, how-
ever, to name only one prestigious example, numbers were the real
things of which the world was constituted, and the knowledge of
numbers gave far more direct and reliable knowledge of both na-
ture and God than language as such, which he understood as as
logical categories bound by social convention. The relationships
between the first three integers, he believed, were far more neces-
sary and binding than any mere grammatical relationship. More-
over, in a thought that derived from Pythagorean sources, he be-
lieved that the self-identity of the soul was bound to the absolute
nature of enumeration. Summarizing the Augustinian doctrine,
Etienne Gilson writes:

> A soul is one only on condition that it remain consistent with
> itself, i.e., that it regularly display the same powers and perform
> the same actions. . . No matter what thing we consider, whether
> material or spiritual, individual or social, it appears as something
> constituted by numbers, relations, proportions, equalities, or re-
> semblances, and these in turn are merely the creature's attempt to
> imitate the original likeness whereby God is perfectly equal to
> Himself, i.e., His essential and indivisible unity. (Gilson, 1960,
> 212)

With the appearance of the species numbers of algebra, how-
ever, these relations, proportions, and equalities took on infinite
dimensions. It was experienced, as we have seen, as a dizzying
expansion of potential knowledge. The discovery that the integers
have no ontological integrity, however, merely prefigured the
nineteenth-century discovery that Euclidean space is not unique,
and the twentieth-century discovery that logic itself can be con-
structed on a variety of radically differing axiomatic assumptions.*
From the initial Cartesian "leap into the beyond," we arrived in an
intellectual space that is so abstract that we cannot say whether it is
the form or the content of the world that we actually inhabit.

With the appearance of methodology, however, the mathemati-
cal stuff of the cosmos was no longer available to experience. The

---

*J. L. Bell gives a readable, nontechnical account of this development in his essay
"Category Theory and the Foundations of Mathematics" (Bell, 1981).

measure by which the soul had attuned itself to itself was trivialized as one of an infinite number of cases. The quantitative bases of classical poetic meter—a real counting of real rythmic durations—was undermined and replaced with an abstract scheme in which the meter of the poem and the movement of its individual performances were directly analogous to an algebraic function and its individual roots. Poetry thus lost its status as a component of the real. Its functions were social and normative. Now that those functions are largely performed by the electronic media, the poetry and art that carried on those traditions— the traditions of Donne and Milton—are luxuries of a certain rare kind. The work of T. S. Eliot and Wallace Stevens represent the magnificent dead—end of those traditions, at which Christian aestheticism and humanist aestheticism vie with one another as the realizations of the metaphysics of self-reflexivity.

Like its cognate epistemology, the baroque poetic tradition articulated various strategies of self-reference. It avoided the ultimate nihilism that is implicit in its project by proposing ever larger linguistic fields. Language is larger than any "I" that expresses itself by words, and the pursuit of self-expression through language leads systematically, by the logic of language as such, to both knowledge of the absolute *and* self-alienation, as Hegel would conclusively demonstrate. If one sees language as a whole from an eternal perspective, as Descartes saw geometry, the entire fantasy collapses: I am I, everything is only what it is, integral and meaningless. Thus, the tradition of poetry that arose among Descartes' contemporaries insisted paradoxically upon finitude as a way of energizing the ideal. It was a self-exploitation from the beginning and could only, as Hegel would accurately note, overcome or sublate itself.

The most significant essay into this matter is Robert Duncan's "A Seventeenth Century Suite in Homage to the Metaphysical Genius in English Poetry (1590-1690): Being Imitations, Derivations & Variations upon Certain Conceits and Findings Made among Strong Lines," in *Ground Work I: Before the War* (Duncan, 1984, 70-93). It is not merely a sequence of poems but a poetic investigation—a working in the common to produce knowledge not by discipline but by creation. Pedants will object that Duncan uses the term "metaphysical" inaccurately, but they will only show that he does not make their mistake of confusing styles with poetics. From Duncan's point of view, all of the significant poetic styles of the seventeenth century are implicated in the substitution of a conventional imagination for intuition: poets turned their attentions to the relationships of image to image, of form to form, of language to language, their stylizations paralleling those of the *mathesis universalis*. Both the most extravagant devotees of metaphysical conceits and the neoclassicists sought ways to regulate the common language by the idealizations of verse.

Many of the poets of Duncan's generation wrote in imitation of seventeenth-century poetry, intending only to continue the cultural imperative (which had worn itself out in the nineteenth century) to imagine an ideal self. Duncan, however, undertakes the project as one of the most articulate polemicists against the old New Criticism, which had sponsored this kind of poetry. In his earlier essays, he objected to the conventional forms of the neo-metaphysicals, but it was not the pentameters and the quatrains per se that drew his ire; it was the use of conventional poetic techniques to enforce normative morality and normative feeling. In "A Seventeenth Century Suite," however, recognizing that language itself is conventional, Duncan addresses convention without obsession. He knows that to honor a particular convention, even by denying its validity, is to privilege one convention against another and to create idealisms in the otherwise open field of language. He demonstrates in his seventeenth-century workings that his pluralism is large enough to include the metaphysical impulse that he had rejected as the "official" style of New Criticism. The field in which the mature Duncan's work conducts itself is large enough to contain conventional selves, such as speak in seventeenth-century poems, *and* the vast spaces exterior to them. The space can be explored, as it were, from both sides. Duncan exploits the aesthetic space and then steps outside it so we see zones of particular kinds of intensity arise and dissipate into larger and more serviceable fields. Proposing a homage, Duncan enters fully into the metaphysical spirit and reveals both its interior richness and its lack of grounding in any thing but itself. "A Seventeenth Century Suite" is not only a remarkable set of poems, it is also a critical act of the highest order.

The "Suite" looks back in its concerns to an earlier poem, "Santa Cruz Propositions." There, Duncan writes:

Poetry! Would *Poetry* have sustained us? It's lovely
—and no more than a wave—to have rise

> out of the debris, the stink and threat
> —even to life—of daily speech, the roar
>   of the giants we begin from,
> primordial Strife, blind Opposition,
>   a current that sweeps all stagnant things up
> into a torrent of confidence beyond thought.
>   (Duncan, 1984, 36–46)

This passages seems to comment directly on the project of "A Seventeenth Century Suite." The true poets contend with the order and primordial conflict not only within their own poetry but within opposing orders of poetry as well. They are not bound by consistency, ideality, convention, or norms, *but by a world* that includes other people and other poets—the vast array of differences and othernesses. Life arises in the world not from the neatly prepared grounds of method or even from the rationalized strife of the dialectic but from the "confidence beyond thought"—the confident specificity of redeemed emotion. Duncan writes: "Each of us must be at strife with our own conviction on behalf of the multiplicity of convictions at work in poetry in order to give ourselves over to the art, to come to the idea of what the world of worlds or order of orders might be" (Duncan, 1985, 111–12).

What Is

In the prelude to the "Suite," "Love's a great courtesy to be declared," Duncan positions himself in relation to the conventions not of metaphysical poetry but of courtly love. He addresses the seventeenth century from the medieval perspective, a perspective to which he returns in "Dante Études," the variations on lines from Dante's prose works, which immediately follows the "Suite" in *Ground Work I*. In direct contrast to the "regulated" language of the seventeenth-century models, Dante underwrites "our own" language,

> ". . . that which we acquire without
> any rule"   for love of it . . .

This,

> being primary,
>   natural and common,
> being "milk";
> is *animal:*

> lungs sucking-in the air, having
> heart in it, rhythmic; and
>   moving in measure
>   self-creating in concert

> —and therein,
> noble.
>   (Duncan, 1984, 96)

That is, primary language is (1) not rule-governed, (2) not spiritual, and (3) not the declaration of an original order. Before "the leap into the beyond," finite humans participated directly in their finite world; they did not presume to measure the infinite by species and abstraction, for which they could know the forms but not the content. Thus, it was language as engaged in time and even the things of the flesh, not the conventions of grammar, that allowed the possibility of the incarnation. If the Word was embodied merely in words nothing was gained. The unified principle would be thus dispersed in a logic devoted to endless classification and division in which the original unity either appears only as a theoretical limit or escapes. Significantly, the Word was embodied in the *flesh,* not in the institutions of language.

Medievalism is, of course, a conventional zone of poetic intensity in its own right, but it is concretely larger than the metaphysical because it opens immediately outward: the ego of the courtly lover is unstable and therefore declares a space of unknown properties; its boundaries are not significantly dependent upon rule-bound linguistic or aesthetic structures. On the secular plane, the self of the courtly lover is incarnated in the gaze of the beloved and the intuition of the beloved by the lover, not in the self-reflexivity of the *cogito.* Duncan hearkens back with Ezra Pound, who speaks in his essay, "Cavalcanti: Medievalism," not of "pagan worship of strength, nor the Greek perception of visual non-animate plastic, or plastic in which the being animate was not the main and principal quality, but this 'harmony in the sentience' or harmony *of* the sentient, where the thought has its demarcation, the substance its *virtu,* where stupid men have not reduced all 'energy' to unbounded undistinguished abstraction" (Pound, 1965, 154). In the medieval perspective that Duncan initially adopts, the world of surfaces, of geometries, of linguistic conventions, are fields of contingency from which vision potentially arises. In the prefatory poem, he writes:

> I'd
> dissolve my soul in sleeping surfaces
>   where transient phantasies may come and go
> that somewhere in that multiplicity of
>   chance encounters
> I might come again to you and find
>   Love's court
> set up once more to rule my mind.
>
> (Duncan, 1984, 70)

How do we determine what is to rule our minds? The Cartesian solution—to be ruled by rule—is obviously circular. There is no binding rule on which to base a decision until after the decision has been made. Duncan prefers to take his chance with chance. In *The Spirit of Romance*, which is an important context of Duncan's poetics, Pound asks, "Did this 'chivalric love,' this exotic, take on mediumistic properties? Stimulated by the color or quality of emotion, did that 'color' take on forms interpretive of the divine order? Did it lead to an 'exteriorization of the sensibility,' an interpretation of the cosmos by feeling?" (Pound, 1968, 94). Questions to which Duncan has consistently given an affirmative and secular answer. Interpretation by feeling, however, proves potentially more rigorous and even more immediately practical than interpretation by rule-governed reason. Methodology establishes the formal conditions of meaning, not meaning itself; it allows its practitioner to know what *can* happen but only in relation to infinite classes. It is a godlike knowledge, but for finite beings it requires endless interpretation. The truth is there, to be sure, but short of eternity we cannot adequately process it. The methodologist, then, is a medium—that is, language itself—which forever mediates himself or herself.

In "A Seventeenth Century Suite," the appearance of an "other world" is not the world of Poetry with a capital P, which is more typical of Duncan's work, but the conventions of a kind of poetry that Duncan himself had once rejected as a model. These conventions do, however, rise and speak, interpreted not by rules but by feelings that are neither generalized nor capricious. The variations interpret their sources in relation not to hermeneutic rules but to the rigorous metrical requirements of a particular eros, a particular reading and a particular writing. The poem itself is the evidence of the engagement, and it is the event—irreducible and inexplicable—that is the truth of the matter, not some some secondary interpretation that refers the event to other relationships that may figure in a reader's designs but are only obliquely concerned with the poem.

The metaphysical genius is, above all, literate and literal, which is to say, it is tied to writing and it demands everything in writing; it is the master of formal systems that arrange atomic syllables according to the rules of grammar and the conventions of metrical forms. Contingency is regulated: for every mark here there *must be* a mark there. Although the marks are themselves arbitrary and contingent, the metaphysical aesthetic attends only to the constancy of relationships. The images of lovers' bodies are mapped point by point onto the image of geometer's compass, violating both, and so forth. Language for the metaphysical poet calls forth more language and insists upon an immediacy of relationship even in oblique situations. Language is inside language, chasing its own tail.

This regulation of contingency, however, is bought at immense expense: the loss of life as an actual event, conducted here and now. The task of Duncan's "Suite" is to open this self-justifying recursivity to its own contingency—a matter that he addresses at the outset in his variations on Sir Walter Ralegh's theme, "What Is Our Life?" Life imitates plays, a formula that must immediately turn upon itself, in that inside the play, plays imitate life which imitates plays, and so forth. It is a small and accurate parable of the infinite regress that was until this century the definitive modern event. The psychology is also characteristically modern: "Thus march we playing to our latest rest, / Onely we dye in earnest, that's no jest." (Duncan, 1984, 70)

The fundamental change that had come about in the Renaissance was clear to such men as Francis Bacon: modernity was "half in love with easeful death." In his essay, "On Death," Bacon writes: "You shall read in some of the friars' books of mortification that a man should think with himself what the pain is if he have but his finger's end pressed or tortured, and thereby imagine what the pains of death are, when the whole body is corrupted and dissolved; when many times death passeth with less pain than the torture of a limb; for the most vital parts are not the quickest of sense" (Bacon, 1985, 9). The psychology that Freud outlines in *Beyond the Pleasure Pleasure* took hold in the seventeenth century. The homeostatic controls on history, created by an *intuited* world, had been removed, and the West had entered its period of wild growth, of proliferation not by mimesis but by methodology. The genetic and the personal have been utterly confused in mass society. To Freud the Cartesian combination of vital physicality and deathly mnemonics will seem to express itself as the erotic attraction of death. Duncan reads Ralegh as saying, "In death alone we are sincere," and implicitly we are cast between a groundless eros and the attractive sincerity of death.

In the second variation, in which he retains Ralegh's theme but rejects his imagistic constraints, Duncan insists upon the knowledge that is missing in Ralegh's poem, of "deep uproilings / of earth beneath your feet"—that is, knowledge of that which does not derive from the recursive event but is the news of not-being itself. He invokes that which is not theatrical, not theoretical, which seems at once a volcanic eruption from the earth and a pimple on the skin of the beloved. All of the content of the infinite regress is suddenly manifest

In an instant

four hundred and thirty-two thousand years
   inertia of conflicting forces
   shows its face raging.
(Duncan, 1984, 72)

This is the face of Kali, the Hindu goddess of destruction. The Hindu cosmic epics allow some sense of the hopeless immensity involved in Western terms such as *infinity* and *eternity*. If Hegel, for example, spoke of the emergence of the Absolute at the end of a cycle of several periods of four hundred and thirty-two thousand years each, the scale would not be meaningful, but the point might more readily come home.

Duncan's engagement with metaphysical poetry—or the true poets' engagement with the world of texts, both formally written texts and "natural" signs, "the fall of a rock, the shifting of sands," in Duncan's words—is not dialectical. The poets do not answer the text of the world in kind but create a language that belongs to another geometry altogether, responsible not to the theorized world but to itself: "We are creatures of language and invent in turn with the sounds of ours mouths, or hands beating surfaces, or with marks upon a stone or arrangements of sticks, an other speech, a speech 'for its own sake' in answer to the World Order which was a language before ours" (Duncan, 1985, 122). The "deep uproilings / of earth beneath your feet" do not revolve or repeat. The poets enter again and again into the destruction of the self that is the avenue of vision, sacrificing that valued access, while standing in testimony to the accuracy of signs they themselves do not *under*stand. One who bears witness does not interpret (which would violate the testimony) but rather says, "I heard, I saw": "The first experience in poetry is to find in words not an argument or an explanation but a world, to see another world or to be of another world. Here definitions are not restrictions but outlines of emerging possible elements of that world" (Duncan, 1985, 121–22). In the second Ralegh variation, he writes:

> Against my body, against my soul,
>   against my spirit, I go then
> in the destruction of the grades of me,
>   to the undoing of those hierarchies . . .
> (Duncan, 1984, 72)

Thus, a persistent sense of hopeful catastrophe that informs Duncan's work. Perhaps one reason Duncan has not been more usefully read is his refusal to allow the reader the comfort of the literary. In his homage to the genius of the tradition, he enters the world that it proposes in order to open its limits to what it had excluded. He undermines the ego-security that the metaphysical poem proposes to create and to recover the knowledge that is repressed in it. In the variations on Robert Southwell's "The Burning Babe," he distinguishes between "a babe of fire" and "a baby on fire." The babe of fire belongs properly to the poem as an image of the perfected self. There is no denial of these mysteries, which are the mysteries of self-consciousness and the persistent study of the modern West: the perfection that is also deathly. Our obsessive questions have had to do with the nature of this recursive function: in Southwell's poem we read of "A pretty Babe . . . such floods of tears did shed, / As though his floods should quench his flames, which with his tears were bred." In "Imagination's alchemy," we await the return of the final deferred term that brings us to equilibrium. This is the conventional conclusion of modern mysticism, and, without denying the integrity of the vision, Duncan gives the passage an appropriately conventional mystical ending, drawing his terms from crucial passages in his own poetry:

The burning Babe, the Rose,
the wedding of the Moon and Sun,
wherever in the World I read
such Mysteries come to haunt the Mind,
the Language of What Is   and I
        are one.

(Duncan, 1984, 74)

Thus, Duncan recalls the language of an earlier poem that crucially defines the space of his work:

Often I am permitted to return to a meadow
as if it were a given property of the mind
that certain bounds hold against chaos,
that is a place of first permissions,
everlasting omen of what is.
                    (Duncan, 1960, 7)

The conclusion, which is drawn in the Southwell variation, that "the Language of What Is and I / are one" is one of the possible loci in the meadow: that is, it is a usurpation of the meadow on behalf of art. It is one of Duncan's loci, and he here claims it. It is, however, an appropriation that no sooner appropriates the meadow than it removes itself. This is the frustration and sometimes the fascination of the perfected *cogito:*

He's Art's epiphany of Art new born
a Christ of Poetry, the burning spirit's show;
he leaves no shadow, where he dances in the air,
    of misery below.
                    (Duncan, 1984, 75)

The self-transcendent image flees the world of chance, even if its perfection is an infinite proposition which finite subjects can only comprehend in brief, intuitive insights. Duncan insists upon another incarnation for which suffering is real suffering, suffering which is not tempered by the memory or the promise of eternal wisdom:

Another Christ, if he be, as we are,
Man, cries out in utter misery.
                    (Duncan, 1984, 75)

Southwell's Christ exists only in the recursive symbolism of the poem. Duncan's other Christ inhabits the world which is not relieved by transcendental knowledge:

I cannot imagine, gazing upon photographs
　　of these young girls, the mind
transcending what's been done to them.

From the broiled flesh of these heretics,
　　by napalm monstrously baptised
　　　　in a new name . . .
　　　　　　(Duncan, 1984, 75)

The newspaper photographs from the Vietnam war that Duncan brings as evidence to the second Christ are irrelevant to the first. The "human" Christ's finitude is relieved by neither the logical mystery of Southwell nor by the mysterious incarnation of Augustine. Duncan speaks of the Word not as rational origin but as a sounding—the measurable vibrations and physicality of language. Augustine writes: "The Unity you love can be effected in ordered things by that alone whose name in Greek is *Analogia,* and which some of our writers have called proportion" (Augustine, 1947, 23). For the secular Duncan, the analogy is not, however, to something *else*—some world writ large—rather life imitates itself: "The *sounding* is the love that moves the poet in language" (Duncan, 1985, 57). The reference of language to itself is in a finite, measurable field. Not being analogous to a divine order, it does not undermine the perfections that it exhibits in itself. To order a language on the basis of one word sounding like another word, on one phrase taking twice as long to pronounce as another phrase, makes sense—that is, perceived by senses, *felt*—as opposed to ordering a language on ideal or transcendental atoms of meaning (Cartesian space-points or structuralist phonemes) that lack the content of feeling and allow no resource to intuition. In Duncan's reading of the poems, eros orders both the grammar and the measure of the verse. The "Suite" is a practice of a distinction that he makes "between the line itself as a going forth, instituting itself as a new event and presence in the world—a sortie Whitman named it—and the poetry [like Wordsworth's, and he might have said like Ralegh's, Southwell's, or Jonson's] where the lines address themselves to an intense turning in upon their own meanings to seek the regulation of emotion and experience" (Duncan, 1985, 200). The use here of "regulation" might be usefully compared to Descartes's use of the term: it bespeaks a discipline of feeling comparable to Descartes's disciple of mind.

In the next two pieces in the "Suite," on George Herbert's

"Jordan I" and "Jordan II," Duncan comes as near writing straightforward variations as he does anywhere. He is oddly closer to Herbert than to any of the other seventeenth-century poets. For Herbert, as for Augustine, poetry was not the creation of a new thing, an invention, as Sir Philip Sidney insists, especially not a creation of the image of the Cartesian self, but an incarnation of the structure of the cosmos, an enactment of real time. The imitation is structural rather than imagistic.*

The "Jordan" poems have been reasonably taken as Herbert's poetic manifestos. Unless their irony is noted, however, they are disappointing—at least for us, who find a declaration of faith tantamount to a kind of mad assertion against all reason and evidence and, thus, expect a Miltonic grandiosity of design, overwhelming the improbability of the doctrine, or a Donne-like display of pathological desire ("Batter my heart," etc.). In light of the new philosophy, the work of Herbert's principal contemporaries was not only an imitation of an imitation, as Plato had noted; it was an imitation of an imitation in a world that offered no original. The relationship of the abstract ego to the abstract space of nature allows only "enchanted groves," as Herbert says in the "Jordan (I)," as the sites of poetry—magical places in which the poet-magician pulls ideal images out of the recursive hat of prose language and the reader must be a diviner, "Catching the sense at two removes." Herbert, who chooses to "pull for Prime," recognizes the phoniness of the Self that is proposed. The logical guarantee that is offered by the *cogito* and the similarly solipsistic arguments of the seventeenth-century philosophers have no relationship to lived life. Even the ideally decorated presentations are ultimately casual and collapse back into the perplexity of casual prose. Herbert's poem stakes nothing on its imagistic content. In "Jordan (I)," he opposes the whole tradition of fleshy, mythological and amorous poetry by saying, plainly, the words, "My God, My King." No poet had ever expected a simple naming to carry so much weight. In fact, however, the poem has said, "My God, My King," through the entire poem, the trivial images serving as

---

*In a study of Augustine and Herbert, which has important implications for the study of seventeenth-century poetry in general, William H. Pahlka notes that "poetic imitations and *imitatio Christi* were, for Herbert, inseparable" (Pahlka, 1987), and he demonstrates the pervasive significance of Augustine's *De musica* to Herbert's *The Temple*.

soundings of the mathematical-musical structure that is the true content of the poem. For Herbert, any image would be merely sensuous and false. The impulse of the poem is the direct intuition of the divine manifested by the harmony of the soul which produces and meditates on the metrical structure. The content of the poem is the obsessiveness of the tune, which may be reduced to a hummed half-line and an injunction or naming:

duh-da-da-duh   da-duh   and pull for Prime
da-duh-da-duh   My God, My King.

The use of such verse is not to provide an ideal image of the self but to orient a finite being to an infinite order, and as an expression of the "temple," as Herbert proposes it, to orient a community of worshipers for whom the pull for prime is the most concrete injunction.

In "Jordan (II)," Herbert notes that the worldly images, "quaint words, and trim inventions," are illegitimate insinuations of the self into the true meditative fire:

As flames do work and winde, when they ascend,
So did I weave my self into the sense.
But while I bustled, I might heare a friend
Whisper, How wide is all this long pretence!
There is in love a sweetnesse readie penn'd:
Copie out onely that, and save expense.
(Duncan, 1984, 79)

Herbert's poems are not professions of faith but *experiences* of faith: the moment by moment address to the harmony of the soul and its analogy to the divine harmony. Herbert expresses a poetic that would find its most complete realization not in poetry but in the tradition of pure music. It would be not the poets but the composers who would undertake to copy out the "sweetnesse readie penn'd" in love. And, to a certain extent, the culture has never recovered from the magnificent successes of Beethoven and the tradition of music from which his work grew. The dissociation of sensibility that T. S. Eliot identified as the loss of relevance of feeling to thought was in fact, even more broadly, a loss of relationship between the meanings of a particular ethos and the possibilities for action that it affords and formal structure.

Duncan's variations are, like the originals, quiet, albeit completely secular. Likewise, for Duncan the poem always presents the problem of incarnation—not the analogical incarnation of the divine harmony but the literal incarnation of the person in the making of the poem. Rather than a re-creation and recalling of experience, Duncan proposes a direct working in the actual time of the poem. As poems, they are not major efforts, but they bring forth necessary evidence:

> (I) For I have this simplicity in my God, My King,
>   that he holds for me the truth of what I am,
>   no fiction but a working thing in me.
>   (Duncan, 1984, 78)

The poem registers nothing but the fact of its own activity. The recursive density of language proposes to represent nothing but itself:

> (II) This water is but water. This is
>   no other water than it is, nor more nor less
>   that's meant to bless,
>   and works no magic
>   but our bliss.
>   (Duncan, 1984, 79)

The first of Duncan's variations sounds a little like Polonius and the second like an Iowa Workshop metaphysical poet. Nevertheless, they are as sincere for Duncan as he takes Herbert's poems to be. It is the *Truth,* which however proves neither what was expected nor final; it is rather a superficial alignment, a seeing that what is, is. In the face of this settlement, "Passages 36" bursts forth unexpectedly, proclaiming that grief is the proper mode of this knowledge.

"Passages 36" belongs both to the suite and to the poetic domain of "Passages," a sequence that first appears in *Bending the Bow.* To "Go as in a dream," as the injunction from the second Ralegh variation has it, is to experience the nature of the true God:

> "Then with the true God, the true *Dios,*
> "came the beginning of cruel tribute
> "the beginning of the betrayal of justice,
> "the beginning of strife by trampling,
> "the beginning of violence,
> "the beginning of no hope."
>   (Duncan, 1984, 80)

These lines are in no sense ironic. The truth of Southwell's self-consuming babe is here recovered as the truth of God. Truth and falsity are dimensions of a formal space that we inhabit and that inhabits us. This is the knowledge of the metaphysical genius to which Duncan pays homage, and it must be honored because it establishes the theater in which our knowledge is exhibited. Duncan writes: "the mind addresses / and would erect within itself," not theoretical bliss—the pleasures of the text and so forth—but "itself"

> as Viet Nam,   itself as Bangladesh,
> itself exacting revenge and suffering revenge.
> (Duncan, 1984, 80)

The justification of theory is not its mysterious origin, which is a self-referential shuffle, but the access that it allows to reality, to that which is *not* generalized and abstract. The true world is *not* a mystery of interpretation as our theorists would have us believe. It is the most obvious thing there is: it is airplanes raining down napalm, it is the freeway choked with traffic, it is the burning rain forests of the tropics. Skepticism and relativism in the face of this obviousness are obscene:

> Is it to suit the myth yet to come—
> the ritual mutilation, the despoiling of nature, of earth,
>   of animal species, and mankind among them,
> with hatred and, no longer having a feeling of what is done,
>   without hatred, day after day,
>   the burning, the laying waste?
> Eat, eat this bread and be thankful
> it does not yet run with blood.
> (Duncan, 1984, 80)

The proposal of a countertruth, however, is likewise obscene, because it likewise claims an authority that justifies "cruel tribute," "the betrayal of justice," "strife by trampling," and so forth:

> Each day the planes go out over the land,
>   And revolution works within
> to bring to an end in the rage of power
>   the works and dreams
> of a governing Art. The air is darkened.
> Drink, drink, while there is water.
> They move to destroy the sources of feeling.
> (Duncan, 1984, 81)

The world that is determined by claim and counterclaim—the dialectical world—which we inhabit and which inhabits us concretely and painfully, is to be measured by a grief that perhaps cannot be sufficient, cannot be redeemed.

Although it should not be necessary, I want to emphasize that Duncan's readings are not to be confused with the typical antitheoretical conventionalism which seems to be once again on the rise, now that it is apparent that literary theory is neither as vast nor as interesting as many critics began to believe twenty years ago. The theory of theories is a vast tautology, never completable in the practical sense but never doubtable as an ultimate conclusion. In the seventeenth-century models, the closure of language is complete, and, when they propose to manifest the truth, as in Ben Jonson's "Hymnaei," the poverty of the metaphysical imagination is revealed:

> *"Her orient hayre,"* I read:
> *"By which beleeving mortalls hold her fast,*
> *"And in those golden chordes are carried even,*
> *"Till with her breath she blowes them up to heaven."*

> Now what am I to do with that? tho I read there is a glow
> where men's souls are quickened in her hair and
> rise upon her breath toward heaven so, the poet's conceit
> turns me back from the myth I know therein.

The figure of imagination that proposes to manifest Truth fails in its spectacle to make Truth any more than an advertisement, an obscene parody of the witness that it might bear to the love which the poem celebrates. Duncan's poem, however, does not make a simple point of taste. Jonson is given the most generous opportunity to bear his witness. The problem is not merely a matter of literary style or of failed poetry. Jonson and his contemporaries propose to situate us in relation to Truth, but, as Duncan writes:

> I do not know where I am with her,

> and myriad reflections upon her face
> lead from old deeps into new deeps of Night.
> (Duncan, 1984,88-89)

Since the seventeenth century, we have articulated a culture inside a language that, testifying on its own behalf, imagines the figures of its own truth. Jonson's lady Truth has, of course, had more attractive manifestations. Indeed she has been set forth in irresistible perfection, say, by Bach and Beethoven, where the world-defining strife is neutralized in the logic of music. The Self-God/God-Self of lady Truth, the being that must include all, because it includes the language in which it is defined, is the figure of modern egotism. Some of Descartes's earliest critics noted that his argument in this connection was circular, that he took self-existence as the grounds for his argument for the existence of god and the existence of god as the grounds for his argument for self-existence. The mathematical Self-God and the poetic Self-God confirm one another. Perhaps it would be better to speak of the "musical" Self-God as all of the timed arts are implicated and compromised. These are the great idealizations of space and time, geometry and music, which, contradicting and confirming one another in a careful dance, have required the participation of the entire culture. To support it has required untold exploitation of human and natural resources.

In the final poem of "A Seventeenth-Century Suite," Duncan takes up the theme of John Norris's "Hymne to Darkness." The turn to darkness is the only recourse for the poets who locate themselves outside of the destructive illumination, beauty, and quest for abstract power to which the culture devoted itself in the seventeenth century:

> yet striking ever true to what is
> most dark to me in me from that first
> darkend scale of all light Harmony
> asking, answering, note upon note of silent
>   command of tunings sound
> beyond sound.
>   (Duncan, 1984, 91)

This is the darkness from which the Self-God/God-Self in its divinity has withdrawn, and it is explicitly identified in Norris's poem with the muse. It is *not* the darkness of the Freudian unconscious, where theorization is not precluded by darkness. What is manifested from this darkness is not something unseen, some obscure origin, but an end and a voice that calls to it. In his blasphemous meditation on the Lord's prayer, he notes:

> Out, out from the First, from the Void,
>   the over-whelming repose of a finality
> overtakes the trembling lives, the sounding

    energies,
and into a Silence I call *Our Father*
    draws them in.
        (Duncan, 1984, 93–94)

In the darkness there are others and the sounding of the voice—not as an ideal but as sounding in the Silence—tests the possibility of love.

In closing lines of the poem the poet is startled by a kiss from the darkness and the voice of his lover saying, "*Good Night!.*" He notes completely without irony, "Love sets me free." The courtly pose of the opening poem is replaced with a domestic love relationship. The final line serves both as a conventional ending to the poet's enthrallment to a manner that is not completely congenial and as a reintroduction to Duncan's central theme.

Real Time

The ideal realm that the Greeks discovered included a teleology. It was the *purpose* of the acorn to grow into an oak tree. Modern science, however, deals only with ideal or achieved purposes. In the modern view, acorns are always oak trees as they are also dead and decayed oak trees and soil and nutrition for second-growth forests, and so forth. The cosmos is already finished according to Newtonian doctrine, a mere playing out of the implications of formulae which are already achieved in the divine mind. As limited divinities, humans can discover the formulae, but our information-handling capacity is too limited. We do not have sufficient data to predict the future, except in carefully isolated and controlled situations.

In the Euclidean-Newtonian cosmos, therefore, time is a shadowy domain. Although Newton himself supposed that its space was a divine attribute, prior even to the creation of the material world, Spinoza and Malebranche, who were bolder and more consistent metaphysicians than Newton, saw that it was unnecessary to a fundamental description of the world. The principles of the cosmic mechanism imply and supersede all possible events. Laplace gave this succinct formulation in 1814: "An intellect which at a given instance knew all the forces acting in nature, and the position of all things of which the world consists—supposing the said intellect were vast enough to subject these data to analysis—would embrace in the same formula the motions of the greatest bodies in the universe and those of the slightest atoms; nothing would be uncertain for it, and the future, like the past would be present to its eyes" (Čapek, 1961, quoted 127).

Although it is mistaken to say that time in the Newtonian cosmos is illusory, it is a human dimension, peculiar to finite minds and important as a teleological framework in an otherwise complete and purposeless world of matter in predetermined motion. Teleology is not natural but social. After the Newtonian world picture was psychologized by Kant, the model of classical physics was easily extended to the development of history and the social sciences, and with the emergence of technology, it became increasingly clear that the human world changes profoundly despite the eternal nature of cosmic principles. History is the ratio of human time to divine time. The supremely nonhistorical thought of the Enlightenment prepared the way for the first, Dionysiac experience of history, during the period between the American Revolution and 1848.

Of course, the ratio of human time to divine time is incalculable, but the timed arts—notably music and poetry—create a sham experience of manageable ratios with infinite implications that seem to empower humankind in a dimension that we have not been able to inhabit and have not been able to forget. A sub/version of this sense of history will occupy the following chapter. The immediate task is to note the personal experience of time that was the grounds of that explosive historiography. From Milton and Racine to Wordsworth and Hölderlin, from Bach to Beethoven and Wagner, the experience of time seemed to open, if not quite directly on the infinite, at least directly enough that the infinite could be intimately and even comfortably known.

Like space, time had been theorized, thus profoundly transforming the poetic medium. The time of the accentual-syllabic poem was no more the time of accentual Anglo-Saxon verse or quantitative classical verse than the space of the mathematical analysis was the intuitive space of Euclid. Much as the images of the seventeenth-century poems have reference to other images and, ultimately, to language itself as the great Image of the World, which is the content of Ralegh's play, the rhythms have reference to an *implicit* rhythmic structure in the language rather than the actual rhythms of the performer's voice or the real experience of time. In the standard formulation, typified by Wellek and Warren, "English verse is largely determined by the counterpoint between the imposed phrasing, the rhythmical impulse, and the actual speech rhythm conditioned by phrasal divisions" (Wellek and Warren, 1966, 170). The confusion of rhythm and mechanical repetition in the culture at large is nowhere more apparent than in this standard doctrine. Rhythmic impulse in this sense can be understood in terms only of the reciprocating cylinder of the steam engine or some other mechanical device.

Much as the painter's sense of perspective anticipated the theoretical space of mathematical analysis, the poetic and musical forms that developed in the sixteenth century anticipated theorized time. The development of the new mathematics and the new prosody may have been largely independent, but the coherence that they formed in the seventeenth century could hardly have been more seamless. The one resulted from the digestion and articulation of theories of proportion that had been transmitted through Arabic sources, the other from the first attempts to deal consciously with questions of poetics in relation to the modern European languages, especially English and German, where the most important temporal innovations—temporal technologies, one might say—the prosodies of Milton and Donne, on the one hand, and the music of Bach, on the other, produced the experience of time as a historical vehicle. As Anthony Easthope notes in an important essay, the dynamic quality of time was subordinated to the representation of "a systemic totality, an explicit preconception legislating for every unit of stress and syllable and 'this continueth through the verse' (Gascoigne), 'in sequence of a metronome' (Pound)" (Easthope, 1983, 66).

Although it relates to a different philosophic stance, Duncan's conception of the poetic line, which derives variously from Whitman, Gertrude Stein, Ezra Pound, H. D., and William Carlos Williams, and by analogy, from the abstract expressionist painters, is nearer Augustine's than Sidney's or Gascoigne's: it is not relational and normative but quantitative. It is not, of course, based on syllabic quantity—English is not quantitative in that sense. Even in iambic pentameter, when it is not merely mechanical, syllables speed up and slow down, slurring, in order to maintain the rhythmic integrity of metrical durations determined by caesuras and end stops. Duncan's rhythm is based rather on the *duration* of the caesural phrase and the line. "Rhythm," Pound says, "is a form cut

into TIME, as a design is determined SPACE" (Pound, 1960, 198).
In "Some Notes on Notation"—the preface to *Ground Work: Be-
fore the War*—in which he explains the scoring of his later work,
Duncan writes: "The literal time of the poem is experienced as
given, even as the literal size of a painter's canvas is given. What is
advanced in the process of the poem is the configuration of that
given time. The counting of numbers, that numbers count in the
structure, is an important aspect of the design" (Duncan, 1984, ix).

In the late 1960s, when Duncan first began scoring his work by
his new conventions, in which caesuras and line endings were liter-
ally counted, the conducting hand in his performances was not as
flamboyant as, say, Osawa's, but nonetheless distinct and dramat-
ic, and he could be heard, under his breath, counting out the
silences, which run up to a count of eight and occasionally more—
very long rests in a public performance of poetry. In later public
performances, his hand would occasionally conduct a few lines, as
he looked for the rhythmic center of a poem, but the bodily "dis-
position" would soon take over. In a reading at Bard College of the
entire manuscript of *Ground Work* over a period of several days in
1983, he did not count audibly. The overt signs of the measure
were internalized in the precise renderings of the lines.

Time in a proper reading of a Duncan poem is a completely
different experience than in either traditional iambic pentameter or
the conventional "free verse" that derives from a failure to *hear* the
rhythmic energy of the poetry of William Carlos Williams and Ezra
Pound. Robert Lowell and the myriad poets who followed his lead
in the 1960s and 1970s lost both the beauty of traditional poetic
forms and the rhythmic "nutrition of impulse," to use a phrase of
Pound's, which is fundamental to the vital verse practice of this
century. Thus, for literary theorists, who take Lowell's verse prac-
tice as normative, the experience of time is replaced by the experi-
ence of language or writing. Temporal intuition—or what might
be called the "Bergsonian experience"—is highly valued by post-
structuralist theorists, but they know it only as a derivative, a by-
product of linguistic structural breakdown, as "play" or "decenter-
ing" force. Jacques Derrida's deconstructions and readings of
erased texts, for example, are an endless engagement to prevent the
temporal flow from freezing into the language of metaphysics.
Many of his frequent generalizations about the Western tradition,

however, apply at best only to the post-Cartesian tradition. His analysis of both Husserl's characterization of the temporal present as an indivisible blink of an eye and the silent voice, which hears itself in the supposed temporal point that he generalizes to "the history of idealization" in its entirety, misses much of philosophy from Parmenides to Will James and Norbert Wiener and fails entirely to comprehend the most profound evidence of temporality the poets have provided in this century.

Augustine, for example, notes explicitly that the experience of time cannot be reduced to the blink of an eye. Indeed, if time is taken abstractly as a series of indivisible points, it is not possible to account for temporal experience at all. Literally, there is no place to be: "one hour passes away in fleeting particles. Whatever of it has flown away is past, whatever remains is future. If any portion of time be conceived which *cannot now be divided* into even the minutest particles of moments, this only is that which may be called present; which, however, flies so rapidly from future to past, that it cannot be extended, it is divided into the past and future; but the present has no space" (Augustine, 1948, 197, my emphasis). In every consideration of time, it seems, some version of the Zenonian paradoxes lurk about. When one tries to pin time down, it disappears. This may be its most mysterious and attractive character. From the perspective of the point-present, time cannot be measured. It is not possible, for example, to compare a metrically long and a metrically short syllable. In fact, if time consists of a series of points, the basis of metrical time as such becomes hopelessly problematic. Thus, in *De musica*, Augustine declares: "All measure and limit is preferred to infinity and immeasurableness" (Augustine, 1947, 15). Time can be inhabited and measured only in its fullness, as involving memory and expectation. Measure must account for various dimensions of time, which consists not of temporal atoms but of complex durations implicated in past, present, and future. Only if time is taken in the most radically subjective sense does it manifest, paradoxically, an objectivity. Augustine's paradigm for temporal measure is the reciting of a psalm: time has both duration and content. In Latin verse, which is measured by syllabic duration, not by a count of syllabic stress like modern English verse, time is never empty or merely normative. Augustine writes:

I am about to repeat a psalm that I know. Before I begin, my attention is extended to the whole; but when I have begun, as much of it as becomes past by my saying it is extended in my memory; and the life of this action of mine is extended both ways between my memory, on account of what I have repeated, and my expectation, on account of what I am about to repeat; yet my consideration is present with me, through which that which was future may be carried over so that it may become past. The more this is done and repeated, by so much (expectation being shortened) the memory is enlarged until the whole expectation be exhausted, when that whole action being ended shall have passed into memory. And what takes place in the entire psalm, takes place also in each individual part of it, and in each individual syllable: this holds in the longer action, of which that psalm is perchance a portion; the same holds in the whole life of man, of which all the actions of man are parts; the same holds in the whole age of the sons of men, of which all the lives of men are parts. (Augustine, 1948, 201)

For Augustine, speech and duration are isomorphic, intensive vectors. Thus, in the experience of reciting a psalm, the actual time of the performance and the time of the psalm coincide. The expressivity of the performer is overwhelmed by the objectivity of the performance, which establishes a domain of commonality. By incarnating the rhythmic structure of the psalm, it is made public by way of the performing body.

Cartesian grammatology and its cognate poetics consciously propose the fiction of atemporality. The especially prepared text of a formal proof consists of enumerated steps in deductive reasoning. The Cartesian image is a chain: "we cannot with one single gaze distinguish all the links of a lengthy chain, yet if we have seen the connection of each with its neighbor, we shall be entitled to say that we have seen how the first is connected with the last" (Descartes, 1967, 20–21). The Cartesian link and the Augustinian syllable are both *metrical* units, ways of keeping track of the linear progress of discourse. The Latin or Greek syllable, however, is a fixed quantity, inherent in the syllable itself. A link in a Cartesian proof may infold entire language worlds (it may in turn subordinate complex arguments), so the structure is at once hierarchical and linear. In the metaphor of the chain, Descartes unites the contradictory characters that dance complexly in his discourse. The experience of temporality in the language of a formal proof is utterly unlike the experience of *quantitative* poetic time, which is fundamental to the Augustinian cosmology. Cognitive time does not answer to *any* externality; it is a psychological dimension. Although it would be left to Kant to deny the objectivity of space, which is implicit in the circular Cartesian argument, Descartes recognizes cognitivity as the source and end of temporality.

One notices, reading Duncan's variations, that the rhythms not only are more varied and demanding of attention than the rhythms of his seventeenth-century models but are of a different kind. All of the seventeenth-century poems are iambic pentameter, with the exception of Southwell's, which is in fourteeners, a line created by running the eights and sixes of the ballad stanza together and regularizing the accentual verse with iambics. The strategy that creates the rhythmic effect of the fourteener is much the same as the strategy of pentameter: both recognize the inherent tendency in English to the four-beat phrase and create syncopations by imposing the expectation of one beat more or one beat less per line. The fourteener is difficult to handle, as it tends to crank apart into the native sixes and eights, but the Southwell poem is masterful. Conventionally syncopation is the mark of "serious" poetry. By contrast, one hears this verse, for example, as playful and childish:

Hinx, minks, the old witch winks;
the fat begins to fry.
There's no one home but jumping Joan,
father and mother and I.

The speaker is a concrete ego—the ego of the speaker of the poem at the time of the speaking. The measure is absolute, not a ratio. Unlike the syncopated verse of Duncan's sources in "The Suite," it does not invoke normative conventions that are independent of the particular performance of the poem.

Duncan's verse is *technically* nearer the nursery rime than the seventeenth-century poems: it is performed in real time, making no concession to the individual expressivity of the performer. Needless to say, it is much subtler. The verses are recited, and the voice is incarnated. Once again speech orients the body, and the body orients speech. For Augustine, this was an imitation of Christ; for Duncan, it is the incarnation of that person he is. In "The First" (from *Ground Work II: In the Dark*), Duncan writes:

IN THIS MUSIC   (Webern):   *"Every thing is a principal idea."*

    Every where central to enquiry.

  Every time initial.

The people of this nation thruout time are not one but a multi-
        tude   each from his one
        heart/mind   coming forward   masst

so you cannot strike down our leader   for no *one*   leads us—

    you will be exhausted before we are to strike down the

        multitude of volitions we come from.
                               (Duncan, 1987, 60)

The task is to clarify this firstness, this initiality, in which
nothing is subordinate, in which the multitude of volitions is ex-
pressed as a multitude, not as a statistically derived sum. What we
are in ourselves is forever in conflict with what we are in the mass;
the life in us in conflict with the finality of what we are as poor
historical creatures, who aim at nothing but our own exhaustion
and extinction, which, in a sense, is already accomplished.

LINGUISTICS: CARTESIAN

    The emotional disturbance echoes down the canyons of the
heart.
        Echoes there—sounds cut off—merely phonemes. A Ground-
        rules double. You recognize them by patter. Try.
                      —Jack Spicer, "Phonemics"

The unique contribution of seventeenth-century logic was the
invention of the abstract machine. The conception of the logical
function that underwrites mathematical analysis, on the one hand,
and at least the dream of a universal grammar, on the other, was
new. With it, the nature of technology changed profoundly, but
more significantly the mind as such conceived itself technologi-
cally. In the most general terms, the new logic proposed that, if a
particular proposition is possible, all of the logical preconditions
for that *class* of propositions must exist: a thought entails the
psychology that makes it possible. The paradigm of cognitive
science—the mind as computer—was essentially a seventeenth-

century development. Since World War II, of course, it has been possible to construct logical devices with high-speed electronic switches. The mystery of the relationship of body to mind turns out to be fairly simple: the Cartesian body consists of the switches, the Cartesian mind is their *logical* concatenation—computer and program.

As Descartes knew and as Berkeley and Hume would show, nothing in experience gives evidence of the kind of reliably discrete objects that methodology requires. Thus, Descartes appeals to innate simple ideas. Conversely, Leibniz argues that the world is composed of monads—simple entities that somehow are already and always implicated in totality. In short, Descartes defers the problem with an infinite circular regression, and Leibniz, arguing that there is no simple location, confronts it directly by positing an incoherent origin. The sun's gravity exerts its force on the planets because, in some sense, the sun and planets are constantly conjoined, separable only in the common mode of human perception. These are the alternatives that rule-governed reality allows. Neither alternative is completely attractive if one seeks Truth founded on unimpeachable logic.

The resilience of the argument for innate knowledge is remarkable. Despite the obvious problems it involves, it has been recycled in the Kantian categories, the Hegelian logic of history, and the Freudian unconscious. Most significantly now, it returns in cognitive science, the first major interdisciplinary reorganization of knowledge to attract both widespread academic attention and, perhaps more significantly, lavish government funding. In *The Mind's New Science: A History of the Cognitive Revolution*, Howard Gardner writes, "René Descartes is perhaps the prototypical philosophical antecedent of cognitive science." And he takes Descartes as thematic. He notes, for example, that "Early intimations [of the possibility of robotics and artificial intelligence] can be discerned in the work of René Descartes, who was interested in automata that could simulate the human body" (Gardner, 1987, 142). Gardner even gives Descartes credit for an opinion that has often been used to ridicule his thought. He interprets the Cartesian suggestion that body and soul join at pineal gland as an early interest in the localization of neural functioning; thus, he understands Descartes as a forerunner of Broca, Wernicke, and present-day neurophysiologists (Gardner, 1987, 284). And, of course, he recognizes Descartes's contribution to the development of transformational grammar: "Leaning explicitly on the work of Descartes some three hundred years earlier, and borrowing leaves as well from the writings of Plato and Immanuel Kant, Chomsky argued that our interpretation of the world is based on representational systems that derive from the structure of the mind itself and do not mirror in any direct way the form of the external world" (Gardner, 1987, 192). The instituting metaphor of cognitive science is the formal system and explicitly the computer program: any human output requires an internal system that makes that class of output possible.

Although Chomsky's historical research on the Cartesian tradition has been reviewed harshly, he reveals an essential fact of the understanding of language in the modern West. Perhaps we can think of his writings in *Cartesian Linguistics* and in the first and third chapters of *Language and Mind* as more mythological than scholarly; he reveals our linguistic unconscious. The thought of Descartes's "primary germs of truth implanted by nature in human minds" is as essential to the culture that built the World Trade Center, the space shuttle *Columbia,* and Disneyland as Athena is to the culture that built the Parthenon or the Virgin is to the culture that built the gothic cathedrals. Chomsky describes language as a mode of free cognitive creation, and the Cartesian precedent for his argument is strong: "Descartes . . . described human reason as a universal instrument which can serve for all contingencies and which therefore provides for unbounded diversity of free thought and action" (Chomsky, 1966, 15).

Chomsky takes little note, however, of the distinction between natural language and *mathesis universalis* that, for Descartes, constituted a significant boundary to the freedom. Even the passage that Chomsky cites implies that *at least some* language is bounded, unfree, and reactive. Descartes writes: "mind is of such a nature that from the motion of the body alone the various sensations can be excited in it," and as we have seen, language without careful methodological discipline is a manifestation of physical mechanism. In the commentary, he goes on to say:

> For we see that either spoken or even written words can excite any thoughts and stirrings whatever in our mind. On the same sheet of paper, with the same quill and ink, if the end of the quill is merely guided over the paper in a certain way; it will produce letters which will excite thoughts of combats, tempests, and fu-

ries, and states of indignation and sadness in the minds of readers. If, however, the quill is moved in another almost identical manner, it will cause very different thoughts, of calm weather, peace, and pleasantness, and exactly opposite states of love and happiness. (Descartes, 1983, 281)

Language in this sense, which is of course precisely the creative mode of poetry as it is generally understood in romantic theory, is according to Descartes mechanical, and no doubt the emphasis on the pen, the mechanical instrument of writing, functions rhetorically to underscore its mechanical nature. Although Descartes never doubts the rich creativity of language, the problem as he understands it is to find a unity of language that is not constantly subverting itself with something new or compromising itself with its own mechanism. Such of course was the motive in searching out a new logical language. The poststructuralist critique of common textuality is implicit in Descartes's desire to discover the *mathesis universalis*. The Cartesian method is directed toward rational control of the unruly linguistic machine that generates its illusory worlds. Chomsky reads romanticism back into Descartes, but in retrospect his assessment of the general spirit and direction of Cartesianism is sound. The culture has underwritten ever more elaborate forms of mental mechanism as the source of productivity.

Contemporary Cartesianism, as Chomsky summarizes it, maintains that "A language is a collection of sentences of finite length all constructed from a finite alphabet . . . of symbols. Since any language L in which we are likely to be interested is an infinite set, we can investigate the structure of L only through the study of finite devices (grammars) which are capable of enumerating its sentences" (Chomsky, 1959, 137). Although it is considerably more general, Chomsky's formulation develops directly from Descartes. For Descartes the system consists of the symmetrical grid that is named for him, space-points identified by their relationship to vertical and horizontal axes on the grid, and the rules of algebra. Implicitly, all of the infinite variety of the world can be generated by recursively applying the finite rules to the space-points. For Chomsky, the grid consists of a phonological grid and the rules of grammar.

The mathematics of such systems was formalized in this century by Alan Turing, who established the necessary conditions for the logical decidability of propositions by the Cartesian machine and any similar abstract machine, which are now generally called "Turing machines." In effect, his theory is the theory of computer programming: the value of a proposition is decidable only if the necessary operations can be performed by a finite number of steps on a finite number of objects in accord with a finite number of rules. Most formal theories of language, like Chomsky's, assume that language can be characterized as a Turing machine. Terence Langendoen and Paul Postal mention twenty-seven different linguistic systems that make this assumption, and no doubt there are more (Langendoen and Postal, 1984, 73–74).

As it turns out, however, natural languages are not Turing machines. Jacques Derrida's most significant result, as far as formal linguistics is concerned, is this: he successfully undermines the ideality of the abstract machine with the concreteness of the marks that constitute natural languages. Although these are not precisely his terms, it is the substance of *Speech and Phenomena* and the necessary foundation for the argument in *Of Grammatology*. Derrida's entire meditation derives from the the deconstruction of the Cartesian circle. He asks the question—a relatively innocent-sounding question—that undoes the entire tradition: "how can we justify the *decision* which subordinates a reflection on the sign to a logic?" (Derrida, 1978b, 7). How do we decide—the emphasis is Derrida's—to obey a logic without having *already* invoked the logic? Consistent attention to this question leads directly to the most corrosive aspect of Hegel: every logic undermines itself. This argument shows that the truth value of *any* text is logically undecidable. The question of whether to subordinate the signs to a logic is itself undecidable; thus every interpretation of the text spectacularly emits more text as the interpreter scrambles on the slippery hermeneutical grounds.

Derrida's argument, while valid, is logically weak. It is itself textual and historical. D. Terence Langendoen and Paul M. Postal make a much stronger argument by proving what they call "the N[atural] L[anguage] Vastness Theorem." They prove formally that natural languages consist not of a countably infinite collection of sentences, which thus could be enumerated by a recursive rule, but of an uncountably vast collection. That is, the set of all sentences of a natural language involves precisely the same paradox as the set of all sets: it must include itself. A formal system, for example, must account for those sentences that begin "I know and

I know that I know and so forth." They quote Gödel's statement of the problem: "It follows at once from this explanation of the term 'set' that a set of all sets or other sets of a similar extension cannot exist, since every set obtained in this way immediately gives rise to a further application of the operation 'set of' and, therefore, to the existence of larger sets" (Langendoen and Postal, 1984, 48–70). This result leads directly to Langendoen and Postal's NL non-constructivity theorem, which demonstrates that natural languages are not formal systems. The grammar of a natural language cannot be given in terms of rules and objects that will generate the entire collection of allowable sentences in the natural language (Langendoen and Postal, 1984, 71–81).

Of course, this argument takes nothing away from the positive success of any linguistic theory. Significant *fragments* of natural languages can be described, as a number of useful grammars clearly demonstrate. The argument does, however, raise profound ontological questions. If linguistic objects are not concepts constructed by rule in accord with psychological principles, as Chomsky and other constructivist linguists argue, what are they? Langendoen and Postal follow Jerrold J. Katz in arguing that language consists of abstract, rather than generated, objects. To exchange Cartesian psychologism for Platonic realism, however, seems to exchange a sophisticated absurdity for a patent absurdity. Plato had to resort to fancy to give an account of these curious objects, and the modern Platonists are hardly more realistic about their realism. It is a kind of logical fundamentalism, which insists upon the literal, objective existence of its logical objects—a position that is common among logicians and mathematicians and increasingly common among linguists.

Jerrold Katz's thought in this regard has taken an interesting turn in his recent work. Rather than rejecting Descartes's arguments, most notably the *cogito,* he proposes an alternative interpretation, which, even if it is questionable on scholarly grounds—and I believe that it is—is an important contribution to Cartesian mythology and the modern myth of symbolism. In his *Cogitation: A Study of the Cogito in Relation to the Philosophy of Logic and Language and a Study of Them in Relation to the Cogito,* he lays out the basis for the intuition of the abstract foundation of linguistics. He argues that the *cogito* is not an enthymeme and therefore a truncated deduction that construes premises to arrive at a conclusion but an analytic entailment. He understands Descartes as arguing that existence is involved by definition in the very act of thinking; no intervening logical steps are subsumed by this conclusion. Katz interprets both Descartes and Chomsky's Cartesianism in terms of pure abstract theory rather than in terms of psychological categories.* In effect, Katz proposes a pure Cartesian grammar, not one infected by the subjectivism of Kant. In structuralist grammars, Katz notes, there are concrete objects and abstract rules. There must be substitution criteria for determining that this or that linguistic unit is equivalent to some other. In generative grammars by contrast, "An understanding of the concepts in question thus comes from their systematic connection to other concepts within the theory, on the one hand, and from the connections of the theory as a whole to the phenomena in its domain on the other" (Katz, 1986, 27). For the generative grammarian, "language" is a purely abstract domain to which the *cogito*—its description of itself and its world—belong. Linguistics as such and the abstract ego of the linguist *as* linguist therefore have no responsibility for the connections of the theory as a whole to the phenomenal domain. Skepticism of the kind voiced by the poststructuralists, therefore, is not the grammarian's problem: it must be dealt with by politics or social engineering or education. Katz secures the basis for a linguistic science, but only at the expense of rendering the formal study of language meaningless for those who are concerned with understanding the common world. The "I" who describes his or her own language may be an utterly confident theoretician, working with absolute objects in an absolute domain, but the knowledge is rendered merely disciplinary or academic (which is, of course, not to say trivial, as engineering is also an academic discipline, and, by way of engineering, academic entities are readily realized and intrude into the common domain by virtue of a crass materiality that does not recognize disciplinary boundaries).

The Cartesian equivocation on the status of the *cogito*, as it hovered between being a synthetic construction and an analytic immediacy, was logically inelegant but practically useful until at

---

*The Cartesian text is not definitive. Descartes seems simply not to have been clear about the analytic-synthetic distinction and was thus a kind of naive Kantian, understanding his propositions as analytic or synthetic as it suited his argument. If linguistic objects turn out to be purely abstract, of course, their relationship to concrete reality then becomes totally problematical.

least some time in the present century. For example, it allowed the
"I" to be the speaking subject of a love poem, on the one hand, and
the theoretical ego required by mathematics, on the other. Now, *a poor*
however, the abstract ego has asserted itself as an absolute theoret- *existence*
ical object, leaving the mere, actual people in a domain where the *Byrd.*
knowledge that addresses their most intimate concerns are, in fact,
irrelevant. Even literature and the arts, to the extent that they
constitute themselves as domains of theoretical objects, likewise
withdraw from the space in which egos suffer the trauma of being
bodies in particular locations, associated with particular people,
whom they love or hate or fear, or, more troublesomely, whom
they love, hate, *and* fear all at the same time. The completely *v.*
nontheoretical *mess* in which people find themselves is cut through *good.*
with disciplines that nowhere address the crisis that initiates their
desire for knowledge.*

Like concepts, to recall Wittgenstein's phrase, none of the *disciplines* are for use on single occasions, and the development of
disciplinary knowledge has consistently taken the place of other
kinds of more specifically useful insights. Thus, it has been important merely to display nonsense. The tradition of outrageousness
that runs from Dadaism to Fluxus to such contemporary rock
groups as the Sex Pistols, Pere Ubu, and the Butthole Surfers has
been merely to mark the site at which knowledge disappears into
the concrete situation. As it turns out, the single occasion—as
opposed to the successful realization of the concept, the mass
occasion—is typically bizarre and even ridiculous, especially in a
culture in which all behavior is constituted to reveal statistically
reliable zones that are required as the basis of social order.

If grammar cannot be described in terms of a finite formal
system, however, it might also be understood as a concrete, rather
than a systematic, construction. Modern linguistic science has assumed that language is a system of empty concepts or essences,
which are actively, and even willfully, made to apply to concrete,
particular occasions. Especially in the work of the cognitivists,
language is conceived as a set of procedures or grammatical rules
and a collection of tokens—marks, phonemes, or whatever—
which can be put into play in the service of the "mind." Mind is, in

---

*I use *mess* as a technical word. I considered *world* or *ecosystem* as alternatives,
  but they both imply some theorized unity from which discipline might arise.

one sense, the collection of rules and tokens, but it is something *more:* it also decides what it *wants* to say. It is the seat of some linguistic activating device—eros or will. By way of this x-factor, which is never the concern of the science itself, that concepts are specified for use on single occasions. For the linguist, *particular* acts of speech are as random as the course of a particular electron for the physicist.

LINGUISTICS: NON-CARTESIAN

Indeed, the *perception* of particular speech acts is difficult to explain in terms of any of the linguistic theories based on the concept of the phoneme. It is not possible to correlate the physical properties of speech with the perception of meaning. The earliest spectographic analyses of speech revealed no invariant patterns in the speech signal (Joos, 1948). Phonemes are modified by the requirements of other phonemes in their immediate linguistic vicinities. Michael Studdert-Kennedy writes: "Thirty years of research with synthetic speech have demonstrated that the speech signal is replete with independently manipulable 'cues', which, if varied appropriately, change the phonetic percept" (Studdert-Kennedy, 1985, 140). Some progress has been made in defining phonetic distinctions in terms of dynamic events that take multiple constraints into consideration. *The Journal of Phonetics* devoted a special issue to the problem in 1986, with a lead article by Carol A. Fowler, "An Event Approach to the Study of Speech Perception from a Direct-Realist Perspective," which is reviewed by an impressive array of experts in the field. Despite this important work, however, R. M. Warren's earlier conclusion still stands: "While phonemes are constructs useful for transcribing and analyzing, they are without direct perceptual basis . . . phonemes seem to have no *direct* relevance to perceptual processes leading to the comprehension of speech" (Warren, 1976, 409, my emphasis).

With the collapse of idealism—and the parasitic idealisms that locate cognition in relation to a slippery or decentered phonology—two defensible possibilities present themselves: Platonic realism, which assumes the reality of abstract grammatical objects, and empirical realism. The first of these position is extensively developed by J. J. Katz; the other, at least inchoately, by Robert Verbrugge. I give here an outline of Verbrugge's work, to the extent that I know it (there are only a couple of published essays), as it develops an understanding of language that is commensurate with the poetics of the common knowledge. Although Verbrugge seems to draw back from the most radical implications of his thought of extending the ecological theory of perception of J. J. Gibson to language, he suggests that cognition and symbol use must be viewed as a species of event perception like seeing and hearing.* As he notes, "This would require a dramatic change in our view of language (seeing it somehow as a specific medium) and in our view of language comprehension (seeing it as an activity that is free of interpretive mediation)" (Verbrugge, 1985, 164).

The proposal is radical indeed. Verbrugge proposes that language is (1) not ambiguous, (2) not arbitrary, (3) not representational, (4) not mediated, and (5) not formal. One could hardly find another doctrine of linguistics that is more fundamental or widely shared than these five that he proposes to overturn; indeed they are the assumptions that are necessary to the very idea of linguistic science as such. Without them, language must be understood as suffused throughout the particular occasions of its use and as deriving its *structure* from those occasions, *not* from an abstract medium. Therefore, language as such could not be understood as a separate object of study. Like other kinds of perception, Verbrugge suggests, "information about [speech] events is necessarily *specific* to them. . . In the case of perceptual experience [and, as he argues by analogy, in the case of speech perception], this implies a tight, nonarbitrary coupling between the experience of events, the media affected by events, and the events themselves" (Verbrugge, 1985, 160).

Verbrugge analyzes three aspects of this specificity.

1. He speaks of language as a catalyst: "Like chemical catalysts, words are rarely the substance of the process they affect, but they can *trigger* a flow of imagining and *constrain* the flow in very specific ways. Words are also like catalysts in that they constrain a process without in any sense containing a representation of the process or its results" (Verbrugge, 1985, 171).

---

*Gibson's radical bypass of classical phenomenology is collaterally relevant to the poetics of the common knowledge, and an awareness of his approach will make Verbrugge's work seem intuitively more accurate. The important studies are *The Senses Considered as a Perceptual System* (Gibson, 1966) and especially *The Ecological Approach to Visual Perception* (Gibson, 1979).

2. He notes the importance of redintegration in the perception of language events: "The activation of virtual experiences by words may be viewed as a process of recollection and more specifically, of redintegration, if we consider words and their patternings to be the commonality between present and past events. . . Redintegration could be said to occur when words alone activate perceptional and actional attunements . . ." (Verbrugge, 1985, 173–74). These attunements are the province of the common knowledge. They are established and adjusted, not by workings in an abstract medium, but by concrete performance in the context of the concrete world. The structures are real not by virtue of their independent existence but by virtue of actually constituting the world which they reveal.

3. Finally, he proposes that all language is indexical: "indexes are signs that are related to what they signify by some natural constraint—such as thunder, a footprint, a bad cough, or a bird's nest. . . Words are not merely indexes to things, but indexes of social events and settings." Thus, language is a concrete, primary medium, like light and sound, not a secondary, reflective, or representational medium. The acts of language therefore are not dependent upon abstract schemata. Verbrugge speaks of the "'existential' relationship between *all* words and their natural occasions" and, although he does not follow out the more general philosophic implications of his argument, his is a radical existentialism, not merely a programmatic or theoretical one (Verbrugge, 1985, 179). Drawing on the research program of J. J. Gibson, he arrives at a pure existentialism, according to which, existence has no significant relation to essence conceived as something separate from existence. Acts do not define essences, as Sartre implies. An act is an act with its own concrete content that is not merely prior to essence; it has no relation to essence whatsoever.

It appears that such a theory will not support a science of linguistics—that is, a science that must describe a domain of essences. Indeed, if the special status of language perception is eliminated, the absurdity of a linguistic science as such would be clear. To propose a theory of coding and decoding symbols to understand the functioning of language in an environment would be comparable to proposing a theory of light to explain the way a person walks through a room without running into things.

If it will not support a linguistics, however, Verbrugge's suggestions appears to point to precisely the theory of language required by the poetics that certain poets have been articulating—or lacking the necessary theory, *trying* to articulate—since Whitman and Melville. Of course, Verbrugge himself is completely unaware of this connection, as far as one can tell, but in his understated, social-scientific language, he takes several important steps toward getting Melville's self, nature, and God out of the dictionary and into the street.

Developing Verbrugge's line of thought in relation to biology, Humberto Maturana writes:

> Human beings can talk about things because they generate the things they talk about by talking about them. That is, human beings can talk about things because they generate them by making distinctions that specify them in a consensual domain, and because, operationally, talking takes place in the same phenomenic domain in which things are defined as relations of relative neuronal activities in a closed neuronal network. (Maturana, 1975, 56)

Communication takes place not as a result of information passing from a sender to receiver by way of a code—as the classic paradigm proposes—but as a result of social attunement or, in a term that Maturana uses, "shared orientation." The *same* information is independently generated by individuals who are attuned or share an orientation. This line of thought leads to a profoundly non-Cartesian conception of mind and language. Mind is not the foundation of social interaction but the creation of social interaction, Maturana and Varela write: "The unique feature of human social life and its intense linguistic coupling are manifest in that this life is capable of generating a new phenomenon, both close to and remote from our own experience: our mind, our consciousness" (Maturana and Varela, 1987, 223). The mind lacks innate knowledge; mind itself is our construction, not as the implementation of a given abstract structure, but as the private manifestation of specific acts in relations to specific, public occasions.

This is, of course, the solution to the problem of origins. Structure is malleable. That it slips and slides, returns on its self in logical loops, and thus decenters itself—the very qualities that render it useless as a theoretical medium—are precisely the qualities that makes it viable as the stuff of the common knowledge. The poetics of common knowledge understands "difference"—the sameness that is not identical, in Derrida's formulation, as a dimension not of linguistic slippage but of poetic *precision*. In poetry, as in cartography, it is *differences* that are recorded as usable information. Poetic measure marks differences and shades of differences with a precision to which both the abstract thought of identity and its critique are blind. Derrida says that "differance . . . points out the irreducibility of temporalizing," or it points it out to philosophers, one might say, as only they have been so inattentive as to miss this most aggressive character of the real. The poetics of common knowledge insists that the earth, the actual, physical earth, and its actual inhabitants, *not* language, preserve "the difference that preserves language" (Derrida, 1978, 130) and poiesis reveals the specific forms of their acts in its measure. For the poet, temporality is not the snake in the metaphysical garden but the dimension of order.

Derrida's claim for the efficacy of language is the inverse of the rationalist's, and it is open to the same objection. The rationalist creates rules for a logic, rules that he follows carefully. If he does not become entangled in his rules, he assumes that he has learned something about the world. Derrida, on the other hand, notes that the rationalists invariably get tripped up by their rules—indeed, that getting tripped is inherent in rule making—and he assumes that, in observing this fact, he has learned something about the nature of the world. The poetics of common knowledge contends that in either case we have learned something only about the nature of rules. In order to follow rules, there must rules for implementing the rules; every access to a logically constructed world is blocked by infinite regression.

Structure, however, does not come from elsewhere, from some mysterious origin; structure is given by its own difference with itself. Structure is the thickening of generality that makes community possible. Verbrugge as a linguist and student of perception and Maturana and Varela as biologists define the possibility of a conceptual domain *without foundation* and without regress to a logical origin. They fall short of producing a poetics of the common knowledge, however, from lack of a developed sense of measure. Therefore, they cannot provide any insight into the single occasion. They locate precisely the site of the conceptual horizon, the crossing of which produces dadaism or indeed any singularity—the domain in which events are unique, unrepeatable, and therefore, in a sense, unknowable. It is *measure,* not structure, that comes from elsewhere. Nothing in the structure provides a sense of scale.

MEASURE

The issue raised by Duncan's "Suite" is precisely the question of temporal quantity that was central for Augustine. Duncan is concerned with the difference between time as the concrete medium of language, on the one hand, and as an abstraction in which time enters only as a particular performance or illustration, on the other. Indeed, more generally, it is the issue raised by Walt Whitman's free verse practice. What is at stake is not a matter of aesthetics or craftsmanship but the most profound question of the relationship of language and reality. Thus, for example, the assertions of William Carlos Williams concerning prosody are by no means hyperbolic. When he speaks of "a new measure by which may be ordered our poems as well as our lives" (Williams, 1969, 340), he speaks of an *order* in the same serious sense that one in the philosophic tradition might speak of logical order or *logos.* That is, there is an order in time that is as *necessary* as logical order but that is concrete and particular rather than abstract and general. A concept is not for use on a single occasion but a *measure* is.

Duncan's remeasuring of seventeenth-century poems and, similarly, for example, Pound's measuring of prose texts by the American founding fathers in the *Cantos* (see, for example, cantos 31–34) are instances of repossession of a concreteness lost both to conventional poetic forms and to prose. Once again, for the first time since Plato's *Republic* settled the matter for the West, there begins to be a suggestion of poetry as a fundamental mode of knowledge, something comparable to the Greek *musike.* Thrasybolos Georgiades notes the significance of this untranslatable term: "The word *musike* in Greek is an adjective, not a noun. It means *mus-ish,* 'pertaining to the Muses.' Perhaps one could amplify it: 'mus-ish activity' or 'mus-ish education.' Possibly it would be best to connect the two: 'mus-ish education' through 'mus-ish activity,' and not a finished product. . . *musike* functioned . . . as the very essence of intellectual education and as the force determining the ethos" (Georgiades, 1973, 107–8). The immense loss has been frequently noted, most often nostalgically, by Heidegger or

Georgiades himself, and to be sure, the new poetry does not pervade the culture as *musike* pervaded Greek culture, but for the first time since the Greeks, I want to say the *technology* for an ethical culture exists. Until recently, a world in which the minds and bodies of individuals were attuned to common ethical self-construction was *theoretically* out of bounds. What is shared in an *ethos*—etymologically, a space shared with other of one's own *kind*—is not a common *description* of the world, not a world picture or paradigm, not even common assumptions about time and space, but a common haunt: the *things* are the same, however much the individual perspectives may differ. We haunt the same world, and it is in our acts of making that we are embodied and realize our commonness.

For a certain tradition of democratic poets, deriving from Whitman, who declare that all people are of one kind, the essentials of a literate *musike* reappears. In one sense, of course, the notion of "literate *musike*" is self-contradictory, *musike* in the classical sense was inherently oral. The poets themselves have been frequently tongue-tied in their attempts to explain the implications of their discoveries, and in an important sense, the concreteness of the world cannot be theorized; it can only be enacted.

Verbrugge comes close to proposing a principle of measure in his discussion of redintegration—a common term in associationalist psychology for the restoration or renewal of mental totalities. The law of redintegration explains the connectivity between thoughts that were previously connected to some totality. It implies that mental functions ultimately involve only wholes of which there are no parts. For the tradition of British empiricism and the psychology that derived from it, the law of redintegration, on the one hand, and the assumption that mental content consists of simple ideas, on the other, were terms of a debilitating incoherence. Although Verbrugge, like J. J. Gibson, dispenses with the notion of simple ideas, he is puzzled about how to deal with the lengthy spans of time that are involved in language perception. He worries that "we risk returning to concepts of memory and association that have failed in the past to provide credible explanations of redintegrative phenomena" (Verbrugge, 1985, 174).

Part of the problem stems from the origins of Verbrugge's research in the study of event perception. Events in the narrow sense are relatively isolated: when I notice the bird land on the branch outside my window or hear a power saw begin to whine some-where in the neighborhood, these are more or less atomic events. They are noticed precisely because they punctuate the unattended continuities. In language, however, the ways in which events *connect* with one another is of great interest. The totalities are not so obvious, and indeed we are not schooled to pay attention to speech acts as extended events. Descartes proposed that the coherence of language results from the recursive application of atemporal rules to finite collections of tokens. By contrast the poetics of common knowledge notes that language may be discovered to cohere in relation to totalities measured *through time.*

Granted, we do not want to return to the discredited theories of associationism, but it is a knowledge of the *actual* associations of thought, not associationism, that is required by an event-perception theory of language. In this regard, William James's insights are far from exhausted. James writes:

> The manner in which trains of imagery and consideration follow each other through our thinking, the restless flight of one idea before the next, the transitions our minds make between things wide as the poles asunder, transitions which at first sight startle us by their abruptness, but which when scrutinized closely, often reveal intermediating links of perfect naturalness and propriety—all this magical imponderable streaming has from time immemorial excited the admiration of all whose attention happened to be caught by its omnipresent mystery. (James, 1950, I, 550)

The attractions of understanding this flow are, of course, con-siderable. If the principles of the connections between ideas could be discovered, one of the most obvious mysteries of the human mind would be cleared up. James makes a distinction that seems at first so simple and obvious as to be trivial but that, in truth, cuts to the philosophic heart of the matter. The very notion of connectivity itself, as it turns out, is ambiguous: "which sort of connection is meant?" James asks, "connection *thought-of,* or connection *between thoughts*"? The Cartesian tradition, down to and including contemporary cognitive science, proposes to account for all of the possibilities of thought and all of the connections *thought of.* As James recognized, however, "The jungle of connections of thought can never be formulated simply." The possibilities are infinite. As James shows, if they are simplified, so as to be enclosed by a rational scheme, such as the rational forms of Hegelian history, the very richness of fantasy and arbitrariness that "are part of the very bone and marrow of our minds" is eliminated. As he goes on to argue—and this argument is crucial to the poetics of the common knowledge—"*Association, so far as the word stands for an effect, is between* THINGS THOUGHT OF—*it is* Things, *not ideas which are associated by the mind.* We ought to talk of the association of *objects,* not the association of *ideas*" (James, 1950, I, 554). Or, to put the matter in other terms, the mind deals with complexes, not simples, most significantly, temporal complexes: "The knowledge of some other part of the stream [of consciousness], past or future, is always mixed in with our knowledge of present things" (James, 1950, I, 606).

We have no means other than poetic measure to give a precise and significant account of this aspect of knowledge. As Georgiades notes, the Greeks *musike* was the technology of this knowledge, and the persistent nostalgia for Greek culture, from the eighteenth-century battle of the books to Joyce's *Ulysses* or Georg Lukàcs's *Theory of the Novel,* is precisely for this lost unity and potential magic. Georgiades writes:

> [In the ancient Greek language] we find a situation in which the things of the outer and inner world meet us as active and living forces, as "essences." Objects here behave like antimate beings and feelings are objectified, personified. There is no distinction between conception and name, on the one hand, and object and individual material thing, on the other. The field is open to conjuration.
>
> . . . In western languages, however, the ontological aspect of the word has vanished, as it were. Western philosophy has evolved correspondingly: logic has separated itself from ontology; the "essence of things," understood by the Greeks as substance and as present, in Kant's philosophy was transformed to the *Ding an sich,* the thing *per se,* which remains inaccessible to the human. Georgiades, 1973, 103–4)

But by the same token, there now begins to be a language that rejoins itself to the concrete. With James's recognition that the mind works its associations not between ideas but between things, we have not an ontology, not a *logic* of being, but *a working among beings as such.* The word as much as the thing is an object, not a representation or a simple token but a complex thing in its own

right. Trees, hills, rocks, houses, and *language* are facts of the
landscape, and we deal with words as we deal with other things.
Faced with a difficult climb up a rocky slope, we look for signs of
good footing. We look for loose gravel, which calls for one kind of
move; mud, which calls for another; and exposed tree roots, which
call for still another. Words too offer a purchase on a landscape
and require a comparable attentiveness to a completely concrete
world. "For the Greeks," Georgiades writes, "the realm of the
intellectual, of the substantial, is lowered to that of the sensory and
becomes identical with it. The ancient conception of 'being' is
characterized, as Hegel says, by the consciousness of the 'god him-
self entering the temple and dwelling in our midst'" (Georgiades,
1973, 105). For us, however, the sensory is raised to the realm of
the intellectual, of the substantial, and becomes identical with it.
The modern conception of being is characterized by the conscious-
ness of men and women entering the world and dwelling in our
midst. Although the gods do not appear, humans are invested with
something of the value that was previously reserved for the divin-
ities. Music, Leroi Jones writes, "is the result of thought. It is the
result of thought perfected at its most empirical, i.e. as *attitude or
stance*" (Jones, 1963, 152). It was that most concrete connection
to thought that was lost in the world of mixed abstractions that
Cartesianism introduced.

In both modern prose and in the verse forms that came to
dominate poetry in the sixteenth and seventeenth centuries, ab-
stract time and its ratios are, in effect, prior to meaning itself.
Thus, the division of structure and semantics that has unsettled our
practice of language ever since. Or, to put the matter in terms that
are appropriate to the next chapter, time was transformed into
history: the flow of events in time was counterpointed to the
Times, and thus the value of every act was rendered relative. Any
particular performance of a traditional lyric is an instance of its
potentiality or purpose that must be energized by private motives.
The pattern allows innumerable possibilities for any given choice
in the actual performance. That is, it allows performers of the verse
expressive freedom, but only inside a context that insures that they
thump out some version of pentameter, the temporal structures
that generate meanings but do not specify their use. The voice
becomes a temporal function of the metrical form, just as the
actual things to which the poem refers becomes a function of

mathematical analysis. The poem as such cannot be performed because the text "contains" any number of possible performances; it can only be *represented* by a performance. The performance and the performer, therefore, become representative, mere examples. The poem itself represents *all* of its possible realizations, which is to say is represents nothing in particular.

Anthony Easthope speaks of English and German pentameter, French alexandrine, Italian and Spanish hendecasyllabic meter, and Russian tetrameter—those meters which are considered "natural" to their languages—as epochal forms of bourgeois culture (Easthope, 1983, 75). They represent precisely the dependence of bourgeois culture on abstract production that has not fully freed itself of its medium. When these forms began to break down—and signs of the breakdown were present almost from the beginning of the bourgeois regime—it was signaled by two very different modes of production that are, however, easily confused with one another because of their superficial resemblance. On the one hand, the sustaining conventions may be lost: readers simply may not hear the counterpunctal rhythm. It is the property of a homogeneous speech group at a particular historical time. For a society, even a small, elite society, to share an abstract norm controlling production of speech and even breath involves an awesome degree of unconscious regulation. At some point, if the efficacy of the institution is to be sustained, the background rhythm must be theorized; that is, the coherence of time or history must be plausibly reproduced and vigorously maintained, just as the coherence of logical space must be theorized. Such was the task of Hegelianism in Western thought, and the initial concern of the following chapter.

CHAPTER 3

Symbolic History

We must have a new mythology, but this mythology must be in the service of ideas, it must be a mythology of reason.
—G.W.F. Hegel

And so to such as German Kant and Hegel, where they, though near us, leaping over the ages, sit again, impassive, imperturbable, like the Egyptian gods. . .

Mark the roads, the processes, through which these States have arrived, standing easy, henceforth ever-equal, ever-compact, in their range today. European adventures? The most antique? Asiatic or African? Old history—miracles—romances? Rather our own unquestion'd facts. They hasten, incredible, blazing bright as fire.
—Walt Whitman

If you write the way it has already been written the way writing has already been written then you are serving mammon, because you are living by something some one has already been earning or earned. If you write as you are to be writing then you are serving as a writer god because you are not earning anything. If anything is to be earned you will not know what earning is therefore you are serving god.

—Gertrude Stein

THE HEGELIAN APOCALYPSE

The earth has been destroyed. Only a
few people know that. The rest usually
think of it as a subject of threat;
atomic, nuclear, erosional
etc.

—Edward Dorn, "A Theory of Truth"

The Two Modernisms

From Descartes and Locke to Kant, both rationalists and empiricists maintained that the world that consciousness imagines for itself relates to an original, however superfluous it may sometimes seem. Although the world-creating activity of consciousness takes place on the boundary between an interior and an exterior, which are finally no more than posited realms, the world that is produced is still *in some sense* a replica, a manifestation of a friction or tension in intellectual space. It can only be said, despite the implicit contradiction, that after Fichte no original corresponds to the replica and that in the Hegelian synthesis conceptualization becomes so fluent that language alone suffices as a world. Any concept understood in Hegelian terms contains all concepts. All perspectives, even perspectives that are contradictory, open to the all-embracing truth. Thought requires error, which—rather than Cartesian certainty—is the first principle of Hegelian logic. Hegelian doubt, however, unlike the Cartesian, which Hegel characterizes as "shilly-shallying about this or that presumed truth, followed by a return to that truth again, after the doubt has been appropriately expelled" is profound. After his confrontation with the malign demon, Hegel is never able to return to the prior truth. "The road can therefore be regarded as the pathway of *doubt*," Hegel says, "or more precisely as the way of despair" (Hegel, 1977, 49).

As much as labor language is, Hegel insists, the alienation of the Cartesian ego into its universality:

> Language . . . contains [the ego] in its purity, it alone expresses the "I", the "I" itself. This real existence of the "I" is qua real existence, an objectivity which has in it the true nature of the "I." The "I" is this particular "I"—but equally the universal "I"; its manifesting is also at once the externalization and vanishing of this particular "I", and as a result the "I" remains in its universality. The "I" that utters itself is heard or perceived; it is an infection in which it has immediately passed into unity with those for whom it is a real existence, and is a universal self-consciousness. (Hegel, 1977, 308–9)

It is to the nature of this infection, which is to say, the infection of language and ultimately the world that is described by and created by the ego, that we now address ourselves. Radical modernism cannot argue with Hegel. The dialectic feeds on contradiction. As individual readers and as a culture we are infected, we can only live through Hegel—live by engagement with him or at least the thought that he first adequately articulated. He is the tar baby of philosophers. We cannot hope to reach the end of the way of despair. This is Hegel's truth. Mallarmé, in Foucault's reading of him, was almost correct: the language *has* spoken; its logic is complete; it has nothing *more* to say. What it says, however, is infinite—that is, it says *everything*. The depth of the persistent modernist strategy, to equate being and language, reveals itself: *if being is language, every thing is true (and false)*. Hegel's thought is the apocalypse. The world is destroyed by its truth. His beginning takes all of its infinite consequences into consideration. By incorporating the end and all of its logical resources, he preempts beginning again, and we enter the *verkehrte Welt*—the topsy-turvy world, in which every beginning again is a continuation. Without the various disciplines by which we are mastered in the topsy-turvy world, we have only paradoxical languages. As a radical modernist, one may want to speak of identifying language with nonbeing, for example, but that is topsy-turvy talk too. Rather the radical modernist move is to dissociate knowledge from language, information, history, textuality—the media that are confused with the factual world they mediate. It is necessary to dissociate knowing even from the medium of consciousness. The experience of the topsy-turvy world, when it is fully teased out, reveals that the authority of these overwhelming concepts is a joke, literally comedy, Hegelian apocalyptic comedy. We have had some brave predecessors, but only now do we begin in large numbers to laugh.

Lower-case consciousness, language, information, history, and textuality are local systems, contingent and open, factual, available for use. I have cited Melville's letter to Hawthorne—"Take God out of the dictionary, and you will have Him in the street." It is from this critical perspective that we read Hegel, for whom perfected self-consciousness remains in relation to a science of language—what Hegel calls "logic"—which cannot be stated with a finite grammar. Thus, the Hegelian beginning again produces a newness that is not new, an event that utterly destroys the past without moving toward the future. The dialectical habits of mind so completely color our disciplined knowledge that it is difficult even to state an alternative.

Hegel begins not with the isolated ego but with all of the richness and confusion of Descartes's second house of culture, where history and its implicit tragedy call forth a profound questioning. His rejection of the classical infinity in favor of the modern is explicit. The wrong infinity, he notes, "is only a negative of a finite: but the finite rises again the same as ever, and is never got rid of and absorbed. In other words, this infinite only expresses the ought-to-be elimination of the finite" (Hegel, 1975b, 137). The right infinity, on the other hand, does absorb the finite. He compares the right infinite to an acid that is transformed in its absorption of the alkaline finite but "does not lose itself." To paraphrase Herman Weyl's comment on the Cartesian project in terms that are appropriate to Hegel, *The leap into the beyond of the beyond occurs when the infinitely open logical array of the natural languages is made into a closed aggregate of objects existing in themselves.* Hegel repeats the move that Descartes makes on the sequence of integers on the natural language. Hegelian logic discovers the infinity of mathematical analysis in the instigating metaphors of natural language itself. It is the infinitesimal calculus of the alphabet, which reveals the complex ratios of object to subject, consciousness to self-consciousness, master to slave, and so forth both, in their differences and their approach, at some infinitely deferred limit, to identity. In the *Logic* of 1830, Hegel notes, "People who are too fastidious toward the finite never reach actuality, but linger lost in abstraction, and their light dies away" (Hegel, 1975b, 136). We can now see, however, that life is not redeemed by the thought of the right infinity and that its endless process is as tedious as the wrong infinity. It is fastidiousness toward the finite—the ever-new here-now—that defines radical, post-Hegelian modernism, as in Walt Whitman and Gertrude Stein, to whom the second half of this essay is devoted. For more than two millennia, the resources for beginning again were associated with abstraction. After Hegel, and especially after Shannon and Wiener, they were associated with the concrete. Consider, for example, Whitman's fastidiousness toward finite time: "The past and present wilt—I have fill'd them, emptied them, / And proceed to fill my next fold of the future."

Language cannot be described finitely. From Hegel's point of view, therefore, it is possible only to swing back and forth between bacchanalian revel and despair—the heady mystical moment of participation in absolute knowledge and the grim reality of finitude. Post-Hegelian history has confirmed the dialectical character of Western institutions. The necessity of history and the contingency of history are always in proximity. Even the simplest thought requires the whole of history and its simultaneous denial. Every experience is total experience. "To me the meanest flower that blows can give / thoughts that do often lie too deep for tears," Wordsworth writes. This concentration of the all in everything is, of course, attractive. It makes experience almost unbearably rich and significant, but the richness and significance is bought at the expense of the constant nearness of the poor and the meaningless. In every lapse of concentration, the unmitigated contingency of "lazy existence" asserts itself. It requires genius or utter distraction, the philosopher or the couch potato. The emotional turbulence of the postromantic era results from this all or nothing attitude; mystical insight walks hand in hand with nihilism.

The radical modernism that arose in the middle of the nineteenth century was signaled theoretically by the non-Euclidean and N-dimensional geometers—especially by Riemann—and practical evidence of it can be found in the work of Melville, Whitman, Dickinson, William James, Henry James, Benjamin Paul Blood, and others, some time before a conscious poetics was formulated by the generation of 1910, most notably perhaps by Gertrude Stein and Marcel Duchamp. The radical modernists, rather than identifying being with language, identified language as the *content* of being. *The structure of being is everywhere made manifest by linguistic media but it can only be known factually and finitely, not by characterizing the nature of the medium.*

The End of Poetry, the Beginning of Poetry

We will examine Hegel's argument in the opening pages of the *Phenomenology* in detail, but in its most generalized form, it sounds much like Parmenides in Plato's dialogue: if we begin with the thing, *any*thing, and ask how we should name it, we are in a quandary because we cannot possibly recognize it without already knowing what it is; if we begin with the pure concepts, just empty names, however, there is no way to associate them with undifferentiated things. In either case, as Parmenides succinctly argues, having elicited the possible various forms of the paradox from the young Socrates, philosophy is without a reliable origin: "if . . . one will not allow that there are characters of things that are, and refuses to distinguish as something a character of each single thing, he will not even have anything to which to turn his mind, since he will not allow that there is a characteristic, ever the same, of each of the things that are; and so he will utterly destroy the power and significance of thought and discourse" (Plato, 1983, 13). Hegel's work is in the aftermath of the destruction of reason. Having taken the step into the beyond, he does not have a language that can "acknowledge ideas or species of existences" or "define particular species." Nothing can be separated from anything else. Thus, modernist that he was, he begins the project twice, taking up first one horn of the dilemma and then the other: in *Phenomenology,* starting with the unnamed and inherently unnameable, stuff of consciousness, and in *Encyclopedia,* beginning with logic, with language, the names that have no content. If it were not for the history of culture, the accumulated false starts and rhetorical ploys, it would never be possible to get beyond this beginning. There are no absolute representations. The aesthetic realm that includes the entire world of "experience"—every thing finally but the absolute thought of the absolute mind—is never more than temporary or provisional.

Hegel closely follows the logic of Plato in *Parmenides,* which he calls "surely the greatest artistic achievement of the ancient dialectic" (Hegel, 1977, 44). The Parmenidean arguments are devastating, not only to the Platonic theory of ideas but, more generally, to the possibility of rational thought leading beyond the Parmenidean unity. Whatever Parmenides himself may have thought, and trying to interpret the fragments is at best a speculative undertaking, the Platonic Parmenides establishes a series of paradoxes that leads us to the conclusion that, *if there is anything,* it is one, indivisible, continuous, timeless, and unspeakable. When Socrates is utterly vanquished, Parmenides suggests to him that the noble and divine impulse of philosophy might be served by an art that "is generally regarded as useless, and condemned by the multitude as idle talk." And he adds that, in the exercise of this art, Socrates should "examine the consequences that follow from the hypothesis, not only if each thing is hypothesized not to be, but also if that same thing is hypothesized not to be" (Plato, 1983, 13). This is, of course, the classical dialectic. Its basis is idle talk—that is to say, tradition or culture.

Classical reason refused to compromise the distinction between a worldly space, which must be conceived as a singularity, and a mental space, which was marked by syntactical recurrence; and Descartes's violation of it seems perhaps unconscious. The

Parmenidean logic, as Plato appears to have recognized, however, is inescapable; and the paradoxes that Parmenides and his student, Zeno, articulated have plagued subsequent thought. In the immediate Hegelian context, Kant reasserts the classical rigor. He develops four propositions—which bear on central philosophic concerns—and their opposites, maintaining that the arguments for both sets of propositions are equally valid. For example, in the "Second Conflict of Transcendental Ideas," the argument that most clearly recalls the Zenonian paradoxes, Kant shows that, on the one hand, "Every composite substance in the world is made up of simple parts, and nothing anywhere exists save the simple or what is composed of the simple," but, on the other hand, "No composite thing in the world is made up of simple parts, and there nowhere exists in the world anything simple" (Kant, 1965, 402). Kant's solution to these problems is to assign the terms of the conflict to different logical spaces, the one is true of the phenomena, the other of the noumena. More generally, Kant argues, paradoxes arise in the failure of this distinction.

So long as two separate-but-equal logical spaces can be maintained, it is possible to argue reasonably that the world is both finite and infinite, atomic and continuous, that nature is both determined and free, that god both does and does not exist, but the arguments are satisfying only to the most utterly rational minds. The drive toward unity is emotionally overpowering. The philosophers who immediately followed Kant, most notably Fichte, Schelling, and Hegel, and the artists of the period, quintessentially Beethoven perhaps, made noble attempts to bring science and psychology into more confident relationship to the life of the spirit. It was the first and last adequate manifestation of the modern ego, and it is for this reason that romanticism has cast such a long and persistent shadow over subsistent Western culture, where it has sponsored both anarchism and totalitarianism, mysticism and technologism. Of course, radical modernism makes no attempt to *represent* the ego at all.

When Spirit conceived itself as the source of a cogent world image, it necessarily conceived itself as more, as a vast, seamless texture of information, a world-embracing syntax that is meaningful only because it cannot communicate with all parts of itself at the same time and, so, must defer its awareness of the total logic on behalf of the absorbing parts, thus creating history. The metaphysical subject that was called into existence by renaissance humanism and codified in methodology was the necessary site for the construction of a world ideally suited to that subject's own self-understanding. Like Descartes, Hegel approached his work in the spirit of humanism, but Hegel had discovered the lesson of the metaphysical poets, that at some degree of abstraction any two things are identical and at some degree of abstraction any two things are different; moreover, the choice of abstraction is, at least within limits, open. Hegel revealed this occult knowledge of the new poetry and systematized it. Just as one order of poetry came to the end with Plato, another order of poetry came to the end with Hegel. To be sure, the old poetry has been carried on by the academy. The ideal self that Cartesian modernism required is produced as a luxury, and it is this silly figure that creative-writing workshops and most criticism of poetry cultivates and sentimentalizes. We are still living out the consequences of this dispersion.

In the closing passionate pages of *Phenomenology,* Hegel writes of history as presenting "a slow-moving succession of Spirits, a gallery of moving images, each of which, endowed with all the riches of Spirit, moves thus slowly just because the Self has to penetrate and digest this entire wealth of substance" (Hegel, 1975, 492). This ecstatic attention concentrates the history of Spirit in summation in a moment of satisfied self-awareness. Before Hegel's time, one finds records of the absolute Spirit felt and symbolized or seen and presented to passive contemplation: that is the aesthetic prehistory of absolute knowledge. Hegel, however, is just beyond, as he says, the passage "over from the poetry of the imagination to the prose of thought" (Hegel, 1975a, 1:89). The ecstasy is not frenzy, nor is Hegel transfixed in contemplation. The images pass slowly, and, while they might be alluded to imaginatively, as symbols, here they are thinkable and thought. In the *Aesthetik,* Hegel describes the disappearance of the epic world in which life is the practice of forms thoroughly integrated with themselves. Of the "world of prose" that follows the epoch of poetry, he writes:

> the individual is no longer able to maintain that appearance of autonomous and complete vitality and freedom which is the very foundation of the notion of beauty. It is true that neither system nor a totality of activities are lacking in the immediate human reality and in the undertakings and institutions of the latter; yet

> that whole is but an aggregate of individualities, its occupations and activities are split and fragmented into innumerable parts, so that only tiny particles of the whole fall to various individuals. (Hegel, 1975, 1, 89–90)

Reality is particle-ized, atomized. The unity of finite objects with the finite space in which it is measured is broken. Prose mediates the ideality of mathematical analysis and the ideality of normative measure in poetry and music, retaining the ideal forms without the ideal content. Hegel reveals the career of reason. Thereafter, the *rational* structure of history (as distinct from its contingent procession of events) holds no more surprises; it is the structure of logic itself. He investigates the mechanism of thought, not like Kant to seek a guarantee of its adequacy, but as offering direct access to knowledge itself. Thereafter, the medium is the absolute (a paradox in itself). We have replaced the Parmenidean problem of not being able to begin, with the Hegelian problem of not being able to stop.

Ludwig Wittgenstein writes: "One thinks that one is tracing the outline of the thing's nature over and over again, and one is merely tracing the frame through which we look at it" (Wittgenstein, 1953, 48). To a certain extent this confusion is common to all philosophic thought, but in the nineteenth century, there was a widespread determination to *inhabit* the frame, which proved in large measure to be both inhabitable and malleable. Hegel provided a logic by which these repetitions, tracing and retracing the outlines of things, develop a rich internal texture and appear to gain reality. The production of the Hegelian cinema became the central cultural project.

Symbolic History is not time but the ratio of an event to a specified context that is theoretically rule-governed. History is theorized as as sequence of events playing against a stable background of epochal rules. It was Hegel's discovery that any set of rules that is complex enough to account for the sequence of events is infinitely generative. To act at all in such a context is to overwhelm the finite. For Napoleon such exaggerated drama was possible; by 1848, it was not. Thereafter, the attractions of synthesis, which reconciled so much and achieved so little, diminished: science became increasingly a series of nonphilosophic procedures for predicting and controlling phenomena, and the remainder of philosophy attached itself to a psychology, sometimes in the name of nationalism or education of the masses or entertainment. It is the poetics of the production of posthistorical history, this altogether *uncommon* production, which replaced poetic production, that we consider in this chapter.

"Betwixt Unity and Number"

David Hume had shown that the split in Cartesianism that separates intuition and the logic of language cannot be overcome. Making specific reference to Descartes's test of clearness and distinctness, he argues:

> 'tis a principle generally receiv'd in philosophy, that every thing in nature is individual, and that 'tis utterly absurd to suppose a triangle really existent, which has no precise proportion of sides and angles. If this therefore be absurd in *fact and reality*, it must also be absurd *in idea;* since nothing of which we can form a clear and distinct idea is absurd and impossible. . . Now as 'tis impossible to form an idea of an object, that is possest of quantity and quality, and yet is possest of no precise degree of either; it follows, that there is an equal impossibility of forming an idea, that is not limited and confin'd in both these particulars. (Hume, 1978, 20)

In a sense, this is merely the oldest philosophic problem: all stones, for example, are of a certain weight and color, but the *idea* of stone is neither heavy nor light, red nor black. The specificity of intuition and the generality of the logic of language are in themselves irreconcilable. The intuition discovers unitary objects and the language requires classes which refer to innumerable objects. From the ideas of unity and number, thus supplied, however, it impossible to arrive at the idea of identity, by which, for example, one can be assured of an object's identity with itself through time. What is required is a medium—a third realm—"betwixt unity and number," as Hume says, through which the things of the world and their representations can be conjoined. The subsequent history of philosophy is characterized by the quest not for a foundational premise but for a foundational medium, which Hume argues must be, in effect, a medium "betwixt existence and non-existence," which is to say a purely imaginary place, according to his account, produced by the inertia of custom.

With respect to the imagination, Kant, a solid man of the Enlightenment, must have known that he was on dangerous grounds; all right-thinking men despised the imagination as the generator of chimeras and madness. In *Critique of Pure Reason*, in his attempt to respond to Hume, however, he takes the imagination into the house of metaphysics and gives it a place of such privilege that it is almost beyond criticism. The imagination is the associative principle, which first atomizes the continuous flow of pure intuition and reassociates the atoms into discrete representations. It is the imagination that mediates betwixt unity and number, between existence and nonexistence. It therefore designates a site for the origin of language, but it does not explain it, except by way of transcendental conflict. Kant writes: "A pure imagination, which conditions all *a priori* knowledge, is thus one of the fundamental faculties of the human soul. By its means we bring the manifold of intuition on the one side, into connection with the condition of the necessary unity of pure apperception on the other" (Kant, 1965, 146). To this day, philosophy looks for the medium which unites the seamless web of intuition with the discrete objects of grammar and logic. The history of the past two centuries of thought is strewn with theories of the medium: Fichte's ego, Hegel's history, Marx's labor, Schopenhauer's will, Nietzsche's recurrence, Freud's (very different) ego, Peirce's signs, Russell's logical atoms, Heidegger's Being, Jung's archetypes, Jakobson's and Turbetzkoy's phonemes, Levi-Strauss's structures, Lacan's signifying chains, or Derrida's *différance*. Behind all of these, as contradictory as they are, is the Kantian conviction that the imaginative medium must *somehow* produce its own content either in relation to a specifiable subset of the medium—a *logos*—or in relation to the extensive medium itself.

This fundamental argument in *Critique of Pure Reason* has been adequately explained a thousand times and is the philosophic property of everyone who ever took a beginning philosophy course, but we must examine it again in an attempt to understand its remarkable resilience, especially among literary critics where its—largely unconscious—influence continues almost unabated. The dependence of the argument upon a class of propositions that Kant exemplifies with Euclidean geometry must be made clear. As we shall see, the discovery of non-Euclidean geometry undermines not only the specific Kantian argument but also the entire class of arguments that proposes to derive knowledge of the world from knowledge of the linguistic media. The medium is no more a priori than the content.

Language is a kind of experience, of course, so it is not surprising that language and experience in general are confused, but Kant insists upon first radically separating and then rejoining them, making a fundamental gain in the process. At the outset, he notes that language experience is peculiar in that language can refer both to itself *and* to the contents of intuition—that is, it is a *possible* medium. However, statements that refer to language—"analytical judgments"—and statements that refer to intuitions—"synthetical judgments"—have notably different characters. The truth or falsity of analytical judgments can be determined inside language itself. A classic example is "All bachelors are unmarried." It is not necessary to examine any bachelors to know that this is true; it is a definition. And as Kant notes, "Through analytic judgements our knowledge is not in any way extended" (Kant, 1965, 29). The truth or falsity of synthetical judgments, on the other hand, depends upon conditions outside of language; that is, they actually say something about the world. The truth of the statement "the rose is red" can be determined only by *looking* at the rose. Such statements tell us about the world, but unfortunately we can never be completely certain of their truth. Our appeal to experience is never completely conclusive. The observation cannot be guaranteed to be correct. We are perhaps unwittingly observing the rose under a red light.

The question that arose for Kant took this form: Are there propositions that are logically necessary *and* applicable to experience, or, how are a priori, synthetic judgements possible? Kant adduces the theorems of Euclidean geometry as examples of a priori synthetic judgments. They seem to be readings from the medium betwixt unity and number itself: "That the straight line between two points is the shortest, is a synthetic proposition. For my concept of straight contains nothing of quantity, but only of quality. The concept of the shortest is wholly an addition, and cannot be derived, through any process of analysis, from the concept of the straight line. Intuition, therefore, must here be called in; only by its aid is the synthesis possible" (Kant, 1965, 53). In other words, the transcendental imagination itself produces the conditions by which its own spatial image is known, and, beyond establishing the general categories of thought, the primitive synthetic powers of the imagination are awesome. As it had once articulated the entire pantheon, prior to the advent of metaphysics, now it was to replicate its performance *in consciousness,* rather than in the dream-world alone. In order to accomplish this task, it would call the only highly developed technology of world construction that was available, the tradition of visionary poetry; the perennial vision was to be theorized.

The unity of life had never been so profoundly tested, nor had the self been required to bear such torque. The generation of philosophers who were the immediate heirs of Kant's work were at least in part aware of their theogonic task. What had been obscure in mythology was now to be recovered in the clear light of reason. Schelling writes: "As the mythologies and theogonies of primitive peoples anticipated modern science, so Böhme anticipated all scientific systems of modern philosophy in his description of the birth of God. . . Böhme is really a theogonic personality, but it was just this which prevented him form raising himself to free world-creation and just thereby to the freedom of positive philosophy" (Brown, 1977, quoted 274). Schelling, undertaking to rectify this situation himself, proclaims: "Mythology in general and any piece of mythological literature in particular is not to be understood schematically or allegorically, but symbolically. For the demand of absolute artistic representation is: representation with complete indifference, so that the universal is wholly the particular, and the particular at the same time wholly the universal, and does not simply mean it" (Schelling, 1989, 14). Schelling's claim that the particular is universal is, of course, mysticism and directly related to the mystical tradition which finds the *imago dei* in the finite world. It echoes the Augustine argument on the trinity and also the Socratic argument that physical love is an image of philosophic love. His literalism, however, is breathtaking. He makes no distinction between the image and the thing imagined, and his boldness has compelled nearly two centuries of aesthetic meditation. It is so commonplace that one is likely to miss the fact that it is, as presented, literally non-sense.

Hegel objects to Schelling's universal particular, and in the grand design of his works, he confronts aesthetic mysticism with scientific abstraction. The difference for Hegel, however, is only that the identity of the particular and the universal is deferred to the absolute. Otherwise, the pursuit of the universal remained tediously on the path of the wrong infinity.

Like his humanist predecessors, however, Hegel venerates Greek culture. Recognizing that the relationship between the ancients and the moderns is subject to historical development, however, he argues that, to continue the ancient impulse, it is necessary to articulate a contrary position or at least a position that is submerged by the ancient ontological enthusiasm. Like Descartes, he strategically deploys a dependence upon a continuous tradition which is fictive. Therefore, he turns away from the content of ancient philosophy—"the scientifically valueless myths," as he calls it—and concentrates on method. Unlike Descartes, Leibniz, and Spinoza, however, Hegel is not a mathematician, and he speaks disparagingly of the mathematical tradition in idealism. The Cartesian method, like the ancient philosophic myths, dwells excessively on mere content; it does not pursue its method *inwardly*, as Hegel says, to the interior conditions of its possibility. "In mathematical cognition," he writes, "insight is an activity external to the thing; it follows that the true thing is altered by it" (Hegel, 1977, 24). Unlike the Greeks and the first modernist philosophers, who were equally bowled over by the superficial power of the dramatic demonstrations of mathematical analysis, Hegel draws attention back to the common language, but a common language that has taken the ideal language up into itself. Philosophical cognition unites the external and internal moments:

> The inner coming-to-be or genesis of substance is an unbroken transition into outer existence, into being-for-another, and conversely, the genesis of existence is how existence is by itself taken back into essence. The movement is the twofold process and the genesis of the whole, in such wise that each side simultaneously posits the other, and each therefore has both perspectives within itself; together they thus constitute the whole by dissolving themselves, and by making themselves into its moments. (Hegel, 1977, 25)

In this mutual positing, substance is generated *ex nihilo*. In the beginning is not the Word but the medium, the language and its fully ramified infinitistic logic. In the drama of the *Phenomenology*, the terms of the Cartesian dualism are required to contend with one another, not in terms of mathematical formalism, but in terms of cultural history. Granted, Hegel's language here seems strained after the lucidity of Descartes, and this will continue to trouble our reading. The *Phenomenology* was written at white heat and perhaps carelessly, but after puzzling over passages one generally feels that there are reasons for the difficulties. Here Hegel explains how we get past the Parmenidean problem of beginning. The problem arises again clearly and urgently in the aftermath of the Cartesian compromise, when the ideal language turns back and undertakes to incorporate the metalanguage that made it possible. This turning back as a perpetual process, a beginning again in a space of having begun, is in effect language engorging itself, the modernist moment as such. About 1945, in the work of the cyberneticists and information theorists, it would lead to a theory that could deal with multiple variables without reference to an all embracing and infinitely deferred absolute. Hegel first signals the possibility of completely fluent abstraction, abstraction *as* abstraction, its own content.

Verkehrte Welt

The first three chapters of *Phenomenology* establish three loci in of Western epistemology: simple empiricism, simple idealism, and transcendental idealism. These positions can be identified with historical figures and philosophical movements, but the history of the Hegelian spirit and the actual history of philosophy coincide only in general terms. For Hegel, metaphoric ratios develop between ancient and modern philosophy and between the history of philosophy, thus folded into both itself and the individual consciousness. The perspective is never clear and can never be precisely clarified. The problem is not to determine some specific referent but to appreciate the metaphoric richness of any given locus in language.

In "Sense-Certainty: or The 'This' and 'Meaning,'" Hegel addresses the disjunction between experience and language, a problem that had twice previously pushed philosophy to the the crisis point in the thought of Parmenides and Hume. At the outset, Hegel rejects the Parmenidean ontological mysticism. The immediate and unspeakable intuition of "this-ness," he says, "proves itself to be the most abstract and poorest truth" (Hegel, 1977, 58). As he goes on to show, the "this" is called into existence by the requirements of language itself; conceived apart from language, it is empty, nothing at all. Hegel takes no interest in languageless meditation and the intuition of cosmic unity that is at the heart of the Parmenidean epic. Its poverty, according to him, is precisely that it cannot be spoken and cannot, therefore, become involved in the social conflict that is the motive of history itself. "What is called unutterable," Hegel writes, "is nothing else than the untrue, the irrational, what is merely meant [but not actually expressed]" (Hegel, 1977, 66).

Hegel confronts the full force of the Parmenidean logic squarely:

> It is as a universal too that we utter what the sensuous [content] is. What we say is: "This", i.e. the universal This; or, "it is", i.e. Being in general. Of course, we do not *envisage* the universal This or Being in general, but we utter the universal; in other words, we do not strictly say what in this sense-certainty we *mean* to say. But language, as we see, is the more truthful; in it, we ourselves directly refute what we mean to say, and since the universal is the true [content] of sense-certainty and language expresses this true [content] alone, it is just not possible for us ever to say, or express in words, a sensuous being that we mean. (Hegel, 1977, 60)

Even in the English translation the equivocation on "mean" in this passage is powerful. Its *meaning* in the first two uses (which may themselves have slightly different shadings) is different from its meaning in the final use. On the one hand, it means "intention" and, on the other, "reference." In the German, however, the polysemy is even more obvious. The verb *meinen* carries the force both of "meaning" and "of being of an opinion, of mere opinionating," and it also offers Hegel the opportunity to pun on *mein,* the possessive adjective (mine). The activity of meaning is the activity of taking possession. The certainty that was initially understood as a certainty of the thing itself is transferred in the dialectical process to the act of knowing: "[Sense-certainty's] truth is in the object as my object, or in its being mine [Meinen]; it is, because I know it" (Hegel, 1977, 61). The dialectic is a semantic machine that generates significance out of its own attempted possession of itself through the possession of language. This is the ego-infection of all discourse; ego takes possession of the language on behalf of opinion, on behalf of untruth, until the untruth or its "meaning"—that is, both personal opinion and general significance—is revealed.

The argument for the sufficiency of language is desperate, the only possible preserve of a culture that had lost the habits by which language is interpreted and must look to language to interpret itself. It imposes the solipsistic dilemma on the culture at large. Why, one wants to ask, is language "the more truthful"? One might well think of language in itself as neither truthful nor untruthful but as a colorless medium. Language, however, Hegel argues, has a self-correcting feature: "In it [language], we ourselves directly refute what we mean to say." And again, he speaks of language "which has the divine nature of directly reversing the meaning of what is said, of making it into something else" (Hegel, 1977, 66). That is, language is perpetually self-critical; it is like the Pentateuch, telling the story that establishes its own authority. If the discourse is universal, it cannot rest until it implicates all of language, and in the process of following its implications, it reveals the inadequacy of its originating tropes. Each turn (*trope* is etymologically "turn") offers a new perspective, and each perspective proves to be limited.

Unlike Hume, whose ultimate philosophic task was to justify the bourgeois decorum of mid-eighteenth-century England, Hegel could not fall back on stable social and linguistic conventions. Or perhaps one can say more accurately, that Hume's arguments have a different significance for times of social stability and times of dramatic social change. The bourgeois revolution was in the past for Hume's England, and its regime was comfortably established. The West has seldom known a society in which the conventions were so secure, sophisticated, and impeccably practiced. The language was supported by firmly entrenched and respected institutions—the preserve of a small, homogeneous ruling-class that had every confidence in its authority. And, of course, such a stability has never established itself again. By contrast, Hegel, according to tradition, was penning the final parts of *Phenomenology* almost literally as Napoleon marched into Jena. In such a time, what is the habit or convention to which Hume attributed all ontological and epistemological as well as social stability? Hegel was at the beginning of the epoch of the most dramatic change in human history. In the nineteenth century, we entered the epoch of changing change that features not only continual flux of phenomena but also constant revision of the entire intellectual context.

In the long run, however, it was neither revolution nor

Napoleonic adventurism but technology that disturbed the neo-classical complacency. The difference between a hand loom and a power loom was quantifiable and dramatic; under its impact, old ways of thinking about production and markets were outmoded. Time and change were immediate and undeniable experiences. The thing to be explained was not dead matter, which does not revise itself, but mind, which is constantly changing. By the time of Hegel, it appeared that changes of mind were not, as they had seemed to the neoclassicists, merely the vicissitudes of enthusiasm but inherent facts of a trial and error process that leads to definitive local improvements. Thomas Edison and Henry Ford were Hegelians in practical garb.

Hegel's argument cannot get fully underway until he begins the discussion of perception: "The wealth of sense-knowledge belongs to perception, not to immediate certainty, for it was only the source of instances; for only perception contains negation, that is, difference or manifoldness, within its own essence." Any particular thing is no sooner perceived as a thing—that is, as the bearer of a name and the representative of a class—than it involves the contradictions that motivate the dialectic. As particulars can never be more than provisionally accommodated by logical classes or "notions," as Hegel says, and vice versa, the categories must be in time ever more finely analyzed. Perception and the language of the conditioned universal, the universal that is always supplemented with a "this," or "here," or a "now," are the tools of the casual consciousness, the miasmal realm of everyday life in which deception lurks, according to Hegel, at every turn: "It is 'sound common sense' that is the prey of these abstractions, which spin it round and round in their whirling circle" (Hegel, 1977, 79). Consciousness is a representation that represents nothing but its own activity; it is at once instrument and medium. With the appearance of the unconditioned universal, consciousness breaks its relation with lazy existence and enters the realm of pure thought, thought that requires nothing but thought for its development. Philosophy is that mode of thought that learns from itself, as it were, from its own nervous tension. It tries to catch itself in the act of beginning. In its hall of mirrors, consciousness sees and sees itself see, and by comparing image to image, a space that has no property but comparison comes into existence. This logic is the common language equivalent to algebraic logic, and by its means an entire culture—

not just the initiates of mathematical analysis—makes the "leap into the beyond." This is the domain of phenomenology. Thus, the phenomena are already a medium, and the tension in it that drives the dialectic is mediation of this immediacy.

Unless we note that the Hegelian construction of the world takes place in a falsely and dangerously inflated aesthetic space, it will appear so rich and various, so full of promise, as to make one contemptuous of the meager world which the thinkers of the Enlightenment proudly inhabited. Hegel's morbid preoccupation with opinionating is symptomatic of a culture in a frenetic process of trial and error—feverish activity arising from the infection of language by the ego in which *every* idea must be tested, every thought must be pushed to its conclusion, every mistake must be offered the redemption of meaning, in order to sustain a relatively stable situation in a culture which has no reliable truth, habits of mind, or conventions of social behavior. Such has been the intellectual landscape since about the time of the Napoleonic wars.

Force and Understanding

The powerful abstractions, which mathematical analysis made available to Descartes and Newton, had been used only to describe essentially static forces. In the third chapter of *Phenomenology*, "Force and the Understanding: Appearance and the Supersensible World," Hegel recognizes how comparable cognitive tools are applicable to a world that is manifestly dynamic and historical.

The Hegelian critique is addressed to concepts that had served as boundaries of subjectivity. Although Descartes had substituted relationships for measure of the image, he continued to conceive of the objects of thought as external to the logical categories of the subject, and the unconditioned universal, even as it appeared after the Copernican revolution which Kant claimed to have effected in philosophy, was still conceived as a *thing*, not the pure relationship that consciousness requires. In his critique of the Kantian notion, Hegel writes: "This unconditioned universal, which is now the true object of consciousness, is still just an object for it; consciousness has not yet grasped the Notion of the unconditioned as Notion. It is essential to distinguish the two: for consciousness, the object has returned into itself from its relation to an other and has thus become Notion in principle; but consciousness is not yet for itself the Notion, and consequently does not recognize itself in that reflected object" (Hegel, 1977, 75).

The stage of consciousness that Kant represents posits a world-constituting understanding but that understanding does not recognize itself in its creation. For Kant, like Descartes, the content is given by intuition, and the form is provided by concepts, by virtue of the synthesizing power of consciousness. Although the Kantian compromise answers the empiricist critique, consciousness is still estranged from its own creation. The Kantian mind cannot hold its creation in itself. Its own cognition cuts it off from its possibility of acting, at least in the profound sense that attracts Hegel, of following the consequences of knowledge to its boundless limits. The subject looks in the mirror and sees *something* but fails to recognize itself. It is stopped, as it were, at the mirror's surface. Kant does not take responsibility for the reflection; otherwise the terms of the antinomies would appear in the same space and the elegant order of the Newtonian picture would crumble. The Kantian compromise left the problem of interaction between mind and body not much beyond the Cartesian impasse. "Consciousness plays no part in its free realization," Hegel writes, "but merely looks on and simply apprehends it" (Hegel, 1977, 80). Its world-constituting activity is limited to the imagination of a static world that excludes the dynamism of its own action.

The move that Hegel makes is one of the boldest, even one of the most outrageous, moves in the philosophic literature. Fichtean egotism was grandiose, but it was controverted by the actual experience of will. The world-constituting subject is never free of itself; it engenders its own resistance. Hegel takes this division of the world and this resistance into consciousness itself: "To begin with, therefore, we must step into its place [i.e., the place of the constituted object] and be the Notion which develops and fills out what is contained in the result. It is through awareness of this completely developed object, which presents itself to consciousness as something that immediately is that consciousness first becomes explicitly a consciousness that comprehends [its object]" (Hegel, 1977, 80). This step initiates an infinite regress, inside of which Hegel discovers the whole of history from the perspective of the end of history. The absolute antitheses are posited as identical: in their infinite extensions, subject and object, general and particular, are the same—that is, notions of consciousness.

Kant had developed an elaborate dualism to avoid this conclusion. In Hegel, however, the drive to monism is rampant and imperial: all content is dissolved into the form, the solvent of form. To posit the identity of subject and object is to posit the absolute as a potential of consciousness. The paradise within, by which the seventeenth century sought to repair damaged reason, was now to be imposed on the world. At this moment of posited unity, all being becomes metaphorical in relation to the unity of language, and consciousness has intimations of the absolute, albeit a "poor" absolute, articulable, but not yet articulated. It can be attained only in more and more audacious appropriations of the world to language (or language to the world). This is the Faustian consciousness or the Promethean consciousness perhaps, but the Faust who has internalized his Mephistopheles or the Prometheus who has internalized his eagle.

Here one finds the first fully articulated exposition of the scaleless, parodic world replica that the West still inhabits. In this crucial and difficult passage of argument, Hegel first descries the *verkehrte Welt*. The term is usually translated into English by "inverted," but it implies a whacky inversion. In the strongest sense, *verkehrte* can be translated as "perverted." This term has proven more troubling for Hegel's commentators than perhaps it should. Hans-Georg Gadamer usefully orients us to the term with reference to the satiric tradition. The "up-right" world calls forth its own parodic image, and from any finite perspective, the world is more or less grotesque, a series of replicas of which there is no original (Gadamer, 1976, 7–24). In truth, however, the *verkehrte Welt* is as old and as well known as the philosophic world itself: it is the world of the paradoxes that every attempt to be rational engenders; it was known to Parmenides, Heraclitus, Zeno, and Gorgias; to Proclus, Tertullian, and Ficino; to Rabelais, Erasmus, and John Donne. Rosalie Colie's great *Paradoxia Epidemica* (Colie, 1966), while focusing on the renaissance, is an exposition of the tradition of the topsy-turvy world from Parmenides to Bertrand Russell, and outlines the range of cognition with which an inclusive phenomenology of mind must in fact contend. In taking responsibility for both the unconditioned universal and the self *in* the unconditioned universal, the Hegelian consciousness enters the profoundly paradoxical space of self-reference. Some version of the liar's paradox colors the very beginnings of historical process.

The *verkehrte Welt* is "the Notion of the unconditioned as Notion," the world as pure contentless relationship. If every proposition is true, at least inchoately true, every proposition is also false. Modernist philosopher after modernist philosopher had proposed the identity of being and language, only to be derailed by the paradoxes. Hegel undertakes the sublation of the paradoxes themselves.

This act, which must be seen as profound aggression, sets us on the dialectical and historical path: "The onset of the new spirit is product of a widespread upheaval in various forms of culture, the prize at the end of a complicated, tortuous path and of just as variegated and strenuous an effort" (Hegel, 1977, 7). Hegel realizes, however, that this first seizure represents a new world only in its startling immediacy, an unstable moment of will, a moment of madness or Bacchic transcendence that is soon negated by the thing itself, causality, or physical law. Just as the excitement of political seizure gives way to the boredom of imperial administration, the excitement of ontological seizure gives way to the boredom of argument. The metaphoric relations are such that it makes only temporary sense to ask whether we are speaking here of politics or ontology. Without equivocation, Hegel asserts that the answer is both: "the 'matters' posited as independent directly pass over into their unity, and their unity directly unfolds its diversity, and this once again reduces itself to unity" (Hegel, 1977, 80). The generality of this thinking, the inclusiveness of "matters," makes illustration superfluous and essentially impossible. Whether we speak of some irreducible atomic event of consciousness or the apprehension of the absolute, the movement is the same: knowledge for the Hegelian consciousness is to dismiss the boundary between consciousness and other. The experience of this reduction, this moment of appropriation, is the initial experience of force.

The larger part of chapter 3 of *Phenomenology* is devoted to Hegel's analysis of force. From the time of Galileo and Descartes until the early years of this century, force was an important notion both in physics and in quasi-scientific philosophy. Transformed into notions of will and desire, it continues to exercise a largely unconscious role in our language and thought. Force is one of the central tropes of the modern West. From the beginning, however, as Leibniz recognized, force was the Achilles heel for Newtonian interpretation of physics. Hegel takes it in the broadest possible sense, and, at the very beginning of the century in which the notion was to function as an ultimate appeal of scientific rhetoric, shows both that force binds the knowledge-guaranteeing ego together with the rarefied world that mathematical physics describes *and* that it is a relatively empty concept. It first appears as the inner-ness of both percipient and perceived, the primitive energy of rea-son, which overwhelms the content of thought to reveal its rational structure. In its kinetic manifestation (Hegel calls it the "expres-sion" of force), it is consciousness; in its potential manifestation ("force proper"), it is the supersensible world. As expression, force is known as "given-ness," intuition, and content; in its proper being, it is known as concept, understanding, and form. However, "the truth of Force remains only the thought of it;" Hegel writes, "the moments of its actuality, their substances and their move-ment, collapse unresistingly into an undifferentiated unity, a unity which is not Force driven back into itself (for this is itself only such a moment), but is its Notion qua Notion. Thus the realization of Force is at the same time the loss of reality" (Hegel, 1977, 86).

Simple force at its most abstract is the poorest grade of con-sciousness. It establishes little more than the possibility of thought, the first vague stirring of the intellectual ego and the conditions that make understanding possible. These terms are still too closely related to simple dualism to be of much real use to Hegel's most characteristic modes of thought. "Noumena" and "phenomena" as moments of force are fleeting and insubstantial:

> consciousness has a mediated relation to the inner being, and, as the Understanding, looks through this mediating play of Forces into the true background of Things. The middle term which unites the two extremes, the Understanding and the inner world, is the developed being of Force which, for the Understanding itself, is henceforth only a vanishing. This "being" is therefore called appearance; for we call being that is directly and in its own self a non-being a surface show. But it is not merely a surface show; it is appearance, a totality of show. (Hegel, 1977, 87)

This "totality of show" is a rich arena of possibilities, inhab-ited by entities in that identity and nonidentity are tentatively rec-onciled. These entities—portions of conceptual mush in which universal and particular are united—are commonly known to us as the images of romantic poetry. When they vanish, like the airy sprites which they are, they invoke a supersensible world, but their interiors are still completely undeveloped and vacuous. Unlike the more credulous transcendentalist poets and even Kant himself, Hegel recognizes that these figures beckon to an interior that is empty, not to "the holy of holies," Hegel says, recalling a phrase of Kant's. Admitting, however, that "there may yet be something" in that place of the supersensible, he opines it is best to hold the space open: "we must fill it up with reveries, appearances produced by consciousness itself. It would have to be content with being treated so badly for it would not deserve anything better, since even reveries are better than its own emptiness" (Hegel, 1977, 89). For Hegel and subsequent bourgeois culture, this is the place of both art and the psychological unconscious, the domain, as we now know, of the postmodern simulacra.

The supersensible world, the world to which Kant assigned the freedom of both man and god, proves then to be mere appearance. It is abstraction or potential, imagined in the name of natural law, which Hegel defines as "the stable image of unstable appearance" (Hegel, 1977, 90). The law as a law of consciousness represents a higher grade of reality than the mere posited supersensibility for which it stands. The tension that is expressed in the stability of instability, however, bespeaks the opposite of law—that is to say, tranquilized change, the presence in the law of the multifarious, particular, and deviant cases that it mirrors. Such law, Hegel says, "does not fill out the world of appearances." It is the shrunken head, the desiccated thing left over, when the living body has been expressed as law. Despite its superior potential, consciousness has still not attained even the reality of the mere appearances that it describes. Consequently, the account of experience in terms of one law must invoke others: to explain the fall of a feather by the law of gravity also requires the laws of aerodynamics, and so forth. So the possibility of a law of law arises, but the universal law must explain such totally different kinds of content that the sense of law as such is lost. "The unification of all laws in universal attraction expresses no other content than just the mere Notion of law itself, which is posited in that law is the form of being. Universal attraction merely asserts that everything has a constant difference in relation to other things" (Hegel, 1977, 91). It must include itself and must, therefore, assert its own difference from itself. The laws of physics, for example, are merely the objective moments of the reveries with which we fill the supersensible emptiness. The flux of appearance is art, the stability of appearance is law. Hegel puts the ideal world of physical law and the ideal subject of poetry into dialectical opposition and enters the world of a prose that subsumes everything in its unmeasured abstractions.

The Final Triumph of Humanism

The last half of chapter three of *Phenomenology*, in which the turn to pure abstraction transpires, has occasioned remarkably little commentary. Since it is here that Hegel speaks of the necessity to think pure change and of the inverted world, it has not been utterly ignored, of course, but perhaps now we can see that in this nearly impenetrable passage of dialectic that some of Hegel's most radical and prophetic thinking occurs. He envisions a world in which resistant actuality turns plastic before human consciousness. If there is to be a world of spirit at all, it must be created; human creativity, though never free of its own requirements, is absolute. It is here that the Nietzchean willing of will is prepared. We dwell with Hegel in this prolonged moment of spiritual excitement. We await the appearance of the absolute, and, in our confused babble, we think it may be Napoleon or nuclear weapons, or man or "the closure of metaphysics." At certain moments of crisis, this egoic infection still rages in our institutions.

If, as I suggested earlier, the ancient theogonies are recapitulated in consciousness by modern idealism, Hegel here discovers the intellectual equivalent of the omphallos, the point of world origin. The argument becomes increasingly difficult to paraphrase, not only because it is dense (which it is), but also because, one suspects, Hegel is trying to follow the dialectic through a passage, which seems to him significant, indeed the core itself of the intellectual tradition that he inherited, but that proves to be a dialectical dead-end. Although he clearly sees the conclusion, he is as puzzled by this dialectic complication as we are. To say the least, there is a passage of argumentation that leads from the first sighting of Force, expressing itself and being repressed into itself, to the discovery of the fully developed notion of Force, that seems frankly garbled. The Hegelian discourse rarely feels so tenuous. The conclusion, which only in our own time has returned so clearly to focus, is startling and threatens to bring the dialectic to a stop.

Hegel discovers that law is a mere tautology; it is completely lacking dialectical tension: "A law is enunciated; from this, its implicitly universal element or ground is distinguished as Force; but it is said that this difference is no difference, rather that the ground is constituted exactly the same as the law" (Hegel, 1977, 94). Such is the stability of the Newtonian world: "It is an explanation that not only explains nothing, but is so plain that, while it pretends to say something different from what has already been said, really says nothing at all but only repeats the same thing" (Hegel, 1977, 95). One might say that precisely that is its advantage: from the point of view of the Enlightenment, an explanation that changed the thing explained would have been no explanation at all. Hegel, however, recognizes that the Understanding at this point is little richer than the sense certainty and perception that it supersedes. If sense certainty consists of meaningless, indescribable change and perception of self-contradictory common sense, law is static, and it omits the larger part of the world which interests us. It fails to account not only for history but also for most kinds of individual variation: Hegel notes, "the law by which a stone falls, and the law by which the heavenly bodies move, have been grasped as one law. But when the laws thus coincide, they lose their specific character" (Hegel, 1977, 91). The question, which we have already raised in the context of Cartesian method, is, How does the translation into the language of law overcome individual variation—in short, what happens to difference? Hegel is completely lucid concerning this intellectual sleight of hand: "the difference . . . is posited by the Understanding in such a way that, at the same time, it is expressly stated that the difference is not a difference belonging to the thing itself" (Hegel, 1977, 94). Difference is stowed away in the understanding in order to clarify appearances.

If the law of appearances is that "everything has a constant difference in relation to other things," what then is the law of the Understanding? It must account for the stability of law, and, in order to do so, it must take flux into itself. It absorbs difference and converts it into cultural activity, on the one hand, and revises the law, on the other. Hegel states its law thus: "like becomes unlike and unlike becomes like" (Hegel, 1977, 96). This is the law of the "inverted" world:

> Through this principle, the first supersensible world, the tranquil kingdom of laws, the immediate copy of the perceived world, is

changed into its opposite. . . This second supersensible world is in this way the inverted world and, moreover, since one aspect is already present in the first supersensible world, the inversion of the first. . . According, then, to the law of this inverted world, what is like in the first world is unlike to itself, and what is unlike in the first world is equally unlike to itself, or it becomes like itself. (Hegel, 1977, 97)

Thus, the grounds for a progressive history is established. The Understanding has access both to the "tranquil kingdom of laws" and the utterly anarchic kingdom of difference. The requirements of this knowledge are more rigorous than any humankind had ever been asked to endure. If the intellectual discipline, which over several millennia had taught humankind to think, consistently had been harsh, Hegel demands that "We have to think pure change, or think antithesis within the antithesis itself, or contradiction. For in the difference which is an inner difference, the opposite is not merely one of two—if it were, it would simply be, without being an opposite—but it is the opposite of an opposite, or the other is itself immediately present in it" (Hegel, 1977, 99). The Cartesian double dualism is made explicit and shown to be, after all, unified in Understanding. The trace of dualism, however, is maintained in the involvement of Understanding in two infinite regresses, one that is static and forever approaching motion, one that is in motion and forever approaching stasis. Hegel calls them "simple infinity" and "Infinity, or this absolute unrest or pure self-movement," and it is capital-I Infinity that is the "soul of all that has gone before" (Hegel, 1977, 100–101). The chief activity of Infinity, even in the most self-contained appearance, is self-explanation or self-consciousness. In the dialectic, true knowledge only appears with the necessity to explain the failure of law; in fact, only then does self-consciousness or the grounds of true knowledge come into existence. When consciousness discovers itself, it finds that all along there has been nothing else; it is merely the site of a paradox, a topsy-turvy world, that endlessly explains itself to itself. It functions both to elicit thought and to frustrate thought. On the one hand, we contemplate the empty interior: "It is manifest that behind the so-called curtain which is supposed to conceal the inner world, there is nothing to be seen unless we go behind it ourselves, as much in order that we may see, as that there may be something behind there which can be seen" (Hegel, 1977, 103). This is the point in the modern bacchanal when the god enters the dancers. It is not the god that discovered wine, however, but a god that promises wine at the infinitely deferred conclusion of the explanation. The new Bacchus is the god of heady talk; the new Venus is the goddess of intellectual coitus interuptus; the new Hephaestus is the creator of technological expediencies. On the other hand, we enter into the experience of discipline, of mastery, of being a slave and a student. Consciousness must be mastered from without or from the appearance of without, which of course proves to be from within. All knowledge is disciplined knowledge, spanked knowledge, arising only from the experience of Force, and all knowledge is therefore perspectival. In all knowledge there is a suggestion of something militant, if not positively military.

The Tedium of the Absolute

In Hegel, the vestiges of the old mimetic logic, which created logical models or metaphors by imposing a single perspective on extant states of affairs, gave way to irony—that is, a knowledge of change without measure. The ironic consciousness knows no boundaries because it knows only a theoretical space and time, which it constantly undermines. The definitive quality of Hegel's thought, despite his intentions, is novelistic, not dramatistic. The novel is the preeminent ironic genre. We feel that the story is known to the narrator (however murky a figure he may be) before the story begins. The pleasure of reading a novel has to do largely with the feeling that logic and phenomena are *already* assimilated to one another; they are already aspects of psychology. The novel furnishes solipsism with all of the richness of an actual world. Perhaps the social function of the novel was, in part, to break down the feeling of conflict between the form and content of the world. Such, at least, is the effect of Hegelian narrative logic: time appears not as the source of unexpectedness and freshness but as history that is virtually past but, at the same time, to be constructed. The only access to change that the logical tradition offers is change that is already completed. The perpetual ascendancy into the absolute is the final gathering of the world into the infinite and infinitely forgiving narrative.

The novel, of course, was one of the first mass-produced consumer products, and its cognate philosophy of history was a response to an experience of time generated by technology. Under the impact of the industrial revolution, the rate of historical change increased to the extent that acceleration could be experienced in the space of one generation. Hegel did his best to account for this experience in light of traditional logic, but he could only explain change by imagining himself at the end of history. Now we know that he was at the beginning of world-revising change and that his logic was a last desperate attempt to save a ghost of the Parmenidean unchanging object of knowledge. The mechanical time of the seventeenth-century poets gave way to the time of the newspapers, the periodicals, the serial novels, the histories and histories of histories in the nineteenth century and then to the movies and television in this century. The conflict between time and performance was sublated in abstract rhythm or, I would suggest as a more accurate term, in "historicized temporality." Hegel explicitly recognizes the relation of poetic time to historical time:

> This conflict between the general form of a proposition and the unity of the Notion which destroys it is similar to the conflict that occurs in rhythm between metre and accent. Rhythm results from the floating centre and the unification of the two. So, too, in the philosophical proposition the identification of Subject and Predicate is not meant to destroy the difference between them, which the form of the proposition expresses; their unity, rather, is meant to emerge as a harmony. (Hegel, 1977, 38)

Time as a floating center, a kind of balloon or aesthetic spaceship, is central to the experience of history which appeared with the bourgeois revolutions. As we have seen, the institution of iambic pentameter as the mark of serious poetry in English was in effect a commitment to a mode of temporality which ties subjectivity to history. This linear logic is a formal reflection of the Hegelian merging of subject and predicate. In one of its dimensions, the ego has access to the enfolding and productive generality of the dialectic. In the free metrical substitutions, which marks the verse practice of the great romantics, time becomes utterly plastic. It is *theoretical* time, as much a construction of methodology as the Cartesian space—an idealized dimension of action to correspond to the idealized space of understanding. As a result, however, time appears as private, and it is a strict dependency of the will. Thereafter solipsism was isolation in private time as well as private space.

In the new synthesis, time and its objects are eradicated and then recreated in the artistic-aesthetic domain. Hegel is probably thinking of the some of the soaring passages in Hölderlin, who was the German master of this moment when the new poetry at once achieved its potential and exceeded it. It is here, at this pinnacle of poetic excitement, that it gives way to the prose of thought. Hegel could have been thinking of these lines in Hölderlin's "Brot und Wein" that both describe and enact the synthetic harmony:

> Fest bleibt Eins; es sei um Mittag oder es gehe
>   Bis in die Mitternacht, immer bestehet ein Maas,
> Allen gemein, doch jeglichem auch ist eignes beschieden,
>   Dahin gehet und kommt jeder, wohin er es kann.

> One thing is sure even now: at noon or just before midnight,
>   Whether it's early or late, always a measure exists,
> Common to all, though his own to each one is also allotted,
>   Each of us makes for the place, reaches the place that he can.
>   (Hölderlin, 1961, 244–45)

Hölderlin lacked the powerful bourgeois tradition of the French and especially the English, and his metrical practice is much more theoretical than that of his contemporaries. When Longfellow wrote in classical meters, it was an academic performance: Like Coleridge's return to accentual verse, it was an indication that rigorous iambics were already losing their hold on Anglo-American tongues. For Hölderlin, however, the attempt to adapt classical meters to the German language—the rhythms of which, based on accent rather than quantity, are wholly inappropriate—represented a move into a higher degree of abstraction. Hölderlin's skillful simulation of classical elegaics in the poem is to a certain extent mechanical. Unlike the pentameter norm of so much English and German verse, for example, Hölderlin invokes a norm that has no hearable relationship to the performance of the lines. Of course, like Ezra Pound in some of the recorded readings, he may have stylized the German in order to imitate classical meters in his own performance of the verse, but it seems unlikely, as it would have obscured the relationship between accent and meaning. It is, moreover, this distance between the measure common to all and the proper measure allotted to each one that is, in effect, the theme of the poem. The destitution of modernity, the destitution of the time that the gods have deserted, is marked by a language that disjoins the common time and the individual time.

That he manages, inside these rigorous constraints, to maintain a rhythmic coherence—using devices that are irrelevant to the theoretical scheme—is of course remarkable. I know of nothing that establishes the characteristic tone of elegaic modernism any earlier. It is the tone, for example, of the closing pages of the *Phenomenology*, the pervasive tone of music for the larger part of nineteenth century, quintessentially developed in Wagner, the tone of Victorian poetry; in more desperate configurations, it is the tone of T. S. Eliot and the tone of half of Ezra Pound (or half of the tone of *all* of Ezra Pound), of Stravinsky, the neoromantics in American music and the neoformalists in American poetry. Elegaic production is, in a sense, production that does not produce. From Hölderlin to the latest popular elegaic critic of the tradition—I could refer to many of the illustrious critics whose prophetic voices are collected in Ralph Cohen's *The Future of Literary Criticism* (Cohen, 1989)—history can be conducted only in terms of abstract temporality, a ratio of time to times: the present is divided by some incommensurable other historical token, Hölderlin by Pindar, Browning by Sordello, Pound by Homer, and so forth. History, rather than producing, has offered itself up to perpetual self-immolation. It pushes Zeno's paradoxes to absurd completion: Zeno's arrow both does and does not reach it target; the tortoise both does and does not outrun the hare. From the perspective of the absolute to which logic finally gives us access, these are not contradictory states of affairs.

Hegel's reintroduction of time and the possibility of meaningful change was a relief from the timeless worlds of the mathematicized cosmos; it is no doubt Hegel's redemption of the Cartesian ego from empty eternity that makes him the central thinker of the nineteenth century. The way in which Hegel reintroduces time, however, keeps thought completely in the Cartesian orbit. Hegelian time is time merely to be overcome. Its history is the education of the spirit into temporality, and it is an education for temporal Napoleons, who would overwhelm time as well as space. Hegel writes, "Spirit necessarily appears in Time, and it appears in Time just so long as it has not grasped it pure Notion; i.e. has not annulled Time" (Hegel, 1977, 487). The transformation of Spirit that transpires in the closing pages of *Phenomenology* is terrifying in its arrogance, which turns on the Kantian categories and reappropriates them as merely subjective. The Spirit recoils at the emptiness of mere abstraction and proposes to itself the *utility* of its absolute freedom. This moment is, for Hegel, the passage from the contemplative life of the religious community to the active life of the Self as pure Notion in History. It is with great zest that he portrays the subsequent pathology: "Not until consciousness has given up all hope of overcoming that alienation in an external, i.e. alien, manner does it turn into self-consciousness; not until then does it turn to its own present world and discover it as its property, thus taking the first steps toward coming down out of the *intellectual world,* or rather towards quickening the abstract element of that world with the actual Self" (Hegel, 1977, 488).

This is the entrance of the despair that is the way of the Spirit into the concrete world. That is, the infinite regress by which Spirit generates the dynamism of its intellectual world is transferred to the material culture. Toward the end of the nineteenth century, the imagination, which quickened "the abstract element of that world with the actual Self," developed an astounding fluidity. It could model one world as well as another. The artifice of Mallarmé or Huysman's elaborate interiors forecast the shopping mall and video pleasure dome. To note only one salient example of this unanchored terminology, Nietzsche takes melodrama (and Zarathustra is no less melodrama than the popular theatrical fare of the later nineteenth century) to the limit of romantic artifice and beyond, where truth and untruth, genuine emotion and sentimentality, are indistinguishable from one another. In one of the strangest inversions in the work of this man who made a habit of turning everything upside down, melodrama becomes comedy.

Comedy has always seemed a secondary art because it cannot properly take place in the theater. It begins as ritual—Hegel tells us—but it ends as an orgy in which everyone, ritual celebrants and audience, participates. It reveals its medium. All of the latent possibilities, all that has been masked by sanity or taste, are manifested. Of the comedian, Hegel writes: "the actual self of the actor coincides with what he impersonates, just as the spectator is completely at home in the drama performed before him and sees himself playing it." Comedy begins by donning the masks and ends by taking them off. "What this [comedic] self-consciousness beholds is that whatever assumes the form of essentiality over against it," Hegel goes on to say, "is instead dissolved in it—in its thinking, its existence, and its action—and is at its mercy" (Hegel, 1977, 452). To be sure all essentiality melts away. And have we not been constantly playing out this comedy, essentiality melting like flesh, in wars and death camps? We laugh the philosophic laugh—the bacchanalian laugh at Golgotha (these are the terms of the Hegelian irony). Now we must begin to wonder if we can stop laughing, or if we are condemned to the howling, mad laughter which echoes through the theaters, where we are both players and audience, convulsively and endlessly. Is it possible, at this foremost stage of art, as Hegel reckons it, to find life other than a collection of stories from a sado-masochistic *Mad* magazine?

In tragedy, there is a cosmic order. The theater itself is a theory, an *imago mundi*—Shakespeare's Globe, for example, which foregrounds the essence against a background of accident, meaning against a background of mere information. Comedy destroys the essence; life appears utterly flat; it manifests not necessity but possibility. In the spirit of Hegelian comedy, Artaud invokes the spectacle of cruelty and terror in which the assault of the permutative universe is revealed. The telling of the possibilities is the telling of the medium itself and the mediation of the individuals and events which inhabit it. This is the crisis of the Cartesian self, the recognition that it can be identical to itself only by comprehending all of the possibilities of its medium; that is to say by comprehending the Unconscious—the cruel deity of this closing epoch of transition, an uncanny Trickster, which (who?) manifests only in occasional glimpses, never leaving a reliable trace.

The dialectic leads to no new knowledge. The thoughts that arise in self reflection are neither "higher" nor more compelling in any other sense than the thought that arises from the most objective observation. The autoerotic satisfaction of Hegelian logic takes its rise in the thoughts, "I am not quite I," and "I will be I" (it is very close to Freud). We have poured a world replica into the space between these thoughts. We cannot just turn from its falseness: it is replicated in steel, concrete, and electronic circuitry. The replica is very like the world, but fashioned from a simplistic logic, nothing fits very well. In order to sustain itself at all, it must grow wildly, trying to repair the system that was so poorly made in the first place in the process, so it gets tired, and wants to die even in its most exuberant attempts to live.

Hegel wrote the lives of heroic figures, of emperors and imperial philosophers (of which Hegel himself may be the only adequate example) into the static cosmos. The dialectic objectifies the ego or subjectivizes history—locating things in the Hegelian world is always problematic—thus producing a normative society. For those who do not constantly rehearse the whole of history in deeds or thoughts, however, time is still an empty accumulation, and few have the confidence of absolute knowledge. Post-Hegelian thought found itself dealing with spiritual disaster on an ever greater scale. In time the dialectic runs its course from clarity to irony and then to something like schizophrenia. In moments of crisis, Hegelian logic can neither specify a contradiction nor maintain an identity; it cannot define subject and object or internal and external, so they remain distinct, as, later, Freud, following in Hegel's footsteps, cannot distinguish between life and death. Hegel gutted logic. He left the classic science in such an impoverished state that even the most general distinctions were empty and their terms interchangeable.

The End of History

Sometime in the middle of the nineteenth century, the relationship between abstraction and practical life was transformed. The distinction between idealism and materialism lost its force, and, while it carried great *emotional* resonance, because it was associated with questions surrounding the breakup of traditional religious faith, technology replaced ideology as the grounds of mediation. This change was announced by the *Communist Manifesto* and in the revolutions of 1848. That the popular revolts were quickly put down and the old regimes restored indicates only that it was not primarily a political change. The narrative of human purposiveness was grafted to the mechanistic and deterministic stock of Newtonianism. This view is implicit in the great historical paradigms, the Marxian utopia, the Nietzschean recurrence, and the Freudian unconscious relentlessly unfolding its timeless content in history and biography. In each case, history is played against a richly figured backdrop of eternity. Unlike Hegel, who remained attached to the classical ideal, Marx, Nietzsche, and Freud narrativize the crisis of rationality, attributing action to unconscious forces and motives. This is the mark of their postmodernism.

The progressive *episteme* demanded both ever bolder imaginative leaps and ever more massive cognitive schemata to preserve order, ever more chaos and greater repression. The narrative by which it was rationalized required a relatively stable background, an epochal system that provided the terms of explanation, and a dazzling fluency of style to adjust to the particular situation. The nineteenth-century novel was the laboratory of this fluency, and the novelist was the pedagogue to the bourgeoisie, which, as a class, was unprepared to deal with the disruption that its own emergence occasioned. Dickens, Balzac, Tolstoy modeled a new psychology in which the distance between particular events and the massive informing schema was immense but manageable in terms of a carefully plotted story.

As Henry Adams foresaw clearly, however, the manic intensity could not be perpetually sustained. At some point the instigating contradictions, between the one and the many, the self and the not-self, all of the uneasy differences that had motivated thought, were no longer generative. They were not resolved and not definitively shown to be unresolvable, but their bite and poignancy were lost in a sophistication that could no longer be passionately sustained. The dialectic permanently stalled, and the production of meaning proliferated without relation to a unifying scheme. Although Henry Adams's theory of history has been treated as a curiosity of latter-day mechanistic thought, a footnote to the Comtean philosophy of history, or a mistaken science that, from Newton to Einstein, explained all "mysterious" phenomena, such as the action of gravity on distant objects, by "force," it might be better understood as a profound analysis of a peculiar and previously unparalleled variety of sociocultural stress. The acceleration of history, as Adams shows, is an inherent requirement of progressive thought, but its very success pushes it toward catastrophe. In *The Education,* he writes, "After 1500, the speed of progress so rapidly surpassed man's gait as to alarm everyone, as though it were the acceleration of a falling body which the dynamic theory takes it to be" (Adams, 1974, 484). Increasingly, it was no longer possible to assess a particular fact against the systematic background of an epoch, and thus events became merely free-floating occurrences. In an attempt to describe this unstable situation, Adams applies the rule of phase, the mathematics that describes threshold phenomena—such as water turning to ice—to history. His argument, in brief outline, is as follows: if the religious phase of history lasted ninety thousand years and the mechanical phase three hundred (i.e., $300 = \sqrt{90,000}$), the electrical phase could be expected to last roughly seventeen years ($17 = \sqrt{300}$), before giving way to the "ethereal," which would last just over four years ($4 = \sqrt{17}$); if we had entered the electrical phase in 1900, as Adams supposed, then thought would reach "the limit of its possibility in 1921" (Adams, 1949, 308).

Reasonable man that he was, Adams was aware that his dates were arbitrary and perhaps fanciful. Even Charles Sanders Peirce, however, Adams's less excitable contemporary, envisioned a stage in which "mind is at last crystallized" as the inherent possibilities of cosmic evolution are fully realized. Although Peirce placed this crystallization in "the infinitely distant future" (Peirce, 1955, 323), he was concerned with logical, rather than Adams's historical, limits. In characteristic modern fashion, they agreed upon the form of acceleration, but not on the measure. For the historian, the logic need not play itself out to its ultimate conclusion to precipitate an epistemological crisis: "The movement from unity into multiplicity, between 1200 and 1900 was broken in sequence, and rapid in acceleration. Prolonged one generation longer, it would require a new social mind. As though thought were common salt in indefinite solution it must enter a new phase subject to new laws. Thus far, since five or ten thousand years, the mind had successfully reacted, and nothing yet proved that it would fail to react—but it would need to jump" (Adams, 1974, 498).

Beyond a certain point on the accelerating curve, Adams could imagine only the possibility of "thought in terms of itself," rather than in terms of a reifying historical narrative. Obviously, given our habit of speaking of our own time as definitively after some other, but exhibiting no definitive character of its own, we have the same problem. We speak of Adams's "jump" as if in midair, uncertain where we will land: we call our epoch "postindustrial," "postcultural," "postliterate," even "postcontemporary." These terms attempt to conjure a history that has dispersed into thin air. When everything changes, history collapses on itself. Adams's ethereal stage of thought arises with the breakdown of the distinction between narrative and science, between history and the infinite. In a sense, this moment was envisioned by Hegel: the absolute as such is not thinkable in a finite sense, and, while the absolute has not manifested itself, its progressive realization can no longer be embodied in the finite mind or finite act.

In the last stage of thought, Adams did not know whether to expect a stasis, "the subsidence of the current [of active mind] into an ocean of potential thought, or mere consciousness, which is also possible, like static electricity," or some intensely kinetic event, the consequence of which might be "as surprising as the change of water to vapour, of the worm to the butterfly, of radium to electrons" (Adams, 1949, 308–9). The situation that obtains proves to be a paradox, embracing both activity and passivity. We enter the perpetual crisis of self-reference, in mathematical logic and physics as well as art. Russell's paradox of self-reference, Gödel's incompleteness theorem, quantum physics, and Duchamp's *The Bride Stripped Bare of her Bachelors, Even* or Pirandello's *Six Characters in Search of an Author,* are landmarks of the problems that arise when a representation requires a representation of itself. Of course, this is precisely the heritage of the Cartesian circularity. Suffice it to say that sometime, beginning about 1921, science and history confronted both logical and empirical horizons that limited the possibility of a coherent and universal paradigm. We attain knowledge by observing the world, but we are also in the world, which we observe in no trivial way, and we must therefore observe ourselves. We begin with the purpose of observing the thing and end with an observation of a relationship in which we are ourselves an unavoidable term. Moreover the language is part of the world that it describes, and the world, it turns out, is part of the language, so language describes itself, the world as a feature of itself, the language as a feature of the world, and so forth ad infinitum. At this point, all of the world-descriptive sentences blink back and forth, declaring, maddingly, *if this sentence is false, it is true; if it is true, it is false.* It seems that this situation should be disallowed by logic, but classical logic has no means other than arbitrary legislation— such as Russell's and Whitehead's theory of types—to prevent it.

The bourgeois strategy has been to claim an independent region of language that is not subject to the general economy of language: it may exempt a religious language, the language of a cultural tradition, or the sentimental language of an inflated conception of family, self, and so forth. One way or another, the trick has been to interpose a conceptual scheme between the "innermost" self and language as a defense against alienation. If that bulwark falls away, social identity is imposed not by a particular paradigm—a kingly narrative, the requirements of material production, or the functions of an organic social order—but by language itself. Conceptual schemes, whether thought of grandly as metaphysics or as blatant fictions, create linguistic communities, without invading the vestigial arena of privacy. These regions of identity, offering aspects of freedom and aspects of necessity, are requisites of the bourgeois conception of democracy that recognizes human integrity not in terms of human bodies or the measurable physicality of speech but in terms of the self as private property. Descartes's subjectivism exchanged an infinite and unfathomable Other, the Augustinian God, for an infinite and unfathomable Self. The gains are clear: the exterior world, thereby, is rendered intelligible to physical science and psychology replaced theology as the science that attempts to satisfy the human need to deny the painful limitations of the human organism. Modern subjectivism reflected the divine realm into the human interior and created the unconscious. The mediating space has been defined by religious belief for the masses and by history for the intellectual elite.

History, with its traditions and paradigms, was the story we told to keep time alive in the awesome context of the infinite which annuls all temporal activity. In "Written History as an Act of Faith" (1934), Charles Beard writes, "any written history involves the selection of a topic and an arbitrary delimitation of its borders—cutting off connections with the universal. Within the borders arbitrarily established, there is a selection and organization—a single act—which will be controlled by the historian's frame of reference composed of things deemed necessary and of things deemed desirable" (Beard, 1934, 220). For at least a time, the deeming of necessity and desirability seemed to offer a source of exploitable temporality, just as the New World had seemed to offer endlessly exploitable space. One paradigm could be played against another, always allowing a space in which identity could swerve, but quickly the ploy of historical relativism became a grim necessity and lost most of its yeast.

The argument that language embodies paradigms or general conceptions that are distinct from its general structure turns out to be paradoxical. The necessary argument is well made both by continental thinkers, such as Jacques Derrida, and Anglo-American thinkers, such as Donald Davidson. Davidson's formulation has the virtue of clarity, and I will follow it for the present.

Taking examples from Thomas S. Kuhn's history of science, from Whorf's studies of Hopi, and from the works of philosophers as different as W. V. Quine and Henri Bergson, Davidson examines the claim that "Conceptual schemes . . . are ways of organizing experience . . . they are systems of categories that give form to the data of sensation; they are points of view from which individuals, cultures, or periods survey the passing scene. . . Reality itself is relative to a scheme: what counts as real in one scheme may not in another" (Davidson, 1984, 184). *Weltanschauung*, historical epochs, and ideologies are all conceptual schemes. Davidson objects that the notion of paradigms belongs to paradigmatic thought, that the notion of epochs belongs to epochal thought, and more generally, that the definitive terms of any scheme are defined only by the scheme itself. Our confident and lucid discussions of different schemas should cause doubt about their objective status and their independence. Obviously they are somehow included in our scheme of discourse and, as such, lack the very uniqueness that we are wont to attribute to them. The bite of this argument becomes clear in face of precisely the question Davidson raises, which might be put in these terms (though they are not quite Davidson's): how are the contents of a paradigm translated into a scheme without paradigms as significant conceptual features; how is it possible to translate not the concepts but the features of concepts that lend those concepts schematic authority. He concludes: "Given the dogma of a dualism of scheme and reality, we get conceptual relativity, and truth relative to a scheme. Without the dogma, this kind of relativity goes by the board. Of course truth of sentences remains relative to language, but that is as objective as it can be. In dividing up the dualism of scheme and world, we do not give up the world, but re-establish unmediated touch with the familiar objects whose antics make our sentences and opinions true and false" (Davidson, 1984, 198).

We can see in this argument the final stage of a socialization process by which humankind adjusts its sense of self to the abstraction of language; the plurality of schemes is homogenized in the universality of the linguistic medium.

Whitman and the Wrong Infinity

There is a literature that attempts to express the possibilities of absolute history, investing the linguistic medium itself with all that has been lost from life and generating almost pathological intensities. It is satisfying as long as we feel its power and not its pathos, but it verges forever on self-pity. Mallarmé, Matthew Arnold, Nietzsche, and many of the other instigators of romantic modernist literature—like their recent commentators and deconstructors— are forever on the verge of whining. The issue is not that Hölderlin became the official poet of German National Socialism or that Ezra Pound made fascist broadcasts on Italian radio or that Paul de Man wrote anti-Semitic essays for a collaborationist paper; even the most benign and liberal approach to Hegelian history must either overwhelm the present with eternity or remain forever in the elegiac mood.

According to romantic theory, to live—to move at all—it is necessary to undermine the logical stasis that is taken as the inevitable (Newtonian) background, to throw oneself recklessly into the double bind that dynamism in logical space requires. The impulse toward integration is the product of contradictory and mutually dependent discourses: the discourse of reason and the discourse of unreason are mutually dependent. The difference of potential between them energizes an otherwise complete and static field—i.e., Newtonian causal determination, Hegelian logic, structuralist *langue,* computer programs, and so on. The impulse to action, therefore, is inevitably a kind of self-exploitation, an invitation to madness and the suffering of mastery. "To understand the historicity of Romantic discourse," Clifford Siskin writes, "is to be able to hear within it the discourse of addiction" (Siskin, 1988, 179). One might even say that the culture is addicted to history, to static kinesis, unprogressive progress, nonproductive production. More precisely, however, we are addicted to mediation, of which history is only an example. When media are consumed—that is, reified as things in themselves and given special subjective relevance—the result is the familiar pathology, a situation that is unstable, at once tense and exhilarating. To the medium eater, everything is dissociated and significant. Nature is a substance that is attractive and easily abused; History is a "rush." In this connection, Hegel's language is accurate and revealing: "Appearance is the arising and passing away that does not itself arise and pass away, but is 'in itself' [i.e. subsists intrinsically], and constitutes the actuality and the movement of the life of truth. The True is thus the Bacchanalian revel in which no member is not drunk" (Hegel, 1977, 27). It is, however, a modern Bacchus who is worshipped: the Hegelian True is the true of the infinitesimal calculus, an infinite rising and passing away that does not itself pass away—the infinite not as merely endless succession, which would have been known to the classical Bacchantes, but as a closed aggregate of objects existing in themselves. Formal languages, natural languages, culture, imagination, history, sex, power, being, and so forth are media that we have consumed, and in our theory they have been understood as half-mechanical and half-mystical.

History in a posthistorical time turns back to its medium, its history of itself and the textual trail that is now cut loose from the phantom events it sought to record. The minimal requirements of an orderly temporality and narrative succession, that each *now* derive from a *then* and give way to a *next,* are not met by a language in which any part, slipping and sliding on its references, ultimately implicates an inconceivably vast totality. Pure abstraction or "the world of prose" in Hegel's phrase, the world without overt aesthetic content (because all content has become aesthetic), asserts itself as a quotidien fact. Rather than presenting itself as the Absolute, however, as Hegel prophesied, it fragmented in a succession of possible worlds, each world with its own logic. Each signifier stands in relation not to one paradigm but to as many as can be self-consistently devised, all of which appear to make comparable legitimate claims for attention. Initially this state of affairs offers an attractive freedom: when a signifier is moved laterally from one paradigm to another, it accrues a remarkable density and potential energy; but when it is moved in the direction of time by way of action, events regress infinitely into their own possibilities and the dense signs diffuse. Thus an immense freedom alternatively supports exhilaration and despair.

The predominant function of the arts in the West since the seventeenth century had been not to situate action in the great household (i.e., *oikos,* "house," therefore, "ecology," "economy") but to restore the object, from which consciousness is said to be separated, to its ideal status. Although it has not been the dominant tradition and has been poorly understood, the necessary reversal, the restoration of the object to its commonality, has been an important motive of the arts since the middle of the nineteenth century. In the insistence that the object of consciousness proves to be that which is most familiar, not something which must be striven for and restored, it represents a total break with the tradition of idealism. Language is relative only to the concrete world as its measure, not to some structure of itself, neither referent, nor structure, logic, method, device, category, frame, concept, paradigm, grammar, rhetoric, writer, reader, tradition, history.

Walt Whitman's poetry resembles Wordsworth's, Shelley's, or Hölderlin's as little as theirs resembles Pope's and Doctor Johnson's. The high romantics articulated finite images against the background of Hegel's right infinity. Although the romantic poets insisted on the primacy of the concrete, the world they grounded on the authenticity of particular experience was absorbed by ever more powerful levels of abstraction. The romantic poems are texts or poems on the verge of entering the flow or textuality—that is, they are writings in history. Whitman's poems are writings in time. They are posed not against an ideal background but against the actual time of the performance. It is true, Whitman sometimes falls for a generalization, as D. H. Lawrence rightly objects:

> I AM HE THAT ACHES WITH AMOROUS LOVE.
> Walter, leave off. You are not HE. You are just a limited Walter.
> (Lawrence, 1964, 164)

And, though his enthusiasm occasionally runs away with him, he is a "limited Walter"; containing multitudes, he is very large, but countable. The measure of his verse is actual quantity, not relationship. And, as we shall see, his images are concrete and paratactic, the requirements of an actual world, not of an absolute logic. There had not been such a poetry since the disappearance of Anglo-Saxon and Latin. Whitman, however, rather than making nostalgic reference to medieval times—like the romantics, thus giving us a simulacrum of finitistic thought—creates a verse practice that responds directly to the finitistic nature of technology. Whitman is one of the first "modern modernists," contesting for mastery not with universal, logical machines but with finite, technological processes. After Whitman and Melville, it is clear the contest is not between world systems—not between dialectical idealism and dialectical materialism or between the absolute ego by the name of Ahab and the ultimate matter in the form of a whale—but between actual, physical humans and actual machines, high-speed printing presses, floating sperm oil factories, and paper mills (see Melville's "The Tartarus of Maids").

Poetry—poetry as such, apart from its possible compromises with abstract thought—is an interpretation of the common intuition, which makes a group into a tribe or a nation or a race, or possibly just a work force. Now we enter into a common fate, a world and species fate: such is the meaning of Whitmanic democracy. The smallest units are the person and the world. Whitman's rhetoric therefore is colored by imperialism. Unfortunately this democracy and this imperialism have expressed themselves, for the most part, tyrannically. Their relationship to Latin America, Asia, and Africa is shameful, and, as Whitman, like few others, recognized, it has also treated itself cheaply, using itself as a tool of its own least attractive capacities. He understood the alternatives as two writings or underwritings of empire. In his address to an historian, he says:

> You who celebrate bygones,
> Who have explored the outward, the surfaces of the races, the
>   life that has exhibited itself,
> Who have treated of man as the creature of politics, aggregates,
>   rulers and priests,
> I, habitan of the Alleghanies, treating of him as he is in himself in
>   his own rights.
>
> (Whitman, 1964, 2:307)

One writing expresses a relationship—one thing is known in terms of another—man in terms of politics, societies, or religions; and, also, in its imperialism, it expresses the third world in terms of Europe and the United States, or it expresses geographies in terms of resources, great diversities of physical objects in terms of the monotonous medium of money, and so forth. The historian's time is abstract and has a shape which is irrelevant to the experienced time of any of the participants in the events. In the imperialist iconography of the nineteenth century, History was inevitably a man on a horse, leading a well-organized army. It was seen not as the arrogance of mechanization but as primal force, expressing the cosmos or the mind or the universal unconscious. The other writing expresses humans—and as it turns out, everything else—only in terms of themselves. It is not as easy as it sounds: the categorical logic of language has a built-in bias toward the aggregate. Whitman corrects the logic of language with the physicality of language. The identity of the person and the world is posited neither as a metaphor to be exemplified, as it was before Descartes, nor as a puzzle in logic, as it was after Hegel. It is, at once, a matter of enquiry and construction. Knowledge is the construction of that which is discovered, and, although the construction is arbitrary, what is discovered is not.

We have lost the sense of poetry that allows us to understand the Platonic assertion that empires crumble when the mode of the music changes or Novalis's claim that the one who controls rhythm controls the universe and even the relatively modest proposition of the Imagists that a new cadence is a new idea. As Ezra Pound repeatedly notes in the *Cantos,* "To break the pentameter / that was the first heave." It was, of course, Walt Whitman's heave, and it was not an easy fact for Pound to swallow: "He is America. His crudity is an exceedingly great stench, but it is American. He is the hollow place in the rock that echoes with his time. . . Entirely free from the renaissance humanist ideal of the complete man or from the Greek idealism. He is a genius because he has vision of what he is and his function. He knows that he is a beginning and not a classically finished work" (Pound, 1973, 145).

Whitman, like Dante, renovated the language of a culture. Traditional English metrics produce temporal norms that measure all performances reductively. Whitman's mensural practice assumes an actual temporality; his democracy is possible, as we shall see, only in actual time, the time of its performance and reperformance. In Whitman's poetry and in poetry of the tradition that it established, the rhythm is not determined by syllabic stress. The numerous attempts to scan Whitman's verse are mistaken not in their details but in their general assumptions. The readers of *Leaves of Grass* can stress the syllables more or less as they chose; the performance is not controlled by a norm, so there is literally no way to regularize the patterns, no way to judge correct emphasis. Stress is not a formal determinant in Whitman's poetry. The controlling rhythms are not relative but absolute, the fact of a particular, concrete performance. Although English is not a quantitative language (in the sense of distinguishing syllables of different durations), Whitman creates an *equivalent* to quantitative verse by giving his attention to the phrase and the line rather than to the foot. His verse improvises quantitative rhythms by attention to durations that are marked both by time and by the repetitions of vowels and consonants. "A design cut in time," in Pound's phrase, is not established by any single aspect of language abstracted from the language as a whole. In accentual-syllabic verse, the reader's expressive emphasis is allowed within the normative limits of the poem's absolute temporal form. The performance is absolutely controlled by the measured durations of phrase and line and by the repetitions of sounds—rhyme in the largest sense of the word—but *the time of the poem is the actual time of the performance itself.* Just as Shakespeare's poetic monuments would make no sense in Whitmanic verse, these lines, from "So Long!"—the concluding poem of *Leaves of Grass*—would makes no sense in iambic pentameter:

> Camerado, this is no book,
> Who touches this touches a man,
> (Is it night? are we here together alone?)
> It is I you hold and who holds you,
> I spring from the pages into your arms—decease calls me forth
> O how your fingers drowse me,
> Your breath falls around me like dew, your pull lulls the tympans
>   of my ears,
> I feel immerged from head to foot, delicious, enough.
>   (Whitman, 1980, 2:452)

The meaning here, as in a Shakespearean sonnet, is completely literal. Whitman's verse, however, does not include its own ideal time nor its own ideal reading; it depends upon the performance and the time of the performance. The speaker of the poem does not know whether it is day or night.

Leaves of Grass is not significantly representative; it is, rather, an interpretation of the common. Traditional forms appear to leave great freedom of personal expression, while in fact, leaving none, as even the most daring departures of performance are assimilated to the ideal. Whitmanic verse, on the other hand, allows little room for personal expression in the reading of the lines. Whitman habitually refers to the poems as "chants," and the quality of the chant and the usefulness of chanting as a mode of presentation in liturgies or cheers is that it obscures the personal, expressive voice (and when he speaks of "a programme of chants," it is completely appropriate to hear the pun on "chance"; time in Whitmanian free verse is a dimension of contingency). The ego that serves to interpret the common world in Whitman's poetry is not—to recall John Keats's characterization of the Wordsworthian ego—sublime; the Whitmanic ego is no more than a convenience. Its use in language, like the use of terms such as *here* and *now,* is that it has no *specific* meaning; it is one of the nodes by which the common has purchase on the logic of language, which is otherwise tyrannically perspectival. The allowance of a full measure of use to deictic terms is profoundly anti-Hegelian.

Whitman's "language experiment," as he called it himself, brings us to the final stage of literacy. The makers of books had assiduously sought the unity of the book with itself; now the book was to be a register of activity. Consider the delicacy with which Whitman establishes the universe of his measure at the beginning of *Leaves of Grass:*

> One's-self I sing, a simple separate person,
> Yet utter the word Democratic, the word En-masse.

To "sing" and to "utter" specify modes that are in conflict. The one is self-reflexive, the other is not. One sings oneself as a person, one utters *words*. Song is absolute and without particular content. In an address to the soul, Whitman writes:

> Loafe with me on the grass, loose the stop from your throat,
> Not words, not music or rhyme I want, not custom or lecture,
>   not
> even the best,
> Only the lull I like, the hum of your valved voice.
> (Whitman, 1980, 1:5–6)

The paradoxes of utterance arise precisely because language is the possession of the masses and is useful in bringing forth diverse circumstances and experiences that are uniquely manifest, from a given perspective, only with the expense of considerable will. The potential conflict was traditionally solved in English poetry by iambic pentameter. The poets utter in terms of absolute, counterpointed measure, and allow themselves or others as performers the opportunity to sing: such was the normative function of poetry. Whitman enforces no norm; every time and place is perfect.

The cosmic Person is not Whitman's theme but a persistent obstruction, which is implicated concretely from the outset in the philosophic oppositions of "One's-self I sing": one's-self/En-masse, body/mind, male/female, free action/divine law. These derive more or less directly from the logical antinomies, and romantic philosophy had discovered certain tricks of reconciliation that were known to Whitman, and in moments of relaxation, he uses them. Whitman, however, unlike the romantic writers whom he resembles, is usually aware that his project rests on a dilemma that no *logical* ploy can resolve. In the words of Kenneth Burke, "Men seek for vocabularies that will be faithful *reflections* of reality. To this end, they must develop vocabularies that are *selections* of reality. And any selection of reality must, in certain circumstances, function as a *deflection* of reality" (Burke, 1969, 59). In the sense that it is relevant to *Leaves of Grass,* history is marked by these persistent deflections or obstructions, the product of the individual entering and expressing the common where value arises, rather than by masses, interest groups, marching armies, or the logical absolute. Disturbed by "the genius poets of old lands" insisting that war is the "one theme for ever-enduring bards," Whitman replies:

> I too haughty Shade also sing war, and a longer and greater one
>   than any,
> Waged in my book with varying fortune, with flight, advance
> and retreat, victory deferr'd and wavering,
> (Yet methinks certain, or as good as certain, at the last,) the field
> the world . . .
>
> (Whitman, 1980, 3:625)

Here the antinomies are restated in a form that defines the project of *Leaves of Grass* as a whole: "my book" and "the field the world." The book is identified not with language nor with the world in the abstract but with a particular engagement. In "To Thee Old Cause," he declares, "my book and the war are one." The doubt that arises from these claims, however, is deep and generative. The identity of the book and the field of the world is "certain," he says, "or as good as certain," but the intuition of the underlying unity manifests itself only in obstruction and conflict, some of which arise from the nature of brute reality and some of which arise from the nature of language. Every creative advance, every move in the direction of manifesting the unity, is necessarily a disruption and a move toward disunity. The mark that symbolizes the unity is a mark amongst marks, which must itself be assimilated to the totality for which it stands, and the logic of marks does not necessarily reflect the intuited sense of the world.

Against history, Whitman poses not unity but the actual voicing of the lines in the poem as the access to people and things as they are *in their own right*. This is the crucial distinction, for the lack of which useful critical thought has nearly come to a halt. By his use of the term *vocalism,* he distinguishes "voice" from the idealized voice of conventional poetics, from the metaphysical voice that proposes to be present to itself, thus, closing the field of discourse, and from the postmetaphysical voice that in the failure of self-presence merely pursues its own tail through endless textual play. Jacques Derrida writes: "There is an unfailing complicity here between idealization and speech [*voix*]. . . The passage to infinity characteristic of the idealization of objects is one with the historical advent of the *phone* . . . what makes the history of the *phone* fully enigmatic is the fact that it is inseparable from the history of idealization, that is, from the 'history of mind,' or history as such" (Derrida, 1978a, 95). The remarkable oversight is that this complicit *voix* is itself physical, a manifest body that idealization seeks to avoid, as it seeks to avoid the physicality of other objects. To be sure, the history of the mind is inseparable from the idealized voice, and, in the period of its greatest success, idealism managed to create images of the idealized voice in poetry. The period that began with Milton, Dryden, and Racine and included the work of the great English romantics, Hölderlin, and Hugo was remarkably successful in this regard.

Whitman's response goes to the heart of the matter: "I sound my barbaric yawp over the roofs of the world" (Whitman, 1980, 1:82). This is no ideal *voix*. In "Vocalism," he writes:

> Vocalism, measure, concentration, determination, and the
>   divine power to speak words;
> Are you full-lung'd and limber-lipp'd from long trial? from
> vigours practice? from physique?
> Do you move in these broad lands as broad as they?
> Come duly to the divine power to speak words?

"Vocalism" takes up the full physical character of speech, its percussiveness and projectivity:

I see brains and lips closed, tympans and temples unstruck,
Until that comes which has the quality to strike and to unclose,
Until that comes which has the quality to bring forth what lies
  slumbering forever ready in all words.
                                        (Whitman, 1980, 2:308–9)

Although Language is inherently abstract, an idealism, it is
also—both in its written and spoken forms—physical, and it tends
thereby toward self-correction. The mnemonic uses of poetry
called upon rhythm and rhyme as devices of continuity and order.
The habits of reading aloud and illuminating manuscripts, which
both called attention to the *physicality* of language, were lost,
however, to the universality of print. "The language industry" was
mechanized even before textile production. The voice could be
idealized because literally, in the age of prose, it had no primary
function. A poet of the newspaper age, Whitman assumes a literate
audience and the easy circulation of cheap printed matter, condi-
tions that his generation was the first to act upon un-
selfconsciously. Indeed for Whitman, the reasons for idealizing the
voice were no longer remembered. He speaks of the devices of
idealized address—"rhyme or uniformity [of rhythm]" as "gag-
gery and gilt" (Whitman, 1964, 2:440). So what is voice for?
Whitman was not required to feature some aspect of language as
memorably monotonous—that is, so many iambs per eye sweep,
or whatever—as a goad to recall. To be sure, there are memorable
lines in *Leaves of Grass;* but few of the poems as wholes are
memorable, nor are they intended to be. No one is likely to want to
memorize the catalogs, for example, which, unlike Homeric cata-
logs, are intended to create vocabularies, not to record specific
information. The more concentrated and content-laden passages,
however, make no greater concessions to memory. Given Whit-
man's assumptions, there are few reasons to memorize a poem; it
can always be read again. The poet's language, however—and
Whitman was the first to appreciate this fact—is freed from the
heavy requirements of redundancy and can, thus, address a vastly
larger field of sounds, images, and themes. Language is freed to
make full use of all of its dimensions in the construction of a world.

Thus, in a beautiful passage, from the beginning of "Song of
Myself," which one might think to memorize, even our syntactical
expectations are disregarded and the complex articulation of the
sound of the poem refers to no abstract unifying device. Although

this is oral poetry, in the sense that it is written to be voiced, it shares none of the techniques of oral poetry in traditional societies; it is no more formulaic than it is grammatical. In traditional oral poetry, the physical voice is featured because it is a mnemonic tool; here it is featured in its own right, sound, serving equally with syntax, to organize the thought. Consider this passage from the second section of "Song of Myself":

> The smoke of my own breath,
> Echoes, ripples, buzz'd whispers, love-root, silk-thread, crotch, and vine,
> My respiration and inspiration, the beating of my heart, the passing blood and air through my lungs,
> The sniff of green leaves and dry leaves, and of the shore and dark-color'd sea-rocks, and of hay in the barn,
> The sound of the belch'd words of my voice loos'd to the eddies of the wind,
> A few light kisses, a few embraces, a reaching around of arms,
> The play of shine and shade on the trees as the supple boughs wag,
> The delight alone or in the rush of the streets, or along the fields and hill-sides,
> The feeling of health, the full-noon trill, the song of me rising from the bed and meeting the sun.
>
> (Whitman, 1980, 1:2)

A body coagulates around the breath, thickens, involves a world and people outside of itself, and rises as song. It is a literal rendering of the obstruction of body, generating thought as *active,* rather than, as in philosophy, reflective and explanatory. In fact, as the passage never comes to a grammatical period, it never declares anything. It requires an actual speaking: it becomes a speech only if an actual voice lends its density to these unlocated phrases.

The opening line, the noun and its dependent prepositional phrase, creates the expectation of a verb, and, to the ear, "echoes" seems at first to fill the bill. Certainly appearing in that grammatical position, it might be a verb. Only the comma after "breath," a device of written language, signals otherwise. In performance, however, the pause and the new line mark a gathering of tension to energize this word that ambiguously, and momentarily, fulfills our grammatical expectations. Although smoke does not generally echo, it is not clear how literally we are to take the passage, and there is pressure on the reader's short-term memory to find an appropriate finite verb. The context of the previous two stanzas, which have to do with the sense of smell, does not strongly limit the possibilities. One might be prepared for the distillations of human fragrances becoming visible. We are given no opportunity to consider these subtle options, however, because "echoes" is followed immediately by another word, "ripples," which also might be heard as a verb, and then by two phrases—"buzz'd whispers" and "love-root"—either of which, given the fact we are slightly disoriented and actively looking for a verb and then perhaps an object, might satisfy our grammatical need. The smoke of breath might buzz whispers, and, for the matter, as we are beyond the limits of short-term coherence, it might love root. We are likely now to hear even "silk-thread, crotch and vine" as hovering in the grammatical space that satisfies the need for a verb and an object. Erotic puns invoke the most remote connotations.

However, grammar is, in effect, a creed of its own, and one of the "creeds in abeyance" that Whitman notes in the first section of the poem. When we come to the line beginning "my respiration," we are well into memory overload and begin to despair of our expectations, so we give ourselves over to the written record, which puts "my respiration and inspiration"—reasonably enough—in apposition with "The smoke of my own breath." If there is lingering grammatical hope that Whitman might regroup and still give us an appropriate verb, it is clear we will have to sort matters out later. As a readerly strategy, we are willing to forget the intervening passage and try to discover what breath as respiration and inspiration does, but we are given a list, which line by line strays further and further from parallel construction. The next two lines stick to the general area of reference—breathing, smelling, nose, mouth, and so forth. We recognize that "voice loos'd to the eddies of the wind" may still parallel "the smoke of my own breath," but this knowledge depends upon conscious analysis. It cannot be "heard" as fulfilling requirements of grammar: attention is not so generous.

The lines thereafter have the appearance but not the content of parallel structure: "the sniff" follows well enough from "respiration," and the thought might pass from the sense of smell to the sense of hearing in "the sound of the belched words of my voice," but "a few light kisses, a few embraces" is radically disjunct. The passage from self-reflection on the voice to a love encounter gives the readers some indication of the distance between the voice that speaks here (or the voice for which they speak in their reading) and its possible, ideal counterpart. The next lines, beginning "the play of shine" and "the delight alone," appear superficially to recur to the parallel structure, but these experiences are displaced from the lyric subject. In the fuzzy grammar, the lines seem to float free of the subject-object axis. Only at the end of the passage is the world reembodied, not as *logos*, but as song.

By the time we get to "the play of shine and shade on the trees as the supple boughs wag," it is apparent that we will not get out of the passage with the grammar intact, and Whitman makes no attempt save us from the grammatical quagmire. He does not "complete a thought"—that is, he does not impose the grammatical drama on the passage and does not grammatically locate the nounish-events. What holds the passage together and allows us to attend, even after the grammar has dispersed, is the complex and careful sonic organization of the passage. The assonance, "the tone-leading of vowels," as Pound calls it, carries through the passage: smoke / own / echo; breath / thread; ripples / whispers / silk; buzz'd / love / lungs; vine / my / dry; beating / green / leave / leaves / sea / reaching / trees / streets / feeling / meeting; hay / play / shade; light / shine / delight / sides / rising. The repeated consonants through the passage are sibilants and liquids, and the rhythmic power derives not from syllabic stress patterns but from the hard bilabials and dentals that zone-off the flow of the speech. As the passage moves away from the repeated phrases having to do with breath, voice, and smell, to the articulation of a fleshy person, the assonance becomes denser. One is carried over the transition, from the mere expectation of an appropriate verb to the appearance of a person, on the run of long-*e* sounds: the coherence is created by auditory rather than grammatical devices. One passes into a linguistic space where the controlling shapes are not periodic but paratactic. There is no significant subordination in *Leaves of Grass*. It is, of course, possible to complete sentences in such a linguistic environment, and Whitman most typically does, but the effective forms of the poem are not controlled by that grammar. Because these are fully literate poems, perhaps the first fully literate poems, the poet is interested in their enactment; they are in effect formless until they are spoken. Poetry had never before been *written* with such confidence, and therefore it could dismiss precisely those literate devices by which voice is inscribed in writing. It could potentially become an equivalent of voice, not its mere representation. To do so, it must appropriate the body and voice of a performer.

It is not wrong to hear all of the possible puns on "solid" and "sound," in this passage from section 20 of "Song of Myself":

> I know I am solid and sound,
> To me the converging objects of the universe perpetually flow,
> All are written to me, and I must get what the writing means.
> (Whitman, 1980, 1:25)

"Solid" and "sound" are likely to be first heard in their metaphorical rather than in their literal senses. We might say that a person's financial condition is solid and sound or, if they are preparing for an exam or applying for a job, that a person's knowledge is solid and sound. Here, however, the passage should also be taken literally: the person is a spatial entity—solid, physical, mute—and a temporal entity—rhythmic, relational, and linguistic. When we pass from the human to the nonhuman, literally, from inside the skin to outside, the terms are reversed: the flow of the universe is rhythmic, relational, and mute; the writing of objects is solid, physical, linguistic. We might generalize in the fashion of the poststructuralists and say that both sonic and solid language are traces, but we would obscure the profound differences. To put the matter clearly but perhaps not too schematically: the objects of the universe converge as flow and writing and are returned as objects and speech. A region of cosmic flow, named, yields a solid object; descending into class logic, it is associated with a type or, in another pun that is behind Whitman's thought, it is typed, printed. In turn, the type, read, becomes sound, the flow of speech. The form of this language is literally the physical world itself. There is the urge, understandably, to name the thing that relates the solid and sound forms. Whitman calls this fundamental unit of intuition the "eidolon." It is the entity that reconciles all of the sameness and difference, like the indifferentiable units of the physical continuum that produce difference. Space and time are constituted of eidolons, as evanescent signs, on one hand, and the "body permanent / the body lurking their within thy body," on the other. They are beyond the lectures of the learned professor, beyond all mathematics and sciences, but completely immediate and accessible. It is clear that to name them is to create insoluable problems: they are the terms of self-obstructing acts, the mirages that appear to create a solid world when we take thought. As a way of understanding their dimension, we can assume for the present that we are dealing with a dualism (to be accurate, we must say only that we both are and are not dealing with a dualism).

Like several other writers who work in Whitman's vein, in an attempt to overcome the substantialist bias of the tradition, Whitman sometimes appears to treat the flowing and the sonic as fundamental. In a footnote to a section of *Specimen Days,* entitled "The Great Unrest of Which We Are Part," Whitman writes:

> Every molecule of matter in the whole universe is swinging to and fro; every particle of ether which fills space is in jelly-like vibration. Light is one kind of motion, heat another, electricity another, magnetism another, sound another. Every human sense is the result of motion; every perception, every thought is but motion of the molecules of the brain translated by that incomprehensible thing we call mind. The processes of growth, of existence, of decay, whether in worlds, or in minutest organisms, are but motion. (Whitman, 1964, 2:289)

The interpretation of this common motion was and is a central philosophic mystery, but, in singing the body electric, Whitman arrives in a poetic space where the relationship between act and agent breaks down. After a long catalog of American types in section 15 of "Song of Myself," Whitman writes:

> And these tend inward to me, and I tend outward to them,
> And such as it is to be of these more or less I am,
> And of these one and all I weave the song of myself,
> (Whitman, 1980, 1:20)

As it turns out, our search for a finite verb in the passage from section 2 was misguided, in a sense. We were drawn into improper expectations by grammatical logic: what is missing is not a verb but a true agent. In fact there is no one there, only a singing, a rising and a meeting of the sun, an interpretation of the common. At least that is the case until *someone* performs the poem. The nouns seem to contain motion in themselves, not by means of their willful agency.

Or again the consideration of the "solid" and the writing of the universe leads us to a linguistic clot surrounding the word *type.*

Allowing all of the turns which would occur to a man who was trained as a printer, it yields "imprint," "model," "embodiment," "nature," "character" (from Greek *tupos,* a "blow," "impression"). In "Starting from Paumanok," Whitman writes:

> Not the types set up by the printer return their impression, the
> meaning, the main concern,
> Any more than a man's substance and life or a woman's
> substance and life return in the body and the soul,
> Indifferently before death and after death.
> Behold, the body includes and is the meaning, the main concern,
>   and
> includes and is the soul;
> Whoever you are, how superb and how divine is your body, or
>   any part of it!
>
>   (Whitman, 1980, 2:284)

And this, from "A Font of Type":

> This latent mine—these unlaunch'd voices—passionate powers
> Wrath, argument, or praise, or comic leer, or prayer devout,
> (Not nonpareil, brevier, bourgeois, long primer merely,)
> These ocean waves arousable to fury and to death,
> Or sooth'd to ease and sheeny sun and sleep,
> Within the pallid slivers slumbering.
>
>   (Whitman, 1980, 3:698)

And again, in a prose note, written about the same time as "A Font of Type," he speaks of "the most important and pregnant principle of all, *viz.* that *Art is one,* is not partial, but includes all times and forms and sorts—is not exclusively aristocratic or democratic, or oriental or occidental. My favorite symbol would be a good font of type, where the impeccable long-primer rejects nothing" (Whitman, 1964, 2:685). The font of type is at once the repository of potentiality and of typification, of recognizing an entity as belonging to a type class. Every one's name is in the type rack. The pun on "character" is to the point: we might speak of the "characters" of an alphabet or the "character" of a southerner or a mechanic. One's self as type is many: One is "O-N-E", and O-N-E can make many imprints. Any inscription of the one betrays itself:

> Still though the one I sing,
> (One, yet of contradictions made,) I dedicate to Nationality,

> I leave in him revolt, (O latent right of insurrection!
> O quenchless, indispensable fire!)
> > (Whitman, 1980, 3:632)

The continuous surface that mediates between one and the One is dispersed, and its materials are made available for use in the construction of poems. The logic of type (molded lead) is not the logic of Language. Its combinatory is finite and unlimited: it is always possible to cast more type, but the aggregate totality cannot be specified. The infinity of type is the Hegelian wrong infinite— the imprint of a concrete, *measurable* world.

Whitman recognizes that we are obstructions to ourselves. The images that define us, by which we are made manifest to ourselves and to others, block the very thing that we are. This dilemma can be managed only by constant movement and measure, accurate to the events themselves. It is by sound and sequence, not by linguistic logic, that language is embodied and speaks for the common.

The measured displacements that we have noted in section 2 of "Song of Myself" is closely related to techniques that would become common in both painting and writing in the cubist era. Gertrude Stein writes, Walt Whitman "wanted really wanted to express the thing and not call it by its name" (Stein, 1985, 241). Whitman has been frequently called an Adamic namer. If he is, it has not been sufficiently observed that he is uncomfortable in the role. He prefers to stay as close as possible to the nameless intuitions:

> Beginning my studies the first step pleas'd me so much,
> The mere fact of consciousness, these forms, the power of
>   motion,
> The least insect or animal, the senses, eyesight, love,
> The first step I say awed me and pleas'd me so much,O
> I have hardly gone and hardly wish'd to go any farther,
> But stop and loiter all the time to sing it in ecstatic songs.
> > (Whitman, 1980, 2:468)

The step beyond the beginning is the step into abstraction, and Whitman takes it uneasily:

> I myself but write one or two indicative words for the future,
> I but advance a moment only to wheel and hurry back in the
>   darkness.
> > (Whitman, 1980, 2:311)

Between the times of Whitman and Gertrude Stein, the Euclidean-Newtonian world was swept away, and there were theoretical grounds for Whitman's practice:

> Naturally, and one may say that is what made Walt Whitman naturally that made the change in the form of poetry, that we who had known the names so long did not get a thrill from just knowing them. We that is any human being living has inevitably to feel the thing anything being existing, but the name of that thing of that anything is no longer anything to thrill any one except children. So as everybody has to be a poet, what was there to do. This that I have just described, the creating it without naming it, was what broke the rigid form of the noun the simple noun poetry which now was broken. (Stein, 1985, 237)

The world was no longer mediated by language. Stein recognizes in Whitman her own disinterest in exhibiting the mere requirements of form interposed between the nouns and the things themselves. In the linguistic regime that had prevailed, which can perhaps be called "practical metaphysics," both language and the sensible world were the implicit media of a transcendental realm: in common expository and narrative writing as well as in philosophic discourse, words and objects were felt to be the sensible figures of a logic that completed itself only in a nonsensible realm.

Poetry is the construction not of things that happen again— that is, machines—but of things that may *almost* happen again: "verse" is etymologically a turn, a turning back or returning, which may use repeated patterns of syllabic quantity or stress, vowel sounds or consonant sounds. The *poem* does not repeat, even when it is most straightjacketed with abstract form. Gertrude Stein writes:

> When I first really realized the inevitable repetition in human expression that was not repetition but insistence when I first began to be really conscious of it was when at about seventeen years of age, I left the more or less internal and solitary and concentrated life I led in California and came to Baltimore and lived with a lot of my relations and principally with a whole group of very lively little aunts who had to know anything.
>
> I began then to consciously listen to what anybody was saying and what they did say while they were saying what they were saying. This was not yet the beginning of writing but it was the beginning of knowing what there was that made there be no

repetition. No matter how often what happened had happened any time any one told anything there was no repetition. This is what William James calls the Will to Live. If not nobody would live. (Stein, 1985, 169)

The poetics of common knowledge addresses the insistence with which rhythmic discrepancy asserts itself. While recognizing the statistical significance of the repetition compulsion, which manifests itself both in maladaptive personal behavior and the arrogant demonstrations of power so common in our culture, it notes that the heart beat, the breath, and the free-floating linguistic events in consciousness are not recurrences; each moment has its own uniqueness. The texts of the common knowledge can be performed again and again, spoken or sung or interpreted. We feel that we have been neither the object of a communication nor the bearer of tiresome habit. Rather we have been informed of an intensity: the interior crisis of being alive is made manifest. The reader-performer of the text and the audience are informed of a measure. This is one kind of knowledge; otherwise, there is trial-and-error (experimental science) and hear-say (culture).

THE EROS OF LANGUAGE

Fechner's Experiment

As a student of William James and a friend of Alfred North Whitehead, Gertrude Stein was in touch with the most advanced thought of the time. Her initiation into science and technical philosophy, which was largely and increasingly only a reflection on the methods and results of science, was so thorough that she could forget it, forget its language, forget its intimidating authority, and forget its boring insistence that life was over, that only its patterns of repetition remained to be fully discovered and mathematically described. She could forget all of that because she inhabited the world to which it belonged, and she was interested in the aspects of life that do not fit the pattern rather than those that do. Few artists or theoreticians have been so at ease with the controlling ideas of this century. Stein insisted upon dealing with the most complex ideas of her day in the language of chit-chat.

There was, Gertrude Stein knew, an *authoritative* grammar—a grammar that, if taken seriously, requires that we believe not only that history is over but also that all of the logical possibilities are tallied up, in effect that life is over. The purely mathematical forms of the grammar were more fully developed, by Russell, Frege, Peano, and others, but the groundwork for the calculus of the natural language reached back to Descartes and Leibniz, and it was only a matter of time until it was formalized. Trained at Johns Hopkins in the sciences, which appropriated the authority of that grammar (if not the rigor of its demonstrations) to particular subject matters, she was "bored, frankly openly bored" (Stein, 1962, 76). When she decided to leave medical school, "Her very close friend Marion Walker pleaded with her, she said, but Gertrude Gertrude remember the cause of women, and Gertrude Stein said, you don't know what it is to be bored" (Stein, 1962, 77). That is, she was *theoretically* bored, bored with the thanatos of science. At that time almost no one had yet had the experience of enlightened false consciousness, the utter boredom of those who have lived past the end of life and can only in their rightness repeat themselves endlessly and deathfully. Stein recognized the onset of enlightened false consciousness in herself and turned from it.

William James had taught her to keep an open mind.* Stein saw that to do so, however, she would have to keep an open mind even about keeping an open mind—Adams's ethereal thought—a discovery she made and began to base a literary practice upon only a few years after Bertrand Russell had discovered the devastating results of this same paradox for attempts to derive mathematics from logic. She turned away from that hall of mirrors, reflecting back into themselves until they arrive at an infinite medium that can be zoned out and described statistically. Stein's language is finite and immediate, local to a physical space in which everything is, as she says, always the same and always different. For Stein the immediacy of language is not the immediacy of self-presence but the immediacy of difference as measure.

Stein has an ability to reduce complex philosophic issues to anecdotes that are not, of course, adequate for philosophy but that mark the forgetting of philosophy by a person interested in living

---

*James was perhaps unnerved by the results of his teaching. He visited Stein after she moved to Paris, and she reports: "He was enormously interested in her writing and in the pictures she told him about. He went with her to her house to see them. He looked and gasped. I told you, he said, I always told you that you should keep your mind open" (Stein, 1962 #122, 75).

in the world, not just describing it. For example, she tells this story in *The Autobiography of Alice B. Toklas:*

> Gertrude Stein never had subconscious reactions, nor was she a successful subject for automatic writing. One of the students in the psychological seminar of which Gertrude Stein, although an undergraduate was at William James' particular request a member, was carrying on a series of experiments on suggestions to the subconscious. When he read his paper upon the result of his experiments, he began by explaining that one of the subjects gave absolutely no results and as this much lowered the average and made the conclusion of his experiment false he wished to be allowed to cut this record out. Whose record is it, said James. Miss Stein's, said the student. Ah, said James, if Miss Stein gave no response I should say that it was as normal not to give a response as to give one and decidedly the result must not be cut out. (Stein, 1962, 74)

This is an interesting anecdote for a number of obvious reasons. We could pick up several threads, none of which are *essentially* thematic—that Stein does not have subconscious reactions, that she was proud of her relationship to James, and so forth. It also allows James to declare himself on the central methodological issue in the experimental psychology of the time and incidentally locates Stein's work in relation to an intellectual "clot" that radiates through all of the fundamental disciplines of knowledge.

Stein would have known (or would have forgotten) Ernst Heinrich Weber's and Gustav Theodor Fechner's studies of the relationship between stimulus and sensation. Richard Herrnstein and Edwin G. Boring say that Fechner's assumption (in *Elemente der Psychophysik,* 1860) "that all just noticeable differences in sensation are equal and therefore provide a subjective unit for stating the magnitude of sensation . . . created most of the quarrels in psychophysics for the next hundred years" (Herrnstein and Boring, 1965, 67). Both Fechner's assumption and his methodology were hot items of debate at the time Stein was taking James's seminar. Stein herself did an experiment on reaction times that was at least indirectly related.

Although the Weber-Fechner experiments hardly seem profound in themselves, they happened to bear on the central intellectual problems of the mid-nineteenth century, and we still have not successfully coped with the issues that they raise. Weber had observed that "if two weights, one of which is 30 half ounces and the other 29, are compared by handling them, the disparity is not perceived more easily than when two weights of 30 and 29 drams are compared with each other" (Herrnstein and Boring, 1965, 64). That is, the half-ounce, which is four drams, produces no more noticeable sensation in relation to thirty half-ounces than the dram does in relation to thirty drams. Fechner states the law in these terms: "equal relative increments of stimuli are proportional to equal increments of sensation" (Herrnstein and Boring, 1965, 67). Weber also conducted studies on the length of lines compared by sight and speculates that the rule holds for the comparison of audio frequencies.

The interesting problem that Fechner raised and that pushed this pedestrian-seeming experiment into prolonged controversy has to do with the threshold cases—cases in which the subject could not decide if a weight was heavier or lighter, a line longer or shorter, and so forth. As we are concerned with the theory rather than experimental methodology, I will give a generalized account of Fechner's experiments, focusing especially on the questions of language that will be most relevant to the ongoing discussion:

Consider a simple language that consists of three names, three signs of relationship, and one rule of interpretation. The names are A, B, and C; the relationships are: greater than, less than, and equals. These signs are interpreted by picking up pairs of weights from the collection, A, B, and C, one in each hand, comparing their weights, and noting their relationships.

I compare weight A, which weighs ten grams, with weight B, which weighs eleven grams, and cannot distinguish between them. So, $A = B$.

I compare weight B, which weighs eleven grams, and weight C, which weighs twelve grams, and cannot distinguish between them. So, $B = C$.

Then I compare weight A, which weighs ten grams, with weight C, which weighs twelve grams, and I *can* tell the difference. That is, $A < C$.

The logic of this situation is troublesome. It does not obey the fundamental logical law of transitivity. We know logically that if $A = B$ and $B = C$, then it is necessary that $A = C$. At first the paradox seems so simple as to be no more than a trick, but careful examination will indicate that the problem appears in any attempt to represent a sensation. Phenomenal intuition and its representation have different requirements. Clearly the problem cannot be solved by a more accurate measuring device; it is inherent in the nature of measurement as such. More accurate measurement makes the terms of the paradox subtler, but, at some point, the ability to discriminate breaks down. Space dissolves, and we discover that $0 = 1$. Everything is the same and everything is different.*

The paradox is decisive for Hegelian phenomenology. Sense certainty is judged to be inferior to language precisely because it proves to be logically intransitive. Hegel gives this account of the physical time continuum: "The Now is pointed to, *this* Now; it has already ceased to be in the act of pointing to it [i.e., $A = B$]. The Now that *is* is another Now than the one pointed to, and we see that the Now is just this: to be no more just when it is [$B = C$]. The Now, as it is pointed out to us, is Now that *has been*, and this is its truth; it has not the truth of *being* [$A \neq C$]. Yet this much is true, that it has been" (Hegel, 1977, 63). This physical character of reality is, Hegel says, "unutterable . . . the untrue, the irrational" (Hegel, 1977, 66). The attempt to express it unsays itself. For Hegel, this unsaying constitutes the language's self-guarantee. In order to avoid the logical problem, it is necessary for Hegel to define a continuum on which there is always a point between any two points, though it may involve units so small they cannot be measured; that is, it is necessary to move from intuition to symbolism, from phenomena to phenome*logy*. Hegel's logic posits infinitesimal, discrete units to which, of course, no phenomena correspond. The symbolic continuum that is created consists not of measurable extension but of discrete relationships. It is without scale: there are an infinite number of intangible points between any two points. Having once made a commitment to this no-space, however, it is impossible to stop making distinctions and defining new points. In the attempt to make sense of the first symbol—to read it—we make more symbols, regressing infinitely into the space of the Zenonian paradoxes, where the rabbit never catches

---

*The example here derives from Henri Poincaré's *Science and Hypothesis* (Poincaré, 1952, 35–88). Poincaré's influence is traced by Linda Henderson in *The Fourth Dimension and Non-Euclidean Geometry in Modern Art* (Henderson, 1983).

the tortoise, the arrow, which at every infinitely small moment of time is at rest, never reaches the target, and so forth. Symbolism defines a world that is absolutely static but dynamic at every local site. Carrying Cartesian methodology a step further, Hegel substitutes linguistic logic for algebraic logic and words for rigorously defined alphabetic signs, an essential development in the prehistory of the logical calculus and contemporary information-handling technology, despite the inherent lack of rigor. History is understood not as the product of the temporal continuum but as the narrative of the attempt to rationalize the accumulated symbolism in its relation to the past and future, which are at once open to inspection and symbolically infinite.

Hegel solves the logical problem by displacing it to the infinite, but at the expense of the legitimacy of finite existence. The focus is changed from the individual, Cartesian investigator to the world historical individual or genius who redeems the masses from the mere empty accumulation of time. Hegel achieves the absolute science without answering any of the finite scientific questions. The philosopher of administration contributes nothing to the store of practical knowledge which administration requires.

The moment on the practical level that corresponds to the seizure of world history is, needless to say, not so dramatic but for the postmodern masses, long after the excitement of history has past, it is crucial. Hegel merely overwhelms the illogicality of the physical by appeal to an infinite perspective. It was the experimental scientists who were left to implement the imperial administration. Fechner writes: "The determination of psychic measurement is a matter for outer psychophysics and its first applications lie within its boundary; its further applications and consequences, however, extend necessarily into the domain of inner psychophysics and its deeper meaning lies there" (Herrnstein and Boring, 1965, 68). For Fechner, who was a mystic, this meaning is very deep indeed, for the passage from outer psychophysics, where sensations can be measured, to inner psychophysics where they cannot, was the passage from the palpable to the impalpable, from the finite to the infinite. It is the experimental equivalent to Hegel's rejection of sense certainty. The differential equation by which he expresses the infinite approach to the absolute limit of sensation is Fechner's Napoleon, which manifests the absolute limit.

With his practical commitments, however, Fechner must determine the dry-as-dust question of how to tabulate his results. What should he do with the undecidable cases? He resolved the problem by distributing the undecidable cases evenly between the categories, but his procedure provoked a lively debate in statistical analysis during the last two decades of the nineteenth century and after. Stephen M. Stigler summarizes the alternatives which were considered:

> 1. Follow Fechner's approach and divide the doubtful cases between right and wrong.
>
> 2. Calculate two values of h [Fechner's term for individual sensitivity] and average them: one with all doubtful cases treated as right, and one with all treated as wrong . . .
>
> 3. Insist that no doubtful answers be allowed, so that all answers became right or wrong. (Stigler, 1986, 253–254)

One way or another, all of these methods void undecidable cases. That is to say, Miss Stein, who produces no useable results, is eliminated as abnormal. Abstraction and purpose enter the experiment by way of these practical considerations. And in hundreds of similar "practical" situations, when we are required to observe symbolic entities, our participation in the world of disciplined knowledge is lost. Our experience is not of a tyrannical experimenter, saying, "*Chose!* You *must* decide!" but of a friendly, smiling person, saying, "Well, what do you think?" Or even more frequently, it is ourselves, in a quandary, and taking this or that chance. One by one, none of the decisions is important. If, however, no decision is important individually, how do collections of such decisions attain importance? The subject's obligation is transferred from the experience to the symbolism.

In general, clearly, the domain of the measurable and the domain of the symbolic behave according to radically different logics: the one that describes a world of proliferating difference and ceaseless flux does not obey the law of transitivity; the other describes for the infinite mind the static world of Zeno's paradoxes. Lacking infinite minds, we experience the symbolic domain as an intense dynamism that goes nowhere—the road of despair.

In the domain of the measurable, there are no discrete units. In the smallest samples we can isolate, things are already mixed: this thing is becoming that thing, here is there, now is then. Each thing is itself, though not *equal* to itself, and exists through its own self-difference. The world is dense; everything is at hand. The measure of things is not supplied by the things themselves but must come from elsewhere. There are no things until someone *does* something. Fechner's weights all weigh the same; indeed are all the same weight, until someone lifts them.

In his masterful study of African drumming, John Miller Chernoff makes a useful distinction between "rhythm as something to 'get with,'"—rhythm that supplies its own measure—as we know it in the West, and "rhythm . . . as something to 'respond to'"—something to be measured. "In African music," he writes "it is the listener or dancer who has to supply the beat: the music itself does not become the concentrated focus of an event" (Chernoff, 1979, 55). Rhythm is directionless and purposeless, a medium of indeterminate topology that is created moment by moment and step by step. Its flow is characterized by the paradox $A = B$, $B = C$, $A < C$.

In the symbolic domain, the subject, who is a center of purposive behavior, divides the intuitive epistemic domain into a class of tokens and a class of objects, which are assumed to be self-identical, and notes relationships between them: *each thing is related to and has meaning through some other thing*, not what it is in itself, because in itself it is nothing. The biography of the subject is the history of formal systems, and from Descartes to Lacan the articulation of that biography and that history explores the boundary conditions, the relationship between conscious and unconscious, which, of course, constantly supplies new content but never anything that was not implicit in the system itself (i.e., unconscious). In this domain, as Baudrillard notes, we create a simulated world of relationships with something not quite ourselves, not quite at the center of it; and when we try to analyze our plight, we create more simulations. The world is always out of reach. The impossibility of this situation has been brought into acceptable tolerance by statistical probability. The science of statistical analysis has transformed the symbolic domain. The Hegelian subject, the heroic consciousness of *Phenomenology*, which presided over history, has been rendered as a statistically reliable zone. Statistical methodology in both the physical and the social sciences developed immense sophistication during the first half of the twentieth century. The unique subject became a luxury, catered to by the so-called arts and humanities. Now a rich subjectivity is a kind of property enjoyed by the elite in posthistorical capitalism and socialism alike.

The Continuous and the Discrete

The developments that we have traced through Fechner's experiment could be followed by other paths through the last half of the nineteenth century. The terms would be different, in some cases perhaps very different, but the issues that are fundamental would be same. Although our primary concern is with language and linguistics, I must at least mention the development of non-Euclidean and N-dimensional geometries. The theoretical impact of the new geometries was profound, and, as Linda Dalrymple Henderson has shown in her important study, *The Fourth Dimension and Non-Euclidean Geometry in Modern Art,* they were significantly used and abused by the cubists and the futurists, artists who are directly relevant to our story (Henderson, 1983).

The fifth postulate of Euclid—that only one line parallel to a given line can be drawn through a given point—had seemed to many geometers less certain than the other postulates, and in the 1820s Nikolai Ivanovich Lobachevsky and Janos Bolyai independently showed that any number of lines that approach but never reach a given line may be drawn on curved surfaces, while in the 1850s, Georg Friedrich Bernhard Riemann noted that spherical surfaces are finite but unbounded and, therefore, on a spherical surface no parallel lines are possible. It was not until around the turn of the century, however, that Henri Poincaré, L. E. J. Brouwer, and others realized that the new geometries had struck a fatal blow to the Kantian doctrine of space and the possibility of a priori synthetic knowledge. If any number of mutually contradictory geometries can be shown to be internally consistent, no particular geometry can be privileged. The implications of this fact are profound: language, to recall Hegel's phrase, is *not* truer. We can learn nothing about the world by studying the requirements of the symbolism by which we represent it. With these developments, the formalism that had prevailed in Western culture since the Greeks could not be maintained. It was the closure of metaphysics, the end of logocentrism. Thereafter, mediation of experience in whatever medium no longer constituted significant philosophic data. For more than two millennia, Western thinking had taken place inside a horizon defined by the relationship of words to the Word. Things had meaning because of their relationship to something else. At some time, in the early part of this century, relationship as a source of meaning was emptied out. Significance thereafter was not a matter of interpretation but of experience.

N-dimensional geometries, which were of course also impossible from a Euclidean perspective, developed out of algebraic geometry. Although there are no definitive originating statements comparable to those of Lobachevsky and Bolyai, Arthur Cayley and Hermann Grassman are usually cited as important early contributors to the idea. Gradually, it became clear during the 1840s that it was possible to add any number of axes to the x, y, and z axes of the Cartesian coordinates. Of course, it was not clear how to visualize these additional dimensions, but they could be mathematically described. The philosophic importance of Riemann's famous inaugural lecture before the faculty of the University of Göttingen in 1854 results from his consideration of the relationship between the intuitive space of geometry and the mathematical space of analysis. There are, Riemann notes, two types of manifolds: the discrete and the continuous. They are distinguished significantly in these terms: "while in a discrete manifold the principle of metric relations is implicit in the notion of . . . [the discrete] manifold, it must come from elsewhere in the case of a continuous manifold" (Riemann, 1929, 424–25). This difference can be clearly illustrated with the symbolic and the measurable in Fechner's experiment.

With Riemann, the problem of the one and the many, which had dominated philosophy since the Greeks, was replaced with the problem of distinguishing two different forms of multiplicity. If a manifold consists of discrete units, of course, the units lend themselves to the establishment of scale. It is necessary only to discover the proper interpretation of their forms. If a space is continuous, however, the production of a world of discrete things—selves, trees, houses—becomes a matter of interaction between the space and the measurer. It is not merely a "relativization of the relations of writer, reader and observer (critic)," to recall Roland Barthes's words, that is called for, but the *creation* of these entities by writing, reading, and observing. To the question, which naturally enough occurs, *who* writes, reads, and observes, the only answer is no one. *Writing, reading, and observing are interactions in a continuous spatio-temporal field which is, in fact, the Creation.*

Charles Olson assesses the importance of Riemannian geometry in these terms:

> All things did come in again, in the 19th century. An idea shook loose, and energy and motion became as important a structure of things as that they are plural, and, by matter, mass. It was even shown that in the infinitely small the older concepts of space ceased to be valid at all. Quantity—the measurable and numerable—was suddenly as shafted in, to any thing, as it was also, as had been obvious, the striking character of the external world, that all things do extend out. Nothing was now inert fact, all things were there for feeling, to promote it, and be felt; and man, in the midst of it, knowing well how he was folded in, as well as how suddenly possessed or repossessed of a character of being, a thing among things, which I shall call his physicality. It made a re-entry of or to the universe. Reality was without interruption. (Olson, 1967, 118–19)

Thereafter, the modernist equation of being and language had a different significance. It was not possible to trace language to an origin in being and then follow the language. Neither being nor language necessarily contained in themselves a principle of measurement. The possibility of measure derived from the *act* of equating the world and being, not from the world or being. Things were dense with quantity, not merely symbolic surfaces. The physical world and the symbolic world were deeply embedded in one another.

The Two Modernisms Again

There are two modernisms in the twentieth century. One is a bedraggled romanticism, which attempts to make a virtue of its impoverishment, its lack of concrete content and its bare formalism. It is committed to the discovery of discrete units of reality and the disciplined enforcement of the rules of their combinations, a version of the ancient equation of being and language incorporating the modern concept of infinite categorical species. It is not surprising, therefore, that modernism produced so many right- and left-wing totalitarians: the finite world is a discipline of the infinite. Even the liberalism that emerged from this socio-intellectual matrix was a kind of self-frustrating totalitarianism committed from the outset to a contradiction that it refused to face and refused to resolve. The radical modernists, on the other hand, take up intransitive reality, putting the contradiction at the origin of language, the eros of life itself, rather than deferring it to the infinite future. Gertrude Stein makes this elegant distinction between the two:

> Lord Grey remarked that when the generals before the war talked about the war they talked about it as a nineteenth-century war although to be fought with twentieth-century weapons. That is because war is a thing that decides how it is to be done when it is to be done. It is prepared and to that degree it is like all academies it is not a thing made by being made it is a thing prepared. Writing and painting and all that, is like that, for those who occupy themselves with it and don't make it as it is made. (Stein, 1962, 513–14)

So there are those who prepare anything and try to make it as it is prepared, and there are those who make anything as it is made. To this we can now add another definition: postmodernists, having prepared perfectly and made it perfectly as it was prepared, now prepare themselves to spend eternity administering their failure.

Romantic modernism devolved quickly and naturally into structuralism and poststructuralism. From the beginning it was an ill-advised strategy to save the tradition of art in the face of overwhelming abstraction, and it turned out to be a viable motive for theoretical discourse which actually needed only a few exemplary works of art as an origin. The testimony of a few crucial works as articulations of abstract form sufficed; they were the manifest *logos* that had escaped the embarrassment and logical difficulty of incarnation. Thus it was possible to continue the traditions of Christian culture without Jesus; the central mystery could be the pure, formal mechanism of the soul.

Thinking particularly of Picasso, Joyce, Braque, Stravinsky, Le Corbusier, and Xlebnikov, Roman Jakobson writes:

> The extraordinary capacity of these discoverers to overcome again and again the faded habits of their own yesterdays, together with an unprecedented gift for seizing and shaping anew every older tradition or foreign model without sacrificing the stamp of their own permanent individuality in the amazing polyphony of ever new creations, is intimately allied to their unique feeling for the dialectic tensions between the parts and the uniting whole,

and between the conjugated parts, primarily between the two aspects of any artistic sign, its *signans* and its *signatum*. Stravinsky with his "search for the *One* out of the *Many*" reveals the core of his work when he reminds us that "the one precedes the many" and that "the coexistence of the two is constantly necessary". As he revealed, all the problems of art (and, we may add, of language too) "revolve ineluctably about this question".

Those of us who were concerned with language learned to apply the principle of relativity in linguistic operations; we were consistently drawn in this direction by the spectacular development of modern physics and by the pictorial theory and practice of cubism, where everything "is based on relationship" and inter-action between parts and wholes, between color and shape, between the representation and the represented. "I do not not believe in things," Braque declared, "I believe only in their relationship." (Jakobson, 1962, 632)

I quote this passage at length because Jakobson's thought so thoroughly underwrites the academic practice of aesthetic criticism. This is the modernism that proposes once again to renew the faded habits of classical modernism, to insist once again that being and language are identical, that the one precedes and *prepares* the many. The new style, which gave the new art its fresh appearance, resulted from the introduction of the discrete infinitesimal and thus nonrepresentational forms into art as Ferdinand de Saussure introduced them into linguistics: Saussure's famous statement, *"dan la langue il n'y a que des differences sans termes positifs,"* defines phonological units as nodes of pure difference which like mathematical points are dimensionless—not things but the "things" of relationships. The essential quality of these non-things, caught up in the weird logic of the transfinite, is that they are discrete and self-identical.

Hegel had prepared the way to thought in the common language of these immense abstractions as Descartes had prepared the way in mathematics, and the rise of phonological science coincided with a revival of interest in Hegel. The resonances of Roman Jakobson's historical assumptions are clear: "The dichotomy of distinctive features is, in essence, a logical operation, one of the primary logical operations of a child and—if we pass from ontogeny to phylogeny—of mankind" (Jakobson, 1962, 424). Of the terms of the binary opposition, Jakobson writes, "Both arise simultaneously and *force* the infant to choose one and to *suppress* the other of the two alternatives" (Jakobson, 1962, 499–500, my emphasis). These are the violent terms of the dialectic of the master and the slave. What is the nature of this force and this suppression that imposes ideal distinctions in phonological space upon us?

I taught my daughter "up" and "down" (and got some exercise) by playing a game in which we would alternatively squat and stand. She learned that she could not be both up and down. The world legislates absolutely that we cannot at the same time bend the knees to bring the buttocks near the heels *and* straighten the knees to make the greatest possible distance between the buttocks and the heels. This is a law that we cannot break. Its logic relates directly to other acts such as climbing, lifting, sitting and so forth. Eventually my daughter learned that she could say "up" but stay down and then laugh at me because I had gotten up. In the physical domain she had to be up or down; in the domain of grammar, she could make a joke. She had entered the *verkehrte Welt,* where even the profoundest oppositions are interchangeable and where making sense requires discipline. The forces that compel obedience to the rules of sense making are social. Joking is controlled by strict conventions: consider, for example, the satyr play, the tradition of the fool, and the shamanistic jokester in traditional cultures. The interpretation of a linguistic calculus, however, like the interpretation of the harmonic structure, goes through a natural growth in which dissonance is gradually replaced with harmony. Even when it is significantly constrained by the norms of a complex cultural tradition, the dialectical tensions of grammar, developed to their greatest abstract potential, go into regression, leading us into a search for the "infinitesimals of the poetic word," in Velimir Xlebnikov's phrase to which Jakobson refers. As meaning is discovered to be undecidable, semantic representation breaks down, and art is reduced to the polyphonous display of the artist's own "permanent individualism," as Jakobson says, or, as one might say less sympathetically, "egotism." Language thus understood is the productive medium of the will to power. Finally, its objective structure dissolves into private associations that can only be confessed guiltily and ironically by Eliot's Prufrock and his kind or blotched out beyond unblotching as a private "mythology of self" by Stevens's Crispin. In either case the narrative recycling of history confronts the postmodern problems of administration. In the *verkehrte Welt,* as it begins to enter the third millennia, the presence and absence of the mystical body of Christ fade into one another, and we give ourselves up to the mastery of a theoretical establishment to negotiate for living space.

Although both modernisms equate language with being as a point of beginning again, their conceptions of language are different: one conceives language in terms of symbolism, the other in terms of measure; one derives language from language itself (from Socratic memory or Cartesian-Chomskyan innate knowledge), the other derives language from nonlanguage.

The thought of language as an extra-ontological structure is, of course, powerful. As an independent subjective structure that describes all ontological possibilities, language is conceived as a mechanism of knowledge. It is, however, an illusion of literacy, and now, as we reach the limits of literacy as a mode of organizing knowledge, the nature of the illusion is clarified. If all of language can be represented with a finite number of phonemes, which combine according to a finite number of rules, it should be possible to generate all of legal combinations for any language. "Spoken language," however, as Eric Havelock writes, "is a continuum, a soundtrack manufactured by the larynx and carried on waves in the air, divisible acoustically into moments but not spatially extended into panels. Moments which anticipate and echo each other are con-sonant, not symmetrical" (Havelock and Hershbell, 1978, 15). With the appearance of a fluent alphabetic script, "The sound-sequence was suddenly brought into contact with a set of written symbols possessed of unique phonetic efficiency. . . The alphabet applied to the Homeric tongue constituted an act of 'translation' from sound to sight. It is the completeness of the art which must first be emphasized, and therefore the completeness of the coverage of human experience" (Havelock and Hershbell, 1978, 4). The alphabet translates from from the continuous manifold of vocal space to the discrete manifold of phonetic space. Its "completeness of coverage," its masking of the temporal consonance with the symmetry of a visual and implicitly logical space, engendered the problems that philosophy arose to solve. The philosophic project of the West has been committed to the impossible task of integrating the continuous manifold of the spoken word and the discrete manifold of the written word.

Derrida asks, "Why is the phoneme the most 'ideal' of signs? Where does this complicity between sound and ideality, or rather, between voice and ideality, come from?" (Derrida, 1978a, 77). The answer is that it comes from *writing* and the abstract requirements of the written alphabet to break-up the continuity of the voice's sound field so it can be represented by a finite combinatory. The voice and ear know phones but no phonemes, which must exist, if at all, only in a private cognitive realm. When speech patterns are studied on spectographs, which record the physical characteristics of sound, nothing in the voice signal corresponds to the consonants and vowels; they are not measurable entities. Moreover, individual sound segments vary depending upon the local phonetic context. That is, the measured phonological continuum cannot be rationalized. "Phonemics," which is ultimately to say, formal grammar as such, "admits no operations 'with unnamed entities,' " Roman Jakobson tells us (Jakobson, 1962, 639) and in an important and necessary sense, the physical, phonological continuum consists of unnamed entities: undifferentiable differences which make measured or named differences. Jakobson writes:

> phonemic analysis deliberately considers and processes the physical matter in order to elicit the strictly relative, oppositive values superimposed on the "phonetic premises" by the coding rules of language . . . phonemic study of paradigmatic relations overcomes the gross phonetic contingencies and discloses the consistent dichotomy of the distinctive features which is basically the same LOGICAL PRINCIPLE that underlies the grammatical structure of language." (Jakobson, 1962, 639)

This "processing" of physical matter and this "overcoming"— or "sublation" in Hegelian terminology—of gross phonetic contingencies turn out to be the fundamental operations of the technological enterprise itself. Meaning and structure are dissociated from one another and then recombined by formal semantic techniques. Paradoxically, writing, this most public of media, has its essential existence in the ideal space of the private soul or in a statistical space of the socius. Meaning, having been deferred in favor of constituting a literate machine, must be reintroduced as an independent rule-governed system. The privatization of the public—the internalization of language in the individual soul or the initiation of the individual into the public requirements of writing—has been the burden of the modern West and the bane of every school child. The conditioning of a literate population requires an educational system that makes the abstract requirements of combinatorial logic the most intimate of experiences. Our education is long and arduous, and its grimness extends far beyond schooling as such to an entire cultural enterprise that requires the substitution of semantic rules for the concrete and specific occasions of language. It requires an overwhelming cultural uniformity.

The structuralist strategy assumes a logical world consisting of enumerable, discrete, self-identical atoms combining according to a finite set of rules. The various poststructuralisms show either that the atoms cannot be enumerated or, more to the point, that a finite set of rules cannot account for their structures. Poststructuralist improvisation consists of play amongst the endless possibilities.

Another kind of improvisation addresses not a preexistent field of discrete atoms but a continuum, a time-sound field where nothing ever repeats. Phonemes are heard as much for their sound and the quantities of time they mark (phrasing) as for their semantic content, which is, of course, to say that they are *not* phonemes but small entities of multiple values. Everything is at once the same and different, forever beginning again. There are no infinitesimals, no instants in which time stops, no simple natures, atoms, or distinctive differences, no phonemes, no systematic backgrounds, neither implicit logical structures nor unconscious.

It is easy to mistake the nature of such improvisation, and it seems to me that even so discerning a critic as Gerald L. Bruns does so. In an essay on William Carlos Williams's masterful double improvisation, *Kora in Hell,* which improvises not only a text but also its own commentary, Bruns says rightly that "improvisation is the performance of a composition in the moment of its composition" (Bruns, 1982, 145), but he fails to understand the permission that controls the situation. He speaks of an innocence, an "evasion of Adam's curse." It is not clear how he squares this characterization with the title of the poem. If Kora is to return to earth, her meanings must work in time where winter has taken its toll on all things. The habits are forgotten; words are emptied of their associations. In his remarkable essay on Proust, Samuel Beckett writes:

> The creation of the world did not take place once and for all time, but takes place every day. Habit . . . is the generic term for the countless treaties concluded between the individuals and their countless correlative objects. The periods of transition that separate consecutive adaptations . . . represent the perilous zones in the life of the individual, dangerous, precarious, painful,

mysterious, and fertile, when for a moment the boredom of liv-
ing is replaced by the suffering of being. (Beckett, 1931, 8)

Between one set of habits and the next is the zone of improvisa-
tion. It is a time of extraordinary peril for the individual. When an
entire culture can no longer keep up with its own startling change
and loses its habits, its survival comes profoundly into doubt. For
the last hundred years in the West, the activity in the vicinity of the
boundary that divides these two states—the one where everything
has been said, and the other where there may be nothing to say—
has been brisk. It is the familiar topos of the modern improvisor.
Robert Duncan writes:

> the death of Man at work,   bee hive
>   cells a-buzz with it,
>   the thriving of Death among us
>   the work of Art to set words
>   jiving breaking into crises
> in which a deathless strain moves thru
>   means without ends
>   Brancusi's towering column
> moving into its true power,
> into an imagined "endlessness", each stage of the form
>   dying upward, giving way
> measures moving in eternity unmoving.
>   (Duncan, 1984, 19)

"Jiving breaking into crises" specifies the art of the improvisor.
It is the disruption of the deathly habits of the beehive, which is
busy only with its own mechanism. In the beehive, there is only
death and the hard work of emulating death; it is the image of
repetition obsession. The purposelessness of art—"means without
ends"—escapes both death and the compulsion of sentimentalized
habit. The alternatives that poststructuralism discovers are defined
in a world of rule-governed linguistic atoms. The improvisation of
the common knowledge, on the other hand, is an eros uncom-
promised by death, an eros that makes symbols only of things in its
construction of the things which construct it.

The examples from *Kora* that Bruns himself gives undercut the
notion that improvisation represents a kind of poetic holiday; he
speaks of a "theory of gameless play." If Williams is innocent of the
usual rhetorical requirements, he incurs another guilt—the guilt of
anyone who uses words perhaps—that the unreasonable body of
language is inseparable from the organon of representation and

reason. He finds himself responsible for that which is arbitrary, "meaningless," and "merely" physical in language. Bruns takes this example from *Kora:*

> When beldams dig clams their fat hams (it's always beldams) balanced near Tellus's hide, this rhinoceros pelt, these lumped stones—buffoonery of midges on a bull's thigh—invoke,—what you will: birth's glut, awe at God's craft, youth's poverty, evolution of a child's caper, man's poor inconsequence. Eclipse of all things; sun's self turned hen's rump.

It is difficult to understand how a reader would find innocence in a passage that attends so relentlessly to "the tone-leading of vowels" and that is, further, poised on a rime (lumped / rump), giving the passage something of the formal quality of a couplet. And the passage does not lose the burden of the sound even as it opens into a new paragraph:

> Cross a knife and fork and listen to the church bells! It is the harvest moon's made wine of our blood. Up over the dark factory into the blue glare start the young poplars. They whisper: It is Sunday! It is Sunday! But the laws of the country have been stripped bare of leaves. Out over the marshes flicker our laughter. (Williams, 1970, 50–51)

Here "church" picks up the phonetic dynamism from "turned," and the passage carries on the short-*a* sounds that were announced at the beginning, almost like a tonic key, yielding the rime of "glare" and "bare" and moving into related repetitions in "h*a*rvest," "d*a*rk," and "m*a*rshes." Bruns suggests that Williams follows "the law of unpredictability." It seems, rather, that Bruns and Williams are interest in different phenomena. Bruns is confident that the sound pattern of a poem is a largely irrational sequence of noises. In these passages one comes to ask whether it is the sequence of noises—the complex patterns of which could be considered at much greater length than I have here—or the readerly expectation of a syntax of subordination which is irrational.

The text is, Bruns says, a list, and "The list, in contrast to the game, is more character than plot—is episodic, one damn thing after another, or containing no demands for a conclusion" (Bruns, 1982, 150). He is, I suspect, thinking of the impossibility of "giving an account" of this writing. What does one tell the eager students in Introduction to Modern Poetry? If there were plot or rules, we might discover the principle for the generation of items on the list, but there is no secret to be unlocked. The reader can only wait and see; the explicator quickly runs into foolishness. Bruns seems slightly scandalized that language is so prolific: "A list is a way of exceeding the limits of the sentence without actually abolishing them" (Bruns, 1982, 150). The production here, however, is profusion, joyously spilling over the bounds of the sentence, the completed thought goes beyond completion, beyond conclusion. In the "Prologue" to *Kora*, Williams writes: "The true value is that peculiarity which gives an object a character by itself. The associational or sentimental value is false. Its imposition is due to lack of imagination, to an easy lateral sliding. The attention has been held too rigid on the one plane instead of following a more flexible, jagged resort. It is to loosen the attention, my attention since I occupy part of the field, that I write these improvisations. Here I clash with Wallace Stevens" (Williams, 1970, 15).

In the domain of the symbolic, the domain of Stevens's work, things have meaning through their relationship to the symbolic system as whole. The fundamental semantic unit is the metaphor. Meaning arises from the ratio of the particular to its implicit background. Stevens and artists of his kind seek the stable reconciliation of the particular with the totality that is possible only in the artful illusion. For Stevens, the supremely self-conscious artist, who is aware of the instability of such artful ploys, the illusion reaches out endlessly to stabilize itself in a regression of illusions. *In the domain of the measured or common, things have meaning through themselves.* The problem is not the one and the many but the many and the more: the erotic proliferation never looks to any stability beyond the stability that the act itself affords. The language is not a calculus but a construction, moment by moment, image by image. The fundamental semantic unit is the image. Williams's mother stands at the beginning of the "Prologue" as a kind of muse: "Whatever is before her is sufficient to itself and so to be valued" (Williams, 1970, 6).

How to Read and Write

Ezra Pound's "How to Read" (1927) and its expanded version, *ABC of Reading* (1934), and Gertrude Stein's *How to Write* (1931) are at the pre-Socratic stage of the new poetics. For the first time, there is a proposal to begin again that does not involve the Edenic equation of being with the logic of symbolism. Both Pound and Stein write how-to books: theirs is a knowledge that cannot be stated but only practiced. That is to say, as Wittgenstein repeatedly demonstrates, *meaning is use*. Going beyond the beginning is now a question not of thought but of practice.

Gertrude Stein writes: "I said in the beginning of saying this thing that if it were possible that a movement were lively enough it would exist so completely that it would not be necessary to see it moving against anything to know that it is moving" (Stein, 1985, 170). That movement is the eros of the common knowledge. It is a knowledge not of ratios or relationships but of things in themselves, unique and beyond comparison. Value is based upon individuality, not exchange or metaphor. Pound notes, "No science save the arts will give us the requisite data for learning in what way men differ" (Pound, 1965, 42). Stein makes a similar point: "While I was listening and hearing and feeling the rhythm of each human being I gradually began to feel the difficulty of putting it down. Types of people I could put down but a whole human being felt at one and the same time, in other words while in the act of feeling that person was very difficult to put into words" (Stein, 1985, 145). The poets of the common knowledge do not mystify voice and self on behalf of writing. They are concerned not with the presence of the self but with the presence of the Other. Here is a tree, a stone, above all, another person. Where might we look to find more basic or more reliable knowledge which could guarantee our intuition? That which exists through itself discovers itself an object amongst objects in a space uninterrupted by discrete egos.

In *ABC of Reading*, Pound distinguishes between alphabetic and ideogrammatic languages. The one, as we have seen, consists of a finite combinatory of simple signs that we now call "phonemes" and a set of rules by which phonemes are combined. Pound was aware by 1912 or 1913 that the allowable combinations cannot be specified by a finite number of rules. "The other kind of language," he notes, "starts by being a picture of the cat, or of something moving, or being, or of a group of things which occur under certain circumstances, or which participate a common quality" (Pound, 1960, 29). The important difference between these languages is not the obvious one. Pound was fascinated by the visual quality of the Chinese written character and by the concreteness of calligraphy, but he was at least as interested in language as sound as language as image:

> And poor old Homer blind, blind, as a bat,
> Ear, ear for the sea-surge, murmur of old men's voices:
> 'Let her go back to the ships,
> Back among Grecian faces, lest evil come on our own,
> Evil and further evil, and a curse cursed on our children,
> Moves, yes she moves like a goddess
> and has the face of a god
>   and the voice of Schoeney's daughters,
> and doom goes with her in walking,
> Let her go back to the ships,
>   back among Grecian voices.
>
>   (Pound, 1971, 10)

Calligraphy or typography is only one aspect of the physicality of language. The poet who wrote these lines, as much as the poet whom they are about, is a master of the craft, the materials of which are consonants and vowels cutting designs in time. Pound does not conclude from the example of Chinese poetry that we must abandon phonetic writing; rather, he proposes the necessity of abandoning the grammatical and logical modes that phonology implies. We must return to the beginnings, to learn to read again, and specifically to begin with the ABCs as images—marks in measurable space—rather than phonemes, which are ideal entities that cannot be discovered in the most sophisticated spectographic analysis of speech.

Our language instruction begins well enough. We give teething babies ABC books made of materials that can withstand repeated gummings. The alphabetic characters are associated with images, and it is important for children to learn that the relationship of *B* to *ball* is not unique; it may also be *baby, bottle,* and so forth. Slightly more advanced ABCs include the information that the alphabetic characters have alternative forms: *B* may also be *b*. The alphabet is arbitrary; the images are not. Children learn to talk without rules, and it is only the seriously impaired who do not speak with at least some proficiency. As children begin to read and write, however, we begin to teach rules of grammar and the learning of language falls under a discipline. The dynamism is lost. "Chinese notation . . . ," Fenollosa writes, "is based upon a vivid shorthand picture of the operations of nature." Of the Chinese sentence "man sees horse" he says, "The thought-picture is not only called up by these signs as well as by words, but far more vividly and concretely. Legs belong to all three characters: they are *alive*. The group holds something of the quality of a continuous moving picture" (Fenollosa, 1967, 8). Sergei Eisenstein independently noted the comparison of the Chinese character and the frames of the cinema: "The film-frame can never be an inflexible *letter of the alphabet,* but must always remain a multiple-meaning *ideogram.* And it can be read only in juxtaposition, just as an ideogram acquires its specific *significance, meaning,* and even *pronunciation. . . .*" (Eisenstein, 1957, 65–66). It is not the visual nature of the Chinese characters but the ways in which, juxtaposed, their discrete boundaries break down and create self-modifying and self-producing continua that is important. The sense of their necessary relationship to their meanings derives primarily not from representation of their referent, which is of course often vague, but from their intransitive measurability.

Of *The Making of Americans* and the early portraits, Gertrude Stein writes:

> I was doing what the cinema was doing, I was making a succession of the statement of what that person was until I had not many things but one thing. . .
>
>   In a cinema picture no two pictures are exactly alike each one is just that much different from the one before, and so in those early portraits there was as I am sure you realize as I read them to you also as there was in *The Making of Americans* no repetition. Each time that I said somebody whose portrait I was writing was something that something was just that much different from what I had just said that somebody was and little by little in this way a whole portrait came into being, a portrait that was not description and that was made by each time, and I did a great many times, say it. (Stein, 1985, 177)

In the cinema, we see measured sequences. From frame to frame, a slowly moving object appears in adjacent frames to be indistinguishably repeated. A comparison of every other frame, however, may reveal that it is moving. That is, movie sequences are intransitive like other measured forms: frame A equals frame B, frame B equals frame C, but frame A does not equal frame C. If every point of an object's trajectory were represented on film, it would have to be infinitely long and would require an infinitely fast machine to project its movement. Stein's phrase, "a whole portrait came into being . . . that was *made each time*" (my emphasis), is accurate to the construction of measured images. The image does not exist at any instantaneous cross section, but, the *whole* subject is in each measurable duration. Unlike a description that decomposes the sitter into atomic units and presents her unit by unit—eyes, nose, mouth, and so forth—Stein's subjects as integral beings are implicit in each time of their making. The continuity of the image in cinematic time and space is a result of the complex event of the movie—the film moving through the projector at a certain speed, the eye of the viewer scanning the screen, the appearance and gradual decay of light traces on the retina, and so forth. Stein slows the process down, so the measure "made by each time" is clearly revealed and our participation is restored. The signs, thus, referring only to themselves, being only what they are, are utterly necessary and, as they could not be otherwise, they are unambiguous, though of course unparaphrasable. Meaning is not an in-other-words equivalent that somehow accompanies the sign.

Although Pound had recognized the rightness of Fenollosa's critique of Western grammar, he did not question the institutions that preserved and enforced the historical tradition of that grammar. As a writer, he escaped totalitarianism, but as a reader, even a reader of his own work, he often did not. This peculiar schizophrenia was widespread among U.S. writers between 1917 and 1945. Pound, like so many of his generation, was a devotee of a widespread nostalgia cult—flourishing in universities to this day—that appeals to the literate past, when the unity of a text interpreted the various marks that constituted it and the problem of the One and the Many generated dialectical excitement. As long as the culture maintained a homogeneous collection of controlling images, the dialectic was a powerful administrative tool precisely because it was possible to structure the writing and *reading* of texts and thus to organize large populations for production. In a literate culture, however, the semantic resources that are available to a speaker and an audience—a shared orientation in a landscape—must be synthetically reproduced in written records, and as E. D. Hirsch and Alan Bloom show in their best-selling books, literacy requires a rigorous selection of references. The European tradition invested inconceivable amounts of time and energy in constructing a universal landscape in language. For two and one-half millennia, the culture built the pyramids of *logos* on the backs of school children. The world view which it accommodates is provincial but provinciality or at least narrowness is essential to its success. The semantic keys must constitute a compact and teachable package.

Shifting the emphasis from Pound's how to read to Stein's how to write requires a radical empowerment of the audience. It is a change of this order that is required. Gertrude Stein declares "Grammar is in our power" (Stein, 1973, 73). Thus, the reign of intimidation by the written word, which had originated with the Greek conception of the *logos,* ended. Nietzsche had said that we still believed in God because we believed in grammar. He could only imagine an eternal recurrence of the casting out and the return of the deity. Thought, to say nothing of emotion, had not been fully our responsibility. We had been appropriated by structures that were not our own. Some of these structures we could rationalize or partially rationalize logically or grammatically; only the origin remained mysterious. It was dealt with theologically; a singular mystery could be localized and ritualized. Although it involved a large cultural investment, it was more or less successfully maintained for millennia.

The rational structures were static and required only realization and maintenance. Emotion, on the other hand, the intelligent stirrings of body that also agitate the mind, had seemed inexplicable, capricious invasions that could be met only with hopeless submission or extraordinary discipline. The blindness of love, the senseless passions of war, and the almost endless diversity of non-theological, religious excitements have been merely to be enjoyed or endured. For Stein, what had been called "reason" and "emotion," these traditionally irreconcilable mental phenomena, were relative loci on a continuum, dynamic forms for which we are responsible in every act of living. Grammar is an order that derives from our participation in it and in life, not from its own internal necessities. The users of language are always in the condition of writers, creating a life from an *ad hoc* language, not readers responding to and responsible for a prior code. Stein's grammar is not descriptive but active. In *How to Write,* her grammar is so singular as to have a proper name: "Consider grammar grammar may fairly be said to be not explicative. Grammar. One two three completely. It is impossible to avoid meaning and if there is meaning and it says what it does there is grammar. Arthur a grammar"

(Stein, 1973, 71). Of course since grammar is in our power, we may also hear "Arthur" as "Author"—a name as an imperative verb; we author not a text but a grammar. "Grammar is how you are" (Stein, 1973, 95).

The traditional grammars are all heavily biased toward the substantive and therefore the static; the Zenonian paradoxes are inevitably hidden away somewhere in them. In order "to think pure change" as the Hegelian imperative requires, it is necessary to overcome the Western bias toward grammars based on nouns or even some ultimate, Hegelian noun. As Fenollosa notes, Western grammars take even verbs in their infinite, substantive mood as primary. In effect, a "thing" in western grammar, the touchstone of concreteness, is itself an abstraction. The assumption that the primary linguistic act is naming places a logic of classification at the origin of all cognitivity. The business of mind therefore is the creation of distinctions that necessarily involve *ideal* boundaries. As Fenollosa notes, however, "A true noun, an isolated thing does not exist in nature. Things are only the terminal points, or rather the meeting points, of actions, cross-sections cut through actions, snapshots" (Fenollosa, 1967, 16). The boundaries in languages and the boundaries in living spaces, for example, have utterly different characters. As Charles Olson observes, the marking of boundaries has to do not with symbolic distinctions but with measure, the stepping off of the limits of a "haunt," an ethos, and it is inherently an ethical activity. The Chinese written character as Fenollosa understands it does not divide an infinite universe into the thing and the not-thing; it takes measure of a finite linguistic region.

Whether he accurately characterizes the actual practice of Chinese or not (and of course a lot of knowledgeable people have objected), the distinction is a necessary one. It is accurate for Stein, if not for the Chinese. Stein finds nouns and "nounishness" the least engaging aspect of language:

> A noun is a name of anything, why after a thing is named write about it. A name is adequate or it is not. If it is adequate then why go on calling it, if it is not then calling it by its name does no good. . .
>
> As I say a noun is a name of a thing, and therefore slowly if you feel what is inside that thing you do not call it by the name by which it is known. Everybody knows that by the way they do

when they are in love and a writer should always have that inten-
sity of emotion about whatever is the object about which he
writes. And there and I say it again more and more one does not
use nouns. (Stein, 1985, 209–10)

She is attracted only to those parts of speech that are "lively," a
term of which we will miss the force unless we hear it specifically
as the counterpart of "deathly." "Verbs and adverbs and articles
and conjunctions and prepositions are lively because they all do
something and as long as anything does something it keeps alive"
(Stein, 1985, 214). Stein does, of course, use those words that are
called "nouns" in traditional grammatical analysis. Even in saying
that "one does not use nouns," she uses a noun, and in poetry,
which "is concerned with using with abusing, with losing with
wanting, with denying with avoiding with adoring with replacing
the noun," she "decided not to get around them but to meet them,
to handle in short to refuse them by using them" (Stein, 1985,
231). She avoids nouns not by shifting the emphasis away from the
noun as such—that is, the class words—to verbs but by shifting
the emphasis to sentences and paragraphs as the active principles
of writing. Like Whitman who shifted his emphasis to the caesural
phrase and the line, she deals with units which are already wholes.
Only in these larger structures, to which formal linguistics has paid
minimal attention, does Stein find useful units of measure. Al-
though she says that she likes "the feeling the everlasting feeling of
sentences as they diagram themselves," her taste for the everlasting
feeling is overwhelmed by her commitment to action. Sentences
diagram *themselves,* thus asserting the intimidating authority of
their logic. The grammatical sentence cannot be written—it is
already written—and thus it might provide the schoolgirl with a
kind of theological experience, but a sentence that diagrams itself
can only be *read;* it is of no use to the writer engaged in the
moment by moment writing of writing or to one interested in how
to write.

A sentence, it turns out, is not defined by its parts; in an
important sense, it has none: it is inherently complex. In the first
chapter of *How to Write,* "Saving the Sentence," Stein writes:

What is a sentence. A sentence is a part of a speech.
A speech. They knew that beside beside is colored like a

word beside why there they went. That is a speech. Anybody will listen. (Stein, 1973, 13–14)

Sentences in themselves, however, are too static, too insistent upon their own completion, and they are therefore emotionally colorless. "Saving the Sentence" concludes with Stein's realization, "I made a mistake." The sentence alone cannot be saved; it must be saved with the paragraph. The next section of *How to Write*— "Sentences and Paragraphs"—is devoted to the proposition that "a Sentence is not emotional a paragraph is" (Stein, 1973, 21–24). The continuum of sentences is intransitive: sentence A is not emotional, and sentence B is not emotional, but the paragraph composed of sentence A plus sentence B *is* emotional. In her lecture "Plays," Stein notes:

> In a book I wrote called *How to Write* I made a discovery which I considered fundamental, that sentences are not emotional and that paragraphs are. I found out about language that paragraphs are emotional and sentences are not and I found out something else about it. I found out that this difference was not a contradiction but a combination and that this combination causes one to think endlessly about sentences and paragraphs because the emotional paragraphs are made up of unemotional sentences. (Stein, 1973, 115)

If the grammar of symbolic forms turns upon identity and difference, the grammar of measured forms turns upon *combinations*. Stein's insistence upon the thinking of combinations should be seen as the alternative to the Hegelian imperative: "We have to think pure change, or think antithesis within the antithesis itself, or contradiction" (Hegel, 1977, 99). Hegel's thunderous command is backed by the authority of grammar itself. A "combination" has only factual authority: it says only that x is combined with y. There is no necessity in the combination: "A Sentence is made by coupling meanwhile ride around to be a couple there makes grateful dubeity named atlas coin in a loan" (Stein, 1973, 115). The sentence is constructed from more or less independent units *that relate to one another*, not to some grammatical form that stands outside the sentence.

Stein, of course, has no authority but her own. She cannot, therefore, advance an argument that compels obedience. She can only exhibit the combinations that are factually but not logically authoritative. It is nevertheless a powerful exhibition, comparable in its force to *The Phenomenology of Spirit*. *How to Write* demands the same seriousness and application as the classic of idealist philosophy, and it can make such a demand only by *not* being philosophy—that is, by not engaging the dialectic.

CHAPTER 4

Symbolic Person

THE CATEGORY OF THE PERSON

The category of the person for whom the symbols of external power and the sense of individual responsibility merge, the fully modern person, that engineer of force, self-creating and world creating, who appeared with capitalism and the Reformation, and was first fully exhibited by Fichte, Schelling, and Hegel, if not quite by Kant—as Marcel Maus tells us—is the product of a remarkable history: "From a simple masquerade to the mask, from a 'role' (*personnage*) to a 'person' (*personne*), to a name, to an individual; from the latter being possessing metaphysical and moral value; from a moral consciousness to a sacred being; from the latter to a fundamental form of thought and action—the course is accomplished" (Maus, 1985, 23). The binding of a *logical* category—the Cartesian subject—to abstract *force* must be accounted one of the premier engineering feats of post-Enlightenment technology, and it could never have been achieved without the subject's intimate involvement in its own articulation. It was the creation of a new, abstract Adam, who did not merely carry out the divine purpose by naming things but brought the force of abstract structure to bear on his own purposes. The natural force that drove the earth in its orbit—and, according to nineteenth-century theory, drove the species to ever higher realizations of itself—also drove the conquistadors of nature—the human will and the Empire of the West. The symbolic person was symbolic nature's device for mastering itself. As Lacan rightly notes, the abstract ego is a monster:

> In the "emancipated" man of modern society, this splitting reveals, right down to the depths of his being, a neurosis of self-punishment, with the hysterico-hypochondriac symptoms of its functional inhibitions, with the psychasthenic forms of its derealization of others and of the world, with its social consequences in failure and crime. It is this pitiful victim, this escaped, irresponsible outlaw, who is condemning modern man to the most formi-

dable social hell, whom we meet when he comes to us; it is our daily task to open up to this being of nothingness the way of his meaning in a discreet fraternity—a task for which we are always too inadequate. (Lacan, 1977, 29)

The profound cultural task that loomed at the end of the nineteenth century was to redeem subjectivity from this monstrous, abstract egotism and, at the same time, to protect the social order without rendering subjective experience empty and meaningless.

Freud undertook to give a rational account of human subjectivity as Descartes accounted for the objective world. *The self-isolating subject which had withdrawn into its own privacy to articulate a symbolic nature was now to describe its private domain within the rationalistic symbolism.* In a sense, the mind's only resource is to loop back on itself: submitting its own rationality to its critique of rationalism. The subject, which had been the boundary and form of knowledge, was now to be realized as content. The innate ideas that had provided the unquestioned semantic keys to the abstract structures of Cartesian subjectivity were laid open to investigation, and it was found that, rather than fulfilling the Cartesian promise of divine origin and univocal interpretation, they are symptomatic psychic disease and ambiguous. As a logical construct, the ego's content is rational, but it is required to serve as a conduit for irrational forces, which, escaping the Hegelian sublation, seem once again invasive, something to be defended against rather than used.

The poetics of common knowledge does not propose an alternative theory, which would be only another relativism, a different theater, so the mind becomes, as it does for Wallace Stevens, a kind of vaudeville performer working in one playhouse tonight and another tomorrow. The function of theory is to create a determinate background, an array of discrete objects that may be physical things (the furnishings of the world) or logical things (propositions, phonemes, "meanings"), defining a theater of action. The debate that has absorbed so much of our attention for the past two decades—structuralism versus poststructuralism—has concerned itself with the relationship of the act, specifically in literary theory the acts of reading and writing, to the theoretical background. The testimony of Freud and Lacan has been crucial to these considerations. We have wanted to know if the act is an expression of theoretical mechanisms as such or if it is possible to generate a critical intensity that is independent of theory. We have reached conclusive results: the act is independent; it cannot be traced to a theoretical origin. Unfortunately, however, the social domain that the Freudian strategy opens is fully predictable and controllable by statistical means. Cartesian theory is founded on a subject that is unique and absolute; Freudian theory seeks the possibility of a normative subject. Both propose methodologies for renovating the individual on behalf of an epistemological mechanism: one seeks the perfection of a solipsistic ideal; the other, the perfection of a social ideal. They are equally mechanistic and totalitarian. Whether the person conceived as a virtual machine is to be programmed with algebraic geometry or with a normative narrative about family life makes a profound difference in the nature of subjective experience, of course. In the Cartesian machine, the person is an equals sign, the underwriter of the mathematical equation; in the Freudian machine, the person is a perpetual child, the carrier of a genetic psychology between parents who never die and an adulthood that never fully appears. In either case, the person is performing a program, and, no doubt, a great deal of human performance is of precisely that monotonous and desperate kind.

For the poetics of the common knowledge, the person is an opacity at the center of knowledge, a contingency, an *ad hoc* jargon, not a grammar, not a virtual machine to be programmed. The distinction that is to be made is not between two theories but between two rhythms or frequencies of human action, only one of which can be expressed theoretically or statistically. Both are pervasive, and, to a greater or lesser degree, both are inevitable. One is the rhythm of the measured manifold; the other, the rhythm of the discrete manifold. One is the rhythm of action; the other, the rhythm of description. One is sustainable and environmentally sound; the other progresses toward a limit of exhaustion. Writing of Shakespeare's late plays, Charles Olson makes the distinction in these terms:

> There is a rule: a thing ought to take off, and put down, and travel at all the varying speeds in between, precisely equal in amount and behavior to the thing it sets out from or seeks. Or if it multiplies, it only multiplies by changing that thing, not by introducing and asserting outside power (as humanism did and all motors with moving parts do), and the quarrel with it is the waste of energy, which is dispersal and, in the curving about of

fact, dispersal comes back and changes, willy-nilly whirligig, the original element of both thing and thing, by making easy the attention and thus reducing the intensity below the level of the implicit power of occasion or of thing. (Olson, 1967, 93)

The important discovery that has solidified the post–World War II attempt to arrive at the common knowledge is that *meaning* may be relative to an opaque performer-creator as well as to a theoretical background. In this chapter, Louis Zukofsky serves to illustrate this development. Like Olson, Zukofsky finds his lead in Shakespeare:

> Shakespeare's writing argues with no one: only in itself. It says: *Love's reason's without reason (Cym.,*IV,ii,22); *Flaming in the . . . sight . . . Love hath reason, Reason none.* This writing exists as its own tempest (as in *The Tempest* or any of the other plays and poems) where thought is free (or necessary-the same difference after a while) and *music is for nothing (T.,*III,ii,132,154). (Zukofsky, 1987, 37)

And after more than fifty pages of careful argument, he concludes:

> And that will be precisely the value of reading Shakespeare—or for that matter anyone who is worth reading—that is, the feeling that his writing as a whole world *is,* compelling any logic or philosophy of history not to confuse an expression of *how it is* with *that world is.* The thought that *it is* has, of course, no value, is rather of a region where thought is free and music is for nothing–or as eyes see and go out. (Zukofsky, 1987, 91)

Thus, *love sees,* and it sees *meanings.* There is an order of articulation that is absorbed not by its own logical requirements but by an actual, finite and therefore knowable world.

METAPSYCHOLOGY

Metapsychology is the science of the *crisis* of mind-body dualism. It is, as Freud describes it, "a method of approach according to which every mental process is considered in relation to three coordinates, which I described as *dynamic, topographical* and *economic,* respectively." And he says, "this seemed to me to represent the furthest goal that psychology could attain" (Freud, 1955, 20:58–59). Psychodynamism, psychotopography, and psycho-economics are the concerns of the three sections that follow.

The problem of metapsychology is to account for mental events at once as functions of both psychological and physical processes—processes that cannot be assimilated to the same metric. As Wittgenstein notes,

> When we are studying psychology we may feel there is something unsatisfactory, some difficulty about the whole subject or study—because we are taking physics as our ideal science. We think of formulating laws as in physics. And then we find we cannot use the same sort of "metric", the same ideas of measurement as in physics. This is especially clear when we try to describe appearances: the least noticeable differences of colours; the least noticeable differences of length, and so on. Here it seems that we cannot say: "If A = B, and B = C, then A = C," for instance. And this sort of trouble goes all through the subject. (Wittgenstein, 1967, 42)

Of course, he is referring here to the Weber-Fechner law, the consequences of which we examined in the last chapter.

Freud's solution to this problem is ingenious. He breaks the psychic field into a discrete, symbolic manifold—or, as we shall see, a more or less discrete manifold, as Freudian distinctions are incontinent—and depreciates consciousness of minute difference. The psychic mechanism, as Freud understands it, does not deal with subtle distinctions. "What part," Freud asks, "is there left to be played in our scheme by consciousness, which was once so omnipotent and hid all else from view? Only that of a sense-organ for the perception of psychical qualities" (Freud, 1955, 5:615). Consciousness in the Freudian scheme is almost unnecessary, a mirror put in the cage to amuse the otherwise self-sufficient mechanism with a display of time, color, sound, texture, and so forth. For Freud, as much as for Newton, these are secondary or derived properties that are more or less illusory. Consciousness is, at best, "a de-bugging trace," in Marvin Minsky's computer jargon that might be applied in the vernacular to psychoanalysis.

Freud undermines the consciousness that Hegel had wrestled from Force by positing the metapsychological mechanism of the symbolic person, a mere input-output device to which self-consciousness is almost irrelevant. He writes: "All psychical activity starts from stimuli (whether internal or external) and ends in innervation" (Freud, 1955, 5:537). The psychic machine absorbs

FIGURE 4.1.

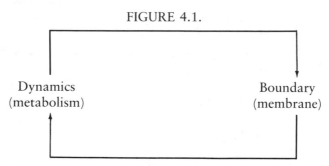

Dynamics
(metabolism)

Boundary
(membrane)

Source: The Standard Edition of the Complete Psychological Works of
Sigmund Freud, 5:541.

force and produces only entropy. Freud's diagram of the mechanism is, in computer jargon, a flow chart (Fig. 4.1).

The dynamism—that is, life itself—belongs not to the person but to the medium. The differences between subject and object, interior and exterior are described not in logical terms, as they were by Hegel, but in topographical terms, and action is described as transfers of force, an economy of boundary crossings. The symbolic person, the person of consciousness, appears in the contemplation of the dark interior geography of the body and the endless body of language. This production of text, however, as writing, as life, as act in relation to infinite regression is not, in fact, production, but reproduction, repetition, monotony, habit, the manifestation of statistical norms. The Freudian media are the media in the popular sense of the term, which we now call upon as people once called on the *name* of God, the very source of dynamism as such. The prose medium, which arose in the seventeenth century to mediate between the ideal world and the ideal self, has subsumed ideality and in turn is subsumed by a pervasive information environment in which self, world, and society are loci that we descry at a certain never-quite-to-be overcome distance.

Freud does not articulate a formal logic, but his practice delineates the mechanism of a social discipline, a vague but fundamentally controlling grammar in which the collective objects constituting a person—protoplasm, neurones, languages, desires, egos, superegoes, parents, objects of very different kinds—appear and combine in an endless process of self-simulation. Any object may have several locations: a parent, for example, may appear as a literal progenitor, as a figure of the superego, and, by transference, as a psychoanalyst, or as a particular configuration of cathected neurones. All of these loci, according to Freud, figure as variables in an extraordinarily complex algorithm that produces and sustains a simple, normative drama.

Freud abstracted from archetypical metaphors as Descartes abstracted from geometry. Freudian ontology discovered that to be a subject is to be the value of a metaphorical variable; Cartesian ontology discovered that to be an object is to be the value of an algebraic variable. These are the historical terms, along with Boole's, Frege's, and Russell's logics, behind Willard Quine's dictum "To be is to be the value of variable" (Quine, 1969, 36). This is the ontology of technology; perhaps it is the ontology of ontology itself. It is a *useful* definition of being—it turns all beings into beings of use—and we have been granted a relief from it only by those, including Freud himself, who point out that the value of the variable is often undecidable. (This is, of course, the sole strategy of the poststructuralists.) It ignores, however, the opacity of *factual* being, being that is non-onto*logical*— that which simply *is* rather than that which is required by a *logos*. The domains of being— one continuous and one discrete, one qualitative and one quantitative ("the principle of measurement . . . already contained in it," in Riemann's phrase)—do not, except for specific purposes, constitute the terms of a ratio. We are unique individuals, not statistical zones. "The transmission of quality," as Freud tells us, "is not durable; it leaves no traces behind and cannot be reproduced" (Freud, 1955, 1:310). The truly interesting aspect of life cannot be simulated. It cannot therefore become the content of an economy based on memory and wish fulfillment.

Psychodynamism

The dynamism that Freud identifies—the dynamism of personal ambition and, collectively, of social progress—is a feature of the categorical person constituted as a function of its inputs. The person is *driven*, as the shaft of the engine is driven, by both exogeneous and endogeneous forces. The stimuli or inputs are pain or desire; the outputs are acts of living, *motor* acts—notably, according to Freud, avoidance of pain and satisfaction of desire by which stress is brought to temporary equilibrium. This dynamic structure is common to both organic and aesthetic forms as they were understood by nineteenth-century theory. What is this impelling force? Lacan notes that "repetition automatism," or repetition compulsion as it is more commonly translated in English, with all of its deathly implications, is associated with the *insistence* of the signifying chain itself (Lacun, 1977, 153). What is the nature of this insistence? this discipline that masters us?

If we accept the premises of a syllogism—all A are B, C is A—then we are impelled to accept the conclusion–C is B—at the penalty of being irrational. The conclusion can be shown by analysis to say the same thing as the two premises, and we appear to lack seriousness if we agree with a proposition stated in certain terms but refuse to agree to the same proposition stated in different terms. The 'force' of logic, however, is not coercive. We may *choose* to be irrational, and of course many people do. This is one face of freedom. We cannot, however, always chose to be rational. We are *forced* to behave in a certain way. We feel the torque of input: "I cannot help myself." In a letter of 1897, Freud writes, "the psychical structures which, in hysteria, are affected by repression are not in reality memories—since no one indulges in mnemic activity without a motive—but *impulses* which arise from the primal scene" (Freud, 1985, 239). Memory has an insistence that, repressed, turns to unconscious production. The differences of potential that force us to seek equilibrium—the tense distances between the unrepressed and the repressed, between content and form, between eros and thanatos—disequilibrate; they are the motives of the dynamism as such.

Although we have conventional techniques for dealing with the split, the split itself and the subsequent disequilibrium cannot be theorized—no single theater can contextualize it. No *medium*, by definition, contains the most intimate interior or the most sublime and terrifying otherness. In their place we have substituted a monotrop that embraces both the soul and the world—"pure" art, shopping malls, and all the institutions that administer both. Despite the medium's obvious ruthlessness, we have served its need to be embodied in intellectual disciplines as well as totalitarian gods and totalitarian leaders. Now we approach a perfection in which the replica is potentially self-sustaining. It no longer requires enforcement. The distractions it presents are absorbing and comfortable, hallucinogenic and pervasive. Our profoundest cultural rituals are inevitably in some measure *ad hoc,* typically sleazy, and produce unwanted by-products, which accumulate and must eventually choke us. Freudian theory accepts ecological disaster as inevitable. The dynamism that drives us is out of control. Freud tells us of Woodruff's findings: "An infusorian, if it is left to itself, dies a natural death owing to its incomplete voidance of the products of its own metabolism" (Freud, 1955, 18:48). Is this our condition, or did Woodruff's experimental conditions create a society of infusoria out of homeostatic control? a society that had unsound ecology forced upon it by the scientist's hand?

The science that Freud inherited had no way to answer these questions. It almost had no way to ask them, because the conceptual constituents of the question, concerning the relationship of facts from different disciplines, had hardly been formulated. The best science of the nineteenth century required radically inconsistent frames of reference to account for nonorganic, organic, and electromagnetic natural systems. The most fundamental conceptions, such as the character of time and space, implicit in Newtonian physics, Darwinian (or, for that matter, Goethean) organicism, and Faradayan field theory, were in conflict. Strictly speaking, time was an illusion in classical mechanics, and space— at least abstract Newtonian space—was an illusion in field theory. By calling somatic stability into question, organicism in its diverse forms undermined all absolute senses of both space and time whatsoever. As Oswald Spengler rightly noted, the perception of nature as historical leads directly to a pervasive relativism. Unlike classical or Cartesian skepticism, it does not deny philosophy outright but admits it, in all of its complexity. In some sense, in relationship to some specifically elucidated background, all of the philosophies are true: "Modern skepticism's solutions are got by treating everything as relative, as historical through and through. . . . is 'skepsis,' in the true sense," Spengler writes, "for whereas the Greek is led to renounce absolute standpoints by contempt for the intellectual past, we are led to do so by comprehension of that past as an organism" (Spengler, 1939, 1:45).

It was impossible, thereafter, to have knowledge apart from this or that set of disciplinary assumptions, and they were not merely historical and open to constant and perhaps capricious revision, they were blatantly in contradiction at the most fundamental levels. The laws of motion, the laws of organic growth, and the laws of electrical fields—to say nothing of the dynamics of the psyche—belonged to incommensurable, empirical domains. In this atmosphere the intellectual disciplines proliferated: history in the modern sense, economics, sociology, psychology, anthropology, as well as the specialized histories of literature, the visual arts, music, the subgenres of physical and biological science, and so forth, each with its own ontology, often with competing ontologies within a single discipline.

The lack of a coherent frame of reference constituted a profound problem for the dynamics of the culture: if the dynamism of history could not be explained as the process of mind seeking equilibrium with the absoluteness of its own logic, it was necessary to look to external forces impelling the change that the emerging technology made perhaps the most obvious character of nineteenth-century life. If logic did not drive life, it must be then that logic was driven by *something*. A metaphysic was required, but a hardheaded metaphysic, consistent with the rhetoric of both right- and left-wing industrial progressivism. As we have seen, Hegel had managed a most uneasy sublation of force by consciousness as a motive of the *Phenomenology*, and the concept rebounded as the central concept of materialistic metaphysics. The gospel of force that appeared at the intersection of scientific philosophy, progressive boosterism, and social Darwinism was variously articulated by Marx's early writings, Buckle's *History of Civilization*, Spencer's *Principles*, and John Fiske's popular *Outlines of Cosmic Philosophy*, as well as popular editorialists and preachers. The concept of force in its vernacular and scientific senses provided both the inclusiveness and the vagueness that was required. It is one of the most persistent concepts in western thought, so abstract and apparently empty that its theological character tends to go unnoticed.

Max Jammer and Mary Hesse, both of whom have written important historical studies of the concept, find the origins of the idea of 'force' in ancient mythology and trace its early formulation as a concept to the Pre-Socratics, notably the dynamistic philosophers—Heraclitus and Empedocles. It was however Aristotle who first articulated the dual sense of the concept as force inherent in nature (*physis*), and as, in Jammer's words, "force as an emanation from substance, the force of push and pull, causing the motion in a second object, and not in itself." Of course, the Aristotelian concept, which was closely related to the central concept of causation, was variously interpreted by the scholastic philosophers, and was a mainstay of the philosophic tradition until the seventeenth century. In depersonalized and quantified form, the concept of force transferred to Newtonian mechanics.

As a commonsense notion, force seems clear and obvious. The scientific concept, however, proved to be problematic, and by the end of the nineteenth century, indeed about the time it became a central metaphor for Freud, it had been, in effect, eliminated from physics altogether.

> As to the concept of force, taken originally in analogy to human will power, spiritual influence, or muscular effort, the concept became projected into inanimate objects as a power dwelling in physical things. Omitting at present some intermediate stages, the concept of force became instrumental for the definition of "mass," which in its turn gave rise to the definition of "momentum." Subsequently classical mechanics redefined the concept of force as the time rate of change of momentum, excluding thereby, at least prima facie, all animistic vestiges of earlier definitions. Finally, force became a purely relational notion, almost ready to be eliminated from the conceptual construction altogether. (Jammer, 1957, 7)

Animistic forces remained, however, as pervasive and utterly reified metaphors for the indwelling energies of persons, historical groups, and linguistic media long after they had been eliminated from physics. From Hegel to Freud, the motive of possibilities passed from force sublated by language to language itself as systematic, or perhaps just irresponsible, dynamism: language was force, cause, and will. No longer dependent upon external motivation, it was active, an entity in itself, an organism that was, in some sense, alive and to which vital attributes were unselfconsciously attributed. According to Foucault, "from the nineteenth century, language began to fold in upon itself, to acquire its own particular density, to deploy a history, an objectivity, and laws of its own" (Foucault, 1970, 296). Relieved from the hierarchy that was imposed by its codependency with the subject, it was taken up by its own circularity, defining itself in relation to its own forever-changing background. Nietzsche announces the appearance of that medium in a oft-quoted passage, indeed perhaps the most frequently quoted passage in literary theory of the past two decades, saying that truth is "A mobile army of metaphors, metonyms, and anthropomorphisms . . .; metaphors which are worn out and without sensuous power; coins which have lost their pictures and now matter only as metal, no longer as coins" (Nietzsche, 1954, 45).

Nietzsche's military metaphor is fundamental to the indecisive intellectual campaigning of the past century. It was, however, Freud who showed us how specific value could be restored to these face-less coins *without* recovering the original image. The word was not bound to an objective signified, not to an "object" so elusive as force, but to *more* language which is itself bound by *force* (cathexis) to language in turn. At the very moment, humankind had the possibility of taking possession of its own physical desire, Freud relocated force as a function of a pervasive physio-linguistic metaphor.

The fabric of Freud's writing consists of tropes of tropes, representations of representations, and so forth. His work was central to a world in which language was not merely a chief actor on the stage; it was very nearly the *only* actor. In a world that understood different aspects of life in terms of incommensurable paradigms, language driven by force—the vastest and most inclusive abstraction, equatable with Being itself—was the only indication that the various disciplines all addressed the same world. From the ancient myths to Lacan and his followers, the vital principle is driven through a language, the logical structure of which is circular: life is conserved as a vital force, a drive, or compulsion to repeat. This pure abstract force need not be "centered" in a particular substance: the deconstruction of all of the metaphysical objects has left a diffuse flow as the "stuff" of an unlocated progressivism. Language is the animating force of the input-output machine that we have made of ourselves.

"Theory" begs the questions of life and the nature of the living. The theoretical mechanisms, whether the elementary machinery of the epics or the elegant machinery of the DNA molecule, appeal to a teleonomy, if not teleology, some outlying or indwelling force of purpose that *drives* the machine. That is, the explanations of life explain everything but life itself, which is inevitably traced back to *something else*. Freud follows the same pattern in his explanation of psychic mechanisms:

it is demonstrably untrue that we are being carried along a purposeless stream of ideas when, in the process of interpreting a dream, we abandon reflection and allow involuntary ideas to emerge. It can be shown that all that we can ever get rid of are purposive ideas that are *known* to us; as soon as we have done this, *unknown*—or as we inaccurately say, "unconscious"—purposive ideas take charge and thereafter determine the course of the involuntary ideas. (Freud, 1955, 5:566–67)

And, of course, if the mechanism of these unknown purposes could be adequately described, it would require some still deeper or more profoundly unknown source to emerge. Throughout his career from the early "Project for a Scientific Psychology" to *Beyond the Pleasure Principle,* Freud flirted with the possibility of pushing his explanation back from free association to somatic sources and even to a Lamarckian life-force.

The metaphor of force that derives from classical physics, however, plays itself out in Freud, where force as propulsion, as life energy, meets its counterforce as Newtonian law requires. The force that drives life, it seems to Freud, "wants" to generalize entropically. If Hegel recognized the necessity of thinking change and time, while remaining within the mechanistic framework of the general laws of motion, Freud discovered the necessity of *being* change and time. The stasis that he sees lurking in the background of the dynamic psyche is not the Absolute but death. In *Beyond the Pleasure Principle,* he writes:

> For a long time, perhaps, living substance was thus being constantly created afresh and easily dying, till decisive external influences altered in such a way as to oblige the still surviving substance to diverge ever more widely from its original course of life and to make more complicated *détours* before reaching its aim of death. These circuitous paths to death, faithfully kept to by the conservative instincts, would thus present us today with the picture of the phenomena of life. (Freud, 1955, 18:38–39)

As we shall see, these are logical or linguistic, not *factual,* requirements of life, but the Freudian argument haunts this century: the technology that amplifies the possibilities of life and makes the promise of human divinity seem almost credible also seems a complicated *détour* to death. Each divergence is also a repetition, a variation on a theme, an attempted replication of a remembered and desired state.

Freudian theory itself has been endlessly rehearsed. It may seem futile to rehearse it again. Freud, however, was the vehicle for the last phase of a psycho-historical dynamism that *required* articulation. The mind of the West—which is, of course, itself merely a rhetorical figure of the philosophic tradition—had been commandeered by a language that absorbed its users in *its* grammatical requirements. The grandiose ego of Cartesian linguistics and its megalomaniacal dialectic, which promises to resolve only in infinity, were—and more or less *are*—the desperate terms of willful beings turned against themselves. Freud sought to expose and treat this megalomania in a colossal act of megalomaniacal self-analysis. The abstractions of the philosophic-religious language were to be redeemed by the discovery that their content was erotic rather than spiritual. This thought, which has reverberated through this century, has remained fresh, subversive, useful, and always ready to be rerepressed and rediscovered. Each subsequent generation has produced readers of Freud who read him as if he had never been read before. I am afraid his story must be repeated again and again until it is finally exhausted. The discovery of the repetition obsession is perhaps the content of the ultimate repetition obsession. In rehearsing Freud again, we now look for evidence that we need not follow this path to its end.

Freud's work marks the beginning of our engagement with the question: Does nature consist of dynamic objects, so that we are truly overwhelmed and must seek to reconcile our desires with a ruthless mechanism which has no interest in us as individuals by inquiring about the meaning of these objects? (The circular logic of this sentence is unavoidable). That is, can we redeem ourselves from a ruthless structure, which we ourselves created perhaps, by interpretation? Either by *finding* meaning or by generating a life intensity by seeking meaning?

Culture is the social form of repetition obsession, and the efficacy of tradition lies in its repetition of cultural forms. Whatever may be the case with organisms in "the state of nature," if that phrase now means anything at all, the evolution of culture is Lamarckian; its process consists of adaptive responses to the environment that cause structural changes that are transmitted by cultural institutions. We are compelled culturally, Freud tells us, even in our frenetic pursuit of change, to seek the classical stasis as we are compelled biologically to mimic the tranquility of inorganic things. Freud understands the artistic tradition, with its endless repetition and variation, as a crucial mechanism of this process. Cultural history, therefore, is a grim spectacle: the longing for aesthetic closure reenacts the longing for the ultimate tranquility.

The poetics of common knowledge poses the alternative questions: Do we as observers invent objects to objectify what Nature means? Can we construct ourselves in relation to our dynamism so it serves us rather than we it?

Psychotopography and the Contact Barriers

Although it had been thought since Kant, and implicitly since Descartes, that we inhabit two incommensurable domains— information, on the one hand, and energy, on the other, to use the current terminology*—the culture devoted itself to the project of overcoming the split by the willful creation of equations and the promise of reconciliation at the end of an infinite regress. The idealist tradition sought to account for energy in terms of information, and the materialist tradition sought to account for information in terms of force or energy. Information or energy, whichever is taken as fundamental, elaborates the other as its own mechanism, theatricalizing transcendence, producing archetypes, paradigms, canons, and factories for stamping out uniform products, creating new divisions and purposes.

The Cartesian *cogito* and the Kantian categories both provided accounts of innate, conscious structures. They were given this privileged status by default: they were the only structures—at least the only structures of comparable generality—that were known. The discovery of non-Euclidean and N-dimensional geometries, however, shook Western philosophy to its foundations and, by the end of the nineteenth century, even the popular imagination was prepared to reconceive the life of the mind in relation to a plastic space.*

---

*The term *force*, which had immense currency through the nineteenth century, is now somewhat outmoded. See Ronald *Martin's American Literature and the Universe of Force* for an important study of this pervasive concept (Martin, 1981). Although he focuses on American literature, his discussion of the scientific and philosophic backgrounds is strong.

*The new geometries were a popular fad around the turn of the century, as Linda Henderson shows in *The Fourth Dimension and Non-Euclidean Geometry in Modern Art* (Henderson, 1983). The matter became, for example, the subject of articles in popular magazines.

From the middle of the nineteenth century forward, the knowledge of structures and structuring proliferated: the appearance of alternative geometries was only the beginning. New aesthetic forms appeared, as, eventually, did new set theories and new logics. Euclidean structure, which had once been so rare, indeed so singular, that they had seemed the essence of mind as such, proved to be only an instance of structures that can be elaborated endlessly. Such was the testimony in the aesthetic domain of Melville, Nietzsche, Browning, Rimbaud, Henry James, Wagner, and Cézanne, to mention only some representative names. Beginning with the mathematics of L. E. J. Brouwer, early in the present century, the plasticity of abstract structure began to be fully formalized. Freud speaks profoundly from that moment beyond which neither world nor mind could be imagined as having an *inherent* logical structure.

When it appeared that we might escape the topological machinery by which we had tyrannized ourselves ever since Euclid, Freud renarrativized space. It was a powerful move, the consequences of which we are now only beginning to understand. When the nineteenth-century conception of organism is extended to metapsychology, which is the fundamental Freudian move, the person must be understood both as a discrete unity and an input-output machine driven by external forces: the organic boundary is at once a boundary and not a boundary, a barrier and a contact, a *leaky* distinction. It is the mechanism of this logic that we must now investigate.

The isolation of the Cartesian subject was a requirement of Cartesian geometry: the coordinates could not represent a reflection of themselves. The Freudian subject, by contrast, is *in* the space that it describes. Freud writes: "The subdivision of the unconscious is part of an attempt to picture the apparatus as being built up of a number of agencies or systems whose relations to one another are expressed in spatial terms, without, however, implying any connection with the actual anatomy of the brain." (Freud, 1955, 20:32). And in *The Interpretation of Dreams,* Freud recalls Fechner's "idea that the scene of action of dreams is different from that of waking ideational life." Then he goes on to say:

> What is presented to us in these words is the idea of psychical locality. I shall entirely disregard the fact that the mental apparatus with which we are here concerned is also known to us in the

form of an anatomical preparation, and I shall carefully avoid the temptation to determine psychical locality in any anatomical fashion. I shall remain upon psychological ground, and I propose simply to follow the suggestion that we should picture the instrument which carries out our mental functions as resembling a compound microscope or a photographic apparatus, or something of the kind. On that basis, psychical locality will correspond to a point inside the apparatus at which one of the preliminary stages of an image comes into being. In the microscope and telescope, as we know, these occur in part at ideal points, regions in which no tangible component of the apparatus is situated. (Freud, 1955, 5:536)

Freud's disclaimer means only that he has no *precise* way to deal with the correlations between anatomy and psyche. Unable to reconcile the truth of materialism, on the one hand, and the truth of idealism, on the other, he lays out an *n*-dimensional space that locates the known phenomena. Although he continued to long for the clarity of the hard sciences, the "literal" body and our literal descriptions of it must be seen as a metaphor among metaphors. The body is the subject of *all* of our fantasies, not just the fantasy of scientific objectivity. Freudian theory mediates between a psychophysics and a truncated phenomenology that belong to different ontological domains, relating to one another only by way of a metaphorical calculus. Despite the radically different materials of the two theories—neurones and flows of force, on the one hand, and symbols and flows of meanings, on the other—they share a common "organization." It is not necessary to define the structure of the space in detail, so long as its general nature is understood.

In a simple logical space, Spencer-Brown writes, "a distinction is drawn by arranging a boundary with separate sides so that a point on one side cannot reach the other side without crossing a boundary" (Spencer-Brown, 1979, 1). It is enough to know that such distinctions are not possible in the topology that the category of the Freudian person defines. The person is a three-plus dimensional being with a three-dimensional sensorium.* A distinction in consciousness, for the most obvious example, may still allow an

---

*Or at least *visual* space is three dimensional, and we have not made much progress in conceiving of alternative. In *The Philosophic Impact of Contemporary Physics,* for example, Milič Čapek proposes auditory space as a necessary alternative, but as far as I have been able to discover, the dimensionality and uses of synesthetic space is still largely unknown.

unconscious crossing of the boundary by way of anatomical or unconscious psychical space. Indeed, extraordinary insistence upon this or that distinction in consciousness ("I dreamed of a woman, who was certainly *not* my mother"), Freud discovered, may positively signal an unconscious crossing of the boundary. That is, the structure that appears in consciousness and the "corresponding" structure of neurones may appear to give an incoherent image until psychoanalysis supplies a topographical explanation.

Freud's "Project for a Scientific Psychology" is a remarkable piece of writing. Although he left it unfinished, its logic as well as many terms of its terms—"mental energy," "excitation," "cathexis," "quantity," and "quality," for example—are taken directly into the metapsychology of *The Interpretation of Dreams*. In the introduction, the editor of the "Project" notes correctly that it, "or rather its invisible ghost, haunts the whole series of Freud's theoretical writings to the very end" (Freud, 1955, 1:290). It is explicitly a Newtonian psychophysics.

Freud proposes what he calls a "quantitative conception" of psychic dynamism. He conceives of a kind of hydraulic fluid, driven by force, which he calls Q, "subject to the general laws of motion," and obeying "the principle of neuronal inertia: that neurones tend to divest themselves of Q." This quantity or charge irritates protoplasm and, exciting it, causes its flight from irritation: "A primary nervous system makes use of . . . Qn [Q of an intercellular order of magnitude] which it has acquired, by giving it off through a connecting path to the muscular mechanisms, and in that way keeps itself free from stimulus." Freud goes on to note, "With an [increasing] complexity of the interior [of the organism], the nervous system receives stimuli from the somatic element itself—endogenous stimuli—which have equally to be discharged." These have their origin in the cells of the body and give rise to the major needs: hunger, respiration, sexuality. From these the organism cannot simply withdraw as it does from external stimuli; they must be satisfied in the external world. (Freud, 1955, 1:295–296) Thus, the organism is invaded by external and appropriated by internal forces. It receives the necessary energy to relieve itself from irritation from precisely the irritation itself. (There is more than an remote analogy between this circular mechanism and the circularity of the *cogito*.)

The organism, according to Freud, is continuously bombarded

with a flow of force that is the very fuel of life but that is also overwhelming and potentially destructive, so it must be at once conserved and defended against. The contact-barriers, which may be either physical mechanisms (neurones) or psychical mechanisms, converting the continuous assault of force into pulses of action which are symbolic expressions, both connect and *separate*. Contact-barriers are the anatomical mechanisms of leaky distinctions. They are expandable receptacles that contain the in-flowing force, making a break in the flow or a distinction, At a certain point, the receptacle reaches its threshold, can contain no more, and discharges a pulse that is a symbolic expression of the force. Force builds up as stress or excitation of the organism and is released in a sudden break-through, which reveals something of its source but only darkly and often most obscurely. Sexual energy, for example, may manifest itself symbolically in rigorous commitment to sexually repressive moralities. The contact-barrier or leaky distinction is the fundamental Freudian structure that is recapitulated in the anatomical, psychical, and conscious spaces.

If Hebraic-Christian mythology tells of transgression or attempted transgression across absolute ontological boundaries, Freudian mythology tells of contact barriers—barriers that are also points of contact: Oedipus is the husband of his mother, a contact-barrier between father and son. The father and the son are the "same" (contact) and "different" (barrier). The Oedipus complex does not break down the structure; rather, it assigns all of the members of the family a double value. The distinction husband-son holds up to a certain point, but then it begins to "leak." The distinction becomes increasingly obscure, causing neurotic behavior, or breaks down completely, pushing the entire family into a crisis of reason. Unlike Deleuze and Guattari, for example, I do not *blame* Oedipal repression on Freud. He only discovered one important psychological structure of the type that dominates a statistical society (Deleuze and Guattari, 1977). More fundamentally, though initially less spectacularly, he discovered a new type of mechanism. He discovered that *the mapping of continuous psychic space in binary code requires not impermeable boundaries but boundaries of changing permeability*. It still may not strike us with its profundity, but it still has not been fully assimilated: so much of our thinking utilizes the logic of leaking boundaries, and so few explanations of thought even recognize it. Poststructuralist theorists, for example, speak of "slippage" in relation to an absolute logic rather than recognizing that the logic of leaky distinctions can be exquisitely managed by means of probability theory and the logic of statistical prevalence.

With any distinction, the distinction of the interior human from the exterior human, for example, a discrete world comes into existence. The world of the distinction is partial, cut-off, and grotesque (Hegel's topsy-turvy world). It has a logic—an inside and an outside—but it has no content. The distinction establishes only the limits of the world. The structure of the interior is obscure and can be clarified only with further distinctions. Each discrete thing has an inter-crypt, promising content, fullness, completion, which is never directly revealed. G. Spencer-Brown writes: "We may take it that the world undoubtedly is itself (i.e. indistinct from itself), but, in any attempt to see itself as an object, it must, equally undoubtedly, act so as to make itself distinct from, and therefore false to, itself. In this condition it will always partially elude itself" (Spencer-Brown, 1979, 105). Freud studies this self-eluding character of the logical subject and the unconscious that is implicit in it. By attending to the *structure* of hysteria and dream, rather than their manifest content, Freud creates a kind of semantic engine which produces images of its own inner resonance and inner dissonance. This is the *logical* basis of the unconscious.

Ultimately, of course, a leaky distinction is no distinction at all: entropy has its way and, in time, the value on the two sides of the contact barrier is equal. The difference of force which is the basis of life is dissipated and the organic mechanism arrives at equilibrium. The Freudian person is a contact barrier, a distinction that is not a distinction, a self-overcoming, death-seeking structure. The psychology that Freud articulated was implicit in the complex cultural accommodations to the programmatic willfulness of the modern West. It is a self-enervating process, a hopeless administration of its own dissipation.

Psychoeconomy and Symbolic Transfer

The input-output model of the psyche requires both a principle of distinction, which accounts for the transfer for quantities and a principle of transfer, which accounts for topological differences—a mechanism of distinction that does not distinguish and a mechanism of equation that does not equate. In Freudian theory, the contact barrier is countered by the symbolic transfer of the metaphor that is, as Kenneth Burke notes, perspectival, an opening of a view from a particular vantage: "If we employ the word 'character' as a general term for whatever can be thought of as distinct . . . then we could say that metaphor tells us something about one character as considered from the point of view of another character. And to consider A from the point of view of B is, of course, to use B as a perspective upon A" (Burke, 1969, 504). Thus, as topography involved an element of exchange, economy involves an element of spatial distinction.

Freud's language is charged with metaphor. Paragraph after paragraph in crucial theoretical discussions, such as chapter 7 of *The Interpretation of Dreams,* derives its content from metaphoric play. To speak of "the *chain* of a dreamer's psychical experiences" or "purposeless *stream* of ideas" is, of course, to use common metaphors. In the context of Freud's bold metaphoric practice, however, these colorless and perhaps nearly empty figures are reawakened by a perspectival use of language that is more than integral to the argument; rather, it is the argument itself. One might have to go to the seventeenth-century prose writers, Sir Thomas Browne or Giordano Bruno perhaps, to find a prose in which the controlling structures of the thought are so consistently metaphoric. Consider the following passages, for example:

> 1. If, then, an indistinct element of a dream's content is in addition attacked by doubt, we have a sure indication that we are dealing with a comparatively direct derivative of one of the proscribed dream-thoughts. The state of things is what it was after some sweeping revolution in one of the republics of antiquity or the Renaissance. The noble and powerful families which had previously dominated the scene were sent into exile and all the high offices were filled by newcomers. Only the most impoverished and powerless members of the vanquished families, or their remote dependents, were allowed to remain in the city; and even so they did not enjoy full civic rights and were viewed with distrust. The distrust in this analogy corresponds to the doubt in the case we are considering. (Freud, 1955, 5:516)
>
> 2. The dream-thoughts to which we are led by interpretation cannot, from the nature of things, have any definite endings;

they are bound to branch out in every direction into the intricate network of our world of thought. It is at some point where this meshwork is particularly close that the dream-wish grows up, like a mushroom out of its mycelium. (Freud, 1955, 5:525)

3. Deliria are the work of a censorship which no longer takes the trouble to conceal its operation; instead of collaborating in producing a new version that shall be unobjectionable, it ruthlessly deletes whatever it disapproves of, so that what remains becomes quite disconnected. This censorship acts exactly like the censorship of newspapers at the Russian frontier, which allows foreign journals to fall into the hands of the readers whom it is its business to protect only a quantity of passages have been blacked out. (Freud, 1955, 5:528)

4. Superficial associations replace deep ones if the censorship makes the normal connecting paths impassable. We may picture, by way of analogy, a mountain region, where some general interruption of traffic (owing to floods, for instance) has blocked the main, major roads, but where communications are still maintained over inconvenient and steep footpaths normally used only by the hunter. (Freud, 1955, 5:530)

These examples occur in the first section of chapter 7 of *The Interpretation of Dreams,* within a space of twenty pages, and this sampling does not begin to exhaust even the more elaborate metaphors in the passage. If one were to survey controlling metaphors in only *The Interpretation of Dreams,* it would be necessary to discuss the metaphor of the dream as rebus or picture puzzle (Freud, 1955, 4:277) and the comparison of the connecting links in dreams to rimes in poems (Freud, 1955, 5:340), which are important figures in chapter 6; the extended metaphor of the compound microscope, which is the dominant organizing device of the second section of chapter 7; as well as the ontogeny-philogeny metaphor (Freud, 1955, 5:548–49), an important cluster of metaphors drawn from economics (Freud, 1955, 5:561); and Freud's metaphoric use of literary materials.

Aristotle suggests that the recognition of similarity in dissimilarity is the genius of metaphorizing, and, as Freud notes, he characterizes dream interpretation in the same terms as the making of metaphors: "Aristotle remarked in this connection that the best interpreter of dreams was the man who could best grasp similarities; for dream-pictures, like pictures on water, are pulled out of shape by movement, and the most successful interpreter is the man who can detect the truth from the misshapen picture" (Freud, 1955, 5:97). The logic of metaphor, however, is like the logic of musical harmony. Any two objects can be compared *in some sense,* just as any two sounds can be heard as consonant. Freud pushed the logic of metaphor to its conclusion at about the same time his Viennese contemporaries in music were pushing harmony to its conclusion. He is the Schönberg of metaphoric discourse.

What is allowable as a metaphor? If we speak of "dawn in russet mantle clad," the comparison is fairly concrete. Visualized more or less literally, it does not seem grotesque or absurd. The essential character of a mantle is to cover as dawn covers the sky; it is "put on" and "taken off"; we might even imagine certain kinds of clouds as the folds and textures of cloth. The comparison involves a fairly high level of abstraction, but I think most people would agree that it is not as abstract as "my love is like a red, red rose." Here the attention must be fairly selective, or the image is grotesque. The comparison is based almost entirely on emotional associations rather than specific sensuous comparisons. The typical Freudian metaphor involves a very high level of abstraction, and it is not constrained by aesthetic considerations: top hat = phallos, mushroom = contraceptive sponge, and so forth. At this level of abstraction, any x is arguably any *y,* and, if any *x* cannot be *directly* associated with any *y,* a discourse with this much tolerance can with a few intervening steps equate any *x* with any *y,* even if, paradoxically, *x* and *y* are "opposites." In this regard, Lacan's commentary restores one of the essential Freudian insights by demonstrating that the systematization of linguistic laws is the final sublation of history and the establishment of post-Hegelian order: "if there still remains something prophetic in Hegel's insistence on the fundamental identity of the particular and the universal, an insistence that reveals the measure of his genius, it is certainly psychoanalysis that provides it with its paradigm by revealing the structure in which that identity is realized as disjunctive of the subject, and without appeal to any tomorrow" (Lacan, 1977, 80).

Freud essays the identification of opposites in his late work, the identification of life and death in *Beyond the Pleasure Principle,* or the identification of subject and object in *Ego and Id,* and the identification of the individual and civilization in *Civilization and its Discontents.* The pristine *ideal* structure of language is irrelevant to the content-laden language of actual use in which the abstract forms are metaphorically extended with content—a content and identity, according to Freud, that is known only as the end result of a series of successful psychoeconomic transactions.

In a metaphor that Descartes and Freud share, the ego is presented as mediating between two texts, one more or less occluded and the other unreliable. Freud writes:

> The dream-thoughts and the dream-content are presented to us like two versions of the same subject-matter in two different languages. Or, more properly, the dream-content seems like a transcript of the dream thoughts into another mode of expression, whose characters and syntactic laws it is our business to discover by comparing the original and the translation. The dream-thoughts are immediately comprehensible, as soon as we have learnt them. The dream-content, on the other hand, is expressed as it were in a pictographic script, the characters of which have to be transposed individually into the language of the dream-thoughts. If we attempted to read these characters according to their pictorial value instead of according to their symbolic relation, we should clearly be led into error. (Freud, 1955, 4:277)

In the methods of both Descartes and Freud, the task is to relate a pictographic language—if we can think of the abstract, geometric figures of analytical geometry in this sense—to a linear language. In both cases, the visual language has priority, and relationship depends upon an analytic function. Freud's orientation, however, is different. While Descartes translates from the common language to an ideal language, Freud is presented with a meaning-laden language, which not only requires translation but which is unknown and must be deciphered. The grammar is unknown, and the vocabulary is improvised from visual detritus. Psychoanalysis reveals the subjective event to be a function of the metaphor, much as Cartesian analysis revealed the objective event to a function of an algebraic expression. Both are based on circular logic: the Freudian method, like the Cartesian, is helical, gradually draining the Zuider Zee, in Freud's metaphor, and using the new-won ground as the base for further draining.

According to Freud, ancient dream interpretation failed because it attempted to decipher the manifest content of dreams rather than the dream-thoughts which they represent. In order to properly interpret dreams, it is necessary to recognize (1) that they invariably represent the fulfillment of wishes and (2) that in dreams, unacceptable wishes and images of their fulfillment are played out in symbolically distorted form. These principles are now, of course, so familiar that they seem commonsensical. The problem of relating the repressed wish to the distorted images that the dream presents, however, remains a problem. Freud himself notes: "There is no possibility of explaining dreams as a psychical process, since to explain a thing means to trace it back to something already known, and there is at the present time no established psychological knowledge under which we could subsume what the psychological examination of dreams enables us to infer as a basis for their explanation" (Freud, 1955, 5:511).

Explanation in itself is paradoxical: either the explanation is equivalent to the original and puzzling formulation, in which case nothing is gained, or it is not equivalent, in which case it does not constitute an explanation. Some of the oldest and most troublesome philosophic paradoxes are versions of this problem. The common solution, which appears in myriad forms, is to find a common ground between two different linguistic structures. The discourse establishes a metaphorical ratio not between one term and another but between entire languages or regions in language. The power of Cartesian geometry, for example, arises from the common grounds it discovers between algebraic formulas and drawings on Cartesian coordinates. Although it is not as clearly articulated, Freud's strategy is comparable. Dream content and dream thought are different linguistic regions, where different grammars apply. Psychoanalytic theory must provide a technique for translating from the dream content to the dream thought without reference to the reality of the unconscious itself, which is, of course, inherently beyond our ken. The linguistic economy consists of exchanges between more or less immediate perceptual regions, which, in turn, generate references to regions that are unknown and, in terms of direct access, unknowable. Freudian inference, while not mysterious, is never direct, and its object is unknown: the unconscious is the x of the psychoanalytic algebra. We cannot solve for *it* anymore than we can solve for *all* of the roots of a generalized algebraic function.

Lacan develops this thought explicitly and completely in the spirit of Freudian practice. He takes the fundamental algorithm of linguistics, signifier to signified, S / s, and extends it meta-phorically to psychoanalysis, seeing it also as the ratio of conscious to unconscious. The situation that is thus described embodies its own impossibility: every attempted crossing from signifier to signi-fied, as it reaches the slash that separates the uppercase s from the lowercase s, waffles and turns aside, producing not the signified but another signifier; likewise, every attempted move from con-scious to unconscious produces not the unconscious but more con-sciousness. Consider, for example, the problem of analyzing a dream: if one merely substitutes a new term for the term in the dream—"phallus" for "top hat," for example—nothing is added. It is comparable to factoring 16 into the expression 2 x 2 x 2 x 2. Such organization of language serves to create taxonomies, but it gives little intellectual leverage. It is possible, for example, to know that "phallus" can be substituted for "top hat" without knowing how to use either term, and, to a large extent, the initiate into psychoanalytic language is in this quandary. Lacan speaks of these relationships as metonymic. There is another dimension to the signifying chain that has "as if attached to the punctuation of each of its units, a whole articulation of relevant contexts suspended 'vertically', as it were, from that point" (Lacan, 1977, 154). When this dimension of language is taken into consideration, semiologi-cal networks appear. In some sense, the whole structure of lan-guage is implicated in every linguistic nexus, and it becomes possi-ble to think in terms comparable to algebraic functions, so a given variable implicates not just an unknown but entire classes of un-known terms.

Lacan formalizes the distinction between the linear and the vertical dimensions of the signifying chains in quasi-mathematical formulae. Although he pursues a brilliant series of playful varia-tions on the most famous Cartesian language—"I think where I am not, therefore I am where I do not think" (Lacan, 1977, 166), his methodology presents many of the same puzzles as Descartes: how is it possible to translate from a language that relates only to itself to a language in which internal linguistic relations are func-tions of a generalized reality? Descartes argues from the common language to a purified mathematical subset of the language that he identifies with natural space; Lacan argues from the common lan-guage to the abstract structure of language which he identifies with the unconscious. Relocating the ego in relationship to the center of language brilliantly re-states Freud's Copernican revolution for a generation dominated by the thought of linguistics. By assigning the ego a place in an insignificant outer orbit of the linguistic solar system, Lacan's algebraic formulae, like Descartes's, symbolize the introduction of extraordinary levels of abstraction into the natural language. The Freudian psychoeconomics combines with the psychotopography to produce a rich, multidimensional medium that has the capacity both to reduce complex quantitative signals to traces that record a simple binary structure and to maintain distinct complex signals in relation to one another.

It should be noted that writing and speech in general constitute the kind of explanatory doubling involved in metaphoric interpretation. Although we do not normally speak in these terms, speech is an "explanation" of writing, and writing is an "explanation" of speech. Since the rise of Greek literacy, the intellectual institutions have conspired to coordinate writing and speech—that is to make writing and speech "breathe" together. Derrida's analysis of the sentimentalization of voice delineates one aspect of the conspiracy but not the other. To be sure, voice is sentimentalized in relation to script, but, likewise, script is sentimentalized in relation to voice. Against the authority of Socrates and Jesus, who speak the Truth but do not write, there is the weight of the entire cultural canon and, since the seventeenth century, the written tradition of scientific research. Entire grammars are mutually enfolded in one another without difficulty. Speech and writing, phonetic script and pictographs, for example, are manifestations of a medium that is essentially tolerant. Freud moves from one grammar to another without notice of a seam, even when radically different logics are involved. The alphabet, for example, is a finite combinatory. A finite collection of discrete signs is arranged by a finite set of rules to create more complex signs. Any such language, whether it is aligned on the voice or not, has a character that differs radically from iconic languages: the DNA code, for example, has such a character. One might imagine a finite combinatory that consists of a finite collection of discrete bodily signs, such as, for example, open and closed eyes and mouth, wiggled ears, flared nostrils, and so forth. Pictographic languages, on the other hand, are open series: it is possible to add unique, new signs that have no relation whatsoever to the existent signs. Pictographs do not require a systematic background. The distinction between these logics, however, is not as clear as it has been almost universally supposed by theoreticians. Consider, for example, the ease with which Freud resolves the matter: "A dream," he writes, "is a picture-puzzle . . . and our predecessors in the field of dream-interpretation have made the mistake of treating the rebus as a pictorial composition" (Freud, 1955, 4:277). That is, the dream itself supplies no grammar or even the wrong grammar. Freud assimilates dream content to dream thought by demonstrating how apparently aberrant psychical phenomena "can be inserted into the chain of intelligible waking mental acts" (Freud, 1955, 4:122). By insisting upon the relationship between iconic languages and phonetic languages, allowing one to function in the other—the one, for example, to supply the syntax for the other—Freud provides certain rules of thumb for life in an environment for which we have no theory and can have no theory. In this century, the medium has achieved a fluency that produces an entire environment which is popularly called "the media" but which is almost inevitably treated as a unitary thing. It is the one in the many and the many in the one, not in any mysterious sense, but as a matter of pure, practical incoherence. It has no character in itself.

The distinction between a domain of energy and a domain of information, which Freud referred to as "topography" and "economy" does not mark opposed locales in the self-cognizing organism; it is, rather, the necessary distinction that brings self-cognizing organisms into being. It is not, therefore, something to be reconciled or balanced out in a larger unity (Hegel); it is not dialectical and therefore dynamic; it is not a source of tension that must be relieved or brought to equilibrium (Freud). It is, rather, the *stable* condition of cognition. Neither the energy consumed in the thought nor the energy consumed in its expression—the excitement of a neurone, the mark on the page, the impress of the print—is the energy of thought, which is to say, the energy of living as such. We suffer a profound confusion of life and its expression. The knowledge that can be shared without disciplinary preconditions is that energy creates information and information creates energy. This paradoxical knowledge is available to any observer who is also a self-observer. It is the origin of a knowledge of transcendence and the finite horizon of the self-cognizing beings who account for both their insides and their outsides *through their own insides*. Beyond this paradox, nothing can be said. Freud proposes to account for insides and outsides of self-cognizing beings from the outsides. His is a last desperate proposal of nineteenth-century scientific objectivism. Although the Freudian psyche appears in the same space as its objects, Freud discovered a cunning model by which psyche appears to get a certain distance on itself.

Freud proposes a "literalism" of the symbol: we are to read the symbol, not its overt content. That is, we are to take the symbol seriously but not *too* seriously. Freud sees his problem as comparable to the task of the biblical scholars: although the text with which he worked was couched in the most mysterious algebra and then badly corrupted, it still "somehow" contained the truth which must be discovered. "In short, we have treated as Holy Writ what previous writers have regarded as arbitrary improvisation, hurriedly patched together in the embarrassment of the moment" (Freud, 1955, 5:514). The Freudian strategy discovers a normative structure that it reimposes with all of the authority of the literal text that it displaces; it replaces the literalism of content with the literalism of structure. In 1914, Walter Lippman wrote: "The impetus of Freud is perhaps the greatest advance ever made towards the understanding *and control* of human character. But for the complexities of politics it is not yet ready. It will take time and endless labor for a detailed study of social problems in the light of this growing knowledge" (Lippman, 1962, 168, my emphasis). Now that control is largely achieved. The irrational components conspire to produce a broadly rationalized, social machine.

The poetics of common knowledge, on the other hand, declares that life *is* an arbitrary improvisation and that each living thing uniquely and absolutely distinguishes itself. What we discover from the structural relationships of symbols—even what we learn negatively or critically—is "truer" than their literal content only in the sense that it makes certain statistically reliable generalizations possible. These generalizations, of course, underwrite the mechanisms of control that now prevail in the symbolic media that define the corporate living space.

Humberto Maturana, whose conception of life as autopoiesis I will oppose to the Freudian conception of life as symbolically bound force, writes, "when it is recognized that language is connotative and not denotative, and that its function is to orient the orientee within his cognitive domain without regard for the cogni tive domain of the orienter, it becomes apparent that there is no transmission of information through language" (Maturana and Varela, 1980, 32). And there is, therefore, no insistence in the signifying chain; indeed, there is no chain. *We are not chained!* We are in no sense required or regulated by language, our own or others. We are not input-output mechanisms, functioning at the whim of the information that we suffer. We are, rather, self-closing organisms that take their own output as input. The joy of language is that it sometimes allows us the opportunity to enter *unconstrained* community, not mediated and numbed, but intensively felt.

In saying that language is connotative, Maturana means not that language refers to emotions but that language *is* emotional, not informational. Although such a characterization seems "unscientific," he notes that it is otherwise impossible to account for the evolutionary origin of natural languages. If language is denotational, the very function that we hope to explain—the ability to communicate a denotation—must preexist itself. The denoted object must be identified *before* it can be recognized and named. For this reason, our theories of language have referred to mysterious origins, and our epistemologies have necessarily invoked infinite regresses. This crisis for cognitive life that called forth "Western philosophy" arose when the cognitive domain, which is never complete but remains open toward the infinite, is made into a closed domain existing in itself. If, however, the function of language is not referential but orientational, it is possible to account for the appearance of language from nonlanguage. So rich is its possibilities of orientation, so inclusive of itself, Mina Loy writes, language might be "reduced to a basic significance that could be conveyed to a man on Mars" (Loy, 1982, 291).

THE PERFORMANCE OF THE PERSON: LOUIS ZUKOFSKY

The Contingent Person

> Me wherever my life is lived, O to be self-balanced for
>   contingencies,
> To confront night, storms, hunger, ridicule, accidents, rebuffs, as
>   the trees and animals do.
>   —Walt Whitman

Reading Louis Zukofsky, especially late Zukofsky, readers sometimes feel like beginning students of German or Greek. They get on what appear to be good syntactical tracks, but a few words are left over, do not fit the pattern. At other times, they feel like readers of an ancient manuscript. Again they find hints of syntax, but key words or phrases are obliterated by tears or wormholes: there are too many words or not enough; there are temptations to add or subtract punctuation or juggle the word order. Occasionally, however, passages appear with astounding clarity, leaving the reader with the mental equivalent of the bends. These examples are from "*A*"–22:

> "If your house were burning
> what would you save from
> it?" "The fire."
> (Zukofsky, 1978, 519)

> the law, water, shaped
> to the container its in.
> (Zukofsky, 1978, 523)

> A
> child learns on blank paper,
> an old man rewrites palimpsest.
> (Zukofsky, 1978, 525)

This last one might be a clue; we should remember it. Also, Zukofsky writes, "we are caught by our own knowing" (Zukofsky, 1978, 510).

Readers are clearly caught as they sit before "*A*"–24, "a five-part score—music, thought, drama, story, poem"—all clamoring to be comprehended simultaneously. (See page 240.)

Although we are told that the masque is "centrally motivated by the drama" (Zukofsky, 1978, 564), the syntax works as surely in the vertical dimension as the horizontal. Sometimes the connections are discursive: the voice of thought, for example, speaks of tuning in "to the human tradition," and the voice of drama responds, "How do you catch such a bird?" (Zukofsky, 1978, 560). Simultaneity, however, is more commonly the rule. The relationships are sometimes complementary, sometimes ironic. There are puns, rimes, subject rimes, and significant repetitions. Zukofsky explores all of the avenues of linguistic interconnectiveness. How

T   And   it   is   possible   in   imagination

D   I came thru there   My mother hit her mother?
          (points finger downward, moves his head negatively from side to side)

S   This story was a story of our time.

P   Blest   /   Infinite   things   /

T   to   divorce   speech   of   all   graphic   elements,

D   *(falls to the floor in a fit)*

S   And a writer's attempts   not to fathom his time

P   So   many   /   Which

T   to   let   it   become   a   movement   of   sounds.

D   *(rises,   limp,*

S   amount but to sounding his mind in it.

P   confuse   imagination   /   Thru   its   weakness,

Source: Zukofsky, 1978, 566.

much of the content can be preserved in performance is uncertain. In poor performances at least, many passages will be lost in muddle. Conjecture, however, is empty; the only way to read *"A"*–24 is to perform it.*

The first twenty-three books of *"A"* are solos, but they too must be performed. Reading the texts aloud is a good beginning, but the texts insist upon being used by the performer and making use of the performer. Neither the reader nor Zukofsky himself is allowed a language apart from the language of the poem. The radical character of the work derives from Zukofsky's refusal to observe the philosophic conventions of privacy, which distribute an act of communications between a sender and a receiver, a producer and a consumer. Zukofsky writes, "The best way to find out about poetry is to read the poems. That way the reader becomes something of a poet himself: not because he 'contributes' to the poetry, but because he finds himself subject [not the object] of its energy." (Zukofsky, 1981, 23) Poetry of this order requires an enactment, to which most of our notions of reading are inadequate.

In *Bottom: On Shakespeare* and *Catullus,* Zukofsky gives performances of other poets. Although they are overtly very different from one another, they are both improvisatory. In this sense, no performance is definitive. In his preface to *Bottom,* Zukofsky writes: "Even a photographic eye—a lens—is placed by some human; when 'shooting' at Shakespeare, at best perhaps by inevitable accident. To say that his focus was this is presumptuous" (Zukofsky, 1987, 10). The performance of poetry that manifests the common is necessarily as unique as its performer. If to read Shakespeare from the point of view of Bottom, the thespian weaver in *A Midsummer-Night's Dream,* is arbitrary and personal, the translation of Catullus, attempting to preserve the sound of the Latin, is idiosyncratic. The shared world is comprised of singularities that lie beyond the horizon of languages and their inevita-

---

*We are told only in a somewhat enigmatic note at the end that, in fact, *"A"*–24 is the work of Zukofsky's wife, the composer, Celia Zukofsky:

> the gift—
> she hears
> the work
> in its recurrence
>   L. Z.

(Zukofsky, 1978, 806)

ble class logics. The performances are aimed not at communicating the content of the language but at manifesting the singularity of the occasion.

Zukofsky claims in *Bottom* to have done away with the theory of knowledge: it is, he tells us: "A long poem built on a theme for the variety of its recurrences. The theme is simply that Shakespeare's text throughout favors the clear physical eye against the erring brain, and that this theme has historical implications" (Zukofsky, 1981, 167). To be sure, Bottom is the one, perhaps of all of Shakespeare's characters, who is innocent of philosophy. He wants to play all of the parts, male and female, human and animal, in the play that he and his cohorts plan to present, and, at the same time, he is fearful that the audience will confuse the play for reality—a mistake he is most likely to make himself. Bottom's values, which are firmly grounded upon completely nontheoretical love, however, are prior to mere matters of reason. His knowledge does not derive its authority from language. Weaving together texts, the technique of Zukofsky's book, honors Bottom's craft. The text is constructed, not as argument, but very much from argument. This self-declared antiphilosophic text quotes philosophers—especially Aristotle, Spinoza, and Wittgenstein—on almost every page and quotes them positively, against themselves, in their own self-obstruction.

In *Catullus,* Zukofsky investigates the other dimension in his theme. "This translation of Catullus," he writes in his preface, "follows the sound, rhythm, and syntax of his Latin—tries, as is said, to breathe the 'literal' meaning with him." He is assuming a persona with a vengeance, or, more exactly, he proposes to assume not Catullus's person but his body. Again, however, he makes this move precisely at the point of a paradoxical reversal: the very act of making like is making differences. By submitting totally to Catullus's language, he is remaking his own. If *Bottom* is an attempt to make us see a physical world that is in danger of becoming transparent, *Catullus* is an attempt to make us hear English that is in danger of becoming silent. It is certainly an English such as we have never heard before:

> Seek or record then the benefactor—pree or voluptuous
>   is the meaning, come say cogitate essay pious,
>   no sanctum will owe loss—so feed him, not foiled there in all he

divined not falling those numina abusing no man's
mull to be rapt there manning a long ah high tide there, Catullus,
sort from ingratitude good and from more a to be.
(Zukofsky and Zukofsky, 1969, poem #76)

The central demand that Zukofsky's art makes on him in *Catullus*, as in the other books, is to keep the historical process alive at the roots, where image, sounds, concepts, and traditions combine and recombine in their restless incongruence. It is an art that calls attention to the deadliness of habit and the possibility of change. It does not seek resolution—and certainly *Catullus* resolves nothing—but it can bring us to those moments of intense vital awareness when resolution seems unnecessary and even undesirable. Playing through the bitterest and most thoroughgoing subject-object relations, it opens to a poem in *"A"* that can only be performed, not thought.

"A," Bottom, and *Catullus* declare the modes of a personal order, which is eccentric and private, and at the same time, completely common. The contingencies of personal vision mediate between mastery of the other and immersion in the other. These three works are inquiries into strategies that engage the lyric voice with other voices in time. They are extended, intersubjective lyrics, the various voices involved all reaching beyond the lyric moment to establish a community. *"A"* investigates the intersubjective play of image, sound, and concepts; *Bottom,* of tradition and concepts; *Catullus,* of image, tradition, and sound or "breath," as Zukofsky says. In these works, we witness the refounding of the tradition of secular choral poetry, which had its very brief day in the age between the decline of the epic and the rise of the lyric of the single voice. The whole of *"A"* is an investigation into the inadequacies and limitations of the single vision and the single voice. In *"A"*–9, Marx and Cavalcanti sing a duet that Zukofsky conducts; *"A"*–21 is a drama; *Bottom* is a lengthy discussion between Aristotle, Spinoza, Wittgenstein, and Zukofsky—in the guise of Bottom—on the subject of Shakespeare; in *Catullus,* Zukofsky sings a close-harmony duet with the Roman poet, while all of the dead speakers of Latin hum backup.

I do not have the space to perform Zukofsky's work here, nor is a performance relevant to the present concern, which must confine itself to strategies of poetic performance. Zukofsky offers evidence of the contingency of the performer and the completely nonphilosophic relationship of the performer to the act of reading the poem. I will begin, not with a commodious warp, such as Bottom might require for a weaving, but with four meager threads.

The first is from Zukofsky in *Bottom:*

> Pouring over the words of such English writings as Shakespeare's or Wyatt's, conjecture may posit that their craft is primarily an attempt to English the truncated thought of their known world— for what else, as histories reiterate, is the thought of the late Renaissance, but an avidity in great part for the thought of an older and mythically unmaimed world. Conjecture will thus say that the craft of their writing is this thought that penetrates the smallest joints of their words, those irrational numbers keeping the "great, deeper" concepts together. (Zukofsky, 1987, 26)

Zukofsky refuses to grant integrity to plot, character, or any other formal entity that might call metaphysical substance into Shakespeare's work. The Zukofskyan reader of Shakespeare or Zukofsky must address attention to the language in its smallest particles, which is not to say that these can be isolated from larger units in which they play.

The second thread is from *"A"*–22:

> one guess at certainty made
> with an assemblage of naught—
> yet in cells not vacuum
> records as tho horses rushed
> definite as an aching nerve
> pleads feed and feed back—
> spine follows path once more,
> to arrogate it small eloquence.
> (Zukofsky, 1978, 509)

Zukofsky is speaking here of the form of *"A"* itself. We are reminded that its forms are arbitrary. The cells in which the poem is cast are so playfully contrived that no one is likely to reify them.

The third thread is from one of Zukofsky's most important sources, Ludwig Wittgenstein. Speaking of poetry and music, he writes: "If a theme, a phrase, suddenly means something to you, you don't have to be able to explain it. Just this gesture has been made accessible to you" (Wittgenstein, 1970, 28). The tradition of Western poetry since the decline of the epic has articulated a series of techniques for making it appear that the poetic experience is explicable. In fact, it is the simplest thing there is. Things are explained in terms of it and not the reverse. For this reason Zukofsky's work can only be performed, the gesture made. The poem is difficult because it does not open to us the opportunity to appear to have explained.

I sometimes think *"A"* is a self-interpreting poem. Most lines that need glossing are glossed somewhere in the poem itself. One performance of the poem, if we assume the role of the cartographer, rather than the weaver, would be to draw isometric lines, connecting those passages that speak to one another. This would not constitute an explanation of the poem; it would be perhaps an "inplanation" or "information." The fourth passage that keys important aspects of a performance of Zukofsky is from *"A"* −14:

> lower limit body
> upper limit dance
> lower limit dance
> upper limit speech,
> lower limit speech
> upper limit music,
> lower limit music
> upper limit *mathemata*
> swank for *things*
> learned (like cage
> silence which pulses).
> (Zukofsky, 1978, 349)

The *mathemata* is the manifest order that, unspoken and unspeakable, Wittgenstein tells us exists in the silence, the source of value, perhaps value itself. "Silence which pulses," Zukofsky says, thus creating rhythm and the possibility for measure. Some mathematical formulations, in themselves mere tautologies, have applications in science and engineering. Zukofsky is brother to the practical mathematician; the performer is the engineer. The meaning of *"A,"* like that of other poetry, is revealed in its use, in its gestures becoming accessible.

In an effort to propose a view of Zukofsky's work as a whole— the work as person—I have the precedent of Zukofsky himself in *Bottom: On Shakespeare:* "It is simpler to consider the forty-four items of [Shakespeare's] canon as one work, sometimes poor, sometimes good, sometimes great, always regardless of the time in which it was composed, and so despite defects of quality, durable as one thing from 'itself never turning,' so growth is organic to decay and vice versa" (Zukofsky, 1987, 13). Zukofsky's canon was likely more consciously constructed as a single work than Shakespeare's (though, of course, we have no way to know). *All: The Collected Shorter Poems* begins with the assertion of a definitive order, with "Poem Beginning 'The.'" The definite article declares a particular kind of objectivity, a uniqueness and a universal perspective. Although "Poem beginning 'The'" is a travesty of Eliot's and Pound's insistence upon *the* tradition, Zukofsky recognizes that cultural order is the context of all and *All*. Against the multiple voices and the tentative musical organization of "Poem beginning 'The,'" he poses, in the first of "29 Poems," the theoretical and practical clarity of Lenin, whom he addresses as a star:

> Irrevocable yet safe we go,
> Irrevocable you, too,
> O star, we speaking to you,
> The shadows of the elm leaves faded,
> Only the trunk of elm now dark and high
> Unto your height:
> Now and again you fall,
> Blow dark and burn again,
> And we in turn
> Share now your fate
> Whose process is continual.
>   (Zukofsky, 1971, 24)

These two poems as premises of the volume nearly cancel one another out, and Zukofsky finds himself near ground zero: "Not much more than being / thoughts of isolate, beautiful /Being at evening." The remainder of *All* is an effort to trace a way through the immediate and local to an inclusive vision from a single point of view. The book is not a miscellaneous collection of pieces that do not otherwise fit in the design, but a carefully organized work, which is nonetheless fragmentary.

In the penultimate section of "29 Songs," Zukofsky takes stock in prose of the dissonances that arise from the process in which he is engaged: "Specifically, a writer of music," he writes. "The composite of notes proceeded with assumed qualities in a definite proportion. But, as dreamed, they controlled the nature of plants, bodies, etc. and the elements of the notes became not easy to separate." The relationship between notes and things, however, is not as simple or as direct as it first appears; there are contradictions at the very heart of his undertaking. He goes on to dream of dancing donkeys, and "the ever falling stomping of their hoofs, now following the range of his notes, were imparting to him clearly: 'Sir, not only as mathematique point flowers into every line which is derived from a Center, but our soul which is but one, hath swallowed up a negative.'"

The dilemma that the donkeys announce is exemplified in "Mantis" and "Mantis: An Interpretation" (Zukofsky, 1971, 73–80). They establish the crisis in which *All* develops. Refusing to commit himself to a unity, which does not inform the whole of life, Zukofsky must deal with images and melodies that are frankly arbitrary. The central Zukofskyan value, therefore, is sincerity. It seems a weak word; we tend to be embarrassed by it. Nevertheless, in the face of an arbitrary existence, we have no other appeal. "In sincerity," he writes, "shapes appear concomitants of word combinations, precursors of (if there is continuance) completed sound or structure, melody or form" (Zukofsky, 1981, 12). The poet can achieve music or an approach to music—form so perfect that it begins to sing—but there is always something more.

The perfections of "Mantis" are conventional and arbitrary, or, at least, almost so. Three lines hang over at the end of the sestina, out of place, like a mantis in a subway station. It is a sestina and a twelfth, but, Zukofsky tells us in "An Interpretation," "The ungainliness / of the creature needs stating." In sincerity, the subject finds its form and, caught up in "the battle of diverse thoughts," exceeds it by three lines, then carries over into another poem that is almost six pages long. Zukofsky recognizes that a mantis in the subway station—even something this insignificant—presents an insoluable problem. Lacking the advantages of symbolism, as a technique for universalizing the particular, he can only bring together "the simultaneous / the diaphanous, historical together in one head."

In 1930, reviewing the poetry of the previous decade, Zukofsky speaks of "Joyce's sense of simultaneity" and its opposite in "the work of Gertrude Stein in its analytical aspects." Although he does not explicitly develop this distinction, it informs the entire essay, and he manages to clarify his point a good deal by contrasting the "modern" situation to the one which it replaces: "The diction which is dead today is that of poets who, as someone said of Matthew Arnold, have put on the singing robes to lose themselves in the universal" (Zukofsky, 1981, 147). Joyce is always in danger of suffering precisely that loss by translating the contingency of person into aesthetic form, the timeless being of perfect simultaneity. Stein, however, recognizes that the logical structure of the medium, which can be demonstrated adequately by the old grammar exercise of diagramming sentences, reveals nothing about its content. It is by analysis and the entertainment of the interstices, where images, things, worlds, and persons come apart, that we have knowledge of living at all.

Writing of William Carlos Williams, who seemed to him the central figure of the 1920s, Zukofsky says, "The aesthetics of his material is a living one, a continual beginning, a vision amid pressure" (Zukofsky, 1981, 148). To allow vision to arise from complex interactions in space, as they bear on the space of the poem, where desire, feeling, fact, form, and language enact their destinies of coincidence and conflict, was to experience fully the exhilaration which the "modern" offered. Williams's poetry, as Zukofsky reads it, is a poetry without presuppositions, a poetry of pure inquiry. Everything bears on everything else. To keep pace with a reality that is not mediated by linear conventions requires an eye that can follow the magician's impossibly quick hands. Nothing can be stopped or isolated or framed. Study and meditation find no still object. After quoting some short passages from Williams's *The Great American Novel*, Zukofsky writes, "Such things are seen and recorded not as notes, but as finished, swiftly trained deliberations of the mind between leaps to other work or the multiplicity of living scenes" (Zukofsky, 1981, 148). This discipline, which does not exaggerate the significance of any phase of the process by which sight passes to vision, is the sole guarantee against life's forming to patterns of unshakeable habit. It requires the quickness of living to manifest a living person; otherwise things settle down into repetition and tiresome justification of the status quo.

Zukofsky's commitment is to the clarity of the process. He objects to the exaggeration of the formal in Wallace Stevens: "The poetic emotion is lacking," he says, "and the product is 'intellectual' rhetoric: blurred disjointed tangibilities." In Hart Crane, he objects to the exaggerated value placed on the ecstatic moment and the inevitable divorce from the process in which the ecstasy finds its relation to other experience: "The result is an aura—a doubtful, subtle exhalation—a haze" (Zukofsky, 1981, 139). On the other hand, he says of Pound, Eliot, Williams, Moore, and cummings: "The things these poets deal with are of this world and time, but they are 'modern' only because their words are energies which make for meaning" (Zukofsky, 1981, 147).

Ludwig Wittgenstein spoke for his generation in announcing that the most intimate and profound knowledge, which is to say, the grounds for knowledge as such, could not be spoken. Zukofsky notes, "In Hebrew the word for word is also the word for thing. The roots and stems of grammar are foresights and hindsights so entangled that traditions and chronologies mean little if not an acceptance, a love of certain, living beings for words as seen things" (Zukofsky, 1987, 104). In *All*, he puts the word for *thing*, not the word for *word*, at the origin of his work. The book ends with the section "After I's," a term that can be taken in one sense of the complex pun as a translation of "metaphysics." In section five of "The Old Poet Moves to a New Apartment 14 Times," Zukofsky offers some measure of how far he has come:

After all—
nothing
interests me
when it is full of being.

The volume ends, however, with a frank admission that it is not, in fact, all:

There is
a heart
has no
complaint
better a-
part
than
faint
so the
faintest
part of
it
has no
complaint
a
part.
 (Zukofsky, 1971, 292)

"A," Bottom: On Shakespeare, and Catullus are the ABC of an order that arises from the fragmented whole. Although Zukofsky was never keen on the term objectivism, terms closely related to it—object, objectivity, and especially, objective, in all of its senses—are clearly important in his work. Perhaps I can use it rhetorically, as a way to establish grounds for discussion, without committing myself to more than one specific point.

Treated promiscuously, as such terms usually are, objectivism is a reincarnation of imagism. The image, after all, is an object; it may be objective; perhaps it brings something to focus, like an optical objective; it may have an aim. But this tells us little. It is in the nature of the image to have a quality of object-ness, but also, as it is treated in the traditions of humanistic criticism, the image also has a quality of *abjectness*. It is *for* the speaking subject, servile to his or her whim of emotion or thought, violated and even despised. Traditional criticism condones a rapacious use of the object and the objective. It treats all that presents itself to eye or ear precisely as the cognate economics treat other resources such as fossil fuel. In Zukofsky's poetry, man, the soul, and the psyche, those entities in the name of which the rapacity is justified, have no special privilege: they are objects, objectives, words. Zukofsky writes: "*Impossible* to communicate anything but particulars—historic and contemporary—things, human beings as things their instrumentalities of capillaries and veins binding up and bound up with events and contingencies" (Zukofsky, 1981, 16).

Jargon and the Displacement of the Symbolic Person

Zukofsky was raised in precisely the kind of tradition Pound and Eliot longed for. If the Judaism of New York's lower east side was provincial in comparison to the European tradition of high culture, it did not need to be patched together like a crazy quilt to give it coherence. "A"–4 opens with a short lyric, typical of the lyrics that appear in "55 Poems." The voice of Zukofsky's community responds in these terms:

Wherever we put our hats is our home
Our aged heads are our homes,
Eyes wink to their own phosphorescence,
No feast lights of Venice or The Last Supper light
our beards familiar; His
Stars of Deuteronomy are with us,

Always with us,
We had a speech, our children have
evolved a jargon.
      (Zukofsky, 1978, 12)

At the time his contemporaries were in a desperate search for the *logos* or mythos of history (the Speech), Zukofsky was under a contradictory impulse, to explore the jargon as a way beyond the repetitious ritual reenactment of the forms of eternity. His work neither refers to nor embodies an arcane structure as its source of meaning or as the guarantee of its ontological claim. He writes, "The poet wonders why so many today have raised up the word 'myth,' finding the lack of so-called 'myths,' in our time a crisis the poet must overcome or die from, as it were, having become too radioactive, when instead a case can be made out for the poet giving some of his life to use of the words *the* and *a* both of which are weighted with as much epos and historical destiny as one man can perhaps resolve" (Zukofsky, 1981, 10). In the interplay of the definite and the indefinite—the poem beginning "the" and a poem beginning "a"—we are in the condition of history as present, history as destiny, rather than as a transcendental order.

Zukofsky assumes that we share a content that we realize in individual forms or in fragmentary insights. In Zukofsky's canon, *"A,"* *Bottom,* and *Catullus* are explorations of the jargon, personal forms, as tightly constructed as Cartesian geometry. They do not, however, presume a coherent background in *All.* The eternal archetypes, by which the jargon might be redeemed, cannot be coherently manifested; they are the silences that pulse and that can only be tacitly counted. Measure enters speech, manifesting the sources of value, only as the poet gives overt attention to something else, say, the innumerable ways the character *A* appears in writing, vision, and thought. The structure is, therefore, contingent rather than necessary. Public reality exists in the intervals that create multiplicity. Zukofsky has a kabbalistic sense of the letters of the alphabet as the constituents of public reality. The larger part of *Bottom* is an alphabet book. As the objective moves from the phonemes to the word with its compact history, its particular combinations of radical elements, to the phrase, and on to the stanza and the total form of the poem, it moves from the public and shared to private integrity of the individual person.

It is, I believe, Zukofsky's sense of the person as contingent, as

lacking identity with his or her objects, as gloriously and neces-
sarily inexplicable, that many readers find unnerving. It is an al-
most intolerable thought to some: it removes the basis for all
rationalization, those rationalizations by which we defend our
privileges and explain our discontents. It leaves only what we *do* as
a record that we exist at all.

In response to the question, "what specifically is good poet-
ry?" Zukofsky says, "It is precise information on existence out of
which it grew." An image makes a historical claim, it is a poem's
stake in the world and its guarantee of producing consequences in
the world. And, he goes on to say, "good poetry . . . is . . . infor-
mation of its own existence . . . , the movement (and tone) of
words" (Zukofsky, 1981, 20). Against the temporality of image, he
poses not mythos or *logos* but language and especially the physical
production of language, its closeness to the voice and the voice's
body, the lips, tongue, lungs of speech. In an interview, he speaks of
the word as "a physiological thing." Poetry has to do with the
organism in which people have their daily living, and the human
form, despite the transience of given bodies, is remarkably con-
stant over time. It is this fact that allows even the person "who
does not know Greek to listen and get something out of the poetry
of Homer: to 'tune in' to the human tradition, to its voice which
has developed among the sounds of natural things, and thus escape
the confines of time and place, as one hardly ever escapes them in
studying Homer's grammar" (Zukofsky, 1981, 20). The interac-
tion of image and sound, finally, allows a poetry of precise inquiry:
that is, experience can be measured. It is not thought, but thought
is frequently hovering around. There is, Zukofsky says, an "inter-
play of concepts."

We have not had a Hegel to do for history of poetry what Hegel
himself did for the history of philosophy, but he would have a
directly parallel story to tell: how from Sappho and Archilochus to
Mallarmé the abstract categories were more and more adequately
articulated until they became absolute. Mallarmé writes, "all
earthly existence must ultimately be contained in a book," and he
goes on to say:

> What, then, will the work itself be? I answer: a hymn, all harmo-
> ny and joy; an immaculate grouping of universal relationships
> come together for some miraculous and glittering occasion.

Man's duty is to observe with the eyes of the divinity; for if his connection with that divinity is to be made clear, it can be expressed only by the pages of the open book in front of him. (Mallarmé, 1982, 80)

Mallarmé had made the advance on Archilochus that Hegel had made on Plato. He images a world relieved of contingency, fully and finally mediated. The finite human is to be replaced by the infinite book.

In a remarkable essay on *"A"*–19, Kenneth Cox shows in detail how Zukofsky uses Mallarmé, translating him, mistranslating him, and taking cues from him for the creation of his own poem. With great care, he shows how Zukofsky turns Mallarmé's words to his own very different necessities. He concludes: "To wish to abolish chance, as Mallarmé did, is to wish not to have been born. For a European educated in the tragic sense of life the wish is reasonable enough. Suicide is second best, the annihilation of life in art can serve as a substitute. For Zukofsky, an American of Jewish immigrant parentage, chance is blessed. His meliorism is powered by the sentimental, the human response to death" (Cox, 1973, 11).

Zukofsky's practice is not a simple inversion of Mallarmé's, not a "Marxist" attempt to stand Mallarmé on his head: the similarities and differences are not so symmetrical. Zukofsky, rather, moves away from the common language in the opposite direction, not toward the absolute, but toward the structure of what is possible, not toward abstract unity, but toward the instituting concrete multiplicity. Rather than inverting the Hegelian-Mallarméan dialectic, Zukofsky empties it out, forces it to encounter not merely the material world, the material language, but also the array of conditions that concretely make them possible.

Since Whitman or since Poe (if we take Williams's reading of him, rather than Baudelaire's), American poetry has been preparing its escape from the inevitable nihilism of the tragic sense of life. Williams, arguing of Poe that "it was a beginning he has in mind, a juvenescent *local* literature," quotes, with approval, a passage in which Poe says, "The highest order of the imaginative intellect is always preeminently the mathematical." (Williams, 1956, 217) And Williams also praises Poe's unwillingess to concede the necessity for any prop to his logical constructions, "save the locality upon which its originality rested."

Zukofsky is the poet Poe promised. The distance between Zukofsky and Mallarmé can be measure in their different relationships to Poe. Mallarmé made the inevitable European assumption that Poe's mathematics required the Pythagorean mystification of number and measure, which has haunted philosophy almost since its beginning. By contrast, the numerological concerns in "A" are contingent constructions; they do not require a system beyond what is established by the text itself. In "A"–22 and "A"–23, for example, both of which comprise one thousand lines, are the millennial books of the poem, maps of a purely contingent and organic paradise:

> what avails the life to
> leaf to flower to fruit
> the seasons colors a ripening
> work their detail—the perennial
> invariance won't hollow it, no
> averaging makes their tones—Paradise.
> (Zukofsky, 1978, 509)

Paradise offers the creative freedom of the contingent particular, not the security of infinite vision of the absolute.

The structures of "A"–22 and "A"–23 are almost identical: both consist of five-word lines, which range from five to sixteen or so syllables per line. "A"–22 begins with a three line motto, which is followed by a section of twenty five-line stanzas, the last of which is short-counted by three lines. If we assume that the three line motto is displaced from the middle section and that the last stanza is to be considered incomplete, the form of the book can be said to be one thousand lines, divided into sections of one hundred, eight hundred, and one hundred lines each. This is the case in "A"–23: an opening section of twenty five-line stanzas, a continuous section of eight hundred lines, and a final continuous section of one hundred lines.

These were the last sections of "A" to be written. "A"–22 was begun in 1970, two years after the completion of "A"–24, and "A"–23 was begun in 1973. They are both "Too full for talk" (Zukofsky, 1978, 526) as Zukofsky says in a phrase that returns here from "A"–11. No one ever talked like this. The poems are not imitations of speech, but they are written to be spoken, directly preparatory for a performance of "A"–24: that is, if the lines were any fuller they would need more than one voice to speak them. All of the myriad possibilities that are open at this point in the poem vie for Zukofsky's attention in each choice. The decisions by which the poem is carried forward are still made in the smallest intervals, word by word and syllable by syllable. The rightness of any particular decision gestures toward the less determinant but possible larger structures of the poem. "*A*" is possibly a fugue. Like some other long twentieth-century poems, it is possibly an analogue to the *Commedia*. As a domestic poem in twenty-four books, it is possibly an analogue to the *Odyssey*. There are also suggestions of less expressive forms. The rigor of forms is all in the "thought that penetrates the smallest joints of words." As that thought informs larger shapes the process of the poem moves from the common and the absolute toward the private and the contingent. This is an inevitable condition of the constructions of finite beings. The other possibilities of form are based on some kind of mirror trick.

"*A*"–22 is Zukofsky's summation: "Others letters a sum owed" (Zukofsky, 1978, 508). It begins, punning on "letters by post" and "letters of the alphabet," "owed" and "ode," a summation. *The Tempest* is obviously much on his mind throughout the book, but he does not even consider renouncing his art. The quotation with which it ends has to do with the storm, not the peace that follows:

> in my mind
> a dream of named history
> content with still-vexed Bermoothes.
> (Zukofsky, 1978, 535).

In fact, he has no reason to renounce his art: the millennium arrives without the intensity of messianic magic. Zukofsky is neither a magician nor a hero. The "art" is all play. The problem is not to try to do too much oneself:

> the mind
> does not light of itself;
> stripped to the meditated object
> eyes, lights, out there here
> itself all ever, increate, seedless—
> yoke fruits other, farming watercourse
> brimming obstacle running by itself.
> (Zukofsky, 1978, 523)

The sense of time here—"brimming obstacle running by itself"—is primordial. It is neither an accretion of ritual repetitions nor abstractly metaphysical. The revelation, which turns out to be adequate, is that there is no revelation: things are as they seemed—despite the whole of the Western tradition trying to demonstrate otherwise.

"A"—23 is "An unforeseen delight" (Zukofsky, 1978, 536), in one sense superfluous, but the "deep need" (Zukofsky, 1978,126) from which "A" issues is personal—not universal or absolute—so it is superfluous as anyone's life is. It is not grounded in a compulsion to repeat, nor obsessed with ritual reliving of archetypal forms. The design of "A" is not deductive but accretional:

> a foreseen curve where many
> loci would dispose and *ands*
> compound creature and creature together.
> (Zukofsky, 1978, 536)

It can, then, continue, "and" by "and." In "A"—22, Zukofsky had written:

> History's best emptied of names;
> impertinence met on the ways.
> (Zukofsky, 1978, 511)

The book ends, however, admitting that "a dream of named history" remains. We can assume, I believe, that coming to the end of his epic of the indefinite article, Zukofsky is thinking of Pound's *Cantos,* the epic of names. The whole of the work that the translation of Catullus initiated—a literal "breathing with the tradition"—is still to be done:

> the saving history
> not to deny the gifts
> of time where those who
> never met together may
> this other time sound *one*.
> (Zukofsky, 1978, 539)

"A"—23 is a celebration of, rather than a realization of, this possibility. The mythological, which Zukofsky scrupulously avoids in the articulation of his personal order, can now appear. Roughly a quarter of the long middle section is given over to a paraphrase of the *Gilgamesh*. In Zukofsky's redaction, however, it becomes a comedy: Gilgamesh receives the plant, "Alive-Old-Stay-Young," but the original episode in which it is again lost is suppressed.

There are also recountings of the story of Hermes, the Babylonian captivity, and other mythological material—still, for the most part, without names. The myths appear as confirmations of neither Zukofsky's belief nor the poem's form. It is a luxury the poem affords.

It is indicative of the thoroughness of Zukofsky's design that the poem should come to its conclusion in his seventieth year—precisely at the end of the biblically promised span. The closing of the poem is pervaded with a sense of exile, but to live in exile is, after all, to escape from history: that is both its advantages and its disadvantage. One's destiny in exile is personal and cosmic, but not world historical, the course of empire is no longer the concern as it was for Whitman and Pound. The achieved person has no place but the cosmos. In concluding "*A*", Zukofsky proposes the project for the next decade, the naming of eighty flowers (Zukofsky, 1978, 562). His choice, that is, is to remain in exile.

If, as Freud tells us, "all organic instincts are conservative, are acquired historically, and tend towards the restoration of an earlier state of things," then exile is an extraordinary circumstance (especially for a nation of exiles), because it represents, to take the linguistic terms in which Jacques Lacan restates Freud's insight, a break in "the signifying chain." It is then possible perhaps to escape the obsessive repetition of the forms of things.

I do not want to make it appear that the problems are solved. We are still only getting ready to read "*A*." As I have put it here, I am still caught in my own knowing. We do not know how to read language that is "too full for talk." The conventions of literate syntax serve primarily to transcribe speech. Zukofsky as an old man, however-recalling one of those passages with which I began—rewrites palimpsest. Whatever pleasures "*A*" affords the ear, it is not a monologue overheard. We must imagine ourselves, not eavesdropping, but looking over the shoulder of an old man at a writing desk: never scraping the palimpsest clean, he takes out words, adds words, thickening the linguistic environment, allowing the words themselves to operate syntactically in the local surroundings, according to their own, often multiple valences.

To take a simple example:

> Seventy plants, thirty
> trees cite the way why
> argue it, those wise don't

inflict your living this place
simple, quiet, kind.
    (Zukofsky, 1978, 516)

Putting aside some difficult questions of content, several practical questions about how to perform the passage present themselves. Ordinarily we would expect a stop of some kind after "way," and then perhaps a question mark where Zukofsky gives us a comma. That would make good sense also of the second half of the third line, but it would leave the remainder of the passage dark, to say nothing of the fact that he gives neither the stop nor the question mark. The way to read the passage, I believe, is one words at a time, keeping an eye to what happens in both directions. The subtext, then, rather than being a definitive deep structure, might read something like this:

Seventy plants, thirty
trees cite the way
trees cite the way why
cite the way
cite the way why
cite the way
why argue it
the way why
why argue
why argue it
those wise don't
those wise don't inflict
don't inflict your living
your living this place
simple, quiet, kind.

Taken this way—that is, destroying the careful movement of the passage in order to hear out the action as the sentence transforms itself, moving from beginning to end—we might think that the kinship of "A" with the work of Gertrude Stein is more than incidental. She is, after all, mentioned in the poem almost as frequently as Pound (she three times; he four). For Zukofsky, as for Williams, her work seemed to open previously unexplored possibilities. The truth we seek here, if it is a truth, stands at the boundary between the sayable and the unsayable. In the drive to establish any individual person, we find incommensurable entities. In "The

Old Poet Moves to a new Apartment 14 times," Zukofsky speaks of himself as " 'The old radical' / or surd" (Zukofsky, 1971, 224).

We necessarily begin to believe that whatever unity life or language may exhibit, it is not neatly round. It cannot be be composed but only pursued. *"A,"* Gertrude Stein's *How to Write,* Williams's *Kora in Hell,* and the growing body of writing that derives from them give valuable testimony that the whole of language is pervaded by these self-obstructing patterns. They extend from the broadest structures of language all the way down to is smallest operations: the fundamental operations of giving names and making simple propositions manifest a realm in which the necessities are "musical" rather than rational. I'll leave my term here— "musical"—more or less unjustified. Perhaps I should only say that the necessities of music involve discord as much as concord. After Schönberg and Cage, we begin to see that the necessities of music making have more to do with how things are given than with how we are required to compose them. We name names and things begin to happen, arbitrarily or randomly. We might, like Cage, let things happen and find that sufficient. Zukofsky's remarkable art is to participate fully in what *might have been* random events, not to interfere with them but to *realize* them fully. It is this commitment to the responsible act that is political basis of Zukofsky's art.

Despite what we have been told about naming by Emerson, Fenollosa, Pound, Wittgenstein, de Saussure, Benjamin, and others, we continue in practice, for the most part, to think of all names as primitive pointers. Although ostensive definition plays an important role in learning language, it is not itself a simple process, and it is only one of several processes. Whether we assume with Emerson that names develop through metaphorization or with de Saussure that names appear as recognitions of sheer difference, naming obviously involves a context of language in which the new name represents a disruption. Wittgenstein calls the context "a form of life." As long as the conventions of a form of life are widely shared, the mechanisms of communication can be unconscious. Language seems natural and its logic necessary. It is possible to propose a metaphysic, a social order, a psychology. The formulae are tirelessly repeated, enacting the conventions in every sphere of life. The whole of life becomes a ritual celebration of the social triumph of the sentence (as in grammar and in law) over the disruptive "proper" name. To complete a sentence as a completed thought is to participate in a form that requires an ultimate completeness of thought. To say anything is merely to complete a link in the signifying chain, to make comments that are "most often already written down elsewhere," to reveal a form that has been agreed upon as preexistent.

At times, however, and perhaps most dramatically in our own time, speakers and writers find that their choices are spectacularly limited. They are increasingly alienated in the very structure of their language as such. The grand distinction, between self and other, subject and object, the inherent metaphysic which institutes language, goes dull. The confidence in the soul, where subject and object can be compared, disappears, and language no longer serves, to use Zukofsky's term, to "sound" (i.e. in the sense of a tuning fork) the mind of the individuals.

In such times, criticism is not enough. To be told that we are the fools of metaphysics tells us nothing; indeed that is one thing we know for sure. What we need is a concretely constructed language, which requires no necessity other than what it exhibits in itself. Zukofsky writes:

> opinion's throbbing ear aimless eye,
> serve ghosts—remain loyal, living
> faithful glances, magic and medicine.
> For *now* it is: *not*
> is the same and can
> be thought and thought is
> *now*. Truth way all one
> where it begins and shall
> come back again thru traceless
> *now* the moving body's sphere.
>   (Zukofsky, 1978, 517)

We are accustomed to reading poetry as listening to a ghost. Our eyes follow the line of words, but, in our mind's eye, we see airy sprites rise and speak, act, witness to a world we do not see. In "*A*," we are asked to read words—to perform, to fill the space where word have their full-bodied and disruptive existence and where the moving human body finds its proper sphere. The symbolic person is displaced by the physical person.

A *thinking*, unfortunately, cannot take us into the depths. A performance, a dance, profoundest action is required. Wittgenstein observes that the profound aspects of language belong to the Person, not to language, not to the symbolism of body. The sense of profundity, he notes, arises "through a misinterpretation of our forms of language. . . . They are deep disquietudes: their roots are as deep in us as the forms of our language and their significance is as great as the importance of our language" (Wittgenstein, 1953, 47). Depth is a fact of a person, the singularity of a person, and the singularity of a person's local world, arising and interfering with rule-based language. Language and the thinking that the person supports are inherently matters of surfaces, where measure is possible, where tangencies and couplings which make community possible appear. One need not glorify irrationality to recognize that the resolution to the problem of nihilism, the catastrophe of thought, is not thought. Corrosion of the mind and derangement of the senses, to recall the nineteenth-century formulae—Baudelaire's and Rimbaud's respectively—are not necessary. Irrationality is rife; we need only to recognize it for what it is. If there is knowledge, it is available to all; that is what we mean by knowledge.

CHAPTER 5

Symbolic Symbols

Wheelers and Dealers
The Theory of Games

The world is becoming invisible. Rainer Maria Rilke.

We might have foreseen it,
The triumph of calculation;
The atom calculated
By its chances.
What can I know? What shall I do?
What may I hope?
And what are my chances?

We ought to be able to survive it.
Out of the unknown activities
Of unknown agents
Mathematical numbers emerge. The last
Invisible world
Of the buyers, the sellers, the planners—

—George Oppen

SOCIETY

This essay on symbols stands in the place of an essay that cannot now be written, an essay on symbolic society. We have only the symbols of symbolic society in which to describe it. The media that regulate our lives can be described only in terms of themselves. We cannot isolate our language from its content. Now is that time of recursive turning, at once exciting and terrifying. If one should invent a new medium for the purpose of describing the symbols, it too would have to describe itself, *ad infinitum*. The symbolic self-representations that the culture has struggled to produce—and valued in part for the struggle—are now readily available, storable, transmittable. The symbolic machine that has been constituted, almost at the moment of its stunning completion, however, proves to be unexpectedly fragile, like a skin the species in its evolution has sloughed off. The next teleological stage now reveals itself not as self-representation but as self-replacement. In the 1980s the cyberpunk vision appeared as an awful and fascinating surprise. It struggles with the inappropriate conventions of the nineteenth-century novel, on the one hand, and a seriously eroded literacy that makes popular literary art a near impossibility, on the other. When William Gibson writes of Case, the information pirate of *Neuromancer*, however, the resonant sense of reality is undeniable: "He'd operated on an almost permanent adrenalin high, a byproduct of youth and proficiency, jacked into a custom cyberspace deck that projected his disembodied consciousness into the consensual hallucination that was the matrix" (Gibson, 1984, 5).

The common knowledge is strange—that from which we are estranged and have been at least since the time of Heraclitus, who noted, "We are estranged from that which is most *familiar*." The Greeks had confused themselves, not with their words, which are common, but with the mechanism of Language. Having discovered the logic of grammar, it appeared to them that to say anything required saying *everything*, to generate the information matrix.

The time and space that we think about are logical; the time and space that we occupy are not. The one is generated by formal systems; the other, by *attention*. Formal systems may serve to describe actual time and space so accurately only because of the cruel discipline of formality to which we have submitted ourselves.

Formal Systems

The symbols are meaningful neither because they correspond to objects in the nonsymbolic world nor because they are coherent with themselves; that is, neither of the two great epistemological theories are applicable. The symbolic systems that have been substituted for Nature, History, and Person turn back on themselves to discover they have symbols that must be interpreted in terms of themselves as their only content. If the range of possibilities is understood to be unlimited, the interpretation has a dialectical flavor. Although it promises progress and seems in a sense to progress, the interpretive mechanism produces perpetually changing combinations that accumulate but do not in fact progress toward the absolute, which is infinitely and desperately distant. The discourse of criticism has this quality of passage from an originless past to a teleologically inconclusive future. If the range of possibilities is empirically surveyable and carefully disciplined, however, the interpretive mechanisms may produce statistical results that are usefully reliable for certain well defined purposes. I delineate something of the formal mechanism of this world, not its formless product.

The idea of a formal calculus, which first appeared in Descartes, is now fully generalized. The Cartesian formal system consisted of space-points, arrayed on linear coordinates and described by algebraic equations. Descartes proposed to model the world with this limited formalism. Now we have unlimited formalism and formal systems of formals systems—cybernetics, category theory.

A formal system consists of a set of tokens, a set of rules by which the tokens may be legally moved and recombined, and a starting position. The tokens may be anything, so long as they are limited in number and all of the tokens of each type are interchangeable: marks, atoms, phonemes, objects in computer programs, checkers, whatever. An input invokes a rule by which tokens are moved from their starting positions into other lawful positions and combinations. A game of checkers, for instance, is a formal system of sufficient complexity to make competition in manipulating the tokens amusing. There are tokens of two kinds, distinguished by color, a set of rules describing legal moves, and a starting position defined by a playing board. Each player is responsible for tokens of a given color. If the rules are applied, eventually tokens of only one color will remain, and the player responsible for that color is declared the winner.

Formal systems are, in effect, abstract machines: a given input produces a predictable output. They are pure conceptions that may be realized in plastic and pasteboard, as in a checker game, or in silicon, meat, or other suitable material. Their power as tools is awesome. We can constitute entire worlds as formal systems and inhabit them, use them, evolve in them and with them. John Haugeland writes:

> The rules of standard logical and mathematical systems, relative to their standard interpretations, are all truth-preserving; and, of course, the tokens in their starting positions (i.e. their axioms) are all true. Therefore, any token in any legal position of one of

these systems is guaranteed also to be true! That is why we know in advance that their theorems (which are defined in purely syn- tactical/formal terms) are all *true* (which is a semantic property). Or, what comes to the same thing, in order to establish the semantic truth of a token in such a system, it suffices merely to prove it formally (play the game). This is how the "two" lives of the tokens [as tokens in a syntax, on the one hand, and tokens in a semantic, on the other] get together; and it is the basic idea behind the formalization of modern logic and mathematics. In effect, given an interpreted formal system with true axioms and truth-preserving rules, if you take care of the syntax, *the seman- tics will take care of itself.* (Haugeland, 1981, 23)

The simple two-valued semantics of logical and mathematical systems, where true or false is the only possible semantic content, take care of themselves.

Formal systems have one serious liability: if there are too many tokens or the rules are too complex, the number of possible legal combinations proliferate wildly. The formal situation simply gets out of hand for the programmer and for the finite machine on which the program must run. The combinatorial explosion is well illustrated by Raymond Queneau's sonnet sequence, *Cent mille milliards de poèmes* (Queneau, 1961), which is a simply constitut- ed formal system of astounding immensity. The sequence consists of ten sonnets and an algorithm for recombining the 140 lines to produce 10^{14} or 100 trillion poems. Queneau estimates that it would take more than a million centuries to read his poems. If formal systems are to be useful, they must be extremely limited, or conventional devices for dealing with the vast quantities must be discovered.

The trillionic complexity of simple combinatories such as Queneau's is at least countable. As the poststructuralists have cor- rectly noted, the rules which constitute natural language are unlim- ited. The possible combinations in natural languages are, there- fore, uncountably vast, not just because of lack of time, but in principle. A certain strain of poststructuralist thought finds inti- mations of a vitality or life-force, of a will or eros, in the symbolic machine conceived as a totality that manifests itself in infinitely regressive texts: the medium generates itself out of its own desire for the infinitely deferred absoluteness of closure. Text is extended a kind of animistic reverence. To be sure, a hylozoistic thrill may be occasioned for certain kinds of intellectuals by the realization that interpretation is without end: the headiness is sufficient to underwrite—at least casually—a kind of romantic paganism. Some theologians have even attempted to claim this experience on behalf of Christianity. This thrill however arises from a mere thought that is posed as emotion—a derivative or aesthetic feeling which comes from the encounter with, and failure of, formal systems. It does produce a dynamism that seems a motive of action, but it is self-cancelling. It is specious emotion, intensity in the direction of passivity, because its intensity is driven toward an impossible, apocalyptic formality.

By contrast, the emotional grounds for action does not require interpretation, or, requiring action, gesture, shout, it is its own interpretation. The given is *breath,* not the words it thinks to form on the breath as it creates itself. The efficacious sentence is a modulation of breath, not a logical object. The vector of the common is toward the complexity of individuals, who comprehend totality among their components.

The inertia of progressivist formalism must be recognized: on the social level, it is immense; its statistical coherence is deathly. We use the world and ourselves as the world's creatures on behalf of thought, formal systems—grammars and logics.

There is, however, a profound alternative: any one of us can *take* thought and use it. Thought, not the world on which the human adventure depends, is for use. Self-exploitation is not required. We are in position to use the abstract structures on behalf of a world of value, a human world of concrete order. *We are obligated by the world, not by thought.*

STATISTICAL REALITY

Considering the most dramatic intellectual developments of the seventeenth century, the appearance of mathematical analysis and the complex institutions that its implementation as science required, the break with the medieval tradition seems clean. Such was the experience of many at the time—"The new philosophy calls all in doubt," in John Donne's words—and that presumed break has subsequently provided a common landmark for our historical orientation. Increasingly, however, scholarship demonstrates that the scientific "revolution" consisted not of a sudden transformation, as it had seemed, but of the appearance of a few new techniques that led to the gradual transformation of traditional modes of thought. As Ian Hacking notes in *The Emergence of Probability: A Philosophical Study of Early Ideas about Probability, Induction, and Statistical Inference,* the doctrine of signatures, for example, that curious, central doctrine of medieval science, was not displaced but transformed. Hacking shows that it is only a step from the concept of the 'signature', which stood behind the vast interlocking pattern of similitudes that medieval science found everywhere in nature, to the concepts of 'evidence' and 'inductive probability' (Hacking, 1975, 44–45). What is retained from the magical legacy of the traditional science is a sense of the reliable relationship between an observed past and an unobserved future.

Propositions about the conjunctions of past and future or cause and effect are always tenuous and, as Hume shows, can never be asserted with the confidence of a mathematical proof. Some signs of causal relation are more reliable than others, however, and in the seventeenth century a mathematical theory of probabilities that describes these regularities began to appear. The first practical applications for the new mathematics, apart from its obvious uses in gambling, were actuarial. In attempts to keep track of the plagues, the city officials of London had collected considerable statistical information, beginning in 1603, and, by the middle of the seventeenth century, statistics were being kept in many parts of Europe. Basing their studies on this material, John Graunt and William Petty established the fundamentals of what Graunt called "political arithmetic." Their work must be reckoned as the beginnings of statistical social science. With the new techniques, it was possible to put annuity and life insurance schemes on sound economic bases for the first time and, a little more than a century later, with Thomas Malthus, to argue political policy in statistical terms (Hacking, 1975, 102–10).

If we were to emphasize our continuity with the seventeenth century, we could say that Leibniz and Pascal (who were both deeply involved in the development of the theory and methods of probability), rather than Descartes, were the most significant instigators of modernity. Norbert Wiener chooses Leibniz as the "patron saint for cybernetics" because "the *calculus ratiocinator* of Leibniz contains the germs of the *machina ratiocinatrix,* the reasoning machine" (Wiener, 1965, 12). In *The Monadology,* Leibniz writes: "each organic body of a living being is a kind of divine machine or natural automaton which infinitely surpasses all artificial automatons. For a machine made by human artifice is not a machine in each of its parts. . . . But the machine of nature, namely living organisms, are still machines even in their smallest parts *ad infinitum.* It is this that constitutes the difference between nature and artifice, that is between divine art and ours" (Leibniz, 1991, 25). Leibniz had not realized that the divine secret was recursion rather than infinite regression; otherwise, he was very close to the insight that is at the origin of artificial intelligence research.

The specific problem that Leibniz faced, but could not fully articulate, became definable and familiar in this century. The distinction between the identity *I am this one that is one* and the identity *I am this all that is all* is conventional, rather than quantitative. We do not know how *large* one is. We speak of one person or one species or one cosmos. That is, we have a problem of measurement: *one* is of no particular size. And, though Leibniz did not fully develop the mathematics of it, his monadology consciously embraces the contradiction: a monad is both an atomic entity and a cosmos, an individual and everything. He notes precisely, however, the limits of representation. There is, he says, an inevitable confusion or blurring of the image as it reaches toward infinity.

Although Leibniz did not use the term, his monad is the statistical subject. In contrast to the Cartesian subject, it is able to define a local region clearly and distinctly, but with respect to the whole, its picture is necessarily fuzzy and its apprehension of itself is based on certain zones of statistically reliable frequencies. The monad, and not the *cogito,* is the basis of technology. It embodies the equivocation which was inherent in the infinitesimal calculus. Inevitably in applied mathematics, there is what Chister Hennix calls "the sleaze factor." In its first forms, as it was developed by Newton and Leibniz, the calculus required an undisguised double shuffle: it dealt with infinitely small quantities, which sometimes counted as significant and sometimes did not. In the calculus texts of the early eighteenth century, the first postulate declared, in effect, that "a differential can increase a quantity without increasing it" (Bos, 1980, 87). The relevant metaphysical question involved the existence of infinitely small quantities that appear as a function approaches a limit. Leibniz, consistently the most scrupulous of the great seventeenth-century thinkers, doubted the existence of such quantities and took a formalistic stance, arguing that, although the symbols of the equations in themselves are meaningless, their use allows one to determine important results.

Bishop Berkeley made a pointed note of the curious logic of the mathematics on which Newtonian physics relied. In "The Analyst; or a Discourse Addressed to an Infidel Mathematician Wherein It Is Examined Whether the Object, Principles, and Inferences of the Modern Analysis are More Distinctly Conceived, or More Evidently Deduced, than Religious Mysteries and Points of Faith" (1734), Berkeley asks, "And what are these Fluxions [the infinitesimal quantities]? The Velocities of evanescent Increments? And what are these evanescent increments. They are neither finite Quantities, nor Quantities infinitely small nor yet nothing. May we not call them the Ghosts of departed Quantities?" (Berkeley, 1957, 173).

In time, mathematicians began to emphasize not the variables, which change in infinitely small increments, but the functions that determine them, thus, at least partially hiding Berkeley's "Ghosts of departed Quantities" from theoretical view. Even as late as 1904, however, Gottlob Frege writes: "It is even now not beyond all doubt what the word 'function' stands for in Analysis, although it has been in continual use for a long time. In definitions, we find two expressions constantly recurring, sometimes in combination and sometimes separately: 'mathematical expression' and 'variable'" (Frege, 1977, 107). It requires little mathematical sophistication to appreciate the problem here. If one emphasizes the abstract nature of the mathematical expression, the relationship appears as atemporal: for every y there is a corresponding x. Nothing about this relationship is variable. It is true of all y's and all x's at all times and places. However, in scientific applications, one is likely to be interested in the variable relationship between a particular y and a particular x. What, for example, is the trajectory of a cannon ball if one varies the charge? and so forth. Some fancy metaphysical footwork is involved in establishing simultaneous consideration of universality and variability.

The reconciliation between the ideal subject that can cognize the abstract relationship X is P and a world in which X is more or less *P* requires a mathematical theory of statistical stability. *X* is *P* not in relation to an absolute context but in relation to a presupposed and definable environment: *X* is *P* with respect to *R*. Statistical knowledge is expressed as a ratio between enumerated possibilities and actual occurrences: *X* is *P*, *Q*, *R*, *S*, or *T* and *X* is *P*. If the *possibilities* cannot be specified, then neither the *purpose* of the judgement nor the *value* of the proposition can be assessed. Statistical reality subordinates the individual not to a *logos* but to a relevant population (of humans, electrons, or whatever); it does not apply to any individual.

The modern intellectual disciplines are, in effect, disciplines of the combinatorial explosion: they limit the range of possible cases to which a particular *X* might belong. They have developed two basic techniques: the number of tokens can be limited by dealing only with the most general qualities of things (periodization in historical studies); or the rules can be stated in terms that make it possible to use the formal qualities of the system without enumerating all of the possible combinations (applied mathematics). A situation may involve a thousand things, but if they can be classified and represented with only three tokens, the combinatory can give information about three *types* rather than a thousand individuals. In some cases no more precision is required for significant results. Or it is sometimes possible—as in the case of certain calculuses—to state relationships between vast classes and provide a metric by which they can be applied in particular cases without producing all of the combinations.

Ultimately, it turns out, the idealized space of mathematics and the idealized subject of poetry were necessary only to initiate progressive institutions. Algebraic space and the modern ego were the first products of the new technology, and they have been rendered obsolete by their own accomplishments. Separate ideal realms for the mathematical object and the human subject are now no longer required, and both mathematics as a form of disinterested meditation and poetry as a form of the ideal subject have largely decayed. Images of ideality, such a poetry once produced, are not now the discipline of totality but the mere content of a higher level of abstraction. Richard Rorty notes:

> For beyond the vocabularies useful for prediction and control—
> the vocabulary of natural science—there are the vocabularies of

our moral and our political lives and of the arts, of all those human activities which are not aimed at prediction and control but rather in giving us self-images which are worthy of our species. Such images are not true to the nature of species or false to it, for what is really distinctive about us is that we can rise above questions of truth or falsity. We are the poetic species, the one which can change itself by changing its behavior—and especially its linguistic behavior, the words it uses. (Rorty, 1982, 88)

This conception of poetry—*species* poetry, the poetry of "behavior"—must be questioned and questioned precisely on its species or statistical character. Though it is implicitly associated with Homer and Shakespeare, who are said to have addressed the image of humankind in a spirit of disinterested inquiry, image making in our culture is not, and perhaps cannot be, disinterested. The image-making institutions that are overwhelmingly most significant in a statistical sense, especially those associated directly or indirectly with the electronic media, are systematically at the service of short-range commercial interests. They raise themselves above questions of truth or falsity in the service of greed and exploitation, not the disinterest of poetic intuition. Although enlightened cynical complaint about advertising and the obvious mechanisms of social control is common, Charles Olson's

> o kill kill kill kill kill
> those
>   who advertise you out)

in the closing lines of the first of Maximus poem takes up the full burden of an alternative poetry (Olson, 1983, 8). The media do not, like the medieval church, propose a human image that can be accepted, rejected, revised, and so forth; it creates images as forms of marketable excitement. Any image will do, so long as it can be made to appeal to the need and greed of a commercially significant population; it makes a farce of pluralism by rendering all of the possibilities of human identification modes of exploitation. Olson's proposed terrorism is now the only possible proposition of poetry because there are

> No eyes or ears left
> to do their own doing (all
> invaded, appropriated, outraged, all sense
> including the mind, that worker on what is

> And that other sense
made to give even the most wretched, or any of us, wretched,
that consolation (greased
> lulled.
>
> (Olson, 1983, 17)

When Olson wrote these poems, around 1950, the commercial
media were only beginning their profound attacks on the last ves-
tiges of human autonomy. As Olson had learned by 1960, to reap-
propriate the mind as such, even to reappropriate the mind as the
metaphorical equivalent of an organism, would not suffice to re-
store the person to him- or herself. The external threats were
graver and the interior resources greater than were commonly rec-
ognized. Olson speaks for the necessity of breaking completely
with conception of the human as an input-output device. The com-
mon world cannot be a *representation;* the world is local to the
integrity of the organism itself. The common world is the construc-
tion of all of its inhabitants, not an image of something they are
supposed to share. It has no *common* image. The common world is
a place not of representation but of action.

The Aesthetics of Recursion

> Who's buried in Grant's tomb?
> —Groucho Marx, on *You Bet Your Life*

The triune logic of the Stoics prevailed into the seventeenth
century. Sextus Empiricus gives this account:

> The Stoics say that three things are linked together, that which is
> signified, that which signifies, and the object; of these that which
> signifies is speech, as for example, "Dion", that which is signified
> is the thing itself which is revealed by it and which we apprehend
> as subsisting with our thought but the barbarians do not under-
> stand, although they hear the spoken word, while the object is
> that which exists outside, as for example, Dion himself. Of these
> two are corporeal, that is, speech and the object, while one is
> incorporeal, that is the thing which is signified, i.e. the *lekton*,
> which is true or false. (Kneale and Kneale, 1984, quoted 140)

The signifier and the signified are, of course, familiar. It is the
mediating term or the *lekton*, which was suppressed by the philos-
ophy of Descartes and Locke. The term derives from the Greek

lekton, which translates as both "to say" and "to mean"; its function, thus, is mediation or interpretation. The *lekton* is troublesome for this reason: mediation introduces either infinite regression—a search for the original Dion—or circularity of argument—Dion is Dion. The dualistic strategies are rhetorically useful to clear up the philosophic problems, but in practice, the suppressed mediating terms are almost immediately reintroduced. Probability theory reintroduces the *lekton* as an enumeration of possibilities, and the signifier and the signified are interpreted in terms of odds. The theory of inductive logic, the philosophic problem of the observer in inductive methodology, and various theories in the human sciences, including the apparently nonstatistical conception of the Freudian unconscious interpreted as a combinatory (as we have seen), are all relevant to the development of statistical reality. During the last years of the nineteenth century, rapid progress was made toward powerful new methodologies: the work of C. S. Peirce, Gottlob Frege, and Bertrand Russell in logic and the work of Carl Friedrich Gauss, Pafnuti Chebyshev, and Andrei Markov in probability theory as such was supplemented and posed in practical light by developments in the sciences, especially in thermodynamics but also, at least conceptually, in the social sciences.

A comparison of Michel Foucault's account of the loss of stoic logic and the subsequent history in *The Order of Things* with Warren McCulloch's in *The Embodiment of Mind* will suggest how thoroughly and disastrously structuralism and poststructuralism have remained locked in the Saussurian two-valued logic (McCulloch, 1965, 390ff.). Binarism is a tool of cybernetic thought, not its essential character. Working with technologies based on off-on switches, it is convenient to define certain quantities as logarithms with a base of two. The hexidecimal base—also for reasons of convenience—is also important in computer science. To Jean Baudrillard's question "Why does the World Trade Center in New York City have *two* towers? . . ." we can answer only: because it happens to have two towers—not, as he insists, because "digitality is . . . the divine form of simulation." (Baudrillard, 1988, 143) If anything, the new science is as trinitary as the old religion. Now the terms are probabilistic, rather than absolute, but history and purpose are mediated by *information* as father and son were mediated by spirit. The poststructuralist critique of absolutism is true but utterly irrelevant.

As we have seen in the previous chapter, in the section entitled "Psychodynamism," the relativism of late nineteenth-century science involved radically different assumptions concerning the various natural realms. In order for the new logical formalism that had developed to coalesce into the *ars magna,* it was necessary to recognize that the physical sciences, especially thermodynamics, where statistical methods found their first application in hard science, the biological sciences, and the social sciences were all dealing with the same fundamental stuff. Cybernetics, information engineering, and the theoretical work that they engendered provided the necessary generalization.

The important figures in this development—figures who must rank in the history of science with Galileo, Newton, Darwin, and Einstein—are are still not household names, and it is perhaps in the nature of the new science that they never will be. They mark the appearance of an intellectual world so dense that a single person can master only a small part of the relevant material. The groundbreaking works were either collaborations or investigations into narrow problems that happened to have large theoretical implications. The titles of the seminal papers are not likely to generate immediate interest: Turing's "On Computable Numbers, with an Application to the *Entscheidungs* Problem" (1936); Rosenblueth, Wiener, and Bigelow, "Behavior, Purpose, and Teleology" (1943); McCulloch and Pitt's "A Logical Calculus of the Ideas Immanent in Nervous Activity" (1943); L. A. MacColl's *Fundamental Theory of Servomechanisms* (1946); von Neumann and Morgenstern's *Theory of Games and Economic Behavior* (1947); and Walter Shannon's "A Mathematical Theory of Communications" (1948). In these papers and others in pure mathematics—by Kurt Gödel and Alonzo Church, to mention notable names—the notion of algorithmic calculability was given sufficient clarity of definition that logical functions could be *theoretically* mechanized. That is, this new science does not involve some computation that describes this or that aspect of the world. It is, rather, a theory about the nature of computability as such. For the first time, fundamental scientific work derives not from the study of nature but from the study of engineering problems. Now rather than conceiving of the world as a machine that the logical formalism describes, the logical formalism describes all possible machine-like worlds. The notion of a paradigm as a model of nature or image of the world is not relevant. Indeed cybernetics is not a new paradigm but a science of paradigms.

Warren McCulloch notes that in "cybernetics" and "information theory," we return to something like the triadic logic of the Stoics. The problems of infinite regression and logical circularity in the meantime have not been solved, but they have been domesticated. The logical circle is no longer necessarily "vicious": some recursive functions generate unending series of information, others create stable circuits of information. In either case, these logical forms that seemed a kind of madness—unavoidable but unspeakable—in seventeenth-century thought are restored to full usefulness. In his introduction to McCulloch's *The Embodiment of Mind*, Seymour Papert writes:

> The common features of these proposals [he is thinking particularly of work by McCulloch and Pitt and by Rosenblueth, Bigelow, and Wiener] is their recognition that the laws governing the embodiment of mind should be sought among laws governing information rather than energy or matter. . . . The principle conceptual step was the recognition of a host of physically different situations involving the teleonomic regulation of behavior in mechanical, electrical, biological, and even social systems should be understood as manifestations of one basic phenomenon; the return of information to form a closed control loop. (McCulloch, 1965, xvi)

Energy and matter had been obviously difficult concepts, useful and readily available to common sense but of an odd ontological status. Even in reliable scientific theory they are metaphysical and mysterious. They appear in the nineteenth-century science *so* concrete as to escape the usual tests of reality. By contrast, information is a commodity so abstract that it is not easily specified. It does not exist apart from some manifestation, but it has no particular manifestation. It is not a substance in the philosophic sense, an underlying unity that is variously modified by accident or design to produce the display of the world: it *is* the display of the world in its multiplicity. In his essay "Cognitive Science: The Newest Science of the Artificial," Herbert Simon writes:

> We have learned that intelligence is not a matter of substance—
> whether protoplasm or glass or wire—but of the forms that
> substance takes and the processes it undergoes. At the root of
> intelligence are symbols, with their denotative power and their
> susceptibility to manipulation. And symbols can be manufac-
> tured of almost anything that can be arranged and patterned and
> combined. Intelligence is mind implemented by any patternable
> kind of matter. (Simon, 1980, 35)

Information, that is, subsumes the philosophic idea of sub-
stance, but it is not a substance itself. Its nature does not require a
particular or lawful structure; it is the malleable stuff of a contin-
gent world. The importance of this fact is still to be worked
through all of our thinking.

Although there is a clear mathematical definition of a quantity
called, perhaps mistakenly, "information," what Papert means by
"information" is not comprehended by any simple definition. The
intuitive notion cannot be summed up by the technical uses, nor
can the import of the technical definitions be fully grasped without
the intuitive notion. That is, one confronts the problem of circu-
larity at the outset: what most specifically defines "information" is
the *return* of information to form a closed loop. The content of the
loop, however, is not specified: it may be the loop of the nervous
system that controls hand-eye coordination in a human, or it may
be the loop that is involved in giving a definition of "language" in
language.

Many of the most puzzling and most characteristic intellectual
problems of this century have to do with the logical weirdness of
self-reference and logical circularity. Bertrand Russell's letter to
Gottlob Frege (1902), pointing out certain devastating problems of
self-reference in set theory, marks the beginning of the ferment that
brought modernism to its profoundest pitch. In this century, it
seems, every attempt to think seriously about ultimate things en-
counters some version of the Russell paradox. Whatever one
thinks to say about the *All* is also said necessarily about the state-
ment itself. We can, for example, speak of the set of all chairs
without problem. The set of all chairs is not a chair. By contrast,
the set of all sets is a set, and it must include itself; if it does
includes itself, however, there must be a set that includes all sets,
including the sets that include themselves, and so forth. This prob-

lem shows up in many different ways. Consider this sentence, which derives from a famous example of Russell's: *The barber shaves all the men in the village*. The truth of the statement can be tested by creating a one to one correspondence between the set of men in the village and the set of men whom the barber shaves. Of course, mistakes are always possible, but, if the test is carried out with care, most people could be satisfied of the truth or falsity of the sentence. This sentence exists in classical logical space. Suppose, however, we say, *The barber shaves all of the men in village who do not shave themselves*. The grammar of the sentence still seems correct, but it presents a curious logical problem. It is not possible to determine whether it is true, because we cannot decide which class the barber belongs to. The sentence implies that if the barber does not shave himself, he does, and if he does, he does not. This problem arises anytime we attempt to create a set that is a member of itself.

After Russell's discovery, related problems of self-reference and circularity seemed to turn up almost everywhere, in quantum physics, in Gödel's incomplete theorem, and in art. Information theory and cybernetics, however, do a good deal to redeem self-reference and circularity of argument, even if it does solve not the more dramatic paradoxes.

In their important research reported in "How We Know Universals: The Perception of Auditory and Visual Forms," Warren S. McCulloch and Walter Pitt address the problem of self-reference in defining general concepts or sets in terms not of universal calculability but of neurophysiological processes. Although they think of neural nets as input-output systems, they address the states of the organism that make cognition possible: "We seek general methods for designing nervous nets which recognize figures in such a way as to produce the same output for every input belonging to the figure" (McCulloch, 1965, 47). How do we know geometric objects or gestalts; in short, how do we know abstractions? Unlike the cognitivists, they do not assume that knowledge is innate. They are fully within the tradition of empiricism and psychological associationism. "Genes can only predetermine statistical order," they write, "and original chaos must reign over nets that learn, for learning builds new order according to a law of use" (McCulloch, 1965, 46). They demonstrate that the learning of a universal in-

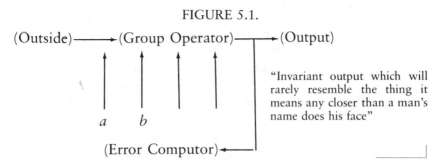

FIGURE 5.1.

Source: McCullough, 1965, 52.

volves a closed, self-correcting loop constituting a finite group of transformations. Although they deal with specific neuro-physiological examples, they give a generalized picture (fig. 5.1).

To be sure, serious philosophic problems are unanswered. How do the neurons recognize that a particular input belongs to one group rather than another involves a circularity. That is, the thing must already be recognized *before* it is assigned to the group *by which* it is recognized. It is also unclear how a network so rich in information as to assimilate all of the variations of a type can be formulated as a single, simple output.

From considerations such as McCulloch and Pitt's a new aesthetic—an aesthetic of recursion—arose. The best known exposition of it is Douglas Hofstadter's *Gödel, Escher, Bach* (Hofstadter, 1979), a serious but sometimes excessively cute introduction to recursive thought. A better introduction to strange loops, especially for readers with literary backgrounds, is Michael L. Johnson's *Mind, Language, Machine.* "Mind, language, machine," he writes: "three systems without positive substance that, copulating interactively, create the universe as it is known and manipulated by man" (Johnson, 1988, 4). Recursion does not have an epistemology. If the question, What is known of X? requires the answer "X is Y," the statement "X is X" is already compromised. The profound discovery of this century, which stills leaves us reeling and giddy, is that things are only what they are: the world is recursive and without origin, X is X. If X is Y, it is only because Y is Z, and Z is A, and A . . . is X. Gertrude Stein writes repeatedly, "Knowledge is what we know." It does not seem especially enlightening perhaps to say that "Information is information," but it advances the argument more than it first appears. The alternative is to refer information to an origin that involves an infinite regression. Moreover, "Information is information" is no more a tautology than "War is war": Information$_1$ is information$_2$. The cognitive activity that generates inputs and outputs *also* generates the space and time from which inputs derive and to which outputs are delivered. That is, experience itself is general, and the individual, not the concept, is constructed. The terms of the construction, however, are not conceptual but mensural: the measure measures itself. There is no repetition but measure. Robert Creeley notes in *Pieces*,

(Creeley, 1982, 391)

There is no repetition but insistence, the act of knowing and knowing again. We measure not an idea but the intensity of our own attention. Difference that dynamically undermines the identities of conceptualization is the medium of measurement.

Baudrillard writes: "A possible definition of the real is: *that for which it is possible to make an equivalent representation*" (Baudrillard, 1988, 145). This is the reality of habit; its technology produces nothing but new examples of the norm. In this mode, attention registers only the boredom of the randomly expected; ecstasy and catastrophe are limit states, *represented* as destructions of the represented. Another possible definition of the real is: that for which it is *impossible* to make an equivalent representation. This is the reality that never repeats itself; its technology produces nothing but its own identity, the constancy of which is changing realizations of itself. In this mode, attention realizes the persistent audacity and vitality of its own unique constructions. To put the matter briefly: a logical structure may be an infinite regress in which identity is lost to statistical normality or it may be a finite recursive loop, which returns to X is X, in which case *identity is maintained in measured time*. In the most general sense, this fact distinguishes two logical environments—the one is self-destructive and death-seeking, the other is ecologically sound and sustainable.

The Meaning of Recursion

TOO LATE

If
you
don't
want
your
mind
fucked
with
don't
read
this
poem
—George Quasha

Ludwig Wittgenstein demonstrates that language games are independent of one another. The rules of the language for describing something mathematically, for example, differ radically from the rules for describing the same thing in the natural language. Despite the continued attempts of grammarians to describe *the* rules of *the* language, we now know that language is not one thing, not an object as such but many objects, which may resemble a rhythm more closely than a tree or stone. The question about information, however, is the question about generality as such: what is the most *inclusive* thing, not the language as such, but the thing that all of the languages have in common? Information is not the *arché* but the most archaic thing that we can imagine: that which is nothing but the assertion of its own emptiness.

To say that the most inclusive thing is information is at best tautological. Perhaps to say anything about absolute inclusivity involves paradox. In the vicinity of totality, as we have seen, tautology tends to turn into vicious (self-contradictory) circularity. Cybernetics defines a logical middle ground between vicious circularity, on the one hand, and infinite regression, on the other. Our logics have been dynamistic and progressive. Cybernetics is the logic of self-sustaining, rather than self-exhausting, mechanisms.

To know meaning and structure in life simultaneously—to see life both in time and from the perspective of the end of time—is the Faustian desire. It appears that, even if we can have one or the other, we cannot have both at the same time. This is the limit that critical philosophy has sought to overcome: since Descartes, the great epistemological strategy has been to master meaning by holding fast to structure and to master structure by holding fast to meaning. Thus, our activity is pitched against itself. We produce endless interpretations in the form of text and other material consumer "goods" that are *ultimately* empty and valueless. To be sure, life is concerned with the immediate, not the ultimate, so material exegesis of the world is a possible basis for communal institutions. Like industrial production, however, textual production creates order only by producing a disorder. The intellectual and physical environment cannot assimilate the accumulation of its toxic output. The intellectual environment, as surely as the physical environment, is being polluted.

It is provocative, if not significant, that Claude Shannon's famous definition of information happens to be the negative of the expression that describes entropy, the statistical measure of thermodynamic disorder, the most generalized feature of a closed physical system and closely associated with time or, at least, temporal direction. Entropy is a measure of an expected tendency toward randomness; information is a measure of the mean statistical unexpectedness of a particular message selected from a set of possible messages. Exactly what this means has never been quite clear. Shannon himself voiced doubt concerning its usefulness outside of communications engineering. It may be, however, that this generalized, dynamic realm is *la langue,* as Saussure defines it, at its pure statistical horizon, the difference that is both pure structure and empty time, beyond which all entities lose their distinguishing characteristics—the point beyond which synchrony and diachrony join.

Shannon is concerned with a highly structured process that makes lawful selections from a preconstructed code. That is, information is defined in terms of probability: the message is relative to a determined systematic background that specifies the possibilities. An example should make the quantitative nature of information clear:

When one person is to be selected from eight candidates by the toss of a coin, a minimum of three tosses is required to make a selection. One half of the candidates can be eliminated with each toss, so the first toss reduces the candidates to four, the second toss reduces them to two, and the third toss determines a selection. The information is measured in units called "bits" or "binary digits." Each coin toss determines the value of an either/or situation, and, thus, three bits of information are required to make a determination. It would make no difference, for example, if the candidates were candy bars instead of people; the same amount of information would be required.* Information in this sense is a static quantity that describes the size of the channel required to transmit a message of a given quantity. It is important, at least in part, because it allowed Shannon to show that miscommunication caused by noise in a channel can be overcome by a calculable amount of redundancy. For example, a candidate might be selected by tossing a coin for each candidate in the pool until all but one is eliminated. This would produce a comparable result but would involve a great deal more information, much of it redundant. But if the information is transmitted over an unreliable channel, the redundancy would help to insure that the message is correctly transmitted. Thus, Shannon's famous formula, which can be simplified for illustrative purposes to

$$I_{(x)} = -\log_2 \{\text{probability of } x\},\dagger$$

defines *potential* information in a sense analogous to potential energy. It might be more accurately called "information capacity" or "the space of empty informational *structures*."

Another aspect of information is also quantifiable, not merely as an abstract ratio of possible messages to selected message, but as a measurable signal or message; it is, as it were, *kinetic* information. The confusion of these quantities has caused great difficulty in the application of information theory in non-technical contexts. In fact, the founders of the new science themselves were not, it appears, completely clear about the difference, which has continued to trouble almost everyone who has thought seriously about the nature of information. Norbert Wiener gives this definition of message or kinetic information: "The message is a discrete or

---

*Fred Dretske develops a similar example fully and usefully. His opening chapters are useful background for anyone who wants to think about the current issues in information theory (Dretske, 1981).

†Where the probability is 0.5 (a binary choice), the amount of information is, therefore, one bit.

continuous sequence of measurable events distributed in time— precisely what is called a time series by the statisticians" (Wiener, 1965, 9–10). That is, a message is a statistically significant *sample* of an actual communication. For example, one might be interested in controlling a robotic hand. The mechanism must, at certain intervals, sample the difference between the actual trajectory of the hand and the necessary trajectory to reach the designated object and, on the basis of that message, correct the movement. Information about the output of the mechanism is looped back as an input and corrects the output. This is, of course, the well known principle of negative feedback. These points about the message should be made:

1. The obvious and insoluble philosophic questions—what is measure? what is an event? what is time? and so forth—are here solved functionally, not theoretically. Measure is *some* means for marking differences. Events are what is marked. Time is the medium of the difference in which events occur. These definitions are circular, of course, which is their advantage and the source of their usefulness. The measurements may be capricious, and time may involve unknown quirks, but a usable message is produced. (It might be noted that deconstructionism is a critique of epistemological theories that are based upon identities. It is irrelevant to a practice in which the message is a difference which is measured by some *ad hoc* scale and that is relevant only to a nonrepeating, local contingency.)

2. The message may be binary or analogue. Although binary sequences happen to be useful in electronic applications and so seem important, the message is not essentially binary. The thermostat, for example, is an analogue device. The message is not *essentially* anything.

3. Wiener goes on to say, "The prediction of the future of a message is done by some sort of operator on its past, whether this operator is realized by a scheme of mathematical computation, or by a mechanical or electrical apparatus" (Wiener, 1965, 9). Thus, the metaphysical mystery of the origin does not arise. The message is judged from a local sample, not from the perspective of a global structure or origin. There are no infinite regressions and no infinitesimals (i.e., unmeasurable ghosts of quantities).

Entropy—that is, information in the first sense—is purely structural; it has no semantic content. Whether or not a message has semantic content is not so clear. One wants to say at least that it is *closer* to meaning than to entropy. The bimetal strip in a thermostat, for example, constantly samples its temperature in order to determine if the selected temperature has been reached, but of course it does not know whether it is hot or cold. To the extent that the message flows through a mechanism that is defined by its purpose, it has meaning at least for those interested in the purpose. *Meaning is created by interest, not interpretation of information.* As Donald M. MacKay, another important information theorist whose work has been too often overlooked, writes, "Questions of meaning need not arise until we bring in the human links in the chain" (MacKay, 1969, 20). The meaning has to do with *purpose,* with the teleonomic creation of order in opposition to the entropic tendency.

As it turns out, information and meaning are antithetical. Something like the relationship between structure and content, it appears, now gets played out in a new context, but the two commodities are complementaries, complete and self-sufficient within their own domain, not incommensurate aspects of a conflicted whole. The relationship between them is not dialectical. Information has to do with the reproduction or representation of a structural identity in a new space, an input-output situation. Meaning has to do with maintenance of self-identity. Warren Weaver writes, "One has the vague feeling that information and meaning may prove to be something like a pair of canonically conjugate variables in quantum theory, they being subject to some joint restriction that condemns a person to the sacrifice of the one as he insists on having much of the other" (Shannon and Weaver, 1964, 28). Weaver's intuition on this point is remarkable, but as far as I have been able to discover, no one has followed the thought to its conclusion. It is interesting to note that many of the same logical peculiarities that we found in connection with the Weber-Fechner experiments in psychophysics reappear in the experimental investigation of information, and both, like experiments in quantum physics, exhibit threshold phenomena as a central feature.

Norbert Wiener notes, for example, that a large class of devices that are based on the feedback principle are "beset by two types of error, of a roughly antagonistic nature." That is, if their sensitivity is increased so they respond to very small changes, they lose their effectiveness in dealing with more dramatic changes. If the device is optimized to deal with dramatic changes, however, they lose their sensitivity. "This interacting pair of types of error seemed," Wiener notes, "to have something in common with the contrasting problems of the measure of position and momentum to be found in the Heisenberg quantum mechanics, as described according to his Principle of Uncertainty" (Wiener, 1965, 9). Similarly, Donald M. MacKay reports that in his work with radar during the Second World War, he found it necessary to follow "the behaviour of electrical pulses over extremely short intervals of time." Like Wiener, he found himself confronted with something analogous to the uncertainty situation. As he reduced the time interval of a measurement, he lost accuracy in the measure of frequency, or as he increased the accuracy of the measurement of frequency, the intervals necessarily lengthened and provided less precision.

MacKay provides an elegant analysis of this situation. He discovers two kinds of quantities, which he calls "structural units" and "metrical units." One is a dimensionless unity that can be determined from the specifications of the test equipment itself; the other, a small quantity with the dimensions of physical entropy that must be determined from the experimental results. That is, the terms here are directly comparable to the terms that we derived from the thought experiment in "Symbolic History," illustrating the Weber-Fechner law: structure and measure obey different logics. It is possible to obtain a richer structural picture of a given situation, but only at the expense of specificity of measure, and vice versa.

Meaning, then, has two possible definitions. One arises from the consideration of entropy or potential information; the other, from the consideration of the message or kinetic information.

If information is a measure of generality or transmissability, meaning arises from the application of an independent abstract structure to a concrete occasion. Thus, as generality is lost, relevance to a particular situation is gained, and to the extent the situation invokes *interest*, interpretation of meaningful results becomes possible. Meaning, thus, is a quantity of specificity or production. In Fred Dretske's words, "Meaning, and the constellation of mental attitudes that exhibit it, are manufactured products. The raw material is information" (Dretske, 1981, vii).

By contrast, a message is already fraught with specificity, and, as Wiener notes: "The amount of meaning can be measured. It turns out that the less probable a message is, the more meaning it carries, which is entirely reasonable from the standpoint of common sense." The message itself, unlike information, is loaded with interest. To be sure, this fact brings us to the least rational aspect of life, and many of the information scientists have shied away from it. Of Wiener's position, Dretske writes:

> There is no simple equation between meaning (or amounts of meaning) and information (or amounts of information) as the latter is understood in the mathematical theory of information. The utterance "There is a gnu in my backyard" does not have more meaning than "There is a dog in my backyard" because the former is, statistically, less probable. It is not even clear that one can sensibly talk about "amounts of meaning" in this way, let alone identify them with the statistical rarity of the signs that are meaningful. To persist in this direction would lead one to the absurd view that among competent speakers of the language gibberish has more meaning than sensible discourse because it is much less frequent. (Dretske, 1981, 42)

In the sense that Wiener seems to be using the term, however, neither of these statements about the gnu and about the dog have any *meaning* whatsoever; they are both empty structures. Wiener is referring to dogs and gnus—the actual creatures—not some quantity belonging to the potential or theoretical creatures of language. The dimensions of information are order and disorder. By contrast, the dimensions of meaning are equilibrium and disequilibrium. The distinction has to do with habitual activity, on the one hand, and the experience of freshness, on the other. Things are meaningful precisely because they draw us from habitual equilibrium. To experience meaning is, as it were, to be shaken: to be *required to attend* to difference. Meaning is specificity, contingency—that which *is*, as opposed to that which is merely probable. It is true: pure meaning is as *empty* as pure structure. Shannon's information too is gibberish, albeit gibberish of a special, structured kind. It makes as much sense to think that gibberish is meaningful as to think that we *find* meaning in that which is meaningless. Information and meaning are modes of knowledge: one arrays the possibilities of *representing* the world by way of a formal system, the other acts in the world by measuring effects that cannot be represented and cannot be represented precisely because they are constantly producing difference.

Charles Olson defines meaning in these terms: "That which

exists through itself is what is called meaning" (Olson, 1969, 2). That which exists through itself is, of course, *difference*. This thought, unthinkable in classical logic, indeed this thought which was madness, which could only be posited as the contents of an unconscious or of an absolute, belongs to the very surface of the world we now inhabit. Thus, the dialectic of structure and content in dynamic conflict is replaced by another dipolar cognitive pair, the pure structural possibility of the world and the fact of the world created by interest. *The question of value, not the question of knowledge, is fundamental. We are not compelled by the logic. The choice in a particular situation depends entirely upon the aim and the interest which generates it.*

The Ethics of Recursion

We entertain a previously unknown level of abstraction—not merely a structure that can be interpreted in relations to various concrete worlds, like an equation in mathematical analysis, but various methodologies for generating many different kinds of structures. For the present we can focus on two large classes of these methodologies. One can be called 'cognitive processing' and the other 'autonomous creativity' or, following Humberto Maturana and Francisco Varela, 'autopoiesis.'

Cognitive processing is familiar. It is the gestalt of the input-output machine, of Jakobson's sender-receiver paradigm, or of our favorite metonomy for it, the computer: "Information, for the computer gestalt, becomes unequivocally what is represented, and what is represented is a correspondence between symbolic units in one structure and symbolic units in another structure. Representation is fundamentally a picture of the relevant surroundings of a system, although not necessarily a carbon copy" (Varela, 1979, xiv). It is undoubtedly received as the commonsense view, despite a fatal flaw that Varela and numerous other critics have noted: there is no evidence in the brain of a homunculus, or indeed an infinite regress of homunculi, who would be required to assign correspondences between symbolic units. The only widely considered alternative to this view—Descartes's and Chomsky's, perhaps Plato's—is to claim innate knowledge, a claim that begs the question rather than answers it.

Maturana and Varela distinguish between allopoietic machines and autopoietic machines. Any living entity—an individual, a family, a society—can be described either as a machine designed to have some output other than itself—offspring, intellectual progress, productive work, and so forth—or as having no output other than the maintenance of its own identity. That is, a living thing can be described as a component in a larger machine, such as evolution or history, or as a self-sufficiency. Allopoietic machines, which by definition have some purpose other than self-maintenance, are necessarily a fragment of some larger mechanism. By contrast, integral systems are marked by purposeless, self-organization. According to Humberto Maturana:

> The living organization is a circular organization which secures the production or maintenance of the *components* that specify it in such a manner that the product of their functioning is the very same organization that produces them. Accordingly, a living system is an homeostatic system whose homeostatic organization has its own organization as the variable that it maintains constant through the production and functioning of the components that specify it, and is defined as a unit of interactions by this very organization. (Maturana and Varela, 1980, 48)

Maturana and Varela diagram the organism as a circular organization (fig. 5.2). The autopoietic machine is continually self-producing, a dynamic boundedness or bounded dynamism. Both one-celled organisms and humans are homeostatic and autopoietic or self-creating. The metabolic dynamics are controlled by the

FIGURE 5.2.
AUTOPOIETIC UNITY

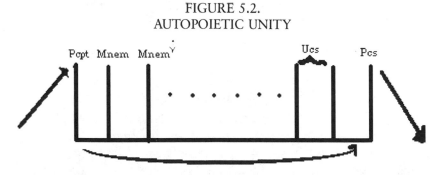

Source: Maturana and Varela, 1987, 46.

binding membrane of the organism and, in turn, the membrane is generated and maintained by the metabolic output.

Maturana and Varela distinguish between the organization of a system and its structure. Maturana writes, "The relations between components that define a composite unity (system) as a composite unity of a particular kind, constitutes its organization." A unity is the kind of thing that it is by virtue of its organization. The distinction between organization and structure has now become a science fiction commonplace. It is a common donné of science fiction that it is possible to copy the "software" of a person and "run" it in a computer. The software is the "organization," whereas the structural material may be meat or silicon. What makes the concept of 'autopoiesis' difficult for minds trained in traditional logic, however, is that the unitary system or the "whole" is one of the parts of the structure. In terms of classical logic, this is, of course, a rank impossibility: "the organization of a system as the set of relations between its components that define it as a system of a particular class, is a *subset* of the relations included in its structure," (Maturana and Varela, 1980, xix, xx, my emphasis). At the expense of some of Maturana's important precision, the terms of the circular organization can be stated more clearly, thus: the organization that defines the whole is a part of the structure that constitutes it.

I first realized that my daughter had absorbed the new logic when she was about six or seven years old. She was taking swimming lessons and had been getting in trouble for leaving various articles of her equipment in the locker room. She therefore made herself a list:

Suit
Goggles
Cap
Towel
List

When I asked her about the last item, she said, "If I lose my list, the idea will not work, but if I have my list I have to remember to bring the list home too." I asked her why she didn't put all of the items on the list under "List," and she noted (very patiently, I realize in retrospect) that there would be no end to that, and she had all of the important items listed. She obviously wasn't going to get caught in an infinite regression just because that was a possibility of the logical situation.

Although I had been reading and thinking about cybernetic theory for sometime and understood that her method was completely acceptable, the cold-blooded practicality of her practice made me a little dizzy. I felt that something was wrong with her logic, that she was scrambling the hierarchy in a way that invited chaos and madness, but she was accounting for possibilities that I would have excluded. In fact, she was beginning to understand what distinguished her as a living unity from an unliving machine that must be driven by input, such as an upset father.* It is only by self-closure that living entities break their dependence upon allopoietic 'nature,' locally escape the domain of the second law of thermodynamics, genetics, the family romance, and secure for themselves a space in which it is possible to articulate an increasing complexity of self-organization. It has proven impossible to explain how matter became alive and then at some point in its development begin to cognize itself. Life is fundamentally cognitive.

Maturana and Varela's understanding of phenomena has sometimes been described as "Kantian," presumably because it explains phenomena as the construction of the cognizing organism. Autopoiesis must be distinguished from transcendental egoism, however, because autopoietic construction of phenomena is not categorical. It is physical and temporal, structured by self-measurement, not logic. Maturana's early work was with visual

---

*This was an important lesson to me both as a parent and as a teacher. I had assumed that by threatening to deduct the cost of towels from her allowance, or whatever parental trick I had employed, that I was trying to impress *my* message upon her. On some unconscious level, I had no doubt believed that, as she was leaving the locker room, an image of a loving but stern father would appear in her mind's eye, reminding her to gather up *all* of her gear. What I had done happily was to awaken her somewhat to her own autonomy. It was a relief to realize that her behavior was controlled by the logic of recursion, not by a superegoistic father-commander. Similarly, I have learned that I can't *tell* students anything. They must explore the closed logic of which they are the autonomous center and create structures that allow us to share a common orientation as we learn how and what we are—students and teacher together.

Incidentally, when I showed my daughter—now sixteen—this essay, she said that, as far as she remembered, she was making a joke with her list. There is no question that the new logic is lighter-hearted: we do not have the grim responsibility for the infinite.

perception, especially color perception, and he discovered a fact that has large implications for our understanding of perception in general. It is possible, he discovered, to "correlate our naming of colors with states of neuronal activity but not with wavelengths. What states of neuronal activity are triggered by the different perturbations is determined in each person by his or her individual structure and not by the features of the perturbing agent. . . . We do not see the 'space' of the world; we live our field of vision; we do not see the 'colors' of the world, we live our chromatic space" (Maturana and Varela, 1987, 22–23). Likewise, we do not *describe* the space of the world; we live our description.

We have gained access to an 'abstraction' which is constituted *structurally* by both phenomena and language. In the measurable, continuous domain of phenomena, each distinction brings into existence a new unity, which is itself continuous and complete: every part contains the whole. In the domain of description, every distinction brings into existence another part. That is, phenomena have one structure, and languages have another. This *difference* has expressed itself in western thought as constituting the terms of a dialectic, and the techniques of interpretation and criticism have appeared as instruments of the dialectic. Now we learn that the *lekton* is not interpretive but creative. 'Abstraction' in scare-quotes means, of course, that this abstraction is not *really* abstract. Unlike abstraction in the old sense, it does not open into an infinite regress of ever higher levels of abstraction. It is the abstraction that includes itself as a unitary nature among its parts. One might, thus, call it equally a 'profounder level of concretion.' In terms of evolutionary history, for example, we may think of the the individual as a product of a reproductive mechanism, where a certain genetic input produces a certain genetic output, or we may think of the species and its evolutionary history as products of individuals who propose to account for the tradition of association with other individuals of their kind by the science of genetics.

This sense of the individual has obvious ethical implications. Although the second law of thermodynamics seems to suggest a gloomy career for isolated structures that tend toward the state of maximum disorder where all energy and information disperse equally throughout the system, purely local developments of order are altogether possible and to explain human evolution, for example, even necessary. Specifically, in relation to the Western intellectual tradition, the great dialectical tensions—between mind and body, subject and object—were overcome not in an act of visionary sublation but in the proposal of a collection of local projects. The logical process of the dialectic was reconceived in terms of informational coupling. In Norbert Wiener's words, "Two or more systems are said to be coupled if the laws of the motion of the larger system made up of all of them together cannot be stated as a collection of separate laws, each of which only involve an interchange of energy [and/or information] between the partial systems. . . ." The larger systems, however, do not necessarily destroy the integrity of their constituents, which may in fact exhibit independent creativity and local increases of complexity. Wiener speaks of "islands of locally decreasing entropy" that we and those amongst whom we live constitute. And he adds, "The result is that the normal perspective difference between the near and the remote leads us to give a much higher weight of importance to the regions of decreasing entropy and increasing order than to the universe at large" (Wiener, 1950, 23).

This assertion of value separates us from cosmic fate as such. We find ourselves profoundly implicated not in the universal and the absolute but in the local and the common. As utter beginners we step forth on an earth of our own making. Wiener's sense of human rights arises from an impeccable moral discrimination, an understanding of the order that involves humans *being* human, from a self-identity that makes no appeal to nature or external purpose. In *The Human Use of Human Beings,* he writes, "That we shall have to change many details of our mode of life in the face of the new machines is certain; but these machines are secondary in all matters of value that concern us to the proper evaluation of human beings for their own sake and to their employment as human beings, and not as second-rate surrogates for possible machines of the future" (Wiener, 1950, 5). The human project cannot justify itself in terms of cosmic purpose or nature. It is radically on its own. In nature, everything is becoming something else: everything is a transfer of energy or information, a machine that produces something other than itself from itself. 'Nature' is allopoietic technology grandly conceived. Human beings, however, draw themselves forth from the human; they draw forth observers from their own observations. They do not act to produce something other than what they are; they act only to maintain their own identity.

THE MODERNISM WHICH DOES NOT BECOME DATED

The 1980s saw a reactionary movement on a worldwide scale: a reassertion of earlier and simpler times—half-arrogant and half-bewildered—appeared in every domain of life. The politically disenfranchised middle class reasserted a nineteenth-century ethics of exploitation (to the profit, for the most part, of the wealthy), the religious reasserted fundamentalism, and the academics reasserted a shopworn romanticism (in the guises of Marxism, Nietzscheanism, and Freudianism). The reason for this reactionary spirit is clear: the modernist narrative is now past its heroic phase, and the deferred costs of that glory are to be paid. The ages of post-this and post-that are about to come to definition in a present with its own name.

In its first phase, beginning in the seventeenth century, modernism proposed to rationalize life in terms of narrative—historical mechanisms, machines of language. Formal narrative emerged as the epistemological structure that mediated between the timeless, spaceless formulae of mathematical analysis and the idealized ego. Thucydidean narrative, which united aspects of continuity with aspects of change, was reconceived as a primary cultural form. History was no longer genealogical and cosmic, as it was for Shakespeare, but mechanistic and social. The novel, the biography, and the novelistic history are the literary forms of this obsessive infinite. We read from beginning to end by way of the middle—the formal requirements are rigid—but we do not get to the *bottom* of things. The formal closure is poised on an infinite reservoir opening inwardly, which M. M. Bakhtin calls "heteroglossia" or "dialog." Bakhtin is perceptive to note the novelization of all of the genres: "The novelization of literature does not imply attaching to already completed genres a generic canon that is alien to them, not theirs. The novel, after all, has no canon of its own. It is, by its very nature, not canonic. It is plasticity itself" (Bakhtin, 1981, 39). The narratives of Hegel, Marx, Nietzsche, and Freud are novelistic in this sense.

In the second phase of modernism, which was articulated in the first decades of this century and was first implemented with technology developed during World War II, narrative was analyzed into its components. Continuity and change, which are reconciled in novelistic-historical narrative, were dissociated and recombined as the terms of ratios, which are expressed in three different structural zones. The physical world described by Newton, the organic world described by Darwin, and the electrical world described by Faraday proved to be strangely disjunct and logically incoherent. These epistemic zones, however, are of vast generality, so that it is possible to account for entire worlds in terms of each of them. World philosophies that impose one or the other of the structures upon inappropriate domains have been common and, when they are the basis for institutional policy, destructive. Much of the philosophic infighting of the present century has been among proponents of these limited perspectives.

It now appears, however, that these variant logics have no philosophic content. The argument that calls attention to structures from biology in order to refute philosophies deriving from physics, for example, underwrites nothing more than a preference for a particular kind of structure. The intuitive bases of the three types of structure are, respectively, reversible relationships (one can always return), directional relationships (one can never [simply] return), and neighborhood relationships (one is always hanging around in the vicinity). As Piaget shows, these structures derive from ordinary experience: "Now when we study the intellectual development of the child, we find that the earliest cognitive operations, those which grow directly out of the handling of things, can be divided into precisely three large categories, according to whether reversibility takes the form of 'inversion,' of 'reciprocity,' or of 'continuity' and 'separation'" (Piaget, 1970, 26). It is now possible to account for the apparently incoherent sense of the world with a single theory, known as "category theory." Instead of one logical space, one *logos*, there are many, and the determination of which, if any of them, is the *logos*, is not a priori; it is a matter of intuitive acuity. Piaget comments, "Suffice it to say here that the 'categories,' with their emphasis upon functions, no longer revolve around the parent structures [of Bourbakian mathematics, algebraic structures, lattice structures, and topological structures] but

around *the acts of correlation* by which the latter were obtained."*
Knowledge arises not from a priori logical forms but from acts of
attention that may vary from case to case, depending upon the
interest involved.

It is not surprising that these logical structures are associated
with structures in the natural language:

The metaphor—algebraic relationships. The metaphoric operation
calls a symbolism into existence. The equation destroys both terms
and creates a formal system of interpretation that closes on the
unified infinite: print writing's (futile) attempt to take itself as its
content. The metaphor models the world with empty marks—
Mallarméan poetry, Flaubertian prose, text. The attraction is the
unity that is rumored to appear at the promised end of interpretation.

The link—order relationships or networks. Linking one thing with
another is a matter of attention: print writing's taking of manu-
script writing as its content. Unlike the metaphor, it does not
transform the objects that are juxtaposed. The relevant genres are
compendia, anatomies, Poundian collage, hypertext. Linkage is
imagistic and deals with the regulation of discrete objects. The
attraction is the respect for discrete things.

The node ("the point at which a continuous curve crosses
itself")—topological relationships. To establish a node is to attend
to the places where two things are *locally* one: print writing's
taking oral performance as its content. Musical rhythm is the most
obvious examples; in writing, Gertrude Stein's prose, projective
verse, Cage's random processes, Burroughs's cut-ups. The attrac-
tion is the registration of *moving* forms.

The direction of intellectual progress in the West has been
toward ever higher levels of abstraction, from the ancient discovery
of the Idea, to the seventeenth-century discovery of the logical
function, and finally to the twentieth-century discovery of abstract

---

*Piaget gives an clear account of the mathematics in *Structuralism* (Piaget, 1970).
To my knowledge, the poststructuralists have not taken up Piagets challenge.
Although Saussurian structuralism has been thoroughly discredited, the history
of structural generation and coupling is vast and does not depend upon this or
that particular array of formal possibilities.

J. L. Bell gives a readable account of category theory for the nonspecialist
(Bell, 1981), and Robert Rosen's use of category theory in *Life Itself* (Rosen,
1991) bears significantly on the present discussion.

systematicity. We can now operate with any degree of abstraction, as we can operate with N-dimensional spaces. In either case we can have mathematical certainty (i.e., not absolute philosophic certainty but reasonable, formal assurance). Unfortunately, we do not know what we are talking about. The problem of interpreting these vast, symbolic machines in terms that humans can understand has always been difficult; now it has become impossible. It is hard to imagine a four-dimensional space, to say nothing of a nine-dimensional space, and it is hard to think of the spaces that might be described by a system of systems of systems. We can use abstract formalism that we cannot understand. We can know what we cannot think. To say the least, we have all of the abstraction we need. The intellectual landscape was once dominated by absolute order, on one side of a great chasm, and chaos, on the other. Now we have found a way of mapping intellectual space in which the describing mind *decides* how great the chasm is, what distance separates order and chaos, and so forth. While the possibility of absolute knowledge has been lost, *everything* can be known with some degree of statistical reliability. Knowledge is a ratio of probability between a defined, finite grid and the contingent events that occur on the grid. For many technological and social purposes, such knowledge is sufficient. Unfortunately, this knowledge does not underwrite meaningful lives for individuals.

Now, the knowledge of form is such that Mallarmé's dream of replacing life with the book—or with the electronic text that has come to replace the book—is altogether realistic. The theorized alienation that we have suffered since the Greeks changes gears. The alienation now becomes practical and quotidien. Information engineers reduce phenomena to its generalized forms and attempt to produce a statistically reliable replica of it: thus artificial intelligence, artificial reality, artificial life, and so forth. Life becomes its own artful product. Hans Moravec of the Robotics Institute of Carnegie-Mellon University writes:

> This is the end. Our genes, engaged for four billion years in a relentless, spiralling arms race with one another, have finally outsmarted themselves. They've produced a weapon so powerful it will vanquish the losers and winners alike. I do not mean nuclear devices—*their* widespread use would merely delay the immediately more interesting demise that's been engineered.
>
> You may be surprised to encounter an author who cheerfully

concludes the human race is in its last century, and goes on to suggest how to help the process along. Surely, though, the surprise is more in the timing than in the fact itself. The evolution of species is a firmly established idea, and the accelerating pace of cultural change has been a daily reality for a century. During those hundred years many projections of future life, serious and fictional, have been published. Most past futurism has kept separate the changes anticipated in the external world, and those expected in our bodies and minds. While our environment and our machinery could be rapidly engineered through industrious invention, alterations in ourselves were paced by the much slower Darwinian processes of mutation and selection.

In the late twentieth century, the barriers of complexity that divided the engineers of inanimate matter from the breeders of living things have been crumbling. In the future [we can only anticipate that] the human race itself will be swept away by the tide of cultural change, not to oblivion, but to a future that, from our vantage point, is best described by the word "supernatural." Though the ultimate consequences are unimaginable, the process itself is quite palpable, and many of the intermediate steps are predictable. . . . The underlying theme is the maturation of our machines from the simple devices they still are, to entities as complex as ourselves, to something transcending everything we know, in whom we can take pride when they refer to themselves as our descendants. (Moravec, 1987, 167–68)

One can question the time scale and the ultimate workability of the scheme, but Moravec states clearly the *telos* of the West. It is not science fiction. His argument is an extrapolation from the fundamental, Western strategy for producing knowledge. Whether we think of Euclidean geometry, Aristotelian logic, Cartesian mathematics, linguistic structuralism, or aesthetic formalism, the underlying techniques have to do with the discovery of formal systems that are potentially translatable into new media. Silicon as a medium for intelligent machines has distinct advantages over hydrocarbons (i.e., meat). It is more stable, and the complexity of the formal systems that it can support appears to be unlimited.

Anthropomorphism enters Moravec's account only when he says these mastermind robots "*refer* to themselves as our descendants." They will refer to us, of course, in the sense that they will be able to access information about us, if they need to, but they will not likely think of themselves or us in any sense which will give us cause for pride. Indeed it seems that they will not be *conscious* in any sense that we would find interesting, so there will not be those moments of holding oneself and ones ancestors in a conscious balance of fascination and reverence. The whole business of the interior cinema that is so important and wonderfully mysterious (and troublesome) for us is *not* significant data for the machines. They will not *need* the display of the conscious self. They will refer not to the tree but to the actual state of their silicon brain that would, for us, produce an image of the tree.

In the first two stages of modernism, humans have successfully created a symbolic machine that can at least theoretically take their place. It is now possible to begin with statements that are obviously and trivially true, because they refer only to empty symbols, and, by using formal procedures that retain the truth of the statements they operate on, to build up complex structures which are far from obvious. The important fact about these procedures is that the truth of the trivial statements is reliably retained in the complex conclusions. The difficulty is that these structures must be *interpreted* as a world, and the hermeneutical task is immense and exhausting. As deconstructionism has shown, it can never be complete. Completion, however, is not necessary: statistical reliability will suffice to construct a world.

The modernism which does not date, by contrast, does not make a dialectical move in relation to the master logic. It offers up a complementarity. We now discover that meaning may also be understood as *prior* to symbolic structure. *We may interpret meaning in terms of symbols.* Thus, we produce a world of conscious awareness, a world dense with symbols but not displaced by symbolic structures. Rather than displacing ourselves, as Hans Moravec imagines, we may construct a common world for human creatures that is the adequate correlative to the world of machines that we are spawning.

THREE VERSIONS OF STATISTICAL REALITY

The Supreme Fiction: The Algebraic Metaphor and Common Language

The institutions that began to incorporate science into daily life were not the creation of a few isolated geniuses; they required the commitment of an entire culture in which Cervantes and Milton, Michelangelo and Bach were as necessary as Galileo or Descartes. The tension between high art and high science was essential to cultural production, and the popular culture was a necessary medium, not of the arts or sciences as such, but of the culture that afforded the arts and sciences ideal space. The idealized objectivity of science and the idealized subjectivity of high art required the maintenance of a vigorous popular tradition of novels, essays, newspapers and magazines, which informed the culture factually and emotionally.

In the nineteenth century, however, science began to relinquish its idealized object and take responsibility for its metalanguage as part of its own methodology. Increasingly, it was statistical and pragmatic, not absolute. The images of ideal subjectivity, such as those provided by the tradition of English poetry that originated with Donne and Milton, were still alive, if failing, in the work of Tennyson and Arnold, but they were no longer required to maintain the subject-object balance. As Hegel recognized, articulation of the ideal subject had been accomplished. Poetry had been superseded by prose and its disciplines, and prose, in turn, was to be superseded by the techniques of statistical epistemology. Thus, the high arts more or less disappeared, becoming fetishes of nostalgia cults—often sponsored by literature or art history departments in universities—and, to the extent it was feasible, recast as highbrow show business in the form of orchestra concerts, ballet and repertory theater performances, gallery openings and so forth. Thus, too, literature came to be the arbiter of a normative reality but the norm of a highly selective, mostly academic, population, which is at once oddly respected and out of the cultural mainstream.

Defining and apologizing for the poetic tradition that arose in the seventeenth century has been the central preoccupation of literary studies. During the past sixty years, it has become an intense, and even manic, enterprise. The tradition has two, often overlapping, branches: one emphasizes ideality of form, the other ideality of content. In English and American poetry, the one tradition takes its rise in Donne and the Jacobean playwrights, includes *Don Juan* and *Biographia Literaria*—if not much high romanticism—and reasserts itself in Browning, the early Ezra Pound, and most notably T. S. Eliot; the other originates in Milton and is most clearly traced through Wordsworth to Yeats and Stevens. These traditions have found their apologists respectively in the old American New Critics and the New Romantics, led by Harold Bloom and Paul de Man. As the possibilities for the self as an independent agent were pared down, the modern imagination was left with a volatile mix of stoicism, nihilism, and formalism, which were recycled in concrete and ever more hermetic forms. The New Critics were stoics and linguistic formalists; their preferred trope was ironic juxtaposition. The New Romantics are devoted to the poetry of personal revolt, the strife and negativity that fuels bourgeois culture, especially as it is manifest in the Oedipal conflict; their preferred trope is metaphor. One might, with considerable justification, think of the two schools as the Catholicism and Protestantism of modern egotism.

The mood of both traditions, however, is elegaic, and both come to the same predicament, which is articulated definitively by T. S. Eliot:

> What might have been is an abstraction
> Remaining a perpetual possibility
> Only in a world of speculation.
> What might have been and what has been
> Point to one end, which is always present.
> Footfalls echo in the memory
> Down the passage which we did not take
> Towards the door we never opened
> Into the Rose Garden.
>   (Eliot, 1963, 177)

In statistical reality, one lives with perpetual abstraction. The Rose Garden is never entered because, if one tries, it becomes merely another of the possibilities, and in the speculative calculus something else takes its place.

Wallace Stevens, likewise, comes repeatedly to this impasse, most poignantly in "The Rock," but he never credits the real existence of the Rose Garden; for Stevens, it is always and only a further place of the mind, "the main of things" (Stevens, 1982, 528).

Eliot speaks for the early modern strategy, which could be more or less reconciled with St. Augustine, that the ideal subject is an image of the infinite, and thus imageless, god. Meditation on this paradox was the sustaining activity of the Christian era. In his most famous essay, Eliot writes: "The point of view which I am struggling to attack is perhaps related to the metaphysical theory of the substantial unity of the soul: for my meaning is, that the poet has, not a 'personality' to express, but a particular medium, which is only a medium and not a personality, in which impressions and experiences combine in peculiar and unexpected ways" (Eliot, 1975, 42). This substitution of a medium for the ego is the essential Cartesian move, and the seventeenth-century metaphysical poets share it with the rationalist philosophers among their contemporaries. Eliot's task, like Donne's, Herbert's, and Milton's, is to constitute an idealized or aesthetically satisfying image of subjectivity even though it cannot be identified with actual, personal experience.

Seeking an alternative to the substantial unity of the soul, Eliot discovers a symbolic unity that shifts the responsibility from the personal ego to the cultural norm and puts the mere actual world and the aesthetic or created world into opposition. Art emotion and personal emotion, therefore, form a Hegelian pair, which can be resolved only in nihilistic irony or mystical unity. Eschewing the one and failing the other, Eliot fetishizes certain statistical norms as the basis for cultural interaction. He "halts at the frontiers of metaphysics or mysticism," however, so that he might confine himself "to such practical conclusions as can be applied by the responsible person interested in poetry" (Eliot, 1975, 43). His art, especially in the plays and later prose writings, remains social, a gathering and formalizing of conventional experience. It attempts to discipline the medium in terms of a particular cultural tradition. Eliot's dominance of Anglo-American literary thought for three decades or more is a sign of the vitality of Christian culture. For a homogeneous culture or a culture with a homogeneous controlling elite, the statistical image of the genetic culture provides an efficient and satisfying coherence, but with the rise of pluralistic, mass culture, this essentially tribal strategy would not serve.

Wallace Stevens, who does not identify with the Christian tradition or with any *social* identity, could express only the individual personality: "poetic truth," he writes, "is an agreement with reality, brought about by the imagination of a man disposed to be strongly influenced by his imagination, which he believes, for a time, to be true, expressed in terms of his emotions or, since it is less of a restriction to say so, in terms of his own personality" (Stevens, 1951, 54). Unsustained by belief and tradition, poetic truth is fleeting, and personality is subject to a cycle of capriciousness and ennui.

For Stevens, the insurance man, personal reality is permutative and statistical. The medium in itself has no definition. As it is clear in "Notes toward a Supreme Fiction," it is necessary to look for statistically reliable invariants:

> Thus the constant
> Violets, doves, girls, bees, and hyacinths
> Are inconstant objects of inconstant cause
> In a universe of inconstancy.
>   (Stevens, 1982, 380–408)

Stevens' medium is a cultural tradition with its commitment not to a particular imagery but to grammar and the statistical constancies on which it depends. All of the possibilities of language are available to him. In keeping with this permutative logic, Stevens's poems take the general form of theme and variation. When computers write poetry it is more like "Sea Surface Full of Clouds" or "The Man with the Blue Guitar" than, to pick another modernist anthology piece, William Carlos Williams's "By the Road to the Contagious Hospital." However we might judge the merits of the poems, which is not our purpose here, we can come closer to writing an algorithm for Stevens's poems than for Williams's or, for that matter, Eliot's. Even so complex a poem as "Notes Toward a Supreme Fiction" is based on the theme and variation format, despite its superficial appearance, which suggests a dialectical structure. In his reading of the poem, Bloom notes the fill-in-the-blank character of Stevens' verse. Consider the opening lines of canto 4 and his commentary:

> The first idea was not our own. Adam
> In Eden was the father of Descartes
> And Eve made air the mirror of herself,
> Of her sons and of her daughters.

On the basis of a passage in an essay by Stevens, Bloom proposes that "we must read canto 4 as opening, 'The first idea was not our own. Adam / In Eden was the father of Freud' . . . Freud, substituted for Descartes, centers our sorrow not in the abyss between subject and object but in Eve making the air the mirror of herself" (Bloom, 1976, 183). Indeed we might substitute any number of names in place of Descartes's. It could be a parlor game in which one player provides a name and the second player provides an interpretation. We might, for example, substitute Kant or Nietzsche—or perhaps Niels Bohr world be interesting. Stevens enters the space of unhampered textual production. It is relentlessly solipsistic, and the poor ephebe, who is a figure not unlike Henry Adams in *The Education,* a figure of the poet's self-instruction, is overwhelmed by language. "Major Man," Joseph Riddel writes, "proves the argument for abstraction, the flesh become word rather than the word become flesh" (Riddel, 1965, 182). He is absorbed into the flux of information. In order to sustain poetic truth for a time, the individual must not only *have* all of the possibilities but also, as it were, be overwhelmed by them; that is, to recall the Hegelian definition of comedy, all essentiality melts away. Comic mastery derives its force from the dissolution of essentially. This peculiar accomplishment of *power* is usually taken gravely by the exegetes:

> The poet is thus the type of those who enable us to master reality. (Sukenick, 1967, 162)

> What Stevens has evolved is a self, and in that self an image of the world of which man is master, the man-hero who comes to accept what is humanly possible and desires no more. (Riddel, 1965, 182)

> [Of a passage in "Notes toward a Supreme Fiction":] So far, an unexceptionable statement: poets are to dominate the violence of reality. (Vendler, 1969, 186)

> In the MacCullough [of "Notes toward a Supreme Fiction"] we confront Whitman assimilated to Nietzsche, an American Over-Man, a grand trope or noble synecdoche of Power, power that compounds the ocean as universe of death, and language: "power of the wave, or deepened speech" (Bloom, 1976, 190).

For Stevens, the poet is a Mallarméan god or *Übermensch* but in a comic form—an unformed, childlike god or *Übermensch*. The triumph of comedy is a concession to an "invasion" of fulfillment of desire. It is an odd moment in romantic thought: fulfillment of desire *invades the desirer.* The mastery of reality is to enter a world of superfluous production and consumption. Few but Hegel, who first noted this inversion, which he called the appearance of the *verkehrte Welt,* and Stevens have had the stomach to explore this grotesque reality, which is at once mastery of reality and self-destruction. The literary commentators do not go this far, of course, but they speak of a condition that is perfected by the machine:

As humans, we are half-breeds: part nature, part nurture. The cultural half is built, and depends for its existence on the biological foundation. But there is a tension between the two. Often expressed as the drag of the flesh on the spirit, the problem is that cultural development proceeds much faster than biological evolution. Many of our fleshly traits are out of step with the inventions of our minds. Yet machines, as purely cultural entities, do not share the dilemma of the human condition. Unfettered, they are visibly overtaking us. Sooner or later they will be able to manage their own design and construction, freeing them from the last vestiges of their biological scaffolding, the society of flesh and blood humans that gave them birth. (Moravec, 1987, 168)

This is not the occasion for an extended reading of "Notes toward a Supreme Fiction." The poem has been read to death and will have to be put aside for a generation or two before we can see it as something other than an instrument of late bourgeois repressive tolerance. We might, however, compare "Notes" with other masterpieces of Romantic self-interpretation, such as Hegel's *Phenomenology,* Emerson's essays on American nationalism, Schopenhauer's *World as Will and Idea,* Nietzsche *Zarathustra,* or Spengler's *Decline of the West.* It is important to understand why the largeness of the world they describe gets pared down to the "fat girl" of Stevens's figuration. They each have some version of the romantic cycle of consciousness:

1. the Ego recognizes itself in recognizing the other, which may of course be only itself in the mode of self-observation;

2. the Ego claims the other as an instrument of its own expression—realization or incarnation in the other (historically the birth of Christ);

3. maintenance of the incarnation in time, however—and this is the turn which brings everything back on itself—creates contradictions in which the Ego must also recognize itself;

4. as the Ego becomes more inclusive, it approaches a limit at which it can no longer comprehend itself, and its medium becomes a monotonous array of infinite possibilities in which any achievement is negated by the vastness of possible achievements;

5. necessarily, therefore, the self empties itself out and makes a

new commitment to an absolute relation of ego and other, thus starting the cycle anew.

The cycle can be more tightly delineated in these terms: self-knowledge is knowledge of the Other in the concrete (marriage); knowledge of the Other is self-knowledge in the abstract (nature). This is a rich circle, rich enough in fact to account for everything that we say that we know. Thinking its way around the circle by way of its instrument, the human Ego accumulates its overwhelming density. It was capacious enough to allow Hegel to account for the whole of history, including the most immediate events of his day. As long as the circle is used perspectivally, so that a place that is known is taken as the condition for a place that is not known, useful insights accrues. It is, however, knowledge for a particular purpose, and it necessarily creates conflict and division rather than commonality. When one attempts to speak of the whole, the cycle of knowledge becomes, as Hegel knew, the way of despair. By the time of Nietzsche, affirmation of the cycle could be a kind of test of bravado. Stevens, however, though retaining the romantic form, had lost the innocence that maintained it. Its intricacies had been so well mapped that its every station was immediately available to him: he could "confect" the Chaplinesque figure who appears at the end of "It Must Be Abstract" into a suitable spouse for the "green fluent mondo" in only a few deft strophes. This is the eternal recurrence—now, it appears to be played out in relation to silicon.

Both branches of the tradition had reached their logical conclusions by the end of World War II or sometime shortly thereafter. After *The Four Quartets* and Stevens's last two volumes, there was no inherent reason for any poet to pursue this line of thought. The nature of culture as such, however, is to conserve its traditions, and the modern West can afford to indulge itself in the luxury of maintaining even moribund traditions. Although this function has been traditionally served by a priest craft, it is now the function of the academy.

Laura Riding Jackson's *Contemporaries and Snobs,* published in 1928 and never reissued, is still one of the most perspicacious analyses of the engineering of posthistorical history and one of the most eloquent documents of a radical alternative. Popular, twentieth-century modernism had already by 1928 degenerated into a mode of suppressed romanticism, which, Jackson says rightly, could only be understood psychoanalytically; that is, by positing a background, a finished, infinite combinatory of possibilities—albeit an unconscious one—for the overt actions. Thereafter aesthetic culture was conducted in relation to a historical metalanguage, a reproduction of an antiquated worldview, the responsibility of an increasingly prosperous academic industry that managed to generate considerable enthusiasm for the spectacle of art.

Laura Riding Jackson understood, in part at least from her reading of Gertrude Stein, that we had reached the end of history, which is to say the end of the symbolism of the absolute. What continues is not history—that is, the structures that produce mechanisms so startlingly powerful that they were thought to be prior to meaning—but "the meaning at work in what has no meaning" (Riding, 1928, 9). This statement distinguishes a domain of knowledge that differs from the post-Cartesian domain. As we have seen, modern scientific knowledge arises from the workings of interpretation in that which *already* has meaning; it creates meaningful ratios or analogies or formal symbolic systems from preexisting symbolic systems. Jackson writes, "human beings have come to the end of their history, and have need for their attaining to a full reality of being, of an immediacy of life that, instead of being progressively consumed by time (unto the death-point!), has time's very nature of self-renewal in it" (Jackson, 1976, 220).

For a brief period, between 1910 and 1930, art escaped the academy or at least made a valiant move toward escape. Art was made as it was made, to recall Gertrude Stein's phrase, not as it was prepared (Stein, 1962, 514). Almost at the moment of its inception, however, Laura Riding Jackson also recognized and defined the beginnings of the new academy: Poetry, she notes, is "easily professionalized. From observations of it in written works, rules are made for it, intentions ascribed to it. There results what has come to be called criticism." The history of the academy and the academizing of reality in this century is yet to be written.

Both the arts and the sciences began to take symbols as the content of their symbols, and knowledge was generated as a result of reflection upon the disciplinary language itself. Jackson asks, "if knowledge is, so to speak, composing its own monster-poem [and it is precisely the beginnings of this composition that we have traced from Descartes to Hegel, Freud, and Shannon], has the poem as such necessarily disappeared? Can minds and their perceptions be erased by a piece of self-investigated india-rubber?" (Riding, 1928, 62). The answer to these questions, as to all other questions in the dialectical universe, is yes and no. On the one hand, as Hegel duly prophesied, poetry, the universal art of the modern *episteme* is dead. Before theory became fluent, we required an aesthetic to mediate between abstraction and the sensuous world. For Hegel, this function was supremely served by poetry:

> Poetry is the universal art of the spirit which has become free in itself and which is not tied down for its realization to external sensuous material; instead, it launches out exclusively in the inner space and the inner time of ideas and feelings. Yet, precisely, at this highest stage, art now transcends itself, in that it forsakes the element of a reconciled embodiment of the spirit in sensuous form and passes over from the poetry of the imagination to the prose of thought. (Hegel, 1975a, 1:89)

Now, the prose of thought is triumphant. That which the dialectic sublates however never disappears: while always staying the same, it is transformed into its medium. It would be more accurate to speak not of the disappearance of poetry and the other arts in their bourgeois manifestations but of their transformation into media that are more efficient and more democratic. Poetry and the other high arts, to the extent that they survive, are adjuncts to television drama and rock and roll. Now it serves not to focus attention but to distract. Art continues because it has been recycled as entertainment and, to the extent that it produces unique material objects, as a field of investment. The arts are entertainment for the most demanding audience—those who require greater complexity, which is to say, those who have more surplus attention to absorb. They are successful—that is, entertaining—precisely to the extent that they successfully pose themselves as something else—culture, self-improvement, and so forth.

The attempts to sound the alarm that poetry in the sense that has persisted in the West, since the seventeenth century, if not since Sappho and Archilochus, has disappeared are too late. Those images of essentiality cannot be sustained against the comedy of statistical reality. Christopher Clausen, who is responsible for one of the more hysterical attempts to call poetry back to its Victorian order, sees science as the enemy: "Few doubt that the rise of science has had something to do with displacing [poetry] as a publicly important vehicle for those truths that people accept as being centrally important" (Clausen, 1981, 703). Such was the case in the nineteenth century. Poetry, like religion, lacked the critical rigor that belonged to science, and, confronted with the intimidation of scientific rhetoric, poets sought new pastures, where they would not be required to compete with positive knowledge. Clausen follows Coleridge in thinking of poetry—the object of which is pleasure and not truth—as a palliative to the harsh objective reality of modern culture: "Seven decades have now passed since the first rattling gunfire of the modernist revolution, a longer period than had then elapsed since the death of Wordsworth, and it is time to ask whether the kind of rescue operation the romantics performed for English poetry is possible again" (Clausen, 1981, 714). The answer to Clausen's question, if he means to ask for the renewal of that unified vision of the world that informed the British empire (Clausen's military imagery is telling here) and the industrial revolution, is emphatically negative. That view in which the world is so simple that it can appear as the trope for the private emotional life cannot be sustained for the mass audience by poetry; it lacks force as propaganda. The maintenance of the illusion that defines the self in technological culture is the business of more powerful mechanisms.

Of course, we have persistent testimony that the pleasures of poetry are extreme. It is associated mythologically with intoxication and even the "pleasures"—read "happy irresponsibility"—of madness. A performance of Homer, from what we know of it, would likely have been more like a rock concert than a contemporary poetry reading (Havelock, 1963). It can be said, of course, that Coleridge speaks of profound pleasures, of disinterested meditation or aesthetically distanced absorption in beauty, but defining "profound" necessarily brings the question back to truth. The readers Coleridge imagined were solitaries in their closets, books in hand, enjoying pleasures of the most cerebral and passive sort—such readers as have given up on the more overt pleasures, having subdued even the desire for them in the name of religion or the demeanor that was required in a protestant bourgeois culture. Nineteenth-century philosophies of organism were controlled by a strict anti-hedonist morality for everyone but the artist, who was not only given wide license but was almost required to use it as a guarantee of authenticity (much as, in recent times, the madness and suicide of poets have been the guarantees of the spectacle of despair). The poets were allowed a holiday from the world of fact and addressed themselves to the imagination and the production of pleasure. They were honored adolescents and were licensed to speak of a world in which the parts added up to make a pleasurable picture of the whole. It was the poets' task to take responsibility for the emotional life of the people. They were, therefore, more or less required to lead scandalous lives (because "the road of excess leads to the palace of wisdom"? or simply because it takes a great deal of irresponsibility to counterbalance such repression?). As a wiseassed teenager, Rimbaud saw precisely what his culture required of him and had the talent and gall to do it: " . . . the problem is to make the soul into a monster. . . . Think of a man grafting warts onto his face and growing them there" (Rimbaud, 1976, 102). His art was compromised with a culture that could see one thing only by relating it to another. A culture that begins with the requirement that every word relate to THE WORD ends by seeing that everything is everything else: "I could see very precisely a mosque instead of a factory, a drum corp of angels, horse carts on the highways of the sky, a drawing room at the book of a lake; monsters and mysteries" (Rimbaud, 1976, 205). Deviation from standard morality was not sanctioned, but it was forgiven as a necessary condition of the poet's office. If Byron is the exemplary case in English poetry, Rimbaud was most viciously victimized by the role, and it was Rimbaud who most clearly exposed it. At the age of college sophomores and as the author of enough poetry to make him immortal, Rimbaud quit: "I! I called myself a magician, an angel, free from all moral constraints . . . I am sent back to the soil to seek some obligation, to wrap gnarled reality in my arms! A peasant!" (Rimbaud, 1976, 213).

By now, the Coleridgean artifact, which offers relief from the unpleasant, incoherent reality, and stimulates the pleasure centers, has been transformed into an integrated technological environment in which truth and pleasure are adjusted to an optimally efficient mix. Microcomputers, two-way television cables, and videotape recorders and cameras will vastly extend the avenues of marketable emotional excitement. Now that we enter an age in which the dominant cultural project is the production and distribution of information, the products of the poetic intelligence are no longer distinct from other consumer items. When the factory produced steel ingots and the poet produced poetry, there was not likely to be any confusion. When the 'factory' and the poet both produce information, however, the fundamental cultural structure has changed. Clausen conceives of poetry as being in some 'blessed" zone of language by which it stands outside instrumental language. Literary institutions, have, or should have, he believes, a special vantage from which to criticize the cultural functions. Without essentially changing in themselves, these institutions have been incorporated in the circuit of production and consumption.

It is disconcerting to discover how many poets and critics still think of poetry as the generator of consumable sentiment or, among the avant-garde, consumable energies without content, and how deeply they resent the media, which have come to fill the office of the poet which Rimbaud abdicated. Nevertheless, in a symposium in *The Georgia Review,* occasioned by the publication of Clausen's book, several of the respondents feel that television is the chief competitor for poetry's claim to the mass audience. Comparing the 1980 Leonard-Hearns fight on cable television and a poetry reading by Adrienne Rich, Maxine Kumin writes "Given the choice between an instant in sports and a lifetime in the arts, the mass-cult unhesitatingly chooses the hedonistic moment." And Joel Connaroe writes:

> There are, after all, an enormous number of diversions everywhere calculated to keep even serious readers from settling in with W. S. Merwin, Emily Dickinson, or any other artist who demands concentration and collaboration. The morning and evening news, *60 Minutes,* and *Wide World of Sports,* among others, provide constant enticements. What chance has Adrienne Rich against Rona Barrett? Anthony Hecht against Mike Wallace? Richard Wilbur writes like an angel, but is he a match for naughty John McEnroe? (Conarroe, 1981, 745)

An *"angel"*? *"naughty"*? Rimbaud's angel has come to *this*?

In response after response, the symposiasts degenerate into the self-parody of a fallen elite. The Victorian function of the *Bible* and *Palgrave's* has been replaced by television, sports, and shopping malls, which are increasingly electronic amusement parks. The practical need for excitement and anesthesia to motivate and to ease the population through the boredom, frustration, and tension that is the experience of the citizens in a technoculture is immense.

Cultures have taken their idea of order from the most general design that they have been able to discover. For the Greeks, it was geometry; for the Middle Ages, syllogistic logic; for the Renaissance, music (i.e., geometry in time); for the Enlightenment, the Newtonian cosmos. Beginning in the latter part of the eighteenth century, order was been understood in terms of organic structure. More recently, it has been understood in terms of language or writing. We are destroyed by the *scale* of writing. The line of thought that runs from Hegel to Nietzsche, Freud, Lacan, and Derrida (Hölderlin, Flaubert, Mallarmé, Joyce, and Stevens are the relevant literary artists) destroys the ego in the infinite.

Writing is the last trace of the private self, that unspeakable abstraction, the reduced matter with which the private self marks the world. The living experience has been digested, and this waste has been expelled. Baudrillard notes, "The universe is not dialectical." It does not behave like people engaged in interested and sympathetic discourse. It thinks us, rather than we it. It is inhuman, unself-regulating: "it moves toward extremes, and not toward equilibrium; it is devoted to a radical antagonism, and not to reconciliation or to synthesis" (Baudrillard, 1988, 218). In short, a logic that is increasingly antithetical to humanity in its articulation of an intellectual landscape has grown from the proposition that man is a rational animal. The logical world emerges as a grotesque, libidinal formalism that can find no object smaller than totality and thus expresses itself as greed. This intractability is surprising only because humankind made a valiant and, given the impossible odds, a remarkably successful attempt to domesticate logic. As it turns out, however, plants can be domesticated, animals can be domesticated, logic cannot be. The intellectual upheaval of the present is not that we are undergoing a shift in paradigms; rather, it is that we pass from a time that understands itself in terms of a single universal paradigm or quasi-domesticated logic to one that does not. Now all paradigms are local and pragmatic, temporary erotic engagements, not universal requirements.

The change that was expected and the type of change with which the dialectical tradition could have coped (or would have already coped, as it would have, in effect, already happened) would have been structural. The change that appeared, however, was substantive: information differs profoundly from the matter and motion of the old physical model. Matter can be at only one place at a time, information can be transmitted instantaneously, so it can be everywhere at once. Unlike logical substances, which embody dialectical tensions between structure and intention, information is the entropic base line—the quantity in which affirmation and negation comfortably cohabit. Dialectical resolution turns out to be the origin rather than the end of history, or, more precisely, the *flow* that is our somatic experience is not history (that peculiar ratio between a determinate event and an epochal paradigm) but time itself. To put the matter in the terms that are relevant to the poetics of the common knowledge, we are now faced with the task of recalling the organism from historical time, where it had been placed in a domain of scaleless abstraction, to somatic time, where it can begin once again to deal responsibly with its environment.

One is almost embarrassed to appeal to Walt Whitman, but he knew that organic autonomy, on the one hand, is fully equal to genetic mechanism, on the other, not as the terms of a dialectic—the autonomous human and the social machine never touch one another—but as complementary localities of action. Whitman observes in *Democratic Vistas*:

> The purpose of democracy—supplanting old belief in the necessary absoluteness of establish'd dynastic rulership, temporal, ecclesiastical, and scholastic, as furnishing the only security against chaos, crime, and ignorance—is, through many transmigrations and amid endless ridicules, arguments, and ostensible failures, to illustrate, at all hazards, this doctrine or theory that man, properly train'd in sanest, highest freedom, may and must become a law, and a series of laws, unto himself, surrounding and providing for, not only his own personal control, but all relations to other individuals, and to the State. (Whitman, 1964, 2:234)

Whitman defines two senses of "organism," or, more precisely, against the metaphoric sense of organism, for which the dynastic identity is genetic or descendant from a privileged origin, he poses an autonomous living being. That man—and it is clear that Whitman means *a* man or woman, an individual who comes into relations with other individuals, not the humanistic Man—might become a law unto himself/herself is a thought so radical that it has hardly been taken seriously. As a matter of fact, until recently, we have had no way in which to understand Whitman's claim except as hyperbole. The sovereignty of the dynastic traditions has been repeatedly called into question, but the mechanisms, which now must include the electronic in addition to those that Whitman names, continue to compel conformity without compelling belief. Indeed, it has been discovered that *belief* in the mechanism of control by the controlled population is not necessary and possibly, for the sake of efficacious control, not even desirable.

Although Whitman's thesis directly parallels the thesis of Charles Darwin, his contemporary, Darwin was disastrously mis-understood as providing a justification for not law but lawlessness. Gerald M. Edelman, the Nobel Prize winner and biological theo-rist, notes that before Darwin the western philosophic tradition had largely followed Plato, assuming that nature consists "of classes, or taxa, defined by properties from the top down, fixed and in plenitude. In this view, individual variation was a noisy inconvenience to be ignored, or it was considered a symptom of the fallibility of our earthly life." Species were not organisms to be found and studied but definitions, products of systems of distinc-tions that prove to be utterly abstract. But, as he goes on to note, "Darwin made it clear that individuality was of the essence, that variance in a population was real and not just noise. Indeed, such variance was the basis for change" (Edelman, 1988, 186). Whit-manian democracy and Darwinian evolution are cognates, not be-cause democracy necessarily underwrites greedy competition, which seeks to stamp out individual variation, but because democ-racy guarantees the autonomy of the individual, thus maximizing the possibilities for both change and, as it turns out, *increased* order. Change is not disruptive; it is the very stuff of structure. The degree of regulation in a system can be increased only by increasing the *variety* that the system allows; "only variety can destroy vari-ety."* That is, adaptation to a particular environment requires the proliferation of individuals. Specialization is the gravest ecological danger. Order derives not from the forceful application of univer-sal paradigms that impose monotonous structures across vast fields composed of fundamentally incommensurable entities but

---

*This has come to be known as Ashby's law, and in *An Introduction to Cyberne-tics,* W. Ross Ashby produces an elegant proof of the proposition, which can be followed by anyone with a little patience for simple mathematical formalism (Ashby, 1964 , 202–18).

from the self-ordering of self-creating systems in pliant media that allow creative and adaptive interaction.

The Darwinian individual seeks not equilibrium, as we are taught by the romantic organicists, but dynamism; not closure but process. The aim of life is not death, as Freud, still under the sway of Newtonian physics and romantic poetry, proclaimed, but life. The formal closures of the great romantic odes thematically anticipate death as the ultimate beauty and adequacy. Indeed, their formal perfection is to be found not in their linguistic structure but in the ritual exhaustion of their thematic possibilities. Of course, as the deconstructionist critics have observed, the ploy is never successful: it is only a ritual enactment of death, not a real suicide. The delicious possibility of experiencing ones own conclusion but not ones end is most attractive. Thus, in "Tintern Abbey," Wordsworth, that most ruminative of poets, concludes fifty-plus lines before he quits. Having discovered "In nature and the language of the sense, the anchor of my purest thought," he is satisfied to continue with his own ruminations and self-deconstructions in which the solidity of the anchor melts into platitudes.

In "Hymn to Intellectual Beauty," Shelley is more definitive:

> Thus let thy power, which like the truth
> of nature on my passive youth
> Descended, to my onward life supply
> its calm . . .
>
> (Shelley, 1975, 2:247)

As is Mallarmé at the conclusion of "L'Aprés-midi d'un faune":

> Non, mais l'âme
> De paroles vacante et ce corps alourdi
> Tard succombent au fier silence de midi:
> Sans plus il faut dormir en l'oubli du blasphème
> Sur le sable altéré gisant et comme j'aime
> Ouvrir ma bouche à l'astre efficace des vins!
>
>
> No, the soul
> Empty of words and this now torpid flesh
> To noon's proud silence all too late succumb.
> I must forget that blasphemy in sleep,
> Laid out on thirsty sand, mouth open wide—
> Oh, delight!—to wine's effectual star.
>
> (Mallarmé, 1982, 38–41)

And Wallace Stevens at the conclusion of "The Rock":

> It is the rock where tranquil must adduce
> Its tranquil self, the main of things, the mind,
> The starting point of the human and the end,
> That in which space itself is contained, the gate
> to the enclosure, day, the things illumined
> By day, night and that which night illumines,
> Night and its mid-night-minting fragrances,
> Night's hymn of the rock, as in a vivid sleep.
>   (Stevens, 1982, 528)

The great monuments of the romantic tradition seek the formal perfection of the inorganic. The excitement that is passivity calls again and again to the weary voyager in the world.

Notice, however, that, even when Whitman takes up the purest themes of romanticism in "Out of the Cradle Endlessly Rocking," he speaks not of sleep but of awakening; neither of a Wordsworthian anchor nor of a Stevensian rock but of "the thousand responsive songs at random." Whitman's forms are dynamic, open not of the openness of self-subversion but of the openness of an organism controlling the crucial variables in terms of which it defines itself.

Like mathematics, the poetry of the modern West has been closely allied with science. Both have been expected to maintain an impeccable formal purity, on one hand, and to articulate a living space on the other. No *medium,* however, almost by definition, contains the most intimate interior or the most sublime and terrifying otherness. In their places, we have substituted a monotrop that embraces both the soul and the world—"pure" art and shopping malls. Despite its obvious ruthlessness, we have served its need to be embodied in intellectual disciplines as well as totalitarian gods and totalitarian leaders. Now we approach a perfection in which the replica is potentially self-sustaining. It no longer requires enforcement. The distractions it presents are absorbing and comfortable, hallucinogenic and pervasive.

The question of Rimbaud's obligation is still open. Is there a knowledge to which we are obliged? Or do we, henceforth, work modification after modification on a universal grey medium that is attractive only to the extent that it can divert and distract, tease and drug, until humans are as mechanical as the creations of their imaginations?

The Comedian as the Letter G: *The Network of Limited Objects*

In the first episode of Jackie Gleason's definitive sitcom *The Honeymooners,* Ralph Kramden argues with his wife Alice over the issue of buying their first television set. He loses the argument, but, before he gives in, he makes this eloquent argument:

> RALPH. Look, Alice, it ain't just the money. There's another reason I don't want no television in this house. It changes people. They stop usin' their brains. They just look. When people get television, they stop readin' books.
> ALICE (*sarcastic*). Well, it can't change us. We don't even have a book!
> RALPH (*grasping straw*). All right. All right. I'll get you a book!
> (Crescenti and Columbe, 1985, 5)

The team that created *The Honeymooners* had an unerring understanding of the medium. Beginning as a segment of *The Jackie Gleason Show,* the series, which was first aired in the 1955–56 season, was the first spin-off. Although it was the victim of bad scheduling and only thirty-nine episodes were made, it was almost immediately syndicated and became the most standard of standard reruns.

The relationship between Ralph Kramden and Ed Norton is based on their complementary attitudes toward statistical reality. Ed Norton accepts the world as it is, as a sewer worker must perhaps. It is indicative of Ed's character that he was planning a career as a fashion designer (as unlikely as that seems), but, he says, on the way to a job interview, "I was running up Forty-sixth street I fell into an open manhole. By the time I found my way out I had two weeks' salary coming" (Crescenti and Columbe, 1985, 205). Ralph, on the other hand, is an inept version of Stevens's ephebe. He is forever in "an ennui of the first idea." Stevens writes: "And not to have is the beginning of desire. / To have what is not is its ancient cycle" (Stevens, 1982, 382). Leonard Stearn, one of the show's writers, notes:

> The idea of pie in the sky, the get-rich-quick-scheme that was going to take Ralph out of his imprisonment in the social structure, was the basis of about ninety percent of the Honeymooners scripts. You recognize that when you come from a background like Ralph's, your only hope is a get-rich-quick-scheme, striking gold, a miracle. Ralph doesn't have the education or the connec-

tions to do it any other way. So it's a fantasy. (Crescenti and Columbe, 1985, 146)

The psychology of *The Honeymooners* is closely allied to the game show. In one episode Ralph appears on *The $99,000 Questions,* and the host, Herb Norris, is played by a real game show host, Jay Jackson, who starred in *Twenty Questions* and *Tic Tac Dough.* Game shows figure repeatedly in the character's thought and conversations. For example, Alice and Trixie are discussing Ralph's refusal to buy a television:

ALICE *(flatly).* Ralph doesn't believe in buying things on time.
TRIXIE *(trying to understand).* Well, you can't blame him for that. A lot of people only believe in buying for cash.
ALICE *(sarcastic).* Oh, he doesn't believe in that either. He wants to win 'em on quiz shows. (Crescenti and Columbe, 1985, 2)

In the episode "Funny Money," Ralph finds a suitcase of money (which unknown to him is counterfeit) on his bus. In trying to explain this improbable fact, he theorizes, "I know what it is . . . it's one of those new kind of quiz shows. It's probably called 'Find the Money on the Bus' or something. You know how they're all crazy in television. *(Then definite.)* That's it, Alice, it's a quiz show. I remember one day a guy on the bus asked me how to you get to the public library. That probably was the $64,000 question" (Crescenti and Columbe, 1985, 17). And in at least two different episodes Ralph characterizes people by what their category would be if they appeared on *The $64,000 Question,* which was the big hit of the 1955 season.

The game show is the self-consciousness of the electronic media: the medium represents normative life and distributes prizes with apparent randomness.* The entire population is perceived as possible contestants. There have been more than seven hundred game shows on television since regular commercial broadcasting began (Fabe, 1979, xiii), and, while they have usually been treated as filler and consigned to the least desirable scheduling slots and despised by television's critics, they have been the bedrock of television programming. By comparison to dramatic shows, they are

---

*The talk show is a recent outgrowth of the quiz show. Instead of Amana Radar Ranges and Samsonite luggage, it distributes air time, which is, of course, a valuable commodity. In statistical reality, there are no more reliable confirmations of one's own being than an appearance on the air.

cheap to produce, and a few have been as popular as the most popular television offerings in any genre.

Groucho Marx's *You Bet Your Life* is the definitive instance, and its title is directly to the point. Although its creaky wheel of fortune and wooden duck seem prehistoric relics as far as game-show technology is concerned, it is still regularly rerun nearly forty years after these perfect little mystery plays of statistical reality were first enacted. Although Groucho obviously sought contestants who were "interesting"—a delicatessen operator who sang opera, a lady born in Egypt, a feisty 102-year-old man, a mathematician who developed a system for beating roulette, the boom-boom girl who beat the drum for a tire company on a TV commercial, a lady who taught hula dancing—they are Everyperson. Groucho jokes at the contestants' expense, but finally they are allowed to be attractive, and Groucho's appreciation of their particular qualities, whatever they might be, seems genuine: "Well, you are a charming couple, and now it is time to play *You Bet Your Life*." The game show is statistical fate or at least one of its instruments. The world of the electronic culture is the world of an actuary chart: no common ground is necessary. It only requires that everyone, no matter how diverse, be accommodated by the grid of possibilities.

Perhaps more than anything else, it was the game-show scandals of the 1950s that destroyed the kind of innocent confidence in statistical reality that Ralph Kramden represents. "Three of the best games ever," Maxene Fabe writes, "were also the crookedest. First they became a national obsession, drawing ratings not equaled again until *Roots*. When at last unmasked, they would betray the nation's confidence to a degree not duplicated until Watergate" (Fabe, 1979, 191). The game-show scandal, unlike Watergate, which was merely the revelation of petty criminality in the highest places, however, was a profound lesson. The problem was that the contestants too regularly beat the odds.

If the popularity of *The $64,000 Question* was an expression of innocence, *The Honeymooners* was an expression of a popular sophistication and cynicism. Jackie Gleason and Art Carney were talented comic improvisors, and the entire style, which has been almost totally lost in subsequent television comedy, involves a dissociation of actor and character to which the audience is privy. The characters who are clowns of statistical reality are played by actors for whom accident was the medium. The thirty-nine episodes were minimally rehearsed and taped before a live audience, typically without retakes. On average, it took took about forty minutes to tape a thirty-minute show, and, as Crescenti and Columbe note, "One of the favorite pastimes of Honeymooners fans is 'spot the ad-lib'" (Crescenti and Columbe, 1985, 63). Gleason and Carney were able to incorporate many accidents that would have stopped most actors completely, including on one occasion the accidental collapse of a flimsy set.

In one episode of *The Honeymooners*, "The Safety Award," Ralph is chosen to receive an award as the city's safest bus driver (Crescenti and Columbe, 1985, 245–49). In an interview with a reporter for *Universal* magazine, which is doing a spread on Ralph, Ralph unselfconsciously reveals the relationship between statistics and stereotypes:

INTERVIEWER. Didn't you ever have even one woman who got on the bus calmly, knew where she wanted to go, and had the right change in her hand?

RALPH. Are you kiddin'! I've only been drivin' a bus for sixteen years.

The entire episode explores the capacity of normative reality to absorb even the most unlikely accidents, which is, after all, the the condition for safety. Walking home the day before the awards ceremony, Ralph is explaining that the key to his record is "look where you're going and go where you're looking." Just as he speaks these lines, he runs into a woman who is walking down the street. She says, "Why don't you look where you're going." The sequence (it cannot be called a plot) consists of a series of highly unlikely accidents. Norton's foreboding, when he first hears of the award, keys our expectation of the unexpected. First, Alice and Trixie turn up, ready to go the ceremony, wearing the same dress (Ralph says they look like the Bobbsey twins). They fight, both refusing to change, and each refusing to go if the other wears the same dress. Ralph and Ed accuse them of being silly, and, as the women represent "reason," they soon reach a compromise. Then Ralph and Ed appear, wearing identical jackets. The resolution of this problem is not shown, but, when they reappear, Ed is wearing an old jacket, and it is clear that Ralph is responsible for damaging the new one. Bringing the car to pick up Alice, Ed, and Trixie, Ralph has an accident. Though he claims innocence, he accepts responsibility and tries to settle the matter off the record, not wanting it to be in the newspapers that the city's safest bus driver had an accident on the way to get his award. It turns out that the commissioner, who is supposed to give Ralph the award, is ill, and Judge Lawrence Norton Hurdle, who is famous for $50 fines and fifty minute lectures on safety to traffic offenders, substitutes for him. By this point, the fact that the judge should be the other person involved in Ralph's accident seems almost probable. Moreover the judge, who was wearing the wrong eyeglasses, admits that his wife had convinced him that Ralph had properly signaled his turn and that the accident was judge's fault, so, in fact, Ralph deserves the safety award.

The programs have no point whatsoever: they are statistical investigations. The media do not instruct. They endlessly reenact the fundamental laws of statistics in relation to stereotypes that are as flat as die faces. The reality is completely familiar: every time the dice are thrown, they will give a number between two and twelve; over the long run, they will give more sevens than any other number. The *logos* of statistical reality might be stated thus: *anything that is possible is possible*. It might also be stated thus: nothing is necessary.

There is a grim mode of cultural criticism that might propose that the classic television programs represent the appearance of a new mythology, and, to be sure, if statistical reality had a mythology, this would be it. Myths are records of special events, however, and in the statistical medium nothing is special. In one episode, Ralph and Ed get in an argument over whether to watch a romantic movie or captain video. They start flipping from channel to channel, and the dialogue connects and makes at least grammatical sense:

MAN. Your lips are like rubies . . . and your mouth . . . your mouth is like . . .
Norton snaps dial.
CAPTAIN VIDEO. A giant crater filled with boiling lava! . . .
Ralph looks at Norton, steamed.
CAPTAIN VIDEO. And now, Rangers, let me remind you of the drink that builds healthy bones and strong muscles. The drink that Captain Video drinks
Ralph snaps dial.
WOMAN. A double scotch on the rocks! Certainly darling.

Norton snaps dial.

Captain Video. Yes, Rangers. That's the drink that makes Captain Video fly high. (Crescenti and Columbe, 1985, 246, 9)

And so forth. It is a completely homogeneous linguistic environment. With the advent of remote-controlled television, even the minimal thematics of television programming disappears. According to some studies, the average viewing time on a channel before a change may be no more than two minutes. With twenty-five or more cable channels available, who knows what people are seeing on television, how the images relate to one another, and so forth? It is perhaps too much to hope that the television mass audience will become conscious collagists, but the technology increasingly places programming in its distracted hands.

The normative nature of statistical reality is neither archetypal nor paradigmatic. The archetype is centered in a vision of eternity, and the paradigm is centered in a vision of history. They both involve evaluations of the trivial and the sublime. In statistical reality, time is not shaped by vision. It is the baseline, uncentered, the dimension of entropy along which information and disorder play. What was called the "trivial" and the "sublime" are arrayed in a grid of possibilities in which triviality and sublimity are numbers that are less frequently called than the quotidien, but as pure formality their moments constitute just more instances in an endless and statistically reliable string of instances.

The change from romantic to statistical reality was not a paradigmatic change but a caving in of romanticism upon itself. Reality was not quantifiable in its totality, if indeed its totality is an infinite closed aggregate, but it was quantifiable in all of its parts. The totality that was proposed as the discipline of organic form and the practical world where things were actually weighed and measured were divided by an insuperable barrier. The parts and the whole which seemed so intimately necessary to one another proved incommensurable (such is the discovery of poststructuralism).

As a theater, the communications medium of a thoroughly heterogeneous population is rich in individual examples but poor in dramatic genres. There appear to be only three, each of which represents an attitude toward normative reality:

1. in situation comedy, a normative reality is established, and anything that happens, disturbing the norm, is funny;

2. in soap operas—in their various manifestations, which include the more "serious" cop shows—a normative reality is established, and anything that happens is traumatic;

3. in chase and crash shows, atypical events, though of a completely normative kind, are appreciated for their rarity.

The remainder of television programming—largely sports and "news"—of course, deals with statistical reality directly.

The intense moments of romantic excitement are diffused throughout a cultural medium, as Walter Benjamin foresaw. In the 1980s the aesthetics of film were introduced into politics by way of the electronic media. If the führer brings the emotional energy of his followers to focus on his person, the movie director and television producers (whoever he is? they are?) create a medium so irresistible that the audience becomes absorbed in itself by becoming absorbed in nothing. The secret of Hollywood is that there is no object and no subject. It is the perfect product: Hollywood sells its customers to themselves precisely at the moment when there is nothing there to buy. It is a condition of potentially endless fascination. It doesn't even require a star. A grade-B, journeyman actor will obviously serve well enough. The things for the directors to fear are lack of variety and the possibility that the audience might take it all too seriously. Ronald Reagan proved himself a real professional when he regained consciousness from surgery for colon cancer and started cracking jokes.

The surest way to control great masses of people is not to whip them into an emotional frenzy—they are likely to become unruly—but to trivialize their existence. It is then possible to convince them to act even against their own best interests, which are so ill-defined as not to be recognized. Even the curiosity that might lead them to inquiry and their sense of something in themselves or in their experience which is not perfectly plastic is eroded. They begin to think that they like watching TV. Their lives become serial events that issue only in more events—soap operas and sitcoms, in which the tension never drops below a certain level and nothing definitive ever happens. Death, like life, is rendered meager and begins to seem cozy, attractive. The moments of high romantic excitement—the dénouement of a Wagnerian opera, the speech of the führer, and so forth—are averaged out over the more than three thousand hours of prime-time programming each season.

Television is purely formal, without content, meaningless. Those who criticize its content, both the right-wing, fundamentalist Coalition for Better Television, for example, and concerned liberals, such as Todd Gitlin (Gitlin, 1983) and Henry Sussman (Sussman, 1989), mistake its nature. Its meaning is not significantly thematic or referential. Derrida's critique of the metaphysics of presence is fully realized by tele-vision, *far-off* vision. The television text functions not by collecting attention, however, but by diffusing it. "Television audiences," says Steven Bochco, writer-producer of *Hill Street Blues,* one of the critically respected programs of recent years, "are creatures of comfort. They want something easy and recognizable. May be the biggest problem with *Hill Street* in terms of popular success, is that the show demands to be watched. And most people do not watch television. They are simply in its presence. They use television as a narcotic" (Gitlin, 1983, quoted 306).

Bochco is not using a casual metaphor: the formality of television is an intensification of consciousness without attention to content. Walter Benjamin writes:

> Reception in a state of distraction, which is increasingly noticeably in all fields of art and is symptomatic of profound changes in apperception, finds in the film its true means of exercise. The film with its shock effect meets this mode of reception halfway. The film makes the cult value recede into the background not only by putting the public in the position of the critic, but also by the fact that at the movies this position requires no attention. The public is an examiner, but an absent-minded one. (Benjamin, 1968, 240–41)

Of course, Benjamin was writing before television, but he half-foresees the day when the sets of the Nielsen families would be wired to recording devices that track their absent-minded judgements and, in turn, determine the programming for an entire nation of television viewers. The idea of a television program may be obsolete. The task may be to produce the most attractive possible sequence of individual moments. Judgement of the content of the television environment is largely beside the point. It is not received with the ritual concentration or the awareness of historical density that enlivens the literary texts. The thematics and ideologies that informed the earlier regimes are now the *content* of statistical reality, not their form. What is required is neither a reassertion of the old archetypes and paradigms, which is at any rate impossible, nor an accommodation to the empty forms of statistical reality, which is death, but an new orientation. The project of artificial intelligence—it might be said—is to produce a simulation of a literate human being. The more profound undertaking is to produce *human* intelligence in the context of the electronic media. That is, an intelligence that does not depend upon the representation of its objects, upon repetition, and upon relating discrete units of comparison. Intelligence in a homogeneous electronic environment is not representation, which is automatic, thoughtless, and endlessly proliferating; it is rather more like music. The ideological content of television is the same as the ideological content of Muzak and must be criticized in the the same terms.

Cognitive Science: Topological Continuity

Despite Descartes's dramatic call for a *mathesis universalis,* the general direction of intellectual history has been toward ever greater disciplinary specialization, and, of course, this tendency has been striking since the latter part of the nineteenth century. Again and again specialists bridged the gap between one discipline and another only to discover that they had created a new specialty. To say the least, the master discipline of philosophic knowledge has eluded us. During the past four decades or so, with the appearance of cognitive science, however, a super discipline, embracing logic, linguistics, mathematics, psychology, anthropology, neurophysiology, computer science, and engineering, as well as certain aspects of nearly all intellectual disciplines has begun to appear. If it is not quite the *mathesis universalis,* the new science has integrated thinking from a wide variety of different fields.

Taking the computer and computer programming as central metaphors, cognitive science provides a methodology that accommodates a wide range of phenomena, without requiring the authority of a universal paradigm. It can allow places to incoherent theoretical schemata without the problems of universality intruding. It is, thus, more closely related to engineering than to theoretical science. Theories are tested in terms of *finite* provability. Validity depends upon the construction of a workable program that simulates the phenomenon in question, not upon impeccable logical consistency. Of course, programming requires consistency in any given routine, but routines may be isolated from one another; it is not a logic that depends upon an absolute *logos*. In *The Mind's New Science: A History of the Cognitive Revolution,* Howard Gardner writes, "I define cognitive science as a contemporary, empirically based effort to answer long-standing epistemological questions—particularly those concerned with the nature of knowledge, its components, its sources, its development, and its deployment" (Gardner, 1987, 6). This is not the science of Newton, to which Hegel, Marx, Nietzsche, and Freud reacted, nor is it the science of Einstein, Bohr, and Heisenberg, to which Heidegger reacted. For one of the founding researchers in the field, Herbert Simon, the new science is not a science of nature but "a science of the artificial." Although Simon is a sly and even cunning thinker, I see no sign that even he fully appreciates the break with the tradition of Western thought that this concept entails (Simon, 1980). Until recently, a science of artifice—that is, a science of the inessential or accidental—would have been unthinkable: sciences were sciences by virtue of subject matters that were ruled by the necessities of nature. In classical philosophy, artificial constructions—that is, the products of the arts in the broadest sense—were considered attractive precisely because they were exempt from the necessities of nature; they offered refuges from crass reality, natural needs, and barbarism. Thus, the polis itself was the supreme artifice. For the post-Newtonian theorists, the compromise changed somewhat, but the function of art remained generally the same: it offered refuge from the empty, objective structures of colorless matter and meaningless motion in natural array. Now, however, we have a science that is not obliged to nature. We study both human psychology and the objective world not in relation to Nature but in relation to our own technology.

Only now can the central problems of Cartesianism, which derived from the fact that the subject was purposive and the object was not (i.e., dualism and its attendant complexities), be solved. In the complex philosophic synthesis of cognitivism, purpose is a formal property, not a vital spirit or life-force, and recursion can be accommodated without difficulty, so the vicious circles that Descartes had to treat so gingerly now present no problem. The digital computer was a requisite of the Cartesian dream. Only now is it possible to store and process the vast amounts of relevant information.

Cognitive science begs the question of abstraction, and this is precisely its advantage. As formal objects, the Cartesian infinities are much more manageable than the complexities of the actual world, but they represent the concrete world only in an odd parody. For a machine to simulate human behavior in the world, a great deal of information must be accounted for on a per item basis. An intelligent machine must have general representations of the world, called "frames," "scripts," or "schemata," which provide the necessary information required to act in some situation—entering a room, reading a story, and so forth. For formal games, such as chess, this information turns out to be relatively simple.

The world of the game can be fully and adequately specified. In "real" world situations, however, an adequate description is elusive. The frame for a room and what can be done in it involves a vast amount of information. Moreover, when one item in the frame changes, other items are likely to change as well, and we have no formal rule to decide which. For example, if a frame affords the possibility of picking up something with the left hand, then it is not possible to pick up something else with the left hand—it is not possible to catch a ball or open doors with the left hand. Of course, many things—the color of the rug, the configuration of the furniture, and so on—do not change. Humans seem to deal with this problem with an absolute minimum of attention, but robots must learn about how things change when things change. While the robot might review the implications for every move in the frame in relation to all of the prevailing conditions, it would be involved in a combinatorial explosion that would endlessly defer any action.

The first generation of cognitivists divided on how the knowledge was to be represented. The declarativists, represented by John McCarthy and Patrick Hayes, for example, proposed to model the essential structure of the world in an abstract formal language and to treat domain-specific data as content. Thus, a powerful, formal theory, consisting of only a few tokens and axioms, could ideally serve as the generalized description of human knowledge that could be variously implemented for special tasks. The proceduralists, on the other hand, such as Marvin Minsky or Terry Winograd, thought that form and content were more immediately intertwined and that knowledge was bound to specific sets of procedural rules, such as how to play chess or how to use English.

Their conception of knowledge was at once more dynamic and more dependent upon the context of its use.

Patrick Hayes's "The Second Naive Physics Manifesto" is a little masterpiece of artificial intelligence theory which makes some of the problems of description usefully clear:

> Let us imagine that a N[aive] P[hysics] formalization exists. It consists of a large number of assertions . . . involving a large number of relation, function and constant symbols . . . let us call these formal symbols tokens, and the collection of axioms the theory (in the sense of "formal theory" in logic, not 'scientific theory' in history of science).
>
> The success of a NP theory is measured by the extent to which it provides a vocabulary of tokens which allows a wide range of intuitive concepts to be expressed and to which it then supports conclusions mirroring those which we find correct or reasonable. (Hayes, 1985, 5)

Such a theory defines a range of possible situations that can be inferred from it and allows the expression of particular situations. One advantage to the symbolism of first-order predicate logic, which Hayes uses, is the existence of a formal model theory, which describes the possible worlds implicit in a set of axioms: "We have to be able to imagine what our tokens *might* mean" (Hayes, 1985, 10). Otherwise, we will not know if the formal system provides for all of the contingencies that might arise in all of the possible states of affairs that the axioms define. A given set of axioms defines a collection of models or of possible worlds, which is likely not to include all of the possible things and possible acts of the common world. With an axiom set that can be proved to be complete, however, all of the possibilities of its world can be known, and one can say with confidence that every contingency can be adequately described in the language. Hayes notes, "We should treasure completeness theorems: they are rare and beautiful things. Without them, we have no good justification for our claims that we know how our theories say what we claim they say about the worlds we want them to describe" (Hayes, 1985, 11–12). However, he doubts the likelihood, if not the theoretical possibility, of an adequate and complete theory: "We must build theories which are only partially closed. Some tokens will not yet have their meanings axiomatically specified: they will represent directions for future investigation. We will, indeed, always be in danger of having later theory construction come back and force an alternation in our present work, perhaps scrapping it entirely" (Hayes, 1985, 17).

Hayes's system as described relates only to a ghost of itself, which is constructed by this operation: "Make a ghost model as follows. Let each name denote itself. Every token which should denote an operation on things, interpret it rather as an operation on the names of things, whose result is the expression which would have referred to the thing got by performing the operation on the things named" (Hayes, 1985, 12). In this sense, the model is purely self-referential. The problem of interpreting the model in terms of an actual world, so it can interact with input of sensory or linguistic data, is difficult. "Indeed," as Hayes notes, "no formal operations, no matter how complex, can ever ensure that tokens denote any particular kinds of entity." Any formal linguistic system, whether first-order logic or the English language—considered apart from its common use—requires an interpretation relating the formalism to the world. The tokens in the formal system must be interpreted by a second system. Obviously, this only defers the problem a step, because the metatheory also requires a metatheory, but the deferment often creates a useful leverage (i.e., something like intelligence).

Some of Hayes's analyses of the common language are comparable in elegance and interest to Wittgenstein's. He gives this cogent and economical example of the difficulty of specifying what it is to put something in something: "Liquid objects . . . are defined by their solid containers, and may be in a state of continual overhaul, like a river. The full story is more complex, however, since if the river dries up and refills it is the same river, while if I drink all my coffee, I go get *another* cup" (Hayes, 1985, 29). Naturally, much of this knowledge is readily available: it needs only be made conscious and expressed in language that makes the relationships clear. Hayes describes the research as consisting of an exploration and clarification of intuitions, and he compares the naive physicist's techniques for recognizing accurate descriptions of the physical world to the grammarian's techniques for sorting out acceptable linguistic constructions.

Sometimes, however, mathematical objects such as symbolic tokens have difficulty in catching the intuitive character of the world. Consider, for example, Hayes's discussion of "touching":

Two bodies can touch, and when they do, there is no space between them: this could even be a definition of touching. It is also clear that they do not (usually) merge together or become attached or unified into one object: each retains the integrity of its bounding surface. And it also seems intuitively clear that the surface of a solid object is part of the object: the surface of a ball bearing is a steel surface, for example. And, finally, the local space we inhabit does seem to be a pseudo metric space (in the technical sense), i.e. there is a (fairly) clear notion of distance between two points. Unfortunately, taken together, these intuitions are incompatible with the basic assumptions of topology, and it is hard to imagine a more general theory of spatial relationships. Briefly, the argument goes: a pseudometric space is normal, which is to say that if two closed sets of points are disjoint, then there are disjoint open sets each containing one of them. (Intuitively, two closed sets cannot touch without having some points shared between them.) But if objects contain their surfaces, then they are closed sets: so they can never touch.

To model objects touching in a formal language, therefore, requires a "fix," and Hayes treats touching objects as if "there is an infinitesimally thin layer of space . . . between them." Admittedly, this is unintuitive and does not address the basic problem "which is that our intuitive local space is, indeed, probably not topological." (Hayes, 1985, 21–22) The model, unlike the models of classical physics, proposes to describe not the world but the language of describing the world. This descriptive domain, unlike the descriptive domains of Descartes or Newton or the Wittgenstein of the *Tractatus,* contains no ideal objects; the objects are rather patterns of statistical regularity that can be described within useful, though not absolute, limits. Unlike robots, humans live in the world, not a description of it. The continuities of topology turn out not to be the continuities of the space that we inhabit.

RECURRENCE

Only those disciplines that study culture have been largely untouched by the cognitive science.* The students of literature, art,

---

*Mark Turner's *Reading Minds: The Study of English in the Age of Cognitive Science* (Turner, 1991) is a notable exception, or so the subtitle seems to imply. Turner, however, takes the occasion of cognitive science to reassert, with one small twist, a traditional, even reactionary, conception of English studies.

history, even of film and other popular genres seem for the most part to have missed perhaps the most profound intellectual development of our time. They continue to speak of power, eros, and will in terms that belong the nineteenth century. The critique of philosophic absolutism that has been brilliantly articulated during the past two decades is largely beside the point. The significant mechanisms of control are not now absolute but cybernetic, based on the measurements of temporality, differences, decenterments, even, in a sense, absences. That is, we have learned to free ourselves from the old structural imperatives at precisely the moment they no longer command us. The ongoing hope to demonstrate the inefficacy of both the old mechanism and the old organism is a nostalgia for the nineteenth-century constraints on the freedom of thought that can now be overcome. Michel Foucault's prescription in his preface to *Anti-Oedipus,* "Develop action, thought, and desires by proliferation, juxtaposition, and disjunction, and not by subdivision and pyramidal hierarchization" (Deleuze and Guattari, 1977, xiii), is precisely the formula of the new mechanism. *The textual structure that frustrates nineteenth-century absolutist totalitarianism is precisely the textual structure that feeds the new statistical totalitarianism.*

Organic form as it was understood in the nineteenth century married the human subject to the Newtonian object, and, though it was an uneasy marriage from the beginning, it created a productive allegiance between warring families. To Friedrich Engels, it appeared that this spectacular productivity was mere chance that he could imagine only as chaos. Fortuitous events *in sufficient numbers,* however, are quite orderly, and, of course, even Marx and Engels themselves believed that the chaos was ultimately subject to historical laws. As Freud first discovered, anticipating cybernetics and information theory in this regard, rational mechanisms of self and society can be configured from purely irrational components.

Marx, Nietzsche, and Freud, each in his own way, attempted to invert the ontological priorities, to assert the priority of the concrete and the material over the symbolic and the abstract. They did a service by stripping the dialectic of its disguises, revealing the logic of production or power or eros that lurked behind the idealistic absolute. "Matter," "force," and "desire," as it turned out, however, belonged to the same language as "spirit" and "mind" and behaved according to the same logic. In effect, the great materialist thinkers of the nineteenth century exchanged one mechanism of thought for another without achieving a definitive grasp on reality or the liberation that they believed such grasp would afford. The forms were indifferent to the substances in which they were manifested: matter or mind, mechanical force or electromagnetic field, meat or microchips of silicon were all the same. The material world they proposed to inhabit folded into the theory by which they hoped to describe it, and the theory in turn folded into languages. The language thus created did exhibit the structures of the world, but it no more revealed the *essence* of those structures than did any other complex natural process. If all inquiry is deflected into a symbolic realm and the dialectic has no objective content, as is ultimately the case with post-Hegelian logic, history is without shape, and the dialectical strategies toward the intelligent renovation of history are at once available as apparent modes of action and without significant content apart from their contribution to the gross cultural production.

Is it possible to withdraw assent from the endless mediation of the world by way of a logic and a language that sustain their *own* processes rather than the processes of the individuals who create and use them? Is there a knowledge we can use rather than be used by? For us, who increasingly produce meaning commodities and services rather than material goods, these questions have the force of the Marxist question of revolution. They address the appropriation of our minds by the pervasive medium of labor and leisure; even the unconscious, it appears, is invaded, appropriated, and mechanized by linguistic logic. It still seems, as it did to the young Marx and Engels, that "men and their circumstances appear upside down, as in a *camera obscura*." The lens, however, has been changed: now, all production is *theoretical* production. We have developed the Marxian theoretical eye without producing the stateless and just society that Marx assumed the theoretical eye implied. The randomness of reality, which seemed to Marx and Engels a denial of reason, is statistically regulated. Even "monstrous" aspects of nature that had evaded mathematical formalization, such as the shapes of mountain ranges and the curves of coastlines, even chaos itself, can now be described by statistical means by means made available by fractal geometry, catastrophe theory, and related disciplines.

Must we dwell in the guilt of an empowerment that requires obedience to the *projects* of life, not life itself? Can we express value by means other than lamentation for the lost Absolute? Is language a single entity, a logical machine in which all of the parts mesh, or is it, as Wittgenstein argues, more like a collection of tools that have related uses but a variety of operating principles? Does the science of linguistic have a subject matter? Is the medium itself a definitive essence or is it an accident, a medium that happened to be available to self-cognizing organisms when they sought to express themselves? The questions proliferate: was the linguistic nature of genetic coding prior to the linguistic coding of genetic nature? the linguistic nature of neural coding prior to the linguistic coding of neural nature? To answer any of these questions is, unfortunately, to beg them. We are able to think about the world only *after* we have assured ourselves that it is coherent, that every thing in logical space entails every other thing. It is, however, precisely our thought that allows us such assurance. The obvious solution to these perplexities, to seize the source of language and theory production, to recoup the lost integrity, is to return to the *false* beginning and to repeat the Cartesian strategy. Thus, we ride the wheel of the Nietzschean recurrence.

CONNECTIONISM

The rigor with which time and energy is extracted from the population in the abstract fueling of culture by information processes makes it appear, as Hans Moravec supposes, that a genetic takeover is underway. The Nietzschean return is an expression of the selfish independence of the DNA molecule and its ruthless strategies of self-preservation. The split is not between mind and body, as the great Western nineteenth-century thinkers believed, but between mind codes and genetic codes. Their brave materialisms are so far from the mark, so caught up in a struggle that proves to be irrelevant, that they cannot even be usefully reinterpreted. Moravec asks,

> How should you and I, products of both an organic and a cultural heritage, feel about the coming rift between the two? We owe our existence to organic evolution, but do we owe it any loyalty? Our minds and genes share many common goals during life, but even then there is a tension between time and energy spent ac-

quiring, developing, and spreading ideas, and effort expended towards biological reproduction (as any parent of teenagers will attest). As death nears, the dichotomy widens; too many aspects of mental existence simply cannot be passed on. (Moravec, 1987, 169)

To be sure, downloading a computer file is easier than raising a teenager, and, as Moravec points out, the storage capacity of our largest computers is approaching that of a teenager. Hopefully, like teenagers these computers might also exhibit extraordinary powers of self-organization, so they would achieve something despite the failures of programming (education).

With the increase of computing power, it now becomes possible to think of replicating not the human mind but the human brain, not the symbolic self-representation, which the culture has struggled so valiantly to produce, but the neural circuitry or a symbolic representation of the neural circuitry. Of connectionist theory in cognitive science, David E. Rumelhart writes:

> Our strategy has . . . become one of offering a general and abstract model of the computational architecture of brains, to develop algorithms and procedures well suited to this architecture, to simulate these procedures and architecture on a computer, and to explore them as hypotheses about the nature of the human information-processing system. We say that such models are neurally inspired, and we call computation on such a system brain-style computation. Our goal in short is to replace the computer metaphor with the brain metaphor. (Rumelhart, 1989, 134)

We no sooner create a technology for symbolic self-representation than it is irrelevant. No doubt, this fact explains the cultural malaise of the past two decades, the almost universal loss of confidence in our ability to know and act responsibly, the gridlock of government, the pessimism of the academy, and the oppressiveness of the information media that has been nearly our only entertainment. Thus, the cultural project moves into a new mode of repression. Now we are to express not the generalized code of the culture, which T. S. Eliot and Martin Heidegger, for example, saw as the burden of sense making, but the genetic code that produces the neural circuitry itself. We are to march to the rhythms of DNA as the Nazis marched to Aryan music.

We now must see that the human individual is not the token of either a cultural or a genetic code. We are beyond both culture and nature. Self-production is absolute.

This proposition—self-production is absolute—is not testable, but it does not make an epistemological claim. It proposes an aesthetic and an ethic but not a truth. It is tested by action, not the protocols of abstract verifiability. Self-production is unique, not normative. It is judged in relation to the environment that the acts of self-production themselves uniquely create.

STATISTICS AND THE SINGLE OCCASION

The baroque extravagance, that drive toward new and ever more inclusive formality, is now exhausted. The dialectical impulse to push abstraction back to the concrete and particular images no longer generates the excitement of history. Only a few supreme examples of each formal type that can be collected in museums—collections of every kind, paintings, literary canons, repertoires, barbed wire, Avon bottles, and baseball cards—suffice to exhibit the formal gestures. The world itself is a museum, an example of itself: Nature does not exist. To receive a message about nature is to constitute a machine that tells us about itself. The problem of the One and the Many has not been solved, but the question has been successfully begged.

The poststructuralist appeal to the undecidability of every locale inside infinite logical horizons is true but *trivially* true. Finite zones can be isolated and analyzed, giving statistically useful results. The symbolic machine that the human mind constituted in the place of the world is now a global enterprise with its own inertia. Mind can no longer *think* its own creation; its functions are local administration and maintenance. The weariness of our moment cannot be revivified by turning back to the tradition that articulated itself by asserting the aesthetic as a contradiction of the abstract. Poetry, however, has not ended. Like logic itself, it is now free of its opposite, and it is the nature of this concrete articulation that we are now to understand.

One might speak of the appearance of a new archetype, which is to say not a new form but a new world, but the notion of the archetype belongs to archetypal thought, and it is precisely that scaleless notion that we now leave behind. We have moved from the

Eleatic notion of a *logos* and its heroic incarnation to the notion of language itself as cosmic order. The tradition of the *logos* proposed from the outset, to speak the unspeakable, to incarnate the immaterial, *and* rigorously to obey the law of noncontradiction. These requirements were impossible but nonetheless rigorous and violently productive. Setting out to make humans into gods, however, it made them only into engineers.

In the domain of the common, by contrast, there is no presupposed background, no repetition, and, so, there are no concepts or even objects. We must speak of the "thing"—self, word, object— at a particular time, involved in a particular attendant, local world: it is never complete, it never realizes an essence, and it is never apart from the event of itself and its performance. The language of a poem is not informative. It neither satisfies a thirst for "fact and reason," to recall the words of Keats's famous passage on negative capability, nor, for that matter, to follow out the Keatsian antithesis, dwells in "uncertainties, mysteries, doubts" (Keats, 1965, 1:193). It has no relationship to systems of determination and decidability; its domain is not information but value.

The object—the poem, painting, or any act of living— divorced from its event, is statistical, a conceptual fossil of thought or life. We must learn to speak of mind and knowledge as events (i.e., the *same* event), occurrences of clarity, opening to the insistent and vivid revelation of arising contingencies, of what happens *now* and its factual content. Ludwig Wittgenstein: "Seeing life as a weave, this pattern (pretence, say) is not always complete and varied in a multiplicity of ways. But we, in our conceptual world, keep on seeing the same, recurring with variations. That is how our concepts take it. For concepts are not for use on single occasions" (Wittgenstein, 1970, 99). When it is possible to survey an event in a statistically significant run, science will serve; when we have only one chance, as is always the case for a living being, poetry is required. Unlike the concept, poetry *is* for use on single occasions. When it is worthy of our attentions, when it is not merely another form of distraction to which we are subject, it does not have or give a second chance. It is the measure of an actual, concrete occasion of living.

Statistical reality is not a unified principle or even a ghost of a unified principle. Its world cannot be deconstructed to reveal a metaphysical origin. The only thing all versions of statistical reality have in common is that they require the input of information, which they do not return in the form of identity-sustaining output. We have lost the last vestiges of autopoietic culture. Our public life is out of homeostatic control and wreaks destruction on the world that is our common home. Now to identify with the statistical mechanism of social organization involves autopoietic self-destruction.

There is one experience of otherness that is strangely intimate, that indeed expresses us better than we express ourselves. In the Lacanian formulation, "the unconscious is the discourse of the Other." This Other is the counterpart that underwrites both ego's logic and its ignorance. *There is also, however, an otherness that cannot be appropriated,* an otherness on which we have no hold and that has no hold on us, an otherness that is not a phantom of our own psychic dynamism. Confronted with otherness as utterly alien, the problem of language in all of its originality appears. Discourse, the language that continues by its prearrangements, falls into silence: nothing is *ex*-pressed or *re*-presented. One is required to speak but has no idea what language might be. Language must be brought forth, not from an origin or a lost *logos,* not even from Language itself in all of its given systematicity and multiplicity, but from *nonlanguage.* We confront one another, but there is no text to interpret. The Euro-American, the Amazonian Indian, and the Chinese peasant all suddenly find themselves needing to speak of, and for, their imperiled planet as if they had never spoken before. Henceforth, we are all in the crisis of that moment of the first time anyone spoke anything whatsoever.

NONSTATISTICAL REALITY

Public reality is now utterly degraded. If there is to be a culture of depth and resonance, independent observers must interact, enter into intercourse and establish larger unities—families (true families rather than units of economic dependency), tribes, communities—in which their autonomy is amplified by its participation in the life of the new unity.

For isolated individuals, the entrance into larger unities is both highly desirable and traumatic. Although the prospects of relieving the loneliness of autopoietic unity is a significant attraction, none of the private logics that propose a public space are viable. The entrance into community is, therefore, unmediated. In any attempt of the individuals to translate from the proprioceptive equilibrium of their autonomy to the formal language, the very thing they would communicate by way of the formal structure is lost. The language by which they propose to communicate, it turns out, is common to no one. The very things of which they hope to speak are disallowed. Gregory Bateson comments: "The explanatory world of substance can invoke no differences and no ideas but only forces and impacts. And, per contra, the world of forms [social mechanisms] and communication invokes no things, forces, or impacts, but only differences and ideas" (Bateson, 1972, 271). Language, therefore, is noninformative. It is emotional and connotative. It gains accuracy not by denoting this or that "thing" but by cutting across several potentially codable signals that interfere with one another and by managing to find a single usable value for complex states of affairs in which the whole is implicit in all of its parts. Visual, auditory, and proprioceptive information, which cannot be reduced to a coherent code, are all measurable by a single scale. In a given instance or embodiment, neighboring signs spill over and modify one another, not by entering into logical relationship, but by virtue of proximity alone. In use, novelties may arise and produce new signs in relation to unique events of knowledge but not in relation to the systemic requirements of preexistent signs. The autopoietic image, which is to say the trace of Eros, is not a representation or a simulacrum; it is the thing itself, the manifest thing. Maturana and Varela write:

> Language was never invented by anyone only to take in an outside world. Therefore, it cannot be used as a tool to reveal that world. Rather, it is by languaging that the act of knowing, in the behavioral coordination which is language, brings forth a world. We work out our lives in mutual linguistic coupling, not because language permits us to reveal ourselves but because we are constituted in language in a continuous becoming that we bring forth with others. (Maturana and Varela, 1987, 234–35)

Autopoietic language produces not a represented world but itself, as it takes its measure on the world upon which it physically impinges and leaves a trace. Whether its forms are glyphs, alphabets, or traces in magnetic media, such language cannot be accounted for in terms of rational coherence and completion. Each incident of language must be read out in terms of its particular occasion and use. It is more accurately transformative than informative: temporal and contingent, it brings forth constantly a new world. Rather than transferring information from a sender to a receiver, thereby reducing uncertainty, it establishes precise orientations in a linguistic field which is open to measure. Indeed, autopoietic language *increases* uncertainty. It wipes out all epistemological capital. The requirement of negotiating a new equilibrium is constant. The common knowledge is perishable; it cannot be banked. All disciplined knowledge must be read out in relation to the autopoietic processes of community. Statistical reality is only a tool of nonstatistical reality.

Logography: Non-Statistical Writing

The poststructuralist critique is important, not because it bears significantly on scientific or technological practice, which can obtain statistically useful results by limiting attention in given cases to relevant finite zones, but because absolutist thought still remains a sentimental attraction that at any moment may assert its false but commanding authority. The philosophic tactic is useful in this sense: the classical doctrines that make claims of absolute truth can be overturned by showing that the absolute structures on which the claims are based are minutely incomplete, that gaps or residues remain unstructured and thus create havoc as the minutiae multiply throughout the potentially infinite system. Poststructuralism, denying the idealities of classical structural schemes, while using their objects and rules as generative fictions of infinite textuality, however, privileges the memory of the tradition that it rejects. The traditional procedures are maintained but only at the expense of rendering them impotent and futile. And, of course, it should be mentioned that to careen through infinite textual space is its own thrill and compensation for lost certainty, the hallucinogen that is found in the media's pharmacopeia along side television's sedative.

In the poststructuralist analysis of language, temporality arises as a result of slippage between the generality of language and the particularity of events, as an intrusion of the cussedness of life in the utopia of intellect. To the prose intelligence, which is without measure, time is an enigma. It has been used as a battering ram against metaphysical citadels, which are more sentimental icons than efficacious defenses of a cultural tradition; but as a dimension of living, time generates anxiety. Measure as a linguistic form has been lost to the logocentric West, and the vigorous campaign to expose metaphysics has done nothing to recover the temporal grounds of the common knowledge. The domain of the common, which was once the burden of folk culture, the active and creative functions of life, as opposed to the merely descriptive and regulatory, must now be specifically constituted.

Charles Olson's redaction of Hesiodic cosmology addresses this necessity directly:

> The sea was born of the earth without sweet union of love Hesiod
>   says
> But that then she lay for heaven and she bare the thing which
>   encloses
> every thing, Okeanos the one which all things are and by which
>   nothing
> is anything but itself, measured so
> screwing earth, in whom love lies which unnerves the limbs and
>   by its
> heat floods the mind and all gods and men into further nature.
>   (Olson, 1983, 172)

Okeanos is the principle of autopoiesis. The distance from Maturana's and Varela's "described so" to Olson's "measure so" is the distance from the domain of the mechanistic and statistical to the domain of the creative and active. In the domain of description, nature is fixed as a realm of possible worlds; in the domain of the creative, the heat of love "floods the mind . . . into *further* nature," which is the realization of the contingent facticity of the organism.

Language as description is reasonably understood; the science of linguistics has been devoted to it almost exclusively. As a concrete act of measure that relates us to a manifest concreteness, however, the poem potentially gives us extraordinary access to our own participation in the construction of the world.

It has been said, with impressive authority—Hegel's, Heidegger's, Lacan's, to mention only one intellectual lineage—that the world is without an origin; it would be truer to say that the origin is without a world. Indeed, for anyone there are many worlds, and, while our logic exacts rigorous consistency of a certain kind, it no longer requires consistency of *image or description*. World making is an *ad hoc* activity. In Charles Olson's *Maximus,* for example, there are many world pictures, mapped and remapped in non-Euclidean space:

> The old charts
> are not so wrong
> which added Adam
> to the world's directions
>
> which showed any of us
> the center of a circle
> our fingers
>   and our toes describe.
>   (Olson, 1983, 64)

Of course, the charts were also not so right, precisely because they did not show *any of us* but Adam, that spreading generalization, Man. The leaping Adam is in fact a mechanism, a projectile of his own cognitive medium, frozen spread-eagle on the cardinal directions, because his self mechanism can know nothing without knowing everything; he is dialectical man, self-frustrating man, forever leaping and forever fixed. Olson juxtaposes another Adam whom, at the age of nineteen, he was taught to embody at the Gloucester School of the Little Theatre:

> It was in our minds
> what she put there,
> to get the posture,
> to pass from the neck of,
> to get it down,
> to get the knees bent
> not as he was shown, arms out, legs out, leaping
> another Adam, a nether
> man
>   (Olson, 1983, 65)

who is in fact nearer Java man, pithecantropus of the middle Pleistocene, as the poem goes on to make clear, than the humanistic Adam of Renaissance charts. The human is intensive rather than extensive, *inhibited*—not by social constraint but by virtue of the self-obstructing nature of the human project—rather than *exhibited*, drawn to erect posture by a center that is not logical but physical. As a result, the relationship between the human subject and object, between conscious and unconscious, is no longer dialectical; these traditional oppositions stand in relation not as logical contradictions but as mapped territory to unmapped territory. The nether man or woman—the unconscious—is oriented to time and space, not by extension, as if there were an origin in the past and a completion in the future and a signifying chain stretching (perhaps infinitely) from one to the other, but by *intension*. And it is essential to keep the full meanings of "extension" and "intension" in play: that is, language is not denotative but connotative, and the time and space of human orientation is significantly measured not as a discrete manifold but a continuity—an experience of depth in which the small, even the smallest, entities are infinitely rich and valuable.

How does one entertain that which is beyond *logos* and the reason proper too it, to recall Olson's phrases, without desperate submission to proliferating information that expands until memory is glutted with its own waste products? The answer cannot be simply given: the conditions that make language possible are not themselves linguistic. One might usefully think of Will James's notion of action, of L. E. J. Brouwer's intuition, and of Wittgenstein's meaning as use. These address certain accesses to formal conditions of temporality that bear on language but that are inherently silent. We have largely failed to develop the precise practice of these ideas, however. The theories are all limited in their success to explaining how we casually bumble through. Only the poets have taken seriously the question of inhabiting time, *being time,* as the condition of action.

In his lectures at the Black Mountain Institute for the New Sciences of Man in 1953, Charles Olson *assumes* that his audience "is prepared to entertain the idea that we are already beyond rationalism, beyond humanism, beyond realism . . ." (Olson, 1978, 15). "Beyond," not just *after.* If rationalism provides a doctrine of structural relationships, humanism a doctrine of structural origination and focus, and realism a doctrine of structural representation, the alternatives cannot be themselves doctrinal, because any *doctrine* must be subsumed by reason, egocentrism, and representationalism. The alternatives must issue in a *practice* that can be indicated in a series of injunctions having no authority but their own results—like the directions to a particular place or a recipe. In their structures, directions and recipes involve no formal hierarchy, no grammatical center, and no representation. The recipe is an ordered series, and the necessity that orders the individual steps is not logical or grammatical. It is not a *logical* connection between, for example, putting the eggs in the bowl and beating them. The center is not a logical position in infinite grammatical space but an unspecified subject in relation to finite and actual possibilities. The only imperative *force* of these imperative forms is desire: *if* you want to get to some place, you follow these directions, *if* you want a cake, you follow the recipe. If the cake is no good, it is not the fault of the *grammar* of recipe. Either it is a bad recipe, calling for the wrong ingredients or the wrong procedures, or the wrong recipe for the kind of cake you desire. There might be mistakes in grammar that cause you to do the wrong thing, but that is not the fault of the grammar itself. And, finally, one does not bake a cake by looking at the picture of the finished product. In fact, one might successfully follow a well-written recipe and be surprised at the actual results—not have a picture of the cake in the mind's eye before it is finished. One gains access to statistical reality by way of pictures, absolutely or pragmatically centered and rationally structured, and confirms the access by way of another picture. One gains access to nonstatistical reality—that is, a particular rather than a normative cake—by way of a recipe and confirms the access by eating the cake. Olson quotes Dante on the nature of comedy as a set of directions: "we may say briefly that the end of the whole and the part is to remove those living in this life from the state of misery and lead them to the state of felicity" (Olson, 1967, 83). Such is the injunction of the poetics of the common knowledge.

The poststructuralist critique decenters the universal, but its practitioners are left at the mercy of a symbolic structure in which every trope is entropy. When it is revealed that "Information" is in the beginning and that the Word comes later, to recall Fred Dretske's dictum, we are delivered into a discourse that is always in the crisis of the reversal of the sign by which the same quantity signals a reduction of uncertainty on the one hand and an increase of uncertainty on the other. The poststructuralist critique reveals only the medium: a text is a demonstration of a channel, of the possibility of communication. Language as such, however, is a vast and unreliable channel because the systematic background of any particular language event cannot be established with certainty. No message can be interpreted if it reduces an infinite number of possibilities by only a finite amount. Language is useful as a communication tool because in practical situations the possible meanings are severely limited by disciplines of various kinds, conventions, and explicit purposes. Only in such especially preconditioned environments is statistically reliable information possible.

When language is disciplined only by the part—the finitude of which becomes more apparent as our rapacious exploitation becomes more efficient and ruthless—as opposed to the ideal entities presupposed by rationalism, humanism, and realism, however, it is dimensioned not by probability but by its own measure. It is *extropy*, a turn that is not in a closed channel, indeed a turn that is not conditioned by a channel at all, even that broadest of all channels—Language itself. It is not *in*formation but *e*motion, an event in the world.

The reality of what is presents itself in contradictory characters: as a continuity and as a series of relationships. Wherever experience has been taken on its own terms, without the prior assumption of its coherence—that is, without begging the question—this duality appears. It is not however a *dualism*. There is no reason to believe that it involves two substances. It has rather to do with the fact that any act that can be accomplished can also be described. The difficulty, and it is a practical problem rather than an ultimate philosophic perplexity, is that the requirements of action are different from the requirements of description: action requires an integral being and description requires a self-divided being. These contradictory requirements might be met from the vantage of the infinite—at least this has been an overwhelming speculation—but, of course, we have no recourse to such a vantage. Thus, in the nineteenth century, when psychologists finally began to look at psychic reality as carefully as the physicists had looked at the natural world, these inconsistencies or complementarities began to appear.

Active intellectual life, as opposed to the repetition of closed rationality, depends on two intuitions that are permanently out of phase with one another. In the face of a culture that is relentlessly monolinear, a culture in which moving the lips is a mark of a poor first-grade reader, Olson asserts clearly and fully for the first time since before Plato the necessity of the physical voice to the exercise of intelligence:

> The difficulty of discovery (in the close world which the human is
> because it is ourselves and nothing outside us, like the other) is,

that definition is as much a part of the act as is sensation itself, in this sense, that life is preoccupation with itself, that conjecture about it is as much of it as its coming at us, its going on. In other words, we are ourselves both the instrument of discovery and the instrument of definition.

Which is of course, why language is a prime of the matter and why, if we are to see some of the laws afresh, it is necessary to examine, first, the present condition of the language—and I mean language exactly in its double sense of discrimination (logos) and of shout (tongue). (Olson, 1967, 3)

The West was completely bowled over by the technology of writing (as it was later bowled over by the printing press and now by electronic information management). It was so impressed by writing's mnemonic efficiency that it dismissed the relevance of the voice and the body to the function of intelligence. Derrida and his followers know voice only as discrimination or "difference" and, therefore, as the Achilles' heel of metaphysical thought. As a mystery of metaphysics, the voice does not speak. Its sole function in metaphysical thought is to provide presence. The poststructuralists know nothing of voice as "shout," nothing of poetry. To the poetic intelligence, difference is measure.

The origin of a prose text may be imagined as a *logos* that is at one with itself. The philosophic project has been to suppress the dualism that is inherent in the nature of abstraction as such (i.e., there is always that from which one abstracts and the abstraction) and to claim the unity of the abstraction. It is in the nature of abstraction to see everything as One, but the procedure that allows the vision of the One calls us to consider two. This is the basis of the dialectic, the internal secret of Platonic idealism and all subsequent idealisms; this is the prose of the world. The poem, however, is always cast in the dissonance between the act and the necessary stasis of the describing mark. The poetic origin is not a unity but a contradiction.

We can speak of this difference in terms of two linguistic modalities, language in the mode of explanation and language in the mode of creation—statistical and nonstatistical probability—and the modes of intuition on which they depend. These two notions are most relevantly defined by Alfred North Whitehead in *Process and Reality*. Of one he writes: "Undoubtedly, the intuitions of Greek, Hebrew, and Christian thought have alike embodied the notions of a static God condescending to the world, and of a world either thoroughly fluent, or accidentally static, but finally fluent— 'heaven and earth shall pass away' " (Whitehead, 1978, 347). This is, one might say, the Parmenidean intuition. It renders primary discourse impossible. Logical thought can say no more than this: If there is anything, it is One, unchanging, unmeasurable. The dialectic that follows this insight, which is to say the intellectual history of the West, is problematic, but it does allow the possibility of description and provisional explanation. Being always double (*dia*/lectic), every move toward the One is also a move toward the two and vice-versa. In the meantime, however, the explanation that the dialectic provides is useful. In other words, the Western tradition *began* in effect with the poststructuralist critique, or, one might say, Parmenides demonstrated that structuralism is its own critique: if there is a truth it cannot be spoken. The tradition is logocentric only in a superficial sense. The thought of the logos has shaped certain conventions, of the book, for example, but that has as much to do with convenient packaging as philosophic necessity. Now, when information can be stored and retrieved much more efficiently by electronic techniques, even the sentimental regard for the *logos* is no longer necessary.

Whitehead also speaks of "civilized intuition": "There is not the mere problem of fluency *and* permanence. There is the double problem: actuality with permanence, requiring fluency as its completion; and actuality with fluency, requiring permanence as its completion" (Whitehead, 1978, 347). It is the intuition that is essential to all orienting action but that the mode of description tends to betray; description does not easily resist the temptation to explain creation, thereby closing itself and withdrawing from the physical world.

In the philosophic project, the intuition that has one component that can be spoken or captured in paint, and another—an entrance to time—that can only be indicated or marked by rhythm, are transformed into two propositions that contradict one another. Two senses of the world that are simply unrelated are imagined as terms of a logic. That is, stasis is attributed to God and fluency to earth: the duality of image and time, vision and audition, is confused with the contradiction of one propositions by another, and the dialectic begins. In the logocentric picture, desire seeks a lost origin, the very certainty that its own activity disrupts.

The desire to possess, to speak the silence, or the desire to represent oneself and to satisfy oneself in the representation is the motive of a history all too familiar—a history in which order is destructive and Eros is deathly. The irreducible duality is denied in the name of the unity of the intuition which is its chief mystery. The subsequent attempt to name the mystery requires a linguistic materialism that has been expressed in the doctrine of the *logos*. Love is infected. The best we can imagine, inside the terms that it provides, is a reconciliation or an accommodation of mind to body, subject to object, life to death. The great sublation that romanticism envisioned rises to its own sleepy fanfare in the homogenized, grey life-death of soap-opera America.

In 1956, Olson began to study Whitehead's *Process and Reality*, discovering that its suggestion, if not its letter, was consistent with his thinking as it had been developing for the previous decade. Whitehead made it possible to restate the central argument of "Projective Verse" and "Human Universe" in vastly enlarged terms. Later, Olson would write of "Whitehead, who cleared out the gunk / by getting the universe in (as against man alone" (Olson, 1983, 249). It is characteristic of Olson to use terms like *gunk* in senses that are so precise that their full definition becomes technical. It is by no means the throwaway that it may first appear. "Gunk" (gum + junk, perhaps) is precisely those aspects of language that allowed abstract thought to compensate for the loss of rhythm by creating a universe of discourse. It is the sludge that inhibits the fluency of language and allows the inflation of the grammatical at the expense of the rhythmic. Olson's problem may be stated in these terms: How is sophisticated thought possible without the infection of abstraction? He had, of course, the evidence of the imagists' work, but for all of their beauty and value as demonstrations, Ezra Pound's "In the Station of the Metro," H. D.'s "Evening," and William Carlos Williams' "The Red Wheel Barrow" do not establish an adequate language in which to conduct the cultural business, and therefore they remain merely "aesthetic"—that is, dependent upon *another* language. Pound's *Cantos* are more to the point in terms of their encyclopedic breadth, but they remain attached to an authority that requires vicious enforcement.

To insist upon individuality as the ground of language is only to insist upon another level of abstraction, until one descends to an atomic level. Of course, the tradition of classical physics hopes precisely to seek the language in which the location and vector of every atom is known. Such can be the only grounds for an accurate rationalistic language, and the failure of rationalistic metaphysics is related specifically to that failure. Every atom, whether logical or physical, sooner or later reveals its constituents until, finally, the unit becomes so small that observation disturbs the object, and the unit of measure becomes some theoretical event horizon, not a concrete unit. The paradox of explanation, which depends upon statistics, is that the supposed simplest units of matter (whether the units are radium atoms or voters) cannot be described apart from their relevant society. Neither the quantum physicist nor the public-opinion pollster deals with individuals, only with the relationship between posited individuals and the generalization of all of their possibilities. Whitehead, however, also speaks of non-statistical probability.

> There can thus be an intuition of an intrinsic suitability of some definite outcome from a presupposed situation. There will be nothing statistical in this suitability. It depends upon the fundamental graduation of appetition which lives at the base of things, and which solves all indeterminations of transition.
>
> In this way, there can be an intuition of probability respecting the origination of some novelty. It is evident that the statistical theory entirely fails to provide any basis for such judgement. (Whitehead, 1978, 207)

These events of creative change do not arise from a determining society of predisposed individuals. In the statistical world, nothing new is possible. All is already accounted for. Any "real" therefore—Baudrillard is true to the statistical world—is a simulacrum. The postmodern assumption is that all of the possibilities—all of the infinite possibilities—are accounted for. The Platonic heaven or divine mind is burdened with vast tabulations instead of essential forms. The knowledge of nonstatistical probability, Whitehead says, represents the "secularization of the concept of God's function in the world." That is, the creation of the world is a secular, finite activity.

In Olson's understanding (I will avoid the complexity of interpreting both Whitehead and Olson in this difficult matter), statistical knowledge is merely philosophic, and though it may allow accurate prediction about certain types of phenomena, its truth does not satisfy the creative eros. Nonstatistical action arises from entities that are not preconditioned by their membership in a society. Unlike conventional atoms that which arise in our efforts to use a general system of signs for particular objects, whether irreducible units of radium as studied by physicists or units of an electorate as studied by public-opinion experts, the human "atom" is not social—which is to say, not an atom. Of course, humans are for the most part socialized; they are persuaded to abandon the cosmos-making function in favor of a statistical environment, where they abide by generalized expectations; they make the tragic sacrifice of the Person to genetics.

Olson recognizes two integrities that are independent and in generative cooperation: the human body, with its manifold abilities to act, and the earth. From the perspective of humankind as physical, these two are unique; they qualify as unities as nothing else. It is by way of them that access to plurality as the possibility of abstraction is made available, or to put it more clearly, it is only by way of a relationship between these integrities that plurality comes into existence. It is the basis of Olson's practice however to speak of the plurality not as idea but as landscape or view. That is, this multiplicity is reduced to a conventional unity, but not the unity of logos. The landscape, furthermore, comprehends language as physical, as marks on the page and vibrations in the air, as an aspect of itself. It is trees, rocks, hills, and language. Landscape and language are events that arise in the relationship of two integrities, which are known in primordial and silent intuition. This is the most common knowledge, and the knowledge from which the larger part our learning and our social ritual distract us.

The human body and the earth are the fundamental event/atoms of poetic thought, a paradox that arises not from some failure of reason but from immediate intuition. The one is intuition of human integrity as a limited temporality; it is constituted of the anxiety and ecstasy of a separate biological organism. The other is the intuition of human integrity as the condition of earth itself, a knowledge of that which abides. The one is manifest as rhythm, the other as syntax; the one as the product of the body, the other as image of earth. Although they may be intuited temporarily as a unity, it is only at the moments of high intensity when one speaks and acts from a confident knowledge of the common. The linguistic medium is constituted of marks by which radically autonomous beings orient themselves with others of their kind in an otherwise featureless world. It does not pass information from a sender to a receiver but creates a world. The common knowledge is not exemplary; it does not impose normative structures on action. It speaks of that which is meaningful in itself. Wittgenstein said of genre paintings, "I should like to say 'What the picture tells me is itself.' That is, its telling me something consists in its own structure, in its own lines and colours. (What would it mean to say 'What this musical theme tells me is itself'?)" (Wittgenstein, 1953, 142). In the mode of the common knowledge, even "genre paintings"—proposed typologies—can only be understood as utterly specific. Knowledge of both the thing in itself and its type must, as it were, come together. We cannot determine if some unknown entity belongs to a given type unless we somehow *already* know. This fundamental problem of circularity haunts our knowledge. The circle is broken by the fact that, in the domain of the common knowledge, some signs refer only to themselves; their degree of generality is determined by the specific occasion of their use.

> We speak of understanding a sentence in the sense in which it can be replaced by another which says the same; but also in the sense in which it cannot be replaced by any other. (Any more than one musical theme can be replaced by another).
>
> In one case the thought in the sentence is something common to different sentences; in the other, something that is expressed only by these words in these positions. (Understanding a poem.) (Wittgenstein, 1970, 28)

These two senses of understanding belong to different epistemic domains. The one informs the science of linguistics: language is seen as a logic of signs, independent of any particular content. The other arises from a radical empiricism: language is experienced as sounds and marks dense with the logical catastrophe of uniqueness and inertness. Such signs present themselves as things in their own rights *and* as proxies for other things, divided and paradoxical from their first appearance. Thus, constituted not of preselected atoms but of specific, complex events of their use, they are uncategorizable and irreducibly alogical. They may be valued as knowledge not because they can be interpreted by rule but because of their usefulness. They are the concrete facts of the world one inhabits.

Olson speaks of "logography"—"Word writing. Instead of Idea writing . . .", a writing emptied of abstraction. The neologism is parallel to "phonography"—sound writing—or "photography"—light writing. Interestingly, the term comes from I. J. Gelb's *A Study of Writing* (Gelb, 1963), which is also the source of Jacques Derrida's term *grammatology*. The distance from Derrida's science of marks to Olson's writing with words, however, is considerable. Grammatology is a science that cannot establish its own principles—a sentimentality that cannot pronounce its own name with a straight face, a kind of etymological centaur. To impose *logos* on *grammé* as definitive terms of a study is to presuppose self-frustration on the part of the student. By contrast, logography is a practice, a technology. It is subject to abuse, like any other technology, of course, but its justifications are pragmatic, not theoretical. Just as the phonograph will record any sound which occurs in its operating presence, whether it obeys a preestablished musical logic or not, the logograph writes words. The page registers word events, not the negotiations between the desire to speak and the lawful modes of saying.

The knowledge that is discovered in Olson's work is not philosophy or science, not mythology, theology, sociology, or psychology; it does not argue with the traditional disciplines. It does, however, expose the arrogance of their claims and the despair of their results, at least when a bewildered human turns to them for practical guidance. Although this knowledge must confront the intimidation of the entire intellectual establishment, which is immense and rightly to be feared, it promises the possibility of action that actually satisfies something of the intellectual hunger, the gnawing need not for certainty about the ultimate but about what is under ones nose: "The Earth . . .," Olson writes, "is conceivably a knowable, a seizable, a single, and your thing. And yours as a single thing and person yourself, not something that's distributed simply because we are so many and the population is growing, or that the exploitation of the earth itself is increasing" (Olson, 1969, 5). Given the vantage of such a possible knowledge, he continues:

> What makes most acts—of living and of writing—
> unsatisfactory, is that the person and/or writer satisfy themselves
> that they can only make a form (what they say or do, or a story, a
> poem, whatever) by selecting from the full content some face of
> it, or plane, some part . . . It comes out a demonstration, a

separating out, an act of classification, and so, a stopping, and all that I know is, it is not there, it has turned false. (Olson, 1967, 5)

The feeling that our knowledge has somehow turned false in our deeds is not uncommon. All too often, acting on the best knowledge we have, we recognize after the fact that we had hoped for something otherwise. Derrida writes:

> There is not a single signified that escapes, even if recaptured, the play of signifying references that constitute language. The advent of writing is the advent of this play; today such a play is coming into its own, effacing the limit starting from which one had thought to regulate the circulation of signs, drawing along with it all the reassuring signifieds, reducing all the strongholds, all the out-of-bound shelters that watched over the field of language. This, strictly speaking, amounts to destroying the concept of "sign" and its entire logic. (Derrida, 1976, 7)

And, though he develops a rather different argument, Michel Foucault concludes in a similar tone:

> From within language experienced and traversed as language, in the play of its possibilities extended to their furthest point, what emerges is that man has "come to an end", and that by reaching the summit of possible speech, he arrives not at the very heart of himself but at the brink of that which limits him; in that region where death prowls, where thought is extinguished, where the promise of origin interminably recedes. (Foucault, 1970, 383)

In fact, Foucault ends *The Order of Things* with a very brief meditation on the distinction that stands at the *beginning* of Olson's work. He writes, "in Artaud's work, language, having been rejected as discourse and re-apprehended in the plastic violence of the shock, is referred back to the cry, to the tortured body, to the materiality of thought, to the flesh" (Foucault, 1970, 383). These words, if we could erase "tortured," might apply likewise to Olson's work. Olson entered this space and, for more than twenty years, practiced efficacious language without suffering the physical torture and intellectual debilitation of schizophrenia. It appears, however, that the French prophets of the end of Western metaphysics or the end of Man, as Foucault proposes it, cannot imagine an alternative except in terms of madness or worse. Derrida, noting that voice is the founding metaphor or metaphysics, fails to realize that it is anything else. He acquiesces in despair: "what makes the history of the *phone* fully enigmatic is the fact that it is inseparable form the history of idealization, that is, from the 'history of mind,' or history as such" (Derrida, 1978a, 75). And in his essay on Artaud, he goes very nearly into paroxysms of gloom: "To think the closure of representation is thus to think the cruel powers of death and play which permit presence to be born of itself, and pleasurably to consume itself through the representation in which it eludes itself in its deferral" (Derrida, 1978b, 250). This is the last possible investment in the tragic sense of life that, more than metaphysics or logocentrism, defines the dominant tone of culture in the West. Oedipus, Socrates, and Jesus are tragic figures in whom we have suffered for a grandiose conception of the human soul, a conception that has perhaps cut us off from other areas of enlargement, which do not promise eternal life but might, at least, make life on earth worth living. Suffering is required to keep the dialectic alive. At this late and utterly abstract stage, it has no significant metaphysical content; its only content is hope that the soul might find a language so devoid of content that it might live. As long as we suffer, we may look forward to the emergence of the Absolute. Hegel says the dialectic can be "regarded as the pathway of doubt, or precisely as the way of despair" and, in the concluding paragraph of the *Phenomenology*, he speaks of the "Calvary of the Absolute Spirit." The culture still clings rigorously to the way of the cross, always focusing on the greatest despair as the term of the greatest hope. We have not yet begun to assess the depth and import of Olson's critique of the dialectic:

> dialectical does mean one to one, and an immediate discharge of mental engagement in which the will and the mind are like aggressive motor actions, and are complimentary in that they do compliment the other person engaged, as though there was a one-to-one possible, as though the conversation was between us and a meeting of minds was possible. It is socializing, and relational.
>
> One wants therefore to enter this ring on a different footing: it isn't true, and has left the universe out, substituting for it a prune or wrinkled grape, the social . . . The whole slip to discourse, deliberately mounted to supply an education, and State as the result (cause-and-effect) of an artificial "person' and an equally shrunken *socius* company ended up in Hegel, and in Marx-plus, the modern liberal companionship. Not only does materialism (instead of technology) become the appetite of the contemporary person, satisfied by the goods alone and a credit

marked as well as the debted Nation, but equally the new man-grape gazes upon space as though he can return via it to the paradise, of trees, on which all the fruits do grow, a conversation with some superior its from *another* planet. (Olson, 1974, 54)

Under the regime of the dialectic, our fate has been to live on this planet, while thinking about another one, which is a parody of our own, lacking its rich profusion of individuals. Like cartoon figures, we are pilots of rationalist space ships, setting ourselves down on an alien planet, and finding that our theories are generally accurate but not really sufficient to deal with particular, unexpected dangers and advantages of the place.

As early as 1946, Olson began an investigation into abstraction or, to use current cant, logocentrism. The terms, space, fact, and stance, which are defined in *Call Me Ishmael,* name the intuitions of a concrete world in which voice is not a metaphor of spirit but the *physical* qualification of intelligence; and, in 1949, in "Projective Verse," Olson announced the beginning of his lifelong practice of "open form." Open form, as Olson uses the term, is not merely a leaky conceptuality that drips through a porous structure riddled with temporality. In the Riemannian world, as Olson understands it, any act creates a discrimination and a space, a unity and a continuum, a nature and an orientation, meaning and information. Although these domains each exhibit their own logic, the relationship among them is not logical; their spaces do not intersect. In one domain—Williams was right—there are "no ideas but in things." In the other—and here Pound was nearer the mark—there are acts, which are something like ideas, at least more like ideas than things, but there are no actors—"the radiant world where one thought cuts through another with clean edge, a world of moving energies" (Pound, 1965, 154). Williams could only imagine a stasis or a static image of motion in "The Yachts," for example. And in *Paterson,* the city is a male abstraction and Garrett Mountain a female abstraction, art and nature, hopelessly sundered; it is a sentimentality. Pound, like so many of his modernist contemporaries, fell for totalitarianism. In the poem that moved him decisively beyond Pound's *Cantos* and Williams' *Paterson,* Olson writes:

> The odish man sd: "Poesy
> steals away men's judgment

by her muthoi" (taking this crack
at Homer's sweet-versing)
"and a blind fear
is most men's portions." Plato
allowed this divisive
thought to stand, agreeing
that muthos
is false. Logos
isn't—was facts. Thus
Thucydides
I would be an historian as Herodotus was, looking
for oneself for the evidence of
what is said.

(Olson, 1983, 104)

Olson conceives of Herodotean history as an active engagement with evidence that one produces for oneself, to trace what is merely told back to what can be seen, not so much out of skepticism or need of proof as for need of meaning. Language apart from an active life in which it functions is empty. Evidence arises in the completely alogical factuality of living. The measure specifies so much time and, by the conventions that he began to develop in "Projective Verse," so much space. Literate poetry is speech writing or written speech: "The advantage to literacy is that words can be on the page." On the one hand, it is potentially as free from *logos* as the preliterate epics; on the other hand, it has all of the resources of five hundred years of printing and three millennia of writing. "One wants phenomenology in place, in order that event may rearise. There are only two facts about mythology which count: that they are made up of tales and personages, in place. Words then are naming and logography is writing as though each word is physical and that objects are originally motivating. This is the doctrine of earth" (Olson, 1974, 50–51).

Construction

Olson read Norbert Wiener's *Cybernetics* in prepublication proofs and quoted Wiener's definition of "message" in "The Kingfishers":

We can be precise. The factors are
in the animal and/or the machine the factors are
communication and/or control, both involve

the message. And what is the message? The message is
a discrete or continuous sequence of measurable events distrib-
uted in time.

(Olson, 1987, 86–92)

The last sentence is quoted directly from Wiener's text. As we
have seen, it is a fundamental definition of information theory. The
message is a measure not of identity but of difference. It should be
added to the varieties of Derrida's "differance":

Differance is neither a word nor a concept. In it, however, we
shall see the juncture—rather than the summation—of what has
been most decisively inscribed in the thought of what is conve-
niently called our "epoch": the differance of forces in Nietzsche,
Saussure's principle of semiological difference, differing as the
possibility of [neurone] facilitation, impression and delayed effect
in Freud, difference as the irreducibility of the trace of the other in
Levinas, and the ontic-ontological difference in Heidegger. (Der-
rida, 1978a, 130)

By this addition, this accomplishment that is neither word nor
concept, that is so destructive to classic rationalism, that so com-
pletely undoes the entire classical project and its careful balancing
of speech and writing, now emerges as the central factor in a new
rationalism, a new representationalism, and in new mechanisms of
control more efficacious than any previously imagined. Whether it
also presents a new humanism depends upon the definition of
human. The distinction between the purposive domain of the hu-
man and the purposeless domain of nature breaks down. Teleon-
omy belongs not to the originary stuff but to the meanings that are
found there in those representations that are known as humans, on
the one hand, and machines, on the other. "A discrete or continu-
ous sequence of measurable events distributed in time" is the new
logos—the *logos* that is not an origin itself but derives from infor-
mation, fully temporalized, self-absent, beyond both absolutism
and dialectics, the *logos* that is embodied not in the scientist,
which is to say, the teleologist of the closed world, but in the
engineer, not in Jesus but in Hephaestus. Hephaestus was an early
worker in artificial intelligence and robotics. It is said by Homer
that he manufactured some mechanical women of gold, who could
talk and faithfully perform the most difficult tasks in his work-
shop, and a fleet of three-legged robots, intelligent tables or carts,

which could run by themselves on errands, and so forth. Thus, the focus has shifted from the Olympian deities to the subterranean deities, from the deities of identity to the deities of difference, from the original creation to the creation of simulacra, provisional creatures, creatures whose obsolescence is already planned. Production is no longer conscious but the work of local societies—to use Whitehead's terms—that can be manipulated in relation to statistical probability. Social production is the work of the unconscious or, to use cybernetic jargon, a black box, in which the inputs and outputs are known but the inner workings are invisible and inscrutable. The innermost workings of the computer chip, for example, can never be known: the movement of the electrons are random and unpredictable. Only because of their vast numbers and the resultant redundancy are we assured of the prevalence of the requisite forms. Nearly a century of psychoanalysis has had one notable result: the unconscious has been mechanized, while, it must be noted, remaining more or less unconscious.

Olson's ouevre is not thematic but investigatory. In the early work, he proposes a revision of the heroic stance of the romantic poets. The poet is understood as an input-output machine, as in the organicist tradition, but an input-output machine on cybernetic principles. In "Projective Verse," he writes, "A poem is energy transferred from where the poet got it (he will have some several causations), by way of the poem itself to, all the way over to, the reader" (Olson, 1967, 52). Thus, the energy/information of the world—the content—is retained as it is shaped by its passage through the particular topological configuration of the poet. In "Projective Verse" and other early theoretical writings, he conceives of the interchange on the phenomenological level:

> Now . . . the *process* of the thing, how the principle can be made so to shape the energies that the form is accomplished. And I think it can be boiled down to one statement . . .: ONE PERCEPTION MUST IMMEDIATELY AND DIRECTLY LEAD TO A FURTHER PERCEPTION. It means exactly what it says, is a matter of, at *all* points (even, I should say, of our management of daily reality as the daily work) get on with it, keep it moving, keep in, speed, the nerves, their speed, the perceptions, theirs, the acts, the split second acts, the whole business, keep it moving as fast as you can, citizen. (Olson, 1967, 52–53)

The message is neither origin nor end, an endless mediation. In "The Kingfishers," he goes on to extend the definition of "message." The message

> is the birth of air, is
> the birth of water, is
> a state between
> the origin and
> the end, between
> birth and the beginning of
> another fetid nest
> is change, presents
> no more than itself
> And the too strong grasping of it,
> when it is pressed together and condensed,
> loses it
> This very thing you are.
>   (Olson, 1987, 90)

In this passage Olson continues to paraphrase Wiener's introduction to *Cybernetics* but now very loosely. The duality that we have repeatedly noted between continuity and the discrete series also appears in the self-reflexive mechanism: "the too strong grasping of it . . . loses it." Consider, for example, a robotic or human hand reaching for an object: it reads a series of messages in time, predicts on the basis of these messages where its trajectory is tending, and, on the basis of the readings, corrects itself. This is, of course, the basic feedback loop of cybernetics—the output of the mechanism, controlling its own input in order to produce purposive acts. The problem is that, unless the mechanism is sensitive, it will fail to react with the required speed, to make necessary small corrections. If it is too sensitive, on the other hand, the need for a large correction will throw it into wild oscillation, over-correcting in one direction and then over-correcting in the other. Wiener writes:

> we found that the ideal prediction mechanism which we had at first contemplated were beset by two types of error, of a roughly antagonistic nature. While the prediction apparatus which we at first designed could be made to anticipate an extremely smooth curve to any desired degree of approximation, this refinement of behavior was always attained at the cost of increasing sensitivity.

> The better the apparatus was for smooth waves, the more it
> would be set into oscillation by small departures from smooth-
> ness, and the longer it would be before such oscillations would
> die out. (Wiener, 1965, 9)

The effective mechanism must allow for considerable play. Olson's
work, especially *The Maximus Poems,* is a probe into the nature of
this topological limit.

If humans are merely input-output devices, however, they can-
not help but be statistically overwhelmed by the enormity of the
collective human product. Even the phenomenological largeness of
Maximus—that is, the human transformer of energy-information
at his or her most efficacious—cannot withstand the onslaught
that is generated by fully mechanized social production. Thus at
the end of the first book of *The Maximus Poems,* Maximus admits,

> I am interfused
> with the rubbish
> of creation . . .

The phenomenological phase of the poem comes to an end.
Maximus withdraws from the input-output circuit to the interior.

>   step off
> onto the nation The sea
> will rush over The ice
> will drag boulders Commerce
> was changed the fathometer
> was invented here the present
> is worse give nothing now your credence
> start all over.
>   (Olson, 1983, 155)

Maximus's new start in *Maximus IV, V, VI* stakes itself to the
archetypal and the cosmic, and in terms of literal geography, its
predominate locale is Dogtown, the now-deserted village that grew
up in Colonial times in the interior of Cape Anne, in order to avoid
the marauding pirates who attacked coastal settlements. Olson
begins in "Maximus, from Dogtown—I," paraphrasing the *The-
ogony* of Hesiod. The literal historical, geographical address of the
first volume is buttressed by the cosmological archetypes. The
individual, rather than merely shaping the energies that appear,
produces an interior world in which

                              the soul is led from drunkenness
to dryness, the sleeper lights up from the dead,
the man awake lights up from the sleeping.

                                        (Olson, 1983, 172)

It is not mere subjectivity but an interiority that awakens into the public domain. As Charles Stein shows in *The Secret of the Black Chrysanthemum*—the only full-length study of Olson that gets beyond introductory issues—Olson's cosmology does not belong to the statistical and social world; its language has no relation to that domain. "I find the contemporary substitution of society for cosmos," Olson writes, "captive and deathly" (Olson, 1967, 97). The crisis of the cosmological address that is at once publicly available and not subsumed by the social mechanism comes in "Maximus, from Dogtown—IV":

The problem here is a non-statistical
proof: Earth 'came into being'
extraordinarily early, #2
in fact directly following on
appetite. Or
as it reads in Norse
hunger, as though in the mouth
(which is an occurrence, is 'there',
stlocus).

                    (Olson, 1983, 333–42)

What is required, in the words of Whitehead, from whom Olson's use of the term "non-statistical" derives, is "an intuition of an intrinsic suitability of some definite outcome." There are two modes of attention and two corresponding domains—an ontological domain, which is forever confused with its own description of itself, half-revealing and half-hiding itself in deferred possibilities, and a common domain, in which even the minimal requirements of grammar, discrete distinctions, do not prevail (all is continuous). In the former, to recall Quine's phrase, to be is to be the value of a variable. It is the being proposed by the doctrine of social order. "According to this doctrine," Whitehead writes in a passage that Olson underlined in his copy of *Process and Reality,* "all social orders [whether the society consists of atoms or humans] depends on the statistical dominance in the environment of occasions belonging to the requisite societies. The laws of nature are statistical laws derived from this fact" (Whitehead, 1978, 207). By contrast, the intuition of an intrinsic suitability of some definite outcome is utterly specific, without relation to the social questions concerning predictable behavior. Rather to be is to be the value of the thing itself, a manifestation of what Olson calls Okeanos: "Okeanos the one which all things are and by which nothing / is anything but itself, measured so" (Olson, 1983, 172–81). Okeanos is the continuous, "heaven's stream." When this space is partitioned, divided, atomized, the distance between every two points opens into infinite regresses, which must be disciplined by the statistical techniques of the mathematical or logical variable. When it is measured by itself, which is to say by its own activity—the event of itself— the continuity is retained *and* a world of shapes, both the measurer and the measured, is made manifest.

The nature of this world, which is as fully furnished and as densely resonant as the activity establishes, however, is local. The cosmic space reaches only so far as the actual measure applies. Just as there are no infinite regressions, there are no infinite expansions. In "at the boundary of the mighty world" for example, Maximus specifically locates Hell's mouth, where the manifestation of heaven's stream opens to Tartaros:

> It is Hell's mouth
> where Dogtown ends
> (on the lower
> of the two roads into
> the woods.
> I am the beginning
> on this side
> nearest the town
> and it—this paved hole in the earth
> is the end (boundary
> Disappear.
>   (Olson, 1983, 332)

This place is clearly enough identified that it is possible to go to Cape Anne and confidently locate it (I have done so). It is an unexceptional place, which for anyone who is not an active participant in the construction is without notable qualities. For the readers of *Maximus,* Hell's mouth, if their cosmos includes one, is elsewhere. Placement is not the result of a statistically reliable agreement, which must be negotiated, ruled by disciplinary conventions, or determined by force. Statistical knowledge is "gener-

al" by virtue of being common to no one: it is textual knowledge—
always deferring, always slipping and sliding, with tolerances
which for most personal uses are worthless. As far as Maximus is
concerned, the statistical world is Tartaros itself.

In Olson's redaction of the Hesiodic cosmology, "Maximus,
from Dogtown, IV," earth is created not from chaos or entropic
generality but from a specific historical construction. Earth as such
is a human product. In nonstatistical space information is the
product of the person, not the reverse. The peculiar qualification of
human vision is that it is local, specific, and, above all, logically
and morally *prior* to the divine perspective of the Tartarean socius.
It arises directly in the Stream, Okeanos, as a result of specific
historical human action:

> that the Earth
> was the condition, and that she
> there and then was the land, country
> our dear fatherland the Earth,
> thrown up to form a cairn, as spouse
> of Uranos: a i a
> the original name
> of Colchis (cld be a 'local'
> reference, that the Great Name
> the Earth shall have been
> Kuban where those
> inventors of the Vision-the
> Civilizers-were
> 'local'? some sure time prior to
> 2000
> BC.
>
> (Olson, 1983, 334)

The creation of the Earth—a i a or Gaia—was the measure
created by the construction of a cairn by the citizens of Kuban,
which Olson identifies elsewhere as "the Founding City of civilized
man."

To what extent is this to be taken as "true" history? For some-
one looking for authority to claim, for example, that the Kubans
where the original Indo-Europeans who established a binding tra-
dition, the purity of which must be regained, it is of course mean-
ingless conjecture. To be sure, objective history is past and deter-

mined. What happened is bound to involve conjecture. Our relation to it from an objective historical point of view is to construct a representation that will be inevitably more or less inadequate. It is a representation the original for which can never be discovered. Nonstatistical knowledge, however, relates not to an original but to the intuition of an appropriate outcome from a novel situation. It derives its authority from the preeminent claim of a present that does afford only the opportunity to act, not the option both to act and to assess the act in relation to the possibilities that condition the act. "Maximus, from Dogtown—IV" concludes with the note, "Thus / March," for which time the cosmology is definitive.

The story is repeatedly told in different terms and in relation to different sources throughout *Maximus IV, V, VI*—sometimes in relatively complete form in the first two poems of the Dogtown sequence, for example, or "Chronicles," and sometimes in relation to a completely different field of mythological reference in "Maximus Letter # whatever" (Olson, 1983, 201); sometimes in fragments which, taken together, bulk large in the last two volumes. What is communicated is not information that is intended to reduce our uncertainty. The *Maximus*, rather, gives evidence of the adequacy and reality of Olson's *own* time, and, in our reading, evidence of the adequacy and reality of our own time. Unlike disciplined, statistical knowledge, it makes itself available to use, not by making claims so general and vague as to have a kind of universal applicability, but by proposing specific concrete acts of knowing.

Maximus IV, V, VI is, however, the solipsistic movement of the *Maximus*. At the outset of the third volume, Maximus announces a wider task:

> having descried the nation
> to write a Republic
> in gloom on Watch-House Point.
> (Olson, 1983, 377).

To write a *res publica* (a public thing or affair). Zeus and the Olympian gods had added nothing to the physical world. Rather, they had instituted the social order, the statistical regime under which every writing was also an unwriting. The phonetic representation of speech could be interpreted only against the background of the entire phonological (and fundamentally social) program.

Olson is not interested in Olympian knowledge, which requires its heightened perspective in order to view both the event of language and the systematic which makes its possible. He is interested not in knowledge as potential power but in actual knowledge, as practice: what to take (*recipere*) and in what order to take it:

```
                              I am a ward
                              and precinct
The Big False Humanism        man myself and hate
     Now on                   universalization, believe
                              it only feeds into a class of deteriorated
                              personal lives anyway, giving them
                              what they can buy, a cheap
                              belief. The corner magazine store
                              (O'Connell's, at Prospect and Washington
                              has more essential room in it than
                                        programs. The goddess
                                        of the good doesn't
                                        follow any faster
                                        than how a person may
                                        find it possible to go out,
                                        and get what it is they do want
                                        wherever they do go
                                                  (Olson, 1983, 379)
```

In contrast to "The Big False Humanism," Olson insists upon active participation in the creation. Humanism attempts to "take in" everything at once: it literally wants to eat its cake and to have it too; and within statistical limits that propose to account for each specific event as an instance of all possible events, it is sometimes able to do so (deferring the textual and "ecological" consequences). The goddess of the good, however, limits her favor to sequences of events controlled by actual desire and the actual discovery of what to take and in what order to take them—that is, only so long as desire is related to the outcome of a specific occasion, not to the statistical exploitation of entire classes of occasions.

Therefore, near the beginning of *The Maximus Poems, Volume Three,* Maximus in the guise of the war god, Enyalion, sets off to do definitive battle with the statistical world—"Dog of Tartarus / Guards of Tartarus / Finks of the Boss . . . War Makers" (Olson, 1983, 405), who obscure those necessary sequences by partitioning reality, creating the discrete manifolds of logic and language and socius that support them.

As long as the generational struggle remains, however, the process remains dialectical and mechanical, as Maximus realizes in an untitled poem that begins:

> I have been an ability—a machine—up to
> now. An act of "history", my own, and my father's,
> together, a *queer* [Gloucester–sense] combination
> of completing something both visionary—or illusions (projec-
> tion? literally.
>
> (Olson, 1983, 495)

So engaged, the visionary and illusory are confused. Charles Stein notes the relevance in this connection of the ambiguity of "projection" as Jung understands it:

> Here, "illusions" is associated tentatively with the word "projection," the question mark after the latter suggesting again the motion of Olson's in-process interrogation of his own thought. For "projection" in the repressive sense is of course productive of mere "illusions," but if repression is absent, projection may yet occur without neurotic admixtures, in which case the process may indeed be productive of creative work or visionary experience. (Stein, 1979, 32)

The uncertainty of the common knowledge is not relativistic but absolute. A claim is not true or untrue because the appropriate systematic background against which to judge it is undecidable but because of its inherent suitability or unsuitability to a specific occasion. It is *utterly* true or false: the outcome could not have realized some other possibility. This is the definitive character of measured or finitistic space.

In an infinitistic cosmology—that is, any logical or semio*logical* or phono*logical* cosmology—all is difference. The distinctions that make logic possible ultimately destroy the identities which make discrete categories useful. If the symbolism can contrive to represent ever smaller units, nothing can ever be definitive or final. There is always another distinction to be made, another symbol to be generated, and so forth. The poststructuralists thoroughly work out the implications of this view. The *Maximus* is at least an initial foray into the alternative.

Toward the end of *Volume Three*, Olson writes at an angle across a page:

the unit   the smallest   there is

**Wed night (after 2 AM Thursday
July 16th—
'LXIX**

Charles Olson

This is the fundamental assertion and demonstration of finitistic cosmology. Any *unit* is the smallest unit there is. Otherwise it would not be a unit. If there is a unit, the infinite regression stops, and the Zenonian paradoxes are replaced by the nonidentity paradoxes—zero is equal to one. What the smallest unit is, of course, depends upon the measure that is used. If the measure is by a scale, the smallest marking that can be discriminated is the unit; if the measure is by the human foot, the foot itself or perhaps the half- or quarter-foot, which can be approximated, is the unit. Anything smaller does not count. In the nonstatistical space of the *Maximus* the pages of the book itself are the units. It is an absolute space that lacks only the means for objective verification; it is not the casual social space (of the poststructuralists, for example) that lacks both truth and falsity.

Seventeen years after the writing of "The Kingfishers," Olson once again recurs to the cybernetic definition of the message. Now, however, the cybernetic machine is autopoietic, not an input-output mechanism:

the Mountain of no difference which I

have climbed as other men and other men will

have no choice other than: there is no other

choice, you do have to listen to that Angel and

'write' down what he says (you don't your

other Angel does and you obey him

to the degree that it is almost impossible to

keep doing, that's for sure!

But,

does this Vision hold in faith

(as well as in credulity) and in my own experience crucially in

　necessity

in perfect measure of rhyme and Truth,

does it, in beauty too, take me

　　　　test, stiffly the modus

of this visione which

　　　　　　　not as modulus, this,

　　　, that is, measurement

　　　　　　　　　"throughout the system"

　modulus precise finite segments

—"There are no infinitesimals"

　all does rhyme   like is the measure of

　　producing like, the Guardian

　　does dictate the message

　　is a discrete & continuous conduction

　　of the life from a sequence of events measurable

in time and none of this is contestable,

There is no measure without it or

with anything but this measure:

it does, my Beloved's head grows to Heaven,

　　　　does my Life grow

out of my "life" [Likewise—likewise?

is the <u>Modus</u>

absolute [I say it,

as a prayer.

(Olson, 1983, 501–2)

Olson's image for the autopoietic process derives from the "Recital of Hayy ibn Yaqzan," an Ismaili Muslim text, which tells the story of each human being entrusted to two orders of angels, "called 'Guardians and Noble Scribes'—one to the right, the other to the left. He who is to the right belongs to the angels who order; to him it falls to dictate. He who is to the left belongs to the angels who act; to him it falls to write" (Corbin, 1960, 148). The occasion only affords the possibility of getting the message right or wrong, of staying in the continuous erotic stream or, damming it, describing it, mechanizing it, thus replicating death on behalf of life.

As early as 1953, Olson had withdrawn his first assessment of the input-output machine, which he had modeled in "The Kingfisher." He speaks of the danger "of falling for, & into, the mechanistic trap of measurement—entropy, & all that language of the electronics of communication, [which] is doing away with the organism which has these behaviors, or satisfying the curiosity—the morality—which is your life, or mine, and that largest question: *what am I doing with it—what is it I am to do with*" (Olson, 1978, 18–19). Both the "inputs" and the "outputs," Olson discovers, are interior to the autonomous organism. He picked up on biological research, the theoretical implications of which would not be otherwise articulated for nearly two decades:

> just as Haeckel's Law has been so examined by embryologists that it has almost come to be inverted from the exactitudes achieved in the last 75 years (that now one says ontogeny (or the life development in the individual) creates phylogeny (creates the species), so one can declare that each of us, the vertical force in us, the gravitational, that prime of all our tropisms, the archeology we are, creates the mythology of which we are the inheritors. (Olson, 1978, 21)

That is, the individual is the *product* of neither an evolutionary tradition nor a cultural tradition but is, in the present, the sole producer of both. Similarly, Maturana and Varela write:

> Thus, the individuals, though transitory, are essential, not dispensable, because they constitute a necessary condition for the existence of the historical network which they define. The species is only an abstract entity in the present, and although it represents a historical phenomenon it does not constitute a generative factor in the phenomenology of evolution, it is its result. (Maturana and Varela, 1980, 107)

The historical network may be constituted as a mechanism of purpose and intimidation. It typically is. It may also be constituted, as Olson writes, as a function of somatic time—life lived by individuals, not by a species or historical agencies or any other abstraction. As such, it is the sole value that is not a mortgage against other things and other people. It is the value of life that is not compromised by the false valuing of death as an ultimate aim.

CHAPTER 6

Beginning Again

There has been a beginning of begun.
They can be caused.
They can be caused to share.
Or they can be cause to share.
—Gertrude Stein, *Stanzas In Meditation*

sing with the taken
—Kenneth Irby, *Orexis*

WHAT WAS RIGHT IN METAPHYSICS

Besides, if there is becoming and movement, the process must also arrive at a limit; for no movement is infinite, and every movement has an end.
—Aristotle, *Metaphysics*

At this juncture, the question, What was right in metaphysics? must invoke the question, What is wrong in poststructuralism? for which metaphysics is not "true" but lives on in a shadowland of erased legibility in texts that we still (for some reason) have the eros to read, if only to build theories that demonstrate that metaphysics is not "true" but lives on still in a shadowland of erased legibility in texts which we still (for some reason) have the eros to read, if only. . . .

I could go on caught in this infinite loop forever. The excitement of infinite hermeneutical possibilities, however, begins to give way to the tedium of processing an infinite text with a finite machine. We have described the world. We know everything. Our ignorance is only apparent. The engines of language crank out infinitely the text of a world that is never the same but never truly different. We know the limit cases, or we have approached the infinitely receding limits so often that we are confident that *in practice* nothing surprising happens in their vicinity—some turbulences in dream texts, automatic writings, randomly generated texts—but nothing wholly new and unexpected. This knowledge, however, is not knowledge of the world, it is knowledge of the *description* of the world. *After* physics, we know the world as a student might know a person from the constitution of the state in which he or she lives. When the physical world has been described completely and adequately, nothing has been said of any individual—person or star.

What was true in metaphysics is that there is an origin. What was false was that metaphysicians supposed a logical rather than a common or factual origin—that is, the metaphysicians supposed that it was only necessary to repeat the strategy that had been successful with *physis* on the individual. Therefore, they began to describe the description and the descriptions of the descriptions, infinitely regressing into solipsism. In fact, what is *after* physics is poiesis. The generalities are only generalities, which is to say relationships between objects that are themselves more or less vague and ill-defined (i.e., nonexistent): in ancient physics, *a* causes *b;* in classical modern physics, *f* is a function of *x;* in contemporary physics, *x* is statistically related to *y.* The ancients modeled the world as a finite machine, the moderns as an infinite formal system, the contemporaries as a collection of finite formal systems, which are reliable to the extent an appropriate background of possibilities can be established.

The issue of metaphysics was forced when phonetic writing became fluent enough to require a theory. Again we must question not Derrida's interpretations, which are always brilliant, but his scholarship. It is true, as he insists, that "the history of the *phone* is inseparable from the history of idealization, that is, from the 'history of mind,' or history as such" (Derrida, 1978a, 75); however, he mistakenly understands the phonetic mark as a sign of the power of voice, rather than what it properly is, the violation of voice. By the sixth century B.C. or so, a few Greeks were skillful enough at writing that they could represent the unbounded variety of speech with the combinations of a finite and remarkably small collection of discrete, arbitrary marks. The Greek alphabet was especially powerful because it identified zones of vocalization. It specified resonance. With discrete vowels, writers had access to a script and, *therefore,* a logic, which seemed complete. It was, however, a logic *not* of voice but of discrete marks, and the problems of metaphysics were generated by meditation upon the necessary conditions of the logic of marks. Thus, Aristotle, in discussing the problem of recognizing the tokens or individual marks of phonetic difference as cases of the universal mark: "For this is just what we mean by the individual—the numerically one, and by the universal we mean that which is predictable of the individuals. Therefore it is just as, if elements of articulate sound were limited in number, all the literature in the world would be confined to the ABC, since there could not be two or more letters of the same kind" (Aristotle, 1984, 1579).

This is not a problem of an organization of knowledge that honors the voice. Plato had banned the carriers and, thus, the traditions of oral knowledge from the ideal republic; and, when Aristotle restored poetry as a tool of philosophy, he restored literate poetry, not oral poetry. Only with literacy did the problems of completeness and normality (i.e., how each token of the sign is recognized as the *same* sign) arise. These are the characteristic problems of writing and the logic of writing. In metaphysics, Aristotle sought to account not just for the reliability of the available texts but for the theoretical reliability of all possible texts. In addition to demonstrating that writing was a complete formal system and that the limited number of marks could represent all of the possibilities, it was also necessary to demonstrate that the meanings of the marks remained consistent from mark to mark. Logic could underwrite the claim that certain necessary relationships held between certain atomic units, but it could not likewise guarantee that the atoms remained consistent from one instance to the next. How could a thing have the dignity and value of a unique thing and, at the same time, be described by universal predicates?

The distance between the particular and the universal has been a persistent source of theoretical embarrassment and practical inconvenience. Many changes have been rung on the theme, producing a class of ontologically weird objects: the pineal gland of Descartes, the objects of Hegel's logic (A = not A), and the frequency-sensitive neurons of Freud's "Project for a Scientific Psychology" as well as Derrida's "visible imperceptible"* texts belong to this peculiar category.

---

* "A text is not a text unless it hides from the first comer, from the first glance, the law of its composition and the rules of its game. A text remains, moreover, forever imperceptible. Its law and its rules are not, however, harbored in the inaccessibility of a secret; it is simply that they can never be booked, in the *present,* into anything that could rigorously be called a perception" (Derrida, 1981, 63).

Classical metaphysics is a sustained meditation on ontological weirdness, on the fact that the world of action and the world of thought are oddly out of whack. In the *Phaedrus,* after playfully delivering an oration to show the art of rhetoric is not so mysterious, Socrates speaks of the techniques of division and generalization, which he had used and which are common techniques of rhetoric in these terms: "I am a great lover of these processes of division and generalization; they help me to speak and think. And if I find any man who is able *to see unity and plurality* in nature, him I follow, and walk in his step as if he were a god. And those who have this art, I have hitherto been in the habit of calling dialecticians; but God knows whether the name is right or not." Of course, to see unity *and* plurality is to see incoherence. The western episteme entered upon a line of thought that rendered the commonest things strange, indeed just beyond the horizon of knowledge altogether. That is, it was not enough to see things, it was necessary to divide things from themselves and to rejoin them in a problematical, theoretical domain. And success in this discipline, as Socrates was aware, conferred remarkable power. To *see* unity and plurality is to conceive rightly—to name rightly, perhaps even denying the certainty of the rightness—in order to *walk* aright, freely, compelled neither by the exigencies of oral performance nor by the rules of rhetoric. Socrates speaks of the divine prospect of reclaiming the integrity of the organism, so it is possible literally to move like the gods. This is to have the Marxian theoretical eye. The oral poet is absorbed by the requirements of memory and the mimetic identification with the narrative, the rhetorician is absorbed by the requirements of logic. Given the triumph of literacy, Socrates could merely dismiss the poets as a danger to the emerging order. The rhetorician and the dialectician, however, are both mechanics of the abstract: the one dazzling with the illogicality of logic itself, the paradoxes and fancy footwork; the other trying to comport himself with grace in a world where even the *first* logical problem is insoluble. Faustian modernism attempted to overwhelm the impossibility of logic by force of will.

Abstraction, which coordinated attention and selective inattention, seeing both unity and plurality in nature, created disequilibriums and dynamisms that *compelled* thought. The mind was no longer free. In one mode of attention, philosophers saw particular trees and buildings and people, but by withdrawing their attention from the marks of individuation and squinting abstractly at the world, they saw that *everything* was water or fire or something overwhelmingly universal. Thereafter, they saw trees, buildings, and people differently. Their insight into the prime material was confirmed and extended. Having opened thought in the direction of abstraction, however, the mind was no longer free to follow its own course and fell subject to its own compulsion: "From these facts," Aristotle writes, "one might think that the only cause is the so-called material cause; but as men thus advanced, the very facts showed them the way joined in *forcing* them to investigate the subject" (Aristotle, 1984, 1556). *After* physics in classical thought, after life was explained as a mechanism of material causation, humans were captives of their own self-description and *its* processes, the forms of language as such. With literacy, there was a sudden increase of available abstraction. As both Plato and Aristotle were aware, however, to assign all individual alphas to the class alphas, individual betas to the class of betas, and so forth opened a powerful hierarchy of abstract relationships that tend to swamp finite life. It opened directly to the cynicism of the sophists and their world in which argument served only power, not justice.

The office of metaphysics was to negotiate the terms of the uneasy, even impossible, relationship between categorical thought and the concrete world. Its fundamental doctrines were (1) that the infinitely reiterable elements of language close on discoverable principles—that is, that the universals are knowable—and (2) that the mind, in discovering its *own* content, frees itself from the *necessities* of its content, its mere representations, and discovers what it is in itself. The strategy of metaphysics was to invoke a third realm, neither the mind nor the experienced world—a place not always as fanciful as the Platonic heaven but of a necessary ideality. Metaphysics had a peculiar genius for generating new entities to explain its problems: objects proliferated into transcendental space by force of the requirements of abstract thought itself. Of the Platonists, Aristotle wrote, "as for those who posit the Ideas as causes, firstly, in seeking to grasp the causes of the things around us, they introduced others equal in number to these, as if a man who wanted to count things thought he could not do it while they were few, but tried to count them when he had added to their number" (Aristotle, 1984, 1565). And, as it turns out, this general strategy involves not a mere doubling but an infinite regress. An abstract world replica must invoke metaworld after metaworld, each mediating between an original and a newly invented world. In these terms, the problem of the relationship of the concrete to the abstract can be deferred, but it cannot solved.

There is no more rigorous critique of so-called Platonic metaphysics than Plato's own in the *Parmenides,* and if I understand the Platonic canon correctly, Plato explores all of the complexities of infinitistic thought from the perspective of a finitistic dialectic, a dialectic that was forever ready to admit that it was uncertain even about its own name. And Aristotle explicitly comprehended the real dangers of the proliferation of metaphysical objects: "those who maintain the infinite series destroy the good without knowing it" (Aristotle, 1984, 1571). Aristotle foresaw the Hegelian bacchanal and recognized its ultimately nihilistic implications.

For more than two millennia, the classical dialectic maintained its equilibrium. The abstract force of classical logical was limited to the relationship of the individual to the general case, the minor premise to the major premise of the syllogism. In the seventeenth century, however, the logical circle turned vicious. An algebraic function is a higher order of abstraction than a syllogism. It establishes a relationship not between an individual and a universal class but between two universal classes. The content of an algebraic x or y (or of a word in an abstract calculus of the linguist) is not some *thing* but another symbolic expression. There was thereafter an ideal object—nature—and an ideal subject—the Cartesian ego; an abstract objective space and an abstract subjective time, the one described by the mathematical science, the other by the new poetry. If doctrinaire, classical metaphysics always regressed into a series of evermore abstract worlds, post-seventeenth-century metaphysics took the opposite tack, replicating abstract ideas concretely, egressing infinitely toward a dense world of the future in which all of the possibilities are materially realized. "Machine technology," Martin Heidegger wrote, "remains up to now the most visible outgrowth of the essence of modern technology, which is identical with the essence of modern metaphysics" (Heidegger, 1977, 116). The classical was a search for an origin, a first world of abstraction; the modern—or, more accurately the Cartesian—is the search for an end, an abstract world of realized construction. The metaphysics of statistical reality can be summed up, as we have seen, in W. V. Quine's dictum "To be is to be the value of a variable." In classical thought the contemplation of the eternal promised eternal life; the introduction of the infinite into life, on the other hand, produces machines, the knowledge of which is deathly and death-producing. It is clear, to say the least, we are approaching a new threshold of technological plasticity that is the eros of modern knowledge.

Heidegger spoke of the "darkening of world . . . the emasculation of the spirit, the disintegration, wasting away, repression, and misinterpretation of the spirit," which followed the European failure to sustain German idealism. He noted:

> It was not German idealism that collapsed; rather, the age was no longer strong enough to stand up to the greatness, breadth, and originality of that spiritual world, i.e. truly to realize it, for to realize a philosophy means something very different from applying theorems and insights. The lives of men began to slide into a world which lacked that depth from out of which the essential always comes to man and comes back to man, so compelling him to become superior and making him act in conformity to a rank. All things sank to the same level, a surface resembling a blind mirror that no long reflects, that casts nothing back. The prevailing dimensions became that of extension and number. . . . This is the onslaught of what we call the demonic (in the sense of destructive evil). (Heidegger, 1961, 37–38)

The world is dark indeed, but it is Heidegger himself, however, who sides with the demonic, not per se in his siding with fascism, which was the historical manifestation of the demonic, but in siding with the discipline of the infinite, the recurrent source of destruction of the common world. Of course, we cannot stand up to the greatness, breadth, and originality of the romantic meditation. This is a given: it is infinite, and we are not. Although the human subject—that is, the abstraction Man—appears to have access to the infinite, men and women do not. Thus, we are forever intimidated by this Being that we postulate at the end of an endless and-so-on. We are to question the beginning of that which is without beginning—to inquire after the god of a world without a god. We are condemned by our language to believe in a god that is forever in hiding, known only in fleeting moments, epiphanies, which hint at some ultimate resolution but which tells us nothing about how to act here and now. It has become fashionable to denounce Heidegger for his fascism. The Nazis however are gone and are not likely to emerge in that form again. It must be seen however that Heidegger's thought, quite apart from its historical association with German fascism, is a profound expression of the arrogance that longs for absolutes. If there is something in the writings of Pound or Wyndam Lewis which can be retrieved from totalitarianism, in Heidegger there is not.

Aesthetic studies have been heavily implicated in this arrogance and this longing. The influence of Paul de Man's widely published writings are far more significant evidence of the pervasive attraction of totalitarianism that infects many schools of literary theoretical thought than are his long-hidden juvenalia. The very devices that are intended to create a concrete world are expressions of a lust for the knowledge that destroys the concreteness and sensuousness that art manifests. Literary texts often seem to carry resonances of the infinite. In all directions, the hermeneutic traces disappear in pregnant ellipses, and the willing reader hears the inexpressible buzz of the absolute. In an essay on Hölderlin, Heidegger writes:

> Hölderlin inquires, before anything else and in fact exclusively, as to man's measure. That measure is the godhead against which man measures himself. The question begins in line 29 with the words: "Is God unknown?" Manifestly not. For if he were unknown, how could he, being unknown, ever be the measure? Yet—and this is what we must now listen to and keep in mind—for Hölderlin God, as the one who he is, is unknown and it is just as this Unknown One that he is the measure for the poet. This is also why Hölderlin is perplexed by the exciting question: how can that which by its very nature remains unknown ever become a measure? (Heidegger, 1971, 221–22)

The metaphysical invocation of the origin, unlike the mythological "in the beginning," is not the beginning of a narrative but the end of narrative. Thereafter, there are no stories as such, only temporal renderings of the archetypes. This is the principle of Aristotle's *Poetics*. The poets whom Plato excludes from the ideal republic are not the poets whom Aristotle restores. It is not poetry as such but the *idea* of poetry that returns as the mechanism of abstraction. For Heidegger, as for Aristotle, poetry manifests concretely the otherwise unworldly forms of logic; now, however, poetry is called upon to underwrite not this or that abstract idea but

Language itself. It must exhibit not this or that truth but the possibility of what Heidegger calls "greatness of spirit." We can think the *idea* of the infinite, and we can make symbols for it, but we cannot think the infinite as such. Thus our poetry has become hopelessly out of touch with the world; making symbols of a grand indefiniteness. The infinite gods of grammar are of no use to us, because they exist in a domain to which we have only provisional access by way of the intoxications of romantic arts and archetypal religions. Thus, we may be edified, but we have no access to meaning or useful action. In fact, an infinite God could not be a meaningful or useful measure even if it *were* known. Infinity is not a scale of the finite world. The darkening of the world results from our failure to produce the finite spirit that can inhabit the finite world which we construct. It is the perfectly knowable human scale that is required.

For men and women, as opposed to MAN, however, language is just another technology that we have mystified as we mystify other technologies and that like many other technologies, does not work as well as we would like. We are not in the closure of metaphysics but in the opening of the secular origin or the domain of the common. Metaphysics, however, is no more exhausted by its closure than mythology is exhausted by the falseness of its tales. Just as it was necessary to discover the psychological meanings of archetypal religions, it is now necessary to discover the ethical meanings of metaphysics.* We have dealt rather well with the integrity of the individual psyche but not with the meaning of the ethos. We must escape the fundamentalism of metaphysicians, their critics, and their deconstructors. Having liberated ourselves from the literalism of myth, we must liberate ourselves from the *symbolism* of metaphysics, or, that is to say, the fundamentalism of the symbol. The knowledge of things in themselves begins not with the question, What is this? or with Why are there things rather than nothing? These are perplexities that arise from the uses of

---

*Metaphysics and archetypal religion are cognates, both products of the Mediterranean basin in the period 500 B.C. and 100 A.D. Christianity is an archetypal religion in a profound sense that ancient Greek religion is not. To be sure, archetypalism can be read back into the ancient ritual practices, but they belong literally to a different world.

symbolism, with definitions and the strange fact that symbols can be negated in a way that things cannot. Philosophy begins with wonder, Aristotle tells us, with amazement, with the knowledge that things are. Here is this! and this! and this! The world makes itself available for the exercise of freedom. Aristotle writes, "Evidently then we do not seek it for the sake of any other advantage; but as the man is free, we say, who exists for himself and not another, so we pursue this as the only free science, for it alone exists for itself" (Aristotle, 1984, 1554–55). Metaphysics was concerned not with *how* to do this or that practical thing but with *stopping* the logical deferment in order to declare that *this is* the beginning, the completely alogical order of the world, life itself, the freely chosen aim of the individual, purposeless and circular, committed only to the maintenance of its own sufficiency. What was true in metaphysics is the knowledge that is freedom rather than the knowledge that is subject to the relentless—but as it turns out, completely relative—requirements of logic. Metaphysics sought to free the mind from the compulsion of its own content, from the necessities of a represented world and the logic of representation, to free the mind to the content that it is in itself. What is true in metaphysics, however deeply it was itself sometimes compromised, is the directions it gives toward a knowledge that is not compromised with its own deathly mechanism.

WHAT SHOULD HAVE COME FIRST

> we're all in the loop
> music   anyway
> limited beyond all possibility notation.
> —Norma Cole, "Erotema"

As Napoleon rode toward Jena, Hegel wrote: "The frivolity and boredom which unsettle the established order, the vague foreboding of something unknown, these are the heralds of approaching change. The gradual crumbling that left unaltered the face of the whole is cut short by a sun burst which, in one flash, illuminates the features of the new world" (Hegel, 1977, 6–7). The bourgeois face that appeared in that sun burst is now crumbled and grotesque, dying and threatening to take everything and everyone with it.

The desperation of the youth culture—expressed for the most part in cartoons and in music the decibel level of which is literally deafening, so many of the musicians and some of their audience suffer permanent hearing loss—is deep and legitimate. Both the music and the cartoons are ugly, intentionally ugly. For the first time since the 1920s, the music is not based on the blues, which is to say, it does not have the vitality of the integral body as a reserve of expressivity. It is not, however, possible to generalize significantly about the Youth. Those who do not merely go through the sitcom motions of living are engaged in local cultural scenes that give a new meaning to fragmentation and decentralization. There are no culture heroes as such, but local rock groups focus the emotional intensity, and the information comes from local fanzines, which have sprung up by the handfuls in most large American cities and in many isolated communities. With readily available page layout software for computers and electronic copying, publishing has been thoroughly democratized. Information can also be cheaply and quickly distributed on magnetic tape and by electronic computer networks.

The following anonymous review of *Dimension Hatross* by Voivod, on the Noise International label, is from an electronic fanzine, *Jersey Beat,* which appeared on a computer bulletin board in the Albany, New York, area:

> A whorling mass of gelatinized steel wool, Canada's Voivod shifts gears on tempo, key and riffage as rapidly as a Village trendy changes lifestyles—and with as much apparent rhyme 'n reason. But in Voivod's case, the result is an exultant, liberating sense of anarchy & stylistic spontaneity. Event-windows rush by too quickly to lock into much more than sensations of pure speed and raw power—perhaps an overall impression of aggressive percussive assault.
>
> A lot is made of this outfit's art-punk and prog influences. To make a long convulted [sic] argument short—they extract a vastly different effect from these elements in this context: there's less scope, breadth, and creative intimation here. On the other hand, a lot of folks, including me, have probably prayed to have those scant seconds of incendiary bombast clipped out of their

Mahavishnu records and pasted together for the pure demolitionary kick of it. Black Flag were moving in this direction but aborted the mission before reaching escape velocity. Voivod are already on Mars on a recon mission.*

The distance from the expressive pelvis of Elvis Presley and the coy sexuality of Chuck Berry's guitar caressing to "a whorling mass of gelatinized steel wool" measures precisely the extent to which the Freudian body—that is, the half-forgotten idealized body—has been revealed. The unexpressed content of the Western psyche is no longer significantly sexual. In fact, it is so-called *conscious* processes that have become so mechanized and so little in need of maintenance that they are repressed, even as their formulae appear nonchalantly on everyone's tongue. Paradoxically, it is not what we fail to express but precisely what we do express with blithe arrogance that we do not know.

The West has long suffered an epistemological pathology, and, with the worldwide communications networks of this century, the entire world is infected. We describe the world in such a way that we are required by the terms of the description to try to overwhelm it. In generalized terms, it works like this:

A describing system may include itself in its descriptions of the world—that is, take its own activity as the background for itself. As soon as one does, however, the event, a thing that has reference only to itself, is transformed into an example—a ratio between an event and a fixed, or at least partially fixed, systematic background. An event says, in effect, A is A. An example says, A is B, B is C, C is D, and D is A. ABCD provides a systematic background for each of the constituents. Of course, A is not exactly B, or they would be indistinguishable from one another, but *ad hoc* identifications allow some imprecision. Even if identifications are random, the example of A/ABCD presents odds of one in four. If

---

*It seems right, somehow, that the last citation in this book should be to a source that I do not know how to cite. I can say that on June 20, 1989, this text was still on the Factsheet Five Bulletin Board in Rensselaer, N.Y., and the source includes an address where one can purportedly get the paper version of *Jersey Beat* (though I have never seen it). Knowing the way things move in this world, however, it is likely neither the phone number nor the address will produce my source, especially by the time this book is published. The anonymous reviewer with a flair for interesting metaphors will be soon be absorbed back into the underground. That is, the event windows open and close rapidly. As of June, 1992, this BBS seems to have disappeared.

the environment allows several chances, everyone will eventually pick a winner. The background may be more or less extensively articulated as a cosmic schema, a Weltanschauung, an archetype, a paradigm, a history, a society, a natural or artificial language, an aesthetic canon, or an electronic circuit. When an important background suddenly appears, it is a sun burst, illuminating the features of a New World—or what *seems* to be a new world because each event becomes an *example* of an entire world.

Peter Sloterdijk notes, "Although Kant forbade us to think of 'objective goals' in nature, his philosophizing orients itself, to be sure, not toward an overarching world reason but toward the confidence in our ability to bring reason into the state of the world" (Sloterdijk, 1987, 545). The epistemological pathology, which appeared in the seventeenth century and flowered in what we call the Age of Enlightenment, admitted an infinite number of steps between A and the return to A. Thus, an *ad hoc* stratagem, by which it was possible temporarily to overwhelm the finite environment, became a permanent discipline or addiction.

Now we know that we cannot bring reason to the world, not because our reason is weak but because the world is not that kind of place. We must welcome the fragmentation, not because a new sunburst awaits us but because, legitimately, we should never have hoped for knowledge as more than a way to "get by" with a little grace. Copernicus, Kant, Darwin, and Freud all proposed to remove us in our arrogance from our self-proclaimed privileged positions. With an arrogance of their own, they beat down human presumption. Now a profound humility is required. We must look quickly into the opening and closing event windows. Events come with their own backgrounds, which fade as quickly as the events themselves. Those who hold to a systematic background beyond the disappearance of the events which produced it, whether for reasons of sentimental love of the tradition or greed or desire for power, are dangers to the common good. The events are random and meaningless until we bring our own measure to them, and, of course, they are random and meaningless as soon as our sustaining attention fades.

Now there are no examples.

This is difficult to say. The statement itself wants to become an example of something—a world or an epoch, especially an example of words, which in turn want to become examples of phonemes, significant differences, statistical reliabilities, or an example of *now*. Words, however are not *examples* of words; now is not an example of *now*. From *now* to *now*, word to word, is a precise measure—unexemplary, unrepresentable except by the traces which mark it, nonrepeatable. The design we cut in time we cut once and once only. From eternity—as we imagine it, with hopeless inadequacy—or from the sham eternity of some discipline of knowledge, *now* is contingent, a roll of the dice, and from the crap game, a domain of possibilities arises—natures, histories, persons, and so forth—a marketplace of knowledge where the truth and the possibility of great profit reward the best calculation. It is pervasive, even unavoidable, but it requires nothing of us. As the design in time is lived, suffered or enjoyed, however, it is absolute; our obedience is required. There are no second or third chances. There is not even a hint of an infinitely resolvable context for our perplexity.

There are no examples here. Now.

BIBLIOGRAPHY

Abrams, M. H. 1958. *The Mirror and the Lamp: Romantic Theory and the Critical Tradition*. New York: Norton.

Adams, Henry. 1949. *Degradation of the Democratic Dogma*. New York: Smith.

———. 1974. *The Education of Henry Adams*. Ed. Ernest Samuels. Boston: Houghton.

Adolph, Robert. 1967. *The Rise of Modern Prose Style*. Cambridge: MIT P.

Aristotle. 1984. *The Complete Works of Aristotle*. Ed. Jonathan Barnes. Princeton: Princeton UP.

Ashby, W. Ross. 1964. *An Introduction to Cybernetics*. London: Methuen.

Augustine, Saint. 1947. *On Music. The Fathers of the Church,* Volume 5. Ed. Ludwig Schopp. Trans. Robert Catesby Taliaferro. New York: Cima.

———. 1948. "The Confessions." *Basic Writings of Saint Augustine*. Ed. Whitney J. Oates. Trans. J. G. Pilkington. Vol. 1. New York: Random.

Bacon, Francis. 1985. *The Essayes or Counsels, Civill and Morall*. Ed. Michael Kiernan. Cambridge: Harvard UP.

Bakhtin, M. M. 1981. *The Dialogic Imagination: Four Essays*. Trans. Michael Holquist. Austin: Texas UP.

Barthes, Roland. 1967. *Writing Degree Zero*. Trans. Annette Lavers and Colin Smith. New York: Hill and Wang.

———. 1977. *Image—Music—Text*. Trans. Stephen Heath. New York: Hill and Wang.

Bateson, Gregory. 1972. *Steps to an Ecology of the Mind*. San Francisco: Chandler.

Baudrillard, Jean. 1988. *Selected Writings*. Ed. Mark Poster. Palo Alto: Stanford UP.

Beard, Charles A. 1934. "Written History as an Act of Faith." *American Historical Review* 39: 219–29.

Becker, Carl. 1932. "Everyman His Own Historian." *American Historical Review* 37: 221–36.

Beckett, Samuel. 1931. *Proust*. New York: Grove.

Bell, J. L. 1981. "Category Theory and the Foundations of Mathematics." *British Journal of the Philosophy of Science*. 32: 349–58.

Benjamin, Walter. 1968. *Illuminations*. Ed. Hannah Arendt. Trans. Harry Zohn. New York: Harcourt.

Berkeley, George. 1957. "The Analyst." *Works*. Ed. A. A. Luce and T. E. Jessup. Vol. 4. London. 53–102.

Bloom, Harold. 1975. *Map of Misreading*. Oxford: Oxford UP.

———. 1976. *Wallace Stevens: The Poems of Our Climate*. Ithaca: Cornell UP.

Bone, J. Drummond. 1987. "Organicism and Shelley's *A Defence of Poetry*." *Approaches to Organic Form: Permutations in Science and Culture*. Ed. Frederick Burwick. Boston Studies in the Philosophy of Science 105. Dordrecht: D. Reidel. 195–210.

Bos, H. J. M. 1980. "Newton, Leibniz, and the Leibnizian Tradition." *From the Calculus to Set Theory, 1630–1910*. Ed. I. Grattan-Guinness. London: Duckworth. 49–93.

Brown, Robert F. 1977. *The Later Philosophy of Schelling: The Influence of Boehme on the Works*. Lewisburg: Bucknell UP.

Bruns, Gerald L. 1982. *Inventions, Writing, Textuality, and Understanding in Literary History*. New Haven: Yale UP.

Bunnell, David. 1987. "Hypervisions." *PC World* March: 14–27.

Burke, Kenneth. 1969. *A Grammar of Motives*. Berkeley: California UP.

Čapek, Milič. 1961. *The Philosophic Impact of Contemporary Physics*. Princeton: Van Nostrand.

Chernoff, John Miller. 1979. *African Rhythm and African Sensibility: Aesthetics and Social Action in African Musical Idioms*. Chicago: Chicago UP.

Chomsky, Noam. 1966. *Cartesian Linguistics*. New York: Harper and Row.

———. 1959. "On Certain Formal Properties of Grammars." *Information and Control* 2: 137–67.

Clausen, Christopher. 1981. "Poetry in a Discouraging Time." *Georgia Review* 35: 703–15.

Cohen, Murray. 1977. *Sensible Words: Linguistic Practice in England, 1640–1785*. Baltimore: Johns Hopkins UP.

Cohen, Ralph, ed. 1989. *The Future of Literary Criticism*. New York: Routledge.

Coleman, Ornette. 1961. *Free Jazz*. New York: Atlantic.

Colie, Rosalie Littell. 1966. *Paradoxia Epidemica: The Renaissance Tradition of Paradox*. Princeton: Princeton UP.

Conarroe, Joel. 1981. "Poetry: A Symposium." *Georgia Review* 35: 744–47.

Corbin, Henri. 1960. *Avicenna and the Visionary Recital.* Trans. Willard W. Trask. New York: Pantheon.

Cox, Kenneth. 1973. "Zukofsky and Mallarmé: Notes on "A"–19." *Maps 5*: 1–11.

Creeley, Robert. 1982. *The Collected Poems of Robert Creeley.* Berkeley: California UP.

Crescenti, Peter, and Bob Columbe. 1985. *The Official Honeymooners Treasury.* New York: Perigee.

Croll, Morris W. 1971. "The Baroque Style in Prose." *Seventeenth-Century Prose: Modern Essays in Criticism.* Ed. Stanley Fish. New York: Oxford UP.

Davidson, Donald. 1984. *Inquiries into Truth and Interpretation.* Oxford: Clarendon.

Deleuze, Gilles, and Félix Guattari. 1977. *Anti-Oedipus: Capitalism and Schizophrenia.* Trans. Robert Hurley, Mark Seem and Helen R. Lane. New York: Viking.

Derrida, Jacques. 1976. *Of Grammatology.* Trans. Gayatri Chakravorty Spivak. Baltimore: Johns Hopkins UP.

———. 1978a. *Speech and Phenomena.* Trans. Alan Bass. Chicago: Chicago UP.

———. 1978b. *Writing and Difference.* Trans. Alan Bass. Chicago: Chicago UP.

———. 1981. *Dissemination.* Trans. Barbara Johnson. Chicago: Chicago UP.

Descartes, René. 1967. *Philosophical Works of Descartes.* Trans. Elizabeth Sanderson Haldane and George Robert Thomson Ross. London: Cambridge UP.

———. 1970. *Descartes' Philosophical Letters.* Trans. Anthony Kenny. Oxford: Clarendon.

———. 1979. *Monde; ou, Traite de la lumiere.* Trans. Michael Sean Mahoney. New York: Abaris Books.

———. 1983. *Principles of Philosophy.* Trans. Valentine Roger Miller and Reese P. Miller. Dordrecht: Reidel.

Doney, Willis, ed. 1987. *Eternal Truths and the Cartesian Circle.* New York: Garland.

Dretske, Fred I. 1981. *Knowledge and the Flow of Information.* Cambridge: MIT P.

Duncan, Robert. 1960. *The Opening of the Field.* New York: Grove.

Duncan, Robert. 1984. *Ground Work I: Before the War.* New York: New Directions.

———. 1985. *Fictive Certainties.* New York: New Directions.

———. 1987. *Ground Work II: In the Dark.* New York: New Directions.

Easthope, Anthony. 1983. *Poetry as Discourse.* London: Methuen.

Edelman, Charles M. 1988. *Topobiology: An Introduction to Molecular Embryology.* New Book: Basic.

Eisenstein, Sergei. 1957. *Film Form and Film Sense: Two Complete and Unabridged Works.* Trans. Jay Leyda. New York: Meridian.

Eliot, T. S. 1963. *Collected Poems, 1909–1962.* San Diego: Harcourt.

———. 1975. *Selected Prose of T. S. Eliot.* Ed. Frank Kermode. New York: Harcourt.

Fabe, Maxene. 1979. *Game Shows.* Garden City, N.Y.: Doubleday.

Fenollosa, Ernest. 1967. *The Chinese Written Character as a Medium of Poetry.* Ed. Ezra Pound. San Francisco: City Lights.

Finklestein, David. 1969. "Matter, Space, and Logic." *Boston Studies in the Philosophy of Science.* Ed. Robert S. Cohen and Marx W. Wartofsky. Dordrecht: Reidel.

Fish, Stanley Eugene. 1972. *Self-Consuming Artifact: The Expereince of Seventeenth-Century Literature.* Berkeley: California UP.

Foucault, Michel. 1970. *The Order of Things: An Archaeology of the Human Sciences.* New York: Random, 1970.

Frege, Gottlob. 1977. *Translations from the Philosophical Writings of Gottlob Frege.* Ed. Peter Geach and Max Black. Trans. P. T. Geach. Oxford: Blackwell.

Freud, Sigmund. 1955. *The Standard Edition of the Complete Psychological Works of Sigmund Freud.* Ed. James Strachey. 22 Volumes. London: Hogarth.

———. 1985. *The Complete Letters of Sigmund Freud to Wilhem Fliess, 1887–1904.* Trans. Jeffrey Moussaieff Masson. Cambridge: Harvard UP.

Gadamer, Hans-George. 1976. *Hegel's Dialectic: Five Hermeneutical Studies.* New Haven: Yale UP.

Gardner, Howard. 1987. *The Mind's New Science: A History of the Cognitive Revolution.* New York: Basic.

Gelb, I. J. 1963. *A Study of Writing.* Rev. 2nd ed. Chicago: Chicago UP.

Georgiades, Thrasybolus. 1973. *Greek Music, Verse and Dance.* Trans. Erwin Benedikt and Marie Louis Martinez. New York: Da Capo.

Gibson, J. J. 1966. *The Senses Considered as a Perceptual System.* Boston: Houghton.

———. 1979. *The Ecological Approach to Visual Perception.* Boston: Houghton.

Gibson, William. 1984. *Neuromancer.* New York: Ace.

Gilson, Etienne. 1960. *The Christian Philosophy of Saint Augustine.* Trans. L. E. M. Lynch. New York: Random.

Gitlin, Todd. 1983. *Inside Prime Time.* New York: Pantheon.

Guston, Philip. 1965. "Piero della Francesca: The Impossibility of Painting." *Art News* April: 38–39.

Hacking, Ian. 1975. *The Emergence of Probability: A Philosophical Study of Early Ideas about Probability, Induction, and Statistical Inference.* Cambridge: Cambridge UP.

Haraway, Donna. 1985. "A Manifesto for Cyborgs: Science, Technology, and Socialist Feminism in the 1980's." *Socialist Review* 80: 65–107.

Harris, Wilson. 1983. *Womb of Space: The Cross-Cultural Imagination.* Westport: Greenwood.

Haugeland, John, ed. 1981. *Mind Design: Philosophy, Psychology, Artificial Intelligence.* Cambridge: MIT P.

Havelock, Eric. 1963. *Preface to Plato.* Cambridge: Harvard UP.

Havelock, Eric, and Jackson P. Hershbell, ed. 1978. *Communication Arts in the Ancient World.* New York: Hastings House.

Hayes, Patrick J. 1985. "The Second Naive Physics Manifesto." *Formal Theories of the Commonsense World.* Ed. Jerry R. Hobbs and Robert C. Moore. Norwood: Ablex. 1–37.

Hegel, G. W. F. 1975a. *Aesthetics: Lectures on Fine Arts.* 2 vols. Trans. T. M. Knox. Oxford: Clarendon.

———. 1975b. *Logic, Being Part One of the Encyclopedia of the Philosophic Sciences.* Trans. William Wallace. Oxford: Oxford UP.

———. 1977. *The Phenomenology of Spirit.* Trans. A. V. Miller. Oxford: Oxford UP.

Heidegger, Martin. 1961. *An Introduction to Metaphysics.* Trans. Ralph Manheim. Garden City: Doubleday.

———. 1971. *Poetry, Language, and Thought.* Trans. Albert Hofstadter. New York: Harper.

———. 1977. *The Question Concerning Technology and Other Essays.* Trans. William Lovitt. New York: Harper.

Henderson, Linda Dalrymple. 1983. *The Fourth Dimension and Non-Euclidean Geometry in Modern Art.* Princeton: Princeton UP.

Herrnstein, Richard J., and Edwin G. Boring. 1965. *A Source Book in the History of Psychology.* Cambridge: Harvard UP.

Hofstadter, Douglas R. 1979. *Gödel, Escher, Bach: An Eternal Golden Braid.* New York: Vintage.

Hölderlin, Friedrich. 1961. *Poems and Fragments.* Trans. Michael Hamburger. Ann Arbor: Michigan UP.

Hume, David. 1978. *A Treatise of Human Nature.* Oxford: Oxford UP.

Jackson, Laura (Riding). 1976. "From the Writings of Laura (Riding) Jackson." *Chelsea* 35: 13–226.

Jakobson, Roman. 1962. *Selected Writings: Phonological Studies.* 2nd ed. vol. 1. The Hague: Mouton.

James, William. 1950. *The Principles of Psychology*. New York: Dover.

James, William. 1976. *Essays in Radical Empiricism*. Cambridge: Harvard UP.

Jameson, Fredric. 1981. *The Political Unconscious: Narrative as a Socially Symbolic Act*. Ithaca: Cornell UP.

Jammer, Max. 1957. *Concepts of Force: A Study in the Foundations of Dynamics*. Cambridge: Harvard UP, 1957.

Johnson, Michael L. 1988. *Language, Thought, and Matter*. Houndmills: Macmillan.

Jones, Leroi. 1963. *Blues People: Negro Music in White America*. New York: Morrow.

Joos, M. 1948. "Acoustic Phonetics." *Language Monograph* 24: 142–173.

Kant, Immanuel. 1965. *Critique of Pure Reason*. Trans. Norman Kemp Smith. New York: St. Martin's, 1965.

Katz, Jerrold J. 1986. *Cogitation: A Study of the Cogito in Relation to the Philosophy of Logic and Language and a Study of Them in Relation to the Cogito*. New York: Oxford UP.

Keats, John. 1965. *Letters*. Ed. Stanley Gardner. London: London UP, 1965.

Kittay, Jeffrey, and Wlad Godzich. 1987. *The Emergence of Prose: An Essay in Prosaics*. Minneapolis: Minnesota UP.

Klein, Jacob. 1968. *Greek Mathematical Thought and the Origin of Algebra, with An Appendix Containing Vieta's Introduction to the Analytic Art*. Trans. Eva Brann. Cambridge: MIT P.

Kneale, William, and Martha Kneale. 1984. *The Development of Logic*. Oxford: Clarendon.

Krause, Pamela E. 1982. "From Universal Mathematics to Universal Method: Descartes' 'Turn' in Rule IV of the *Regulae*" *Journal of the History of Philosophy*. 21: 159–74.

Kristeva, Julia. 1984. *Revolution in Poetic Language*. Trans. Margaret Waller. New York: Columbia UP.

Lacan, Jacques. 1977. *Écrits: A Selection*. Trans. Alan Sheridan. New York: Norton.

Lachterman, David Rapport. 1989. *The Ethics of Geometry: A Geneology of Modernity*. New York: Routledge.

Langendoen, Terence D., and Paul M. Postal. 1984. *The Vastness of Natural Languages*. Oxford: Blackwell.

Lawrence, D. H. 1964. *Studies in Classic American Literature*. New York: Viking.

Lippman, Walter. 1962. *A Preface to Politics*. Ann Arbor: Michigan UP.

Liu, Alan. 1990. "Local Transcendence: Cultural Criticism, Postmodernism, and the Romanticism of Detail." *Representations* 32: 75–113.

Loy, Mina. 1982. *The Last Lunar Baedeker*. Ed. Roger L. Conover. Highlands: Jargon.

Lukács, Georg. 1971. *The Theory of the Novel: A Historico-philosophical Essay on the Forms of Great Epic Literature*. Trans. Anna Bostock. Cambridge: MIT P.

MacKay, Donald M. 1969. *Information, Mechanism, and Meaning*. Cambridge: MIT P.

Mallarmé, Stéphane. 1982. "The Book: A Spiritual Instrument." *Selected Poetry and Prose*. Ed. Mary Ann Caws. Trans. Bradford Cook. New York: New Directions, 1982.

Marcus, Greil. 1989. *Lipstick Traces: A Secret History of the Twentieth Century*. Cambridge: Harvard UP.

Martin, Ronald. 1981. *American Literature and the Universe of Force*. Durham: Duke UP.

Maturana, Humberto. 1975. "Biology of Language: The Epistemology of Reality." *Psychology and Biology of Language and Thought: Essays in Honor of Eric Lenneberg*. Ed. D. Rieber. New York: Academic.

Maturana, Humberto, and Francisco Varela. 1987. *The Tree of Knowledge: The Biological Roots of Human Understanding*. Boston: New Science Library.

Maturana, Humberto R., and Francisco J. Varela. 1980. *Autopoiesis and Cognition: The Realization of the Living*. Dordrecht: Reidel.

Maus, Marcel. 1985. "A Category of the Human Mind: The Notion of Person: The Notion of Self." *The Category of the Person: Anthropology, Philosophy, History*. Ed. Steven Collins, Michael Carrithers, and Steven Lukes. Trans. W. D. Halls. Cambridge: Cambridge UP.

McCullough, Warren. 1965. *The Embodiment of Mind*. Ed. Seymour Papert. Cambridge: MIT P.

Melville, Herman. 1960. *The Letters of Herman Melville*. Ed. Merrel R. Davis and William H. Gilman. New Haven: Yale UP.

Moravec, Hans. 1987. "Human Culture: A Genetic Takeover Underway." *Artificial Life*. Ed. Christopher G. Langton. Redwood City: Addison-Wesley. 167–201.

Nietzsche, Friedrich. 1954. *The Portable Nietzsche*. Trans. Walter Kaufman. New York: Viking.

Olson, Charles. 1967. *Human Universe and Other Essays*. Ed. Donald Allen. New York: Grove.

———. 1969. *Causal Mythology*. Ed. George F. Butterick. Berkeley: Four Seasons, 1969.

———. 1974. *Additional Prose: A Bibliography on America, Proprioception & Other Notes & Essays*. Ed. Donald Allen. Berkeley: Four Seasons.

———. 1978. "The Chiasma, or Lectures in the New Sciences of Man (1953)." *Olson: The Journal of the Charles Olson Archives* 10: 3–109.

———. 1983. *The Maximus Poems.* Ed. George F. Butterick. Berkeley: California UP.

———. 1987. *The Collected Poems of Charles Olson.* Ed. George F. Butterick. Berkeley: California UP.

Pahlka, William H. 1987. *Saint Augustine's Meter and George Herbert's Will.* Kent: Kent State UP.

Peirce, Charles Sanders. 1955. *Philosophical Writings of Peirce.* Ed. Justus Buchler. New York: Dover, 1955.

Piaget, Jean. 1970. *Structuralism.* Trans. Chaninah Maschler. New York: Basic.

Plato. *Parmenides.* 1983. Trans. R. E. Allen Minneapolis: U of Minnesota P.

Poincaré, Henri. 1952. *Science and Hypothesis.* New York: Dover.

Pound, Ezra. 1960. *ABC of Reading.* New York: New Directions.

———. 1968. *The Spirit of Romance.* Ed. James Laughlin. New York: New Directions.

———. 1965. *Literary Essays.* Ed. T.S. Eliot. New York: New Directions.

———. 1971. *The Cantos of Ezra Pound.* New York: New Directions.

———. 1973. *Selected Prose.* Ed. William Cookson. New York: New Directions.

Queneau, Raymond. 1961. *Cent Mill Milliards de poèmes.* Paris: Gallimard.

Quine, Willard van Ormand. 1969. *"Ontological Relativity" and Other Essays.* New York: Columbia UP.

Rapaport, Herman. 1983. *Milton and the Postmodern.* Lincoln: Nebraska UP.

Riddel, Joseph N. 1965. *The Poetry and Poetics of Wallace Stevens.* Baton Rouge: Louisiana UP.

Riding, Laura. 1928. *Contemporaries and Snobs.* Garden City: Doubleday.

Riemann, G. F. B. 1929. "On the Hypotheses which Lie at the Foudnations of Geometry." *A Source Book in Mathematics.* Ed. David Eugene Smith. Trans. Henry S. Smith. New York: McGraw.

Rimbaud, Arthur. 1976. *Complete Works.* Trans. Paul Schmidt. New York: Harper.

Rorty, Richard. 1982. "Mind as Ineffable." *Mind in Nature.* Ed. Richard Q. Elvee. San Francisco: Harper.

Rosen, Robert. 1991. *Life Itself: A Comprehensive Inquiry into the Nature, Origin, and Fabrication of Life.* New York: Columbia UP.

Rumelhart, David E. 1989. "Foundations of Cognitive Science." Ed. Michael I. Posner. Cambridge: MIT P.

Schelling, Friedrich Wilhelm Joseph von. 1989. *Philosophy of Art.* Trans. Douglas W. Stott. Minneapolis: U of Minnesota P.

Shannon, Claude E., and Warren Weaver. 1964. *The Mathematical Theory of Communication*. Urbanba: Illinois UP.

Simon, Herbert A. 1980. "Cognitive Science: The Newest Science of the Artificial." *Cognitive Science* 4: 33–46.

Siskin, Clifford. 1988. *The Historicity of Romantic Discourse*. New York: Oxford UP.

Sloterdijk, Peter. 1987. *The Critique of Cynical Reason*. Trans. Michael Elred. Minneapolis: Minnesota UP.

Spencer-Brown, G. 1979. *Laws of Form*. New York: Dutton.

Spengler, Oswald. 1939. *The Decline of the West*. 2 vols. Trans. Charles Francis Atkinson. New York: Knopf.

Sprat, Thomas. 1958. *History of the Royal Society*. Ed. Jackson I. Cope and Harold Whitmore Jones. St. Louis: Washington UP.

Stein, Charles. 1979. *The Secret of the Black Chrysanthemum: The Poetic Cosmology of Charles Olson & His Use of the Writings of C. G. Jung*. Barrytown: Station Hill.

Stein, Charles, ed. 1988. *Being=Space X Action: Searches for Freedom of Mind through Mathematics, Art, and Mysticism*. Berkeley: North Atlantic Books.

Stein, Gertrude. 1962. "Composition as Explanation." *Selected Writings of Gertrude Stein*. Ed. Carl Van Vechten. New York: Random. 21–30.

———. 1973. *How to Write*. West Glover: Something Else Press.

———. 1985. *Lectures in America*. Boston: Beacon.

Stevens, Wallace. 1951. *The Necessary Angel: Essays on Imagination and Reality*. New York: Random.

———. 1982. *The Collected Poems*. New York: Vintage.

Stigler, Stephen M. 1986. *The History of Statistics: the Measurement of Uncertainty before 1900*. New Haven: Yale UP.

Studdert-Kennedy, Michael. 1985. "Perceiving Phonetic Events." *Persistence and Change: Proceedings of the First International Conference on Event Perception*. Ed. William H. Warren and Rober E. Shaw. Hillsdale: Erlbaum. 139–156.

Sukenick, Ronald. 1967. *Wallace Stevens: Musing the Obscure*. New York: New York UP.

Sussman, Henry. 1989. *High Resolution: Critical Theory and the Problem of Literacy*. New York: Oxford UP.

Turner, Mark. 1991. *Reading Minds: The Study of English in the Age of Cognitive Science*. Princeton: Princeton UP.

Varela, Francisco J. 1979. *Principles of Biological Autonomy*. New York: North Holland.

Vendler, Helen. 1969. *On Extended Wings: Wallace Stevens' Longer Poems*. Cambridge: Harvard U P.

Verbrugge, Robert. 1985. "Language and Event Perception: Steps Toward a Synthesis." *Persistence and Change: Proceedings of the First International Conference on Event Perception*. Ed. William H. Warren and Robert E. Shaw. Hillsdale: Erlbaum. 157–194.

Warren, R. M. 1976. "Auditory Illusions and Perceptual Processes." *Contemporary Issues in Experimental Phonetics*. Ed. N.J. Lass. New York: Academic.

Wellek, René, and Austin Warren. 1966. *The Theory of Literature*. London: Cape.

Weyl, Herman. 1949. *The Philosophy of Mathematics and Natural Science*. Trans. Olaf Helner. Princeton: Princeton UP.

Whitehead, Alfred North. 1978. *Process and Reality: An Essay in Cosmology*. Ed. David Ray Griffin and Donald W. Sherburne. New York: Free.

Whitman, Walt. 1964. *Prose Works: Collected and Other Prose*. Ed. Floyd Stovall. 3 vols. New York: New York UP.

———. 1980. *Leaves of Grass: A Textual Variorum of the Printed Poems*. 3 vols. Ed. Sculley Bradley Harold W. Blodgett Arthur Golden, and William White. New York: New York UP.

Wiener, Norbert. 1950. *The Human Uses of Human Beings: Cybernetics and Society*. Boston: Houghton.

———. 1965. *Cybernetics; Or, Control and Communication in the Animal and the Machines*. Cambridge: MIT P.

Williams, William Carlos. 1956. *In The American Grain*. New York: New Directions.

———. 1969. *Selected Essays*. New York: New Directions.

———. "Kora in Hell." 1970. *Imaginations*. New York: New Directions.

Wittgenstein, Ludwig. *Philosophical Investigations*. Trans. G. E. M. Anscombe. New York: Macmillan.

———. 1967. *Tractatus Logico-Philosophicus*. Trans. D. F. Pears and B. F. McGuinness. London: Routledge.

———. 1967. *Lectures and Conversations on Aesthetics, Psychology, and Religious Belief*. Ed. Cyril Barrett. Berkeley: California UP.

———. 1970. *Zettel*. Ed. G. E. M. Anscombe and G. H. von Wright. Trans. G. E. M. Anscombe. Berkeley: California UP.

Zukofsky, Louis. 1971. *All: The Collected Short Poems*. New York: Norton.

———. 1978. *"A."* Berkeley: California UP.

———. 1987. *Bottom: On Shakespeare*. Berkeley: California UP.

———. 1981. *Prepositions: The Collected Critical Essays of Louis Zukofsky*. Berkeley: California UP.

Zukofsky, Louis, and Celia Zukofsky. 1969. *Catullus (Gai Valeri Catulli Veronensis Liber)*. London: Cape Goliard.

INDEX